50
FROM THE
50's

Books by David Zinman

The Day Huey Long Was Shot
50 Classic Motion Pictures
Saturday Afternoon at the Bijou

50 FROM THE 50's

Vintage Films From America's Mid-Century

DAVID ZINMAN

ARLINGTON HOUSE·PUBLISHERS
NEW ROCHELLE, NEW YORK

P10987654321

Designed by Pat Slesarchik

Manufactured in the United States of America

Library of Congress Cataloging in Publication Data

Zinman, David H
  50 from the 50s.

  Includes index.
  1. Moving-pictures—Plots, themes, etc.
I. Title.
PN1997.8.Z55   791.43'7   78-14988
ISBN 0-87000-318-6

Photo Credits

Once again to my beloved Sara

Acknowledgments

I am indebted to the Theater Collection of the New York Public Library, Astor, Lenox, and Tilden Foundations, especially to Paul Myers, curator, and his professional staff who helped me use the library's vast collection of film material. Thanks also to Don Madison of Photographic Services.

I owe a special debt of gratitude to John Cocchi, who checked my manuscript for accuracy and helped identify character actors in stills—although I take full responsibility for any errors. Also thanks to Monty Arnold who proofread the galleys.

For helping me locate stills, I am thankful to *Movie Star News* and the now defunct Kier's Celebrity Photos of New York. For lending me stills from their collections, I am grateful to Lewis Archibald of New York City; Garnett J. Harris Jr. of Austin, Tex.; Ivan Maule of El Monte, Cal.; Larry Gonclaves of Sacramento, Cal.; Hans Siden of Partille, Sweden; Gordon Samples of San Diego, Cal.; Marilyn Henry of Evansville, Ind.; and John Cocchi of Brooklyn, N.Y.

Thanks also to: Lydia Kowal of Des Plaines, Ill.; Joseph Buoncore of Youngsville, N.Y.; Constance K. Bandy of Los Angeles; Lawrence D. Adams of Hesperia, Cal.; Madeline Israel of Wantagh, N.Y., my hard-working typist; and Martin Gross and Kathleen Williams, my helpful and perceptive editors.

Contents

Introduction

A few years ago, I watched an editor's forehead wrinkle quizzically when I proposed a book on the movies of the 1950s.

His response came in the way of a challenge. "I doubt if you could list half a dozen really outstanding pictures from those years," he said.

Even I was surprised at the strength of my reply. For starters, I named *On the Waterfront* (1954), *All About Eve* (1950), and *Vertigo* (1958). I went on to cite *Paths of Glory* (1958), *High Noon* (1952), *Rashomon* (1952), and *La Strada* (1956). Then I mentioned *The Third Man* (1950), *Some Like It Hot* (1957), *Sunset Boulevard* (1950), *Wild Strawberries* (1955), *Singin' in the Rain* (1952), and *Les Diaboliques* (1955).

Many have dismissed this decade as merely a transitional era in filmmaking. But when one takes a closer look, one finds an untapped mine here. And that was how the idea began to write a book on this much underrated movie decade.

That's not to say the 1950s was a golden age for films. I would never contend, for example, that the decade could match the 1930s in sheer number of four-star pictures. But I think the 1950s can hold its own with any like era in terms of its top fifty films.

This is no small achievement when you consider how politically sterile and repressed those years were—and, particularly, how difficult they were in Hollywood. The movies was an industry under siege. It was trying to overcome exploding television competition, skyrocketing production costs, a Communist scare that brought about blacklisting, and declining audiences and revenues. It was the perfect formula for bankruptcy. Some thought Hollywood would never survive.

But it did survive, even though it failed to blunt the meteoric rise of television. The movie industry's key blunder was that it did not take seriously the new media that intrigued a postwar generation. And so it contributed to its own demise. It failed to concentrate on better stories, new and original scenarios—the kind of productions that the infant television medium could not provide.

Instead, it put its money in public relations and technological innovations. Audiences didn't buy its slogan "Movies are better than ever." And they quickly tired of wearing plastic Polaroid glasses at 3-D films and going to gimmicky productions called Hypno-Vision, Smell-o-Vision, and AromaRama. "I didn't understand the picture," quipped Henny Youngman. "I had a cold."

How badly did Hollywood flounder in the 1950s? Statistics tell the story. In 1946, an average of seventy-eight million people went to the movies each week. By 1959, that audience fell off more than sixty percent to a low of twenty-nine million. In the same span of years, box office receipts tumbled from $1.7 billion to $900 million.

Yet, Hollywood plowed new ground in the 1950s. Out of these economically troubled times came the transition from the formula pictures of the big studios to the individualistic themes of independent producers. Filmmakers developed CinemaScope and the wide screen. Marlon Brando and James Dean anticipated the upcoming decade of rebellious youth. The New Wave directors made their first films. And Otto Preminger broke the puritanical Production Code.

Most important, the films of the 1950s gave us some magical moments. Who will forget the double twist ending of *Les Diaboliques*? Or little Brandon de Wilde calling after Alan Ladd in *Shane* (1953)? There was the gripping Ferris wheel confrontation of Orson Welles and Joseph Cotten in *The Third Man*. The war of nerves between Sessue Hayakawa and Alec Guinness in *The Bridge on the River Kwai* (1957). Kim Novak's chilling fall from the monastery tower in *Vertigo*. The brief reunion of the young Russian infantryman and his mother in *Ballad of a Soldier* (1959). Joe E. Brown's relentless pursuit of Jack Lemmon in drag in *Some Like It Hot*. And Gene

Kelly dancing through puddles in *Singin' in the Rain.*

It was a movie decade that had more than its share of problems, but it left us more than a few indelible memories. Here, then, are fifty of them that I submit not as a definitive list but as one man's opinion of what for him were some of the top movies when America was at mid-century.*

*My own rating of 1950 movies are as follows: (1) *On the Waterfront,* (2) *Paths of Glory,* (3) *Rashomon,* (4) *Ballad of a Soldier,* (5) *Sunset Boulevard,* (6) *Wild Strawberries,* (7) *Vertigo,* (8) *The Third Man,* (9) *Shane,* and (10) *Invasion of the Body Snatchers.*

All About Eve

Bette Davis as the fading stage actress Margo Channing, one of her most memorable roles.

All About Eve*
(1950)

Directed by Joseph L. Mankiewicz.* Screenplay by Mankiewicz,* based on the short story "The Wisdom of Eve" by Mary Orr. Music, Alfred Newman. Photography, Milton Krasner. Editor, Barbara McLean. Costume design, Edith Head* and Charles LeMaire.* Produced by Darryl F. Zanuck. A 20th Century-Fox Picture. 138 minutes.

Margo Channing	*Bette Davis*
Eve Harrington	*Anne Baxter*
Addison De Witt	*George Sanders**
Karen Richards	*Celeste Holm*
Bill Sampson	*Gary Merrill*
Lloyd Richards	*Hugh Marlowe*
Birdie	*Thelma Ritter*
Miss Caswell	*Marilyn Monroe*
Max Fabian	*Gregory Ratoff*
Phoebe	*Barbara Bates*
Aged Actor	*Walter Hampden*
Girl	*Randy Stuart*
Leading Man	*Craig Hill*
Doorman	*Leland Harris*
Autograph Seeker	*Barbara White*
Clerk	*William Pullen*
Stage Manager	*Eddie Fisher***
Pianist	*Claude Stroud*
Frenchman	*Eugene Borden*
Reporter	*Helen Mowery*
Captain of Waiters	*Steve Geray*

(The 1969 stage musical *Applause* with libretto by Betty Comden and Adolph Green was based on the film *All About Eve* and the short story "The Wisdom of Eve." It starred Lauren Bacall, and later Anne Baxter, in the role of Margo Channing.)

*Academy Award Winner. (Another Oscar also went to the 20th Century-Fox sound department for best sound recording.)
**Fisher's role was cut from the final version.

Bette Davis and Anne Baxter, playing Davis' understudy, exchange icy stares while Marilyn Monroe and Hugh Marlowe look on.

A pretty teenage girl steps before a three-faced, full-length mirror. She is clutching a trophy to her breast. A fur wrap is on her shoulders. With the utmost grace, she steps forward and bows to an imaginary audience.

This is the famous finale of *All About Eve* (1950), as Barbara Bates poses enviously and narcissistically with Anne Baxter's Sarah Siddons Award.

All About Eve. No other movie received as many Academy Award nominations (fourteen). Few have ever had such bright and witty dialogue.* Fewer have held up so well. It has become a cult film—like *Casablanca* (1942)—spawning legions of admirers who have committed to memory large blocks of dialogue, and, who, at the slightest urging, stand ready to recite them.**

*The most quoted line is probably George Sanders' colorful description of Marilyn Monroe, his protégé of the moment, as an "actress," a "graduate of the Copacabana School of Dramatic Arts." A less celebrated, but equally witty, retort comes from MM a few moments later. When Miss Baxter deferentially tells Sanders that he will find her boring before too long, Miss Monroe cracks: "You won't bore him, honey. You won't even get to talk."

**The script, issued in hard-cover edition in 1951, was the first to be so published. A first edition now sells for more than $25.

The film represents a milestone in more than one career. It is unquestionably the masterwork of Joseph L. Mankiewicz—*Dragonwyck* (1946), *A Letter to Three Wives* (1949), *Guys and Dolls* (1955)—who wrote its screenplay and then directed the picture.†

It was a high-water mark for Celeste Holm and Miss Baxter. For Bette Davis, it has been called her "quintessential performance." For George Sanders, who won the only acting Oscar (for supporting performance), it was the greatest characterization in his familiar role as a waspish cad.

Yet, ironically, none was picked for the original cast. Darryl F. Zanuck, 20th Century-Fox's production chief, had the foresight to envision a major movie coming out of Mankiewicz's script. He decided to choose the players personally. His choices were Marlene Dietrich as Margo Chan-

†Originally entitled *Best Performance*, the screenplay was based on Mary Orr's short story "The Wisdom of Eve," which appeared in the May 1946, *Cosmopolitan*. Miss Orr, an actress and later a playwright, said her story idea stemmed from a conversation with the Austrian actress Elisabeth Bergner and her husband, Paul Czinner. They told her about an experience they "had had with an unscrupulous young actress they had befriended."

ning, Jeanne Crain as Eve Harrington, and Jose Ferrer as Addison De Witt. Mankiewicz objected strenuously both to Dietrich, whom he admired but thought wrong for the part, and to Crain, whose talent he felt was lacking. ("I could only rarely escape the feeling that Jeanne was, somehow, a visitor to the set," Mankiewicz said. "[She had] an absence of emotional involvement with acting.") For some reason, lost to movie historians, Ferrer's casting never materialized.

Claudette Colbert was Mankiewicz's choice for Margo, but she injured her back shortly before production was to start. Gertrude Lawrence was his second pick. However, she was such a lofty and remote figure that Mankiewicz said he was never able to get her to see his script. He said he had to submit it first to her attorney, Fanny Holtzman. It never got past this formidable lady. She insisted on two changes. First, the drunk sequence at the party scene was out. Second, in the same scene, the pianist was to accompany Miss Lawrence in a torch song instead of playing "Liebestraum."

In the book More About All About Eve, Mankiewicz said he turned down both of these demands. Said Mankiewicz: "Since my own lawyers had already admonished me to respond to other lawyers with either 'yes' or 'no' and urged me to keep the witty ripostes for when you're shaving—I said nothing but 'no.' And that's how Gertrude Lawrence didn't get the part."

Bette Davis was the next choice. She was a long shot, indeed, because she was still filming Payment on Demand (1951). But she was so taken with the script that she skipped her vacation between pictures to play the role. It was a decision she never regretted.

The movie, of course, is remembered as a bitter satire on ambition in the theatre. What Mankiewicz is saying is that success comes to those ruthless enough to climb over the bodies of others to achieve it—although it often turns out to be an empty achievement, devoid of warmth and humanity.*

Actually, what intrigued Mankiewicz was the chance to write an "inside" story about theatre folk, particularly the women who live in this fantasy world. In his insightful book, which film historian Gary Carey actually wrote after several extended interviews with the director, Mankiewicz said that three types emerged in the filmplay:

—Margo. She represents the actress just turned forty, a "star in the theatre" with a limited number of roles to play. She is filled with the fear of transitioning from actress to plain married woman. To add to her trauma, she is about to be married to a man "who will always be thirty-two years old." Mankiewicz modeled her after aging stars he remembered in Hollywood: "In the 1930s, I'd watch them roll into Paramount and Metro at 6:30 in the morning on their way to hairdressing and make-up. Drive in usually with their top down, their hair all blown by the wind, no lipstick, their own eyelashes, wearing anything from a poncho to a polo coat—and I'd think Percy Westmore should be arrested for so much as touching a powder puff to their loveliness. Well, by the late thirties, they were driving with the top up. Then, in the forties, they started wearing scarfs—and, by 1950, large hats. The pancake was getting thicker, the make-up took longer, the cameraman started using specially built little banks of 'inkies' to iron out wee bags and sags. . . . Fortyish. . . . It is a bitterly sad point of no return for an actress."**

—Karen. She is the director's wife whose entrée to the theatre world derives solely from her marital status. In many ways, she is the most vulnerable character. "Of all the females that inhabit the society of theatrefolk," said Mankiewicz, "the one for whom I have always felt the greatest compassion is she for whom, in that society, only one role is available: that of 'wife to _____.' . . . They're in waiting, all right, these 'wives to _____.' Day and night, increasingly as time goes on, waiting. For the axe, the heave-ho, the marital pink slip."

—Eve. She is an obscure little girl who plots until she gets exactly what she wants. Bright-eyed, designing, ruthless—willing to undergo anything from adultery to blackmail to achieve her ends—she comes with a layer of meanness hidden well under

*One dissenting voice to all the acclaim All About Eve won came in a letter to the New York Times from one Esther Margolin of New York City. She lamented the fact that no one thought to criticize Mankiewicz for his harsh portrayal of actors. There was, in her view, nothing in the plot to explain the naked and satanic actions of the movie's characters. "It is significant," she said, "that he [Mankiewicz] has omitted the notorious sins and foibles of some producers in the profession against whom even the sweeping caricatures of the 'critic' and the 'actress' in the film fade into nothingness. . . . If it were not for the brilliant acting of the cast who, as is characteristic of too many performers, allowed themselves to be exploited to the destruction of their own interests, the picture would go in the ash heap."

**Many have suggested that Margo was patterned after Tallulah Bankhead. Mankiewicz and Miss Davis always denied this. Instead, he insisted he had in mind an eighteenth-century actress named Peg Woffington. Skeptics have pointed out that Miss Davis spoke in a husky voice and wore her hair shoulder-length à la Bankhead. Davis said the truth is she had practically lost her voice then due to emotional stress stemming from her divorce from William Grant Sherry, husband number three. The haircut? It was just an expedient choice, Mankiewicz said, attractive and easy to keep in place. (In 1952, Bankhead played the part in a one-hour radio version on the "Theatre Guild on the Air." Mary Orr played Karen Richards.)

an outer garment of modesty. However, there is, in my opinion, a flaw in her development in this movie. While Eve convinces everyone in the picture of her sincerity as a star-struck kid, her killer instinct is so obvious that her sharp claws are utterly transparent to the audience. Nevertheless, she is a real celluloid creation, and as a predatory female she represents a personality by no means limited to the theatre. She is, Mankiewicz says, a universal type. "Watch little girls," he says. "Eve's the one who always seems to wind up at the head of the line for cookies—she'll make or steal her own gold stars to take home if teacher can't be conned into giving her one—she'll throw fits, even run up fake fevers if the prize is worth it to her. Full-grown, in the workaday world, Eve is everywhere . . . in the theatre, the movies, in show business, she's there because there lies the particular loot she's after. . . ."*

*For her performance as Eve, Anne Baxter got an Oscar nomination for best actress. Davis and the studio wanted her to accept a supporting Oscar nomination instead. They reasoned correctly that Baxter and Davis would cancel each other out. But Baxter refused because, she said, Eve was named in the title and "the film was, after all, how different people saw Eve." As it turned out, Judy Holliday won for *Born Yesterday*.

The movie opens at a formal banquet in an oak-paneled old actors' club where the Sarah Siddons Award**—the most distinguished trophy for an actress in the American theatre—is about to be presented to Eve Harrington (Anne Baxter). As she steps to the podium amid warm applause, the camera focuses on the bemused face of Karen Richards (Celeste Holm), the wife of playwright Lloyd Richards (Hugh Marlowe) whose play Eve has appeared in. And we hear her think back to when she first met Eve.

It was a rainy October night, she recalls, when she went backstage to meet her husband. As Karen walks into the theatre alley, she notices the familiar face of a young girl who has haunted the stage door for weeks. With a cold rain falling, Karen takes pity on her and asks her backstage to meet her idol Margo. In her dressing room, where she has been discussing her next play with Karen's

**The award, a gilded statuette, was a fictitious bauble contrived for the story. Yet, some years after the picture was released, a real Sarah Siddons Society came into being in Chicago and established a genuine award for distinguished achievement in the theatre in Chicago. Helen Hayes won the first such trophy. Later, Deborah Kerr and Geraldine Page picked up the award. Fittingly, so did Celeste Holm and Bette Davis.

Davis presents a young Marilyn Monroe (in her sixth movie) and George Sanders to Baxter. The scene produced one of the picture's classic lines. Sanders introduced MM, his protégée of the moment, as a "graduate of the Copacabana School of Dramatic Arts."

husband Lloyd, the actress greets Eve in her best grande dame manner. Eve, with her combination of shyness, good manners, and adoration, quickly ingratiates herself with everyone. She tells them about her husband, Eddie, who was killed in the South Pacific during World War II, and how, as one who loves the theatre, she first saw Margo in San Francisco, then followed her across the country during months of one-night stands.

On impulse, Margo takes Eve along to the airport where she puts her fiancé, director Bill Sampson (Gary Merrill), on a plane to Hollywood. Then she invites Eve—"a lost lamb loose in our stone jungle," Margo says—into her home. It is an act Margo lives to regret.

Eve immediately starts running everything. As Margo later recalls, "Eve became sister, mother, friend, psychiatrist, and cop." Birdie (Thelma Ritter), Margo's gal Friday, sees bad tidings ahead. "She's like she was studying you," Birdie says, "like you were a play or a book or a set of blueprints."

The dark side of Eve begins to show some weeks later at a welcome home party for Bill. Bill's usual practice on arrival is to rush upstairs to see Margo as soon as he gets in the door. This time, however, Margo comes downstairs to find him telling Hollywood stories to Eve.

A fight erupts. But when Margo rages at him, Bill fires right back. He accuses her of petty jealousy, of being plagued by "paranoid insecurity" and "age obsession." Furious, Margo gets roaring drunk and serves notice on her guests that she is in a nasty mood. "Fasten your seat belts, kids," she tells Bill and critic Addison De Witt (George Sanders), "it's going to be a bumpy night."

During the party, Eve drops a hint to Karen that she'd like a chance to be Margo's understudy. A few days later, Eve gets an audition and turns in a stirring performance. Even the cynical De Witt is taken with her talent. He meets Margo in the theatre foyer. "Margo," says De Witt, "I have lived in the theatre as a Trappist monk lives in his faith. I have no other world, no other life—and once in a great while I experience that moment of revelation for which all true believers wait and pray. You were one. Jeanne Eagels another. . . . There are others, three or four. Eve Harrington will be among them."

"I take it she read well," Margo says coldly.

"It wasn't a reading," De Witt says. "It was a performance. Brilliant, vivid, something made of music and fire."

Enraged that Eve has gotten an audition without her knowledge, Margo marches backstage and lets loose a scathing tongue, railing in turn at Richards, Bill, and producer Max Fabian (Gregory Ratoff).

While the brawl goes on, Eve slips away. Bill, sick and tired of Margo's prima donna-like outbursts, walks out, too.

That weekend, Margo, Karen, and Lloyd drive out to the Richards' home. Bill is conspicuously absent and the atmosphere is strained. Then Karen gets an idea. She decides she is going to give Margo the kick in the pants she so richly deserves. While the others are sleeping, she steals out and drains the gas tank.

On the way to the railroad station for the Monday night show, Richards' car runs out of gas, stranding them in the snow. Eve goes on in Margo's stead and turns in a magnificent performance. She wins rave notices, including a glowing review from De Witt. Overnight, she becomes the toast of Broadway.

Now that her career has finally been launched, Eve starts a campaign to win the starring role of "Cora" in Richards' new play. He had written the part for Margo. But since the character is a woman in her early twenties, Margo herself has had second thoughts about playing such a youthful role. And Eve cruelly preys on the aging actress' own doubts.

One day, De Witt's column quotes Eve about "the lamentable practice in our theatre of permitting, shall we say—mature—actresses to continue playing roles requiring a youth and vigor of which they retain but a dim memory."

To insure her effort, Eve blackmails Karen into persuading her husband to give her the role. If she doesn't, Eve warns her, she will reveal how Karen engineered Margo's missed performance. The consequences could be far-reaching. "Your friendship with Margo—your deep, close friendship," Eve reminds her. "What would happen to it, do you think, if she knew the cheap trick you'd played on her for my benefit?"

Karen now sees Eve for what she is—a blindly ambitious girl who would do anything to become a great actress, hiding her evil in an affectation of innocence and shyness.

Her insight comes a little late. Eve fails to entice director Sampson away from Margo. (They reconcile after Margo decides to give up the youthful role.) So she sets her sights on Richards whom she sees as a stepping stone to stardom. While the new play is on tour in its tryout run, Eve calls Richards to her side, saying she is having on-the-road jitters. He leaves, despite Karen's objections.

But Eve has finally overstepped her bounds. In New Haven, where the play is opening for a try-out, Eve confides to De Witt that she is planning to marry Richards as soon as he gets a divorce. That doesn't fit De Witt's plans. "It's important that we

The closing sequence as Barbara Bates, playing Phoebe, pleads with Baxter not to call the police.

talk—killer to killer," he says. When she laughs at him contemptuously, he slaps her face.

Then he proceeds to demolish her carefully stacked house of cards as he tells her that he knows of her duplicity. She had no husband killed in the South Pacific, De Witt says. She did not follow Margo across the country. Instead, she had to flee her Wisconsin home when the wife of her boss caught her with the boss. If she doesn't accept the terms he will now offer, De Witt says, he will tell the world about her checkered past and how she betrayed her friends. "You're an improbable person, Eve, and so am I," he says. "We have that in common. Also a contempt for humanity and its book of rules, an inability to love or be loved, insatiable ambitions—and talent. We deserve each other."

She will never take Lloyd Richards away from Karen, De Witt says, because he will not permit it. "I am your rightful possessor. After tonight, you will belong to me."

The camera flashes back to the awards celebra-

tion.* There is Eve, holding her statuette, her voice sweet and touching as she thanks the Sarah Siddons Society with humility, giving credit for her acting to her friends. Although she is leaving for Hollywood, she tells the audience, her heart remains in the theatre. After the ceremony, Margo tells her, "I wouldn't worry too much about your heart. You can always put that award where your heart ought to be."

Eve begs off going to Max Fabian's party with De Witt and he leaves her at her door. Inside her apartment she is startled by a sleepy girl (Barbara Bates) rousing herself from the divan. She turns out to be a stage-struck teenager who says she is

*The award is, of course, a takeoff on the Tony or, really, its predecessor, the Oscar, which, according to one version, got its name from Miss Davis. After she won her first Academy Award for *Dangerous* (1935), she allegedly said: "I have always liked the statue's backside best. It reminds me of my husband (bandleader Harmon Oscar Nelson—the first of her four spouses)." Miss Davis has disavowed this tale. A second version attributes the name to columnist Sidney Skolsky. Another to Margaret Herrick, former executive director of the Academy.

president of the Erasmus Hall High School Eve Harrington Fan Club. When there is a knock at the door, Eve sends her to answer it. De Witt has come back to bring the statuette that Eve forgot.

"Tell me," he asks the girl, "do you want to have an award like that of your own?"

"More than anything else in the world," she says breathlessly.

"Then you must ask Miss Harrington how to get one. Miss Harrington knows all about it."

From the bedroom, Eve tells the girl to put the statuette on one of her trunks she is packing. As she does, she sees Eve's luxurious fur wrap. She quietly puts it on, picks up the award, and walks to a large three-mirrored cheval.

Then, as if she is taking a curtain call before a cheering audience, she bows low and with great dignity, letting the ripples of silent applause sweep over her.

Anatomy of a Murder

Defense lawyer Paul Biegler (James Stewart) objects as state prosecutor Claude Dancer (George C. Scott) cross-examines Laura Manion (Lee Remick). That's Joseph Welch, of Army-McCarthy hearing fame, playing the judge.

Anatomy of a Murder
(1959)

Produced and directed by Otto Preminger. Screenplay by Wendell Mayes, based on the novel by Robert Traver. Music by Duke Ellington. Camera, Sam Leavitt. Editor, Louis R. Loeffler. Filmed in Ishpeming, Mich. A Columbia Release of a Carlyle Production. 160 minutes.

Paul Biegler	*James Stewart*
Laura Manion	*Lee Remick*
Lt. Frederick Manion	*Ben Gazzara*
Parnell McCarthy	*Arthur O'Connell*
Maida	*Eve Arden*
Mary Pilant	*Kathryn Grant*
Judge Weaver	*Joseph Welch*
Mitch Lodwick	*Brooks West*
Claude Dancer	*George C. Scott*
Alphonse Paquette	*Murray Hamilton*
Dr. Smith	*Orson Bean*
Dr. Harcourt	*Alexander Campbell*
Mr. Burke	*Joseph Kearns*
Mr. Lemon	*Russ Brown*
Dr. Dompierre	*Howard McNear*
Dr. Rachid	*Ned Wever*
Madigan	*Jimmy Conlin*
Sgt. Durgo	*Ken Lynch*
Duane Miller	*Don Russ*
Pie-Eye	*Duke Ellington*
Distinguished Gentleman	*Irv Kupcinet*
Juror	*Mrs. Joseph Welch*

A closeup of Dancer interrogating Miss Manion.

An army lieutenant (Ben Gazzara) shoots and kills a tavern owner, then tells police he did it because the bartender had beaten and raped his wife (Lee Remick). The wife supports her husband's story and a lie detector test backs up her account.

But the medical examiner finds no evidence that the woman was raped. Moreover, the young woman is a striking brunette given to flaunting her charms in tight sweaters and slacks. And the husband has a reputation as a hothead.

Was the woman really raped? Or did she have an affair and then subsequently fight with her jealous husband? Did he beat the truth out of her and then, enraged, rush off and empty his gun into her lover?

These are the intriguing questions that led Otto Preminger to make *Anatomy of a Murder,* a picture based on the 1958 best-selling novel by Robert Traver (pen name of Michigan Supreme Court Justice John D. Voelker).

Actually, the story was really a clinical dissection of a courtroom case. And Preminger saw in the high drama of a trial—particularly a trial about rape—an opportunity to film a realistic and gripping melodrama. The movie, which had the longest

trial scene ever filmed, did, in fact, temporarily run afoul of the censors in some cities. They blanched at such frank expressions as "intercourse . . . contraception . . . spermatogenesis . . . sexual climax." They also objected to the lengthy discussions about what legally constituted rape. ("Violation is sufficient. There need not be a completion . . . on the part of the man.")

Certainly the book's extended discussions over the sex act played a part in its successful sale, and Preminger probably realized that he could exploit this on the screen in a way never done before. But it is also true that those key passages were necessary to the development of the theme, and, for the most part, were done with the propriety and objectivity befitting a courtroom setting.

At any rate, Preminger found the plot engrossing. He bought the movie rights and set out to make a major picture. His choice for the lead was James Stewart, who read the script and immediately agreed to take the role of the middle-aged lawyer. But he ran into a problem on the distaff side. Lee Remick, whom Preminger saw in *A Face in the Crowd* (1957), was one of the actresses considered for the female lead. She was pretty in a

11

fresh and unusual way, unfamiliar to most movie-goers, and talented. She was also in her eighth month of pregnancy. Although she was to have had her baby by the time shooting started, Preminger would be taking a chance to cast her.

So, less than twenty-four hours after he gave her the script, he called her. "I'm sorry," he said. "I've signed Lana Turner." However, Preminger was still impressed with Miss Remick's screen charisma. He offered her the second lead—the part of Mary Pilant, thought to be the murdered man's mistress.

Miss Remick, stung by Preminger's rejection, turned down the lesser role. "I did a very brave, or, perhaps, foolish thing," she said later.

It turned out to be the former. While Miss Turner was learning her part, a disagreement developed over her wardrobe. She turned down a pair of cowboy pants. Lana, expecting a glamorous outfit, wanted her clothes created by Hollywood designer Jean Louis.

Preminger was shocked. He wanted clothes that looked real. After all, he said, she was playing the wife of an army officer who lived in a trailer.

Neither side would budge. Both were used to having their own way. "If she doesn't like it," Preminger finally told her agent, "she can get out of the picture." Lana called Preminger's bluff, but she had made a serious misjudgment. He wasn't bluffing.

No sooner had Lana quit than Preminger was on the phone again to Miss Remick. Since her baby had been born a month earlier, she had had time to regain her figure, and at twenty-four she was at the peak of her beauty. He asked her to come to his office in Hollywood. Before their meeting was over, she had the part. Her performance in *Anatomy*, her third picture, was to launch her career.

For another key role, that of the judge, Preminger considered Burl Ives who looked the part of a midwestern jurist. Then someone suggested: Why not get a real judge? The name of Joseph Welch came up. He was the soft-spoken, folksy but flint-hard lawyer who represented the army and bested Joe McCarthy in the famous Senate hearings.

Preminger called Welch in Boston and made the proposition then and there over the phone. Welch said he'd like to think it over. His wife was against the idea, and so was Welch's friend, Ed Murrow. The television commentator said that he thought the movie might damage Welch's public image. But in his book, *Behind the Scenes of Otto Preminger*, author Willi Frischaver says that Welch himself was fascinated.

"What are the hours?" asked Welch, who was then sixty-four.

"Nine to five," Preminger said.

"What would my wife be doing all this time?"

"She can join the cast and play a member of the jury," Preminger suggested. That clinched it.

To capture the full flavor of the novel, Preminger decided to shoot on location. He moved the company to Michigan's Upper Peninsula and used local people in his courthouse scene. He also gave himself a tight, eight-week deadline because the novel was then leading the best-seller list and a paperback was scheduled to hit the market soon. Shooting started March 23, 1959. Preminger's goal was to have the movie in the theatres by summer. There were bets down that he wouldn't do it, but he had the film edited in a trailer as the movie was shot, and he made his deadline.

As the movie opens, Paul Biegler (Stewart), a small-town lawyer, is deciding whether to defend Lieutenant Frederick Manion (Gazzara) on a murder charge. Everything tells Biegler to turn down the case. Manion has no defense. His only offer of payment for Biegler's legal work is a promissory note if he gets off. And handling the state's case is the attorney who beat out Biegler in the district attorney's election. Finally, the defendant's attitude is so cocksure and confident that it quickly turns off Biegler. "Barney Quill raped my wife," says Manion. "I have the unwritten law on my side."

"The unwritten law is a myth, Lieutenant," Biegler says. The so-called "law" says a jury will automatically acquit a man for killing someone who has attacked his wife. "Anyone who commits murder under this belief is reserving himself room and board in the state penitentiary . . . maybe for life," Biegler says.

The next day, Biegler interviews the lieutenant and his wife separately and hears their account of the crime. Laura Manion (Lee Remick) says she had slipped out of their trailer home when her husband fell asleep early. She had some drinks at a local gin mill and the bartender, Barney Quill, offered to drive her home.

Instead, she says, he took her to a deserted lover's lane and raped her. When she got home, battered and bruised, she woke her husband and told him what happened.

Manion says he got his loaded Luger pistol, set out for the bar, and then his mind went blank. "I remember hearing shots. But they don't seem to be connected with me," Manion says. "They seemed far away . . . like somebody else was doing the shooting."

Biegler sees his defense—temporary insanity—and agrees to take the case.

Lt. Frederick Manion (Ben Gazzara) explains to Biegler why he shot bartender Barney Quill. Manion's defense is that he had an "irresistible impulse" to commit the crime.

But a complication arises right away. Laura Manion, far from being a loyal wife, seems to be a floozy who is ready to flirt with every male she sees, including Biegler. And her husband, she says, is insanely jealous.

"He likes to show me off," she says. "He likes me to dress the way I do. Then, he gets furious if a man pays any attention to me."

"Does your husband have any reason to be jealous?" Biegler asks.

There is a pause. Then Laura says, "No, not once. Not ever."

Nevertheless, a few nights later, Biegler has to drag her out of a roadhouse when he finds her socializing with soldiers. "Until the trial is over, you're going to be a meek little housewife with horned-rimmed spectacles," Biegler says angrily. "You're going to stay away from men and juke joints and pinball machines. And you're going to wear a skirt and low-heeled shoes and a girdle."

Preparing the case is an uphill battle. A key witness, the other bartender at the tavern, Alphonse Paquette (Murray Hamilton), volunteers no information. Nor does Mary Pilant (Kathryn Grant), a pretty brunette who was employed by Quill and was rumored to be his mistress. Biegler suspects

they may be motivated by loyalty to their dead employer and possibly a share in the estate.

Meanwhile, Manion is examined by an army psychiatrist who finds that when Manion shot Quill he was suffering from "dissociative reaction." It means that Manion had an "irresistible impulse" to kill. At the same time, the psychiatrist feels that Manion knew the difference between right and wrong and was therefore legally sane.

This crumbles Biegler's defense of temporary insanity. So he and his associate, Parnell McCarthy (Arthur O'Connell), go into the library to see if anyone has ever used the plea of irresistible impulse as a defense to murder. To their surprise, they find a precedent in an old Michigan case dating back to 1886. It says that even if a person was aware that his action was wrong, he will be excused from punishment if he was forced to commit the crime by an impulse he was powerless to control. Now they have to convince the jury that Manion was acting under an irresistible impulse.

Presiding over the courtroom struggle is veteran Judge Weaver—played by Welch in such a dry, quaint, showmanlike fashion that it belied his amateur status. Except for a stint on the now defunct television show "Omnibus," it was Welch's only appearance before the cameras. Because he had worked with a teleprompter on the TV show, Preminger saw that he had one for his scenes in the picture.

But fluffing lines wasn't his main worry. "I did that often—but so did others—and that meant retaking whole scenes," Welch said. "I was worried about even more basic things. Walking, for example. I'd done it all my life without ever thinking about it. But you have to think about it when making a movie. Jimmy Stewart, for example, as the defense attorney, would stand up and move to just where he was supposed to be. Then they'd make chalk marks on the floor around his shoes so that he'd get right into the same spot for the next take. Little things like that astounded me." Nevertheless, Welch, who died a year after the movie was made, occasionally stole scenes from some of the professionals.

At the opening of the trial, the district attorney (Brooks West) introduces Claude Dancer (George C. Scott) from the attorney general's office. Dancer has been assigned to assist in the prosecution "because of the peculiar nature of the case."

The prosecution's first witness, Dr. Dompierre (Howard McNear), testifies that Quill was killed by five gunshot wounds. One bullet hit him in the heart. On cross-examination, the doctor says that his examination found "spermatogenesis" (the production of sperm) occurring at the time of death. He also says that the failure to find sperm in a woman—as happened in Laura Manion's examination—is not definitive proof that she did not have intercourse. "There could be some reason why the test was negative—the use of a contraceptive or possibly there was no completion on the part of the man."

"Were you also asked to see if the deceased had reached a sexual climax shortly before his death," the doctor is asked.

"No, sir."

"Could you have made such an examination?"

"Yes, sir."

The jury does not know the reason for these questions because Biegler has not been able to introduce the Manions' contention that a rape had preceded the murder and precipitated it. The prosecution's contention is that the rape never occurred because Mrs. Manion was a willing participant in the act. Even if she were raped, the prosecution contends that this would have no bearing on the trial because no evidence has been introduced to link her to the murder charge.

Police Sergeant Durgo (Ken Lynch) finally opens

The panties Biegler holds play a key part in the trial, the longest in any movie. Mary Pilant (Kathryn Grant, Mrs. Bing Crosby), who retrieved them, looks on uncomfortably.

the door for the evidence on the rape when he testifies that Manion told him that he shot Quill after his wife had had "some trouble" with the bartender. When Biegler starts questioning Durgo, the sergeant admits that Manion had not used the words "some trouble." Those were the words the prosecution suggested he say in court. This admission gives Biegler the chance to introduce the motive for the crime to the jury.

> *Biegler:* Tell the court how Lieutenant Manion described the trouble his wife had had with Barney Quill.
>
> *Durgo:* He told me that Quill had raped his wife.

Durgo goes on to say that Mrs. Manion took police to a lane in the woods, the scene of the alleged rape, where they found tire marks and a pair of glasses in a case. However, doubt is cast on the rape story when Durgo says that the panties Mrs. Manion said had been ripped from her body were nowhere to be seen. The rape scene, Durgo adds, was a well-known lover's lane.

While the trial is going on, Biegler's associate, Parnell McCarthy, has driven off to Canada to run down a hunch. McCarthy has noted that Quill had hired Mary Pilant from a little Canadian town. McCarthy thought that it was curious that Quill would have gone so far just to hire someone looking for a job. In the town courthouse, McCarthy finds her birth certificate, which states that she was born out of wedlock and that her father was a lumberjack named Barney Quill.

On the stand, Laura Manion's story of the rape is shrouded in doubt. She admits that she sometimes goes out alone to bars. "Sometimes I'm restless," she says. On the night of the crime, according to her testimony, she went without her husband because he had fallen asleep early, and when she came back she had to swear on her rosary to get her husband to believe that she had been raped. She admits that Manion slapped her. But, she says, that was because she was hysterical. However, she denies that she fabricated the rape story to keep Manion from beating her.

The next witnesses, two psychiatrists, one for the defense and one for the prosecution, take opposite sides of the medical issue. Dr. Smith (Orson Bean), testifying for the defense, says that Manion was in the grip of an irresistible impulse and couldn't help himself on the night of the crime. Dr.

Arthur O'Connell (left) playing Stewart's legal sidekick in the courtroom drama.

Harcourt (Alexander Campbell), testifying for the prosecution, says that in his opinion Manion was in sufficient possession of his faculties so that he was not in the grip of an irresistible impulse.

A prisoner, Duane Miller (Don Russ), throws the courthouse into an uproar when he testifies that while he shared a jail cell with Manion, the lieutenant said he had everybody fooled. "I fooled my lawyer," Miller quotes the lieutenant as saying. "I fooled that head shrinker. And I'll fool all the corn cobs on the jury."

But Biegler quickly destroys Miller's credibility. He shows that Miller has a long criminal record about which he lied in his testimony and that he is hoping for a light sentence in return for his cooperation.

However, the biggest surprise is yet to come. Mary Pilant unexpectedly asks to take the stand and testifies that a day after the killing, she found a pair of panties in the laundry bin at the motel where she and Barney Quill lived. The bin is at the bottom of a chute next to Quill's room, and the panties match those worn by Mrs. Manion. When she produces them, the jury can see that they are badly torn. As a result, she says, she isn't sure now whether Quill did or did not rape Mrs. Manion.

Now Dancer moves in to try to attack the credibility of Mary Pilant's crucial testimony.

Q: Do you know for a fact that Barney Quill dropped the panties down the chute. Or did you just assume it?
A: I assumed it.
Q: Had you thought that perhaps someone else put the panties there?
A: I hadn't thought of that.
Q: You wanted to crucify the character of the dead Barney Quill, didn't you? Your pride was hurt. You were jealous. Are you Quill's mistress?
A: No. It's not true. Barney Quill was my—
Q: Barney Quill was what, Miss Pilant? Barney Quill was what, Miss Pilant?
A: Barney Quill was—my father.

A gasp sweeps through the courtroom. Dancer's head drops.

Hours later, the jury returns with its verdict:

"Not guilty by reason of insanity." Mary Pilant's surprise testimony has tipped the scales.

There remains one more surprise for Biegler and McCarthy. The next day when they drive out to the motor court to have Manion sign a promissory note for their fee, Manion and his wife are gone. All they have left is a short message: "So sorry. But I had to leave suddenly. I was seized by an irresistible impulse."

Some critics felt that although the picture was skillfully done, it was quickly forgettable because Manion and his wife were less than noble characters. "Worthless persons are really not worth our complete attention," said Alan Dent in *The Illustrated London News*. "Crooks with nothing at all but their crookedness to recommend them do not engage my interest on the screen."

In Russia, some moviemakers felt that Manion should not have been acquitted because he was a bad man. "The evidence was not conclusive," Preminger explained during a trip to Moscow. "And in our country, every man is presumed to be innocent until he is proved guilty beyond a shadow of a doubt."

Despite these reservations, the movie was big box office. On its first run, it earned $4 million in the United States and another $1 million abroad. Preminger, who had a share of the profits, reportedly made more than $500,000.

There was one final legal skirmish. In 1965, Columbia sold the TV rights, allowing stations to shorten the picture to insert commercials. But when Channel 7 in New York cut the two hour and forty minute picture and then interrupted the shortened version thirteen times with a total of twenty-nine commercials, Preminger went to court. He contended that the deletions and the commercials destroyed the movie's integrity. "Audiences are seeing the film in a way I did not intend them to see it," Preminger said. "It is not my film anymore."

As a filmmaker, he felt that he should have a say in the number of cuts and where they were made. Nevertheless, Preminger lost the case. And the effect of that adverse decision is still felt by every frustrated TV viewer who suffers through endless commercials to see a butchered version of what once was a feature-length motion picture.

The Asphalt Jungle

Cops frisk Sterling Hayden, playing a small-time holdup man, as he has coffee in a diner run by James Whitmore. Officers are Ralph Dunn and Pat Flaherty.

The Asphalt Jungle
(1950)

Directed by John Huston. Based on the novel by W. R. Burnett. Screenplay by Ben Maddow and John Huston. Art directors, Cedric Gibbons and Randal Duell. Photography, Harold Rosson. Editor, George Boemler. Music, Miklos Rozsa. Produced by Arthur Hornblow, Jr. Released by Metro-Goldwyn-Mayer. 112 minutes.

Dix Handley	*Sterling Hayden*
Alonzo D. Emmerich	*Louis Calhern*
Doll Conovan	*Jean Hagen*
Gus Minissi	*James Whitmore*
Doc Erwin Riedenschneider	*Sam Jaffe*
Police Commissioner Hardy	*John McIntire*
Cobby	*Marc Lawrence*
Lt. Dietrich	*Barry Kelley*
Louis Ciavelli	*Anthony Caruso*
Maria Ciavelli	*Teresa Celli*
Angela Phinlay	*Marilyn Monroe*
Timmons	*William Davis*
May Emmerich	*Dorothy Tree*
Bob Brannon	*Brad Dexter*
Dr. Swanson	*John Maxwell*
Maxwell	*Alex Gerry*
Janocek	*James Seay*
Older Officer	*Ralph Dunn*
Younger Officer	*Pat Flaherty*
Driver	*Benny Burt*
Private Policeman	*Saul Gorss*
Eddie Donato	*Alberto Morin*

Jean Hagen tries on a diamond ring as she looks over a fortune in stolen gems that Hayden has lifted in a jewelry store burglary.

His movies chronicle the cause of the loser. His heroes are antiheroes—unsuccessful goldminers, small-time hoods, B-girls, washed-up fighters, seedy private eyes. Violence is stamped into their nature.

"When you're slapped, you'll take it and like it. . . . You stay on my back any longer, they'll be pickin' iron out of your lungs. . . . If I ever see you running over a cat, I'll kick your teeth out. . . ."

These are characters out of John Huston movies—tough, sordid, humorless. To be sure, Huston's more than thirty pictures include a wide assortment of protagonists and range over a variety of storylines (including the discovery of psychoanalysis, nineteenth-century Paris nightlife, and biblical days). But his most memorable works have had a consistent theme—unrealized fortunes, lost opportunities, unfulfilled ambitions. And his people are mostly of the same ilk—unlucky, ill-starred people, pessimistic, fateful souls for whom failure seems inevitable.

If Huston is a champion of defeatism, his place among America's great filmmakers is still to be decided. His pictures all project a tight, stylized professionalism. He is as well known to the public as Hitchcock and Ford. Yet, the final assessment of Huston's work remains controversial. Some critics say he is more a technician than anything else. In his famous rating of Hollywood directors, Andrew Sarris relegates him to the "less-than-meets-the-eye" category. His films, says Sarris, "owe more to casting coups than directorial acumen."

Others have taken him to task for a too casual attitude toward the performance of some of his stars. Says Eugene Archer in *Films and Filming:* "His [Huston's] successes with personality performers (Bogart, Mitchum, Audie Murphy) are counterbalanced by the crucial failure of his work with Gregory Peck in *Moby Dick* (1956), Edward G. Robinson in *Key Largo* (1948), and Jose Ferrer in *Moulin Rouge* (1952) who floundered without proper directorial assistance."

Certainly, Huston's career, which spans four decades, has had checkered moments. But there are as many film writers who extolled him at the start as there were when his days as a filmmaker were drawing to a close. Consider: *The Maltese Falcon* (1941), *The Treasure of the Sierra Madre* (1948), *The Asphalt Jungle* (1950), *The Red Badge of Courage* (1951),* *The African Queen* (1951), *Beat the Devil* (1954), *The Night of the Iguana* (1964), *Reflections in a Golden Eye* (1967), and *Fat City* (1972).

Writing in 1950 about Huston's first eleven movies, James Agee said "There is nobody under fifty at work in movies, here or abroad, who can excel Huston in talent, inventiveness, intransigence, achievement, or promise."

"He is," said *New Yorker* magazine, twenty-two years later, "the quintessential American artist-as-movie-director, and he has placed his unique stamp on every one of his movies."

Says Norman Mailer: "Huston is of course the only celebrated film artist to bear comparison to Hemingway."

Like Hemingway, Huston works from a keen sense of intuition. When he starts directing, some of the best scenes are played behind the camera. In *Beat the Devil*, the company found itself on location without an acceptable script. Every day, he and Truman Capote improvised scenes only hours before shooting was to start.

In *The African Queen*, Huston felt that he wasn't getting the austere but sensitive performance he wanted from Katharine Hepburn. "So one day I said: 'Play her like a lady, Kate.' She said, 'Whom would you suggest?' I said, 'Eleanor Roosevelt.' From then on, she was totally different."

In *The Night of the Iguana*, the press predicted fireworks when Huston, Tennessee Williams, and such stars as Elizabeth Taylor, Richard Burton, Ava Gardner, and Deborah Kerr assembled on a tropical locale. Huston gave everyone a derringer pistol with the names of all the rest engraved on the bullets. "We got along famously," he said.

The son of actor Walter Huston, Missouri-born John left high school to start a multifaceted career. Before he was twenty-one, he had become a boxer (he was the lightweight champion of California), an

actor, and a cavalryman in Mexico. Later, he studied painting in Paris, wrote short stories, bummed around London, and returned to the U.S. to play Abe Lincoln for the WPA Theatre in Chicago.

Then came the turning point. To prove to a girl he wanted to marry that he could amount to something, he went to Hollywood and became a screen writer. However, when he got tired of watching hack directors butcher his scenarios, he asked to change jobs. He got his chance in 1941 when Warner Brothers let him direct his own screenplay of *The Maltese Falcon*. The picture, which James Agee called "the best private eye melodrama ever made," became a classic.

There was no slowing him down thereafter. Within six years he won two Oscars (for writing and directing *The Treasure of the Sierra Madre*).** His lean (six-foot, four-inch) frame, leathery features, and owlish eyes (his friends call him "double-ugly"—his enemies "monster") became a Hollywood landmark.

He became known as the antithesis of the despot director. "Unless an actor needs help," said Huston, "I try to interfere with him as little as possible. Otherwise, they'd be weaker shadows of myself." However, he was a fiercely independent filmmaker and would not allow anyone to bully him. Rather than compromise, he walked off *A Farewell to Arms* (1957) and *Madwoman of Chaillot* (1969).

Huston, who has been married five times, emigrated to Ireland in the 1950s and became an Irish citizen in 1964, purchasing a hundred-acre estate on the west coast. Although he eventually sold it— "I was having to stay away and work just to support the house and staff of fifteen"—he lived like a country squire and rode with the hounds.

In the 1950s, he began getting a reputation as an actor as well. After appearing briefly in his own films, he played an Irish-American prelate in Otto Preminger's *The Cardinal* (1963). While he did a creditable job, he unquestionably will be remembered for his directing talent.

Perhaps the best insight into his films comes from a man who never lived to see the bulk of his work. What distinguishes Huston's movies, said James Agee who died in 1955, is a unique feeling that the sequence on the screen is actually happening just then—as if it were coming to life right before your very eyes.

*There is controversy, though, as to whether *The Red Badge of Courage* was the picture it could have been. In Lillian Ross' book *Picture*, a story of the filming of the Stephen Crane Civil War novel, Huston was depicted as being shocked by the preview audiences' poor reception of the movie. Then, apparently tired of having to compromise artistic intentions, he deserted the still unreleased picture, flying off to direct *The African Queen*. He left his movie vulnerable to scene changes and cuts by others. They were done in a frantic attempt to make the film more commercial, but they were unsuccessful, and some feel that they weakened the movie. "It's now like a different picture," said a saddened producer, Gottfried Reinhardt.

**One of his actors was his father, who also won an Academy Award for best supporting performance. It was their second pairing because the elder Huston had unbilled bit parts in *The Maltese Falcon* and *In This Our Life* (1942), the first films the younger Huston directed.

It's the end of the line for Sam Jaffe, playing a burglary ring leader who has masterminded one caper too many.

Some of these rare moments happen in *The Asphalt Jungle,* a fast-moving melodrama that Andrew Sarris rates as Huston's best.*

The movie opens by introducing us casually to four figures who will try to pull off a million dollar burglary. First, there is Doc Erwin Riedenschneider (Sam Jaffe), the brains of the soon-to-be-formed team. He has masterminded the caper while in state prison. On his first day out, he hails a cab and goes to see Cobby (Marc Lawrence), a bookmaker with dreams of grandeur who operates a warehouse office in a rundown section of a midwestern town.

"I got a proposition," Doc says. "A big one."

"How big is big?" Cobby asks.

"Too big for you."

Doc tells the bookie that the plan is so airtight he could sell it for a cool $100,000, but that would be throwing money away. Instead, Doc, a mild-mannered professional with a German accent, wants to execute it himself and make $500,000—maybe more. He needs $50,000 to go

*The picture earned for Huston the 1950 Screen Directors Guild Award.

into action. The money would pay for a safe-cracker, a reliable gunman, and a getaway driver.

The $50,000 hard cash is what has sent Doc to Cobby. Doc says he has heard that Alonzo D. Emmerich, a shady, big-time criminal lawyer with whom Cobby is in contact, would stake them to the $50,000 and put them in touch with a fence for a share of the loot.

Just then, Cobby is interrupted by a caller and steps out. Doc, left alone for a minute, notices a pinup calendar. He puts on his glasses and, with bulging eyes and pursed lips, starts scrutinizing the girlies. His attraction for a shapely figure will later prove to be his undoing. This unexpected detail is a device that Huston will use over and over to add irony to the unfolding plot and to give depth to his people.

The next scene, for example, introduces us to a hunchback luncheonette operator, Gus Minissi (James Whitmore), who is to become the getaway man. This steely-nerved underworld hanger-on is an animal lover. His first action is to throw out of his diner a truck driver who talks about the pleasure he takes in running over cats.

In the diner, too, is Dix Handley (Sterling Hayden), a small-time holdup man and hooligan. Dix is a surly, cold-blooded blond giant embittered by a lifetime of failures. His weak spot is his penchant for horses, but he is more than just a gambler. He grew up on a horse farm in Kentucky. He knows how to raise and breed horses, and he longs to return to the innocent joys of his boyhood.

Next we see the lawyer, Emmerich (Louis Calhern), a distinguished-looking man in his fifties who is consumed by his lust for high living and his infatuation for his expensive blonde mistress Angela (Marilyn Monroe).

"Some sweet kid," he says, appraising her charms. This was not Marilyn's first speaking role, but it was considered her breakthrough film. Huston later was frank enough to admit that he did not realize her potential then. "I could feel that she was going to be good in this film," Huston said, "and I chose her over a number of others. But still I didn't dream of the places she would go."*

At a meeting with Emmerich, Doc assures him that his plan is foolproof. The target of the caper is Belletier & Co., a kind of midwestern Tiffany. Doc says he has researched everything. He knows the routine of the workmen, the alarm system, the locks on the doors, the safe. The loot is valued at one million dollars. "This is a ripe plum ready to fall," says Doc.

Emmerich shows his knowledgeability in underworld matters. He points out that the take will only be $500,000. "You know as well as I do," Emmerich says, "that in no case will a fence give you more than fifty percent." Nevertheless, Emmerich opts to come in.

Doc says he needs money to operate and hire personnel and then a fence to dispose of the take. Surprisingly, Emmerich says he might be willing to handle the disposal phase of the operation himself. By doing so, this would save the extra money they would have to split with a fence. Doc, although somewhat leery, shakes on the deal.

The men who are recruited to help execute the job are:

—Louis Ciavelli (Anthony Caruso), a safe-cracker who can open a safe "like the back of a

Anthony Caruso wires a jewelry store safe holding a million dollars in gems as he gets ready to blow it open with nitroglycerin.

watch." He's also a family man, and this is to figure in his downfall.

—The hunchback, Gus. "He'll take all the heat," Cobby says, "and won't flap his lip."

—Dix. "A very determined man and far from stupid," says Doc. Cobby adds: "[Also] you can get him for nickels and dimes."

At first, Emmerich tries to stick to his end of the bargain. He hires Bob Brannon (Brad Dexter), a private detective, to collect $100,000 from debtors still holding out on him. But when Brannon returns empty-handed, Emmerich confides that he has the opportunity of a lifetime in his grasp—and he is bankrupt.

Emmerich explains that he is to be a fence for a big burglary caper, promising cash on delivery. When the loot is delivered, however, he wouldn't have any money. He would tell the gang it would take a few more days to raise it. "I'm certain I could get them to leave the stuff with me while we're waiting," Emmerich says. "Then I'd disappear. I'd take a plane to another country, another life."

Brannon is offered a fifty-fifty split for his help. But there is one problem. Emmerich says he does not have the $50,000 to pay the gang's start-up

*Monroe tried out for the part in Huston's studio office. Huston remembers her hands were shaking when he gave her the script. "Listen, kid, don't worry about this," he said. Angela spoke while reclining on a couch in the first of her two scenes. There was no couch in Huston's office so Monroe kicked off her heels, stretched out on the carpet, and played the scene reclining on the floor. Before Huston could comment, she asked to run through the sequence again. After the second reading, she stood up nervously to hear his reaction. "You didn't have to do it twice, honey," Huston smiled. "You had the part on the first reading."

expenses. Brannon has the solution. He suggests that Emmerich ask Cobby for an advance to cover it. "Cobby wants to feel big. Here's his chance," Brannon says. "Advancing money to the great Alonzo D. Emmerich."

On the night of the burglary, Doc and his men slither cautiously down a manhole, through an underground labyrinth of tunnels, and into the store. This is the picture's tensest moment and Huston makes the most of it. Wearing a burglar's coat with pockets for a crowbar, chisel, and bits for his electric drill, the safecracker slides flat on his back on the jewelry store's floor to get past an electric eye burglar alarm. With infinite care, he removes the cork from a bottle of nitroglycerin and sets off a charge next to the huge safe. To his horror, the blast trips alarms in all the stores in the area.

Outside, police are fanning out to locate the source of the explosion, but Doc insists that they stay until they finish the job. Minutes tick off. Then, suddenly, the safe is open, and in a flash they start ransacking it.

It looks as though they are home free until a night watchman happens on the scene. Dix slugs him, but when the watchman's gun falls to the floor, it goes off, sending a slug into the safecracker's stomach. He refuses to let Gus take him to a doctor. Instead, he insists on going home to his wife where he will die hours later.

Meanwhile, Doc and Dix manage to get away and immediately take the stolen gems to Emmerich. With his pal Brannon looking on, Emmerich goes into his carefully rehearsed act. "Gentlemen, I must admit at this moment, I-ah-I'm embarrassed," Emmerich says.

"You haven't got the money!" Doc says, astonished.

Ah, but Emmerich says, no need to get excited. He has the assurance of the entire sum in just a few days. Until then, he suggests that Doc leave the jewels with him.

No one is buying Emmerich's obviously transparent story, so Brannon has no choice but to whip out his gun and demand the jewels. However, Doc and Dix have not risked everything to lose it in a

Louis Calhern playing gin rummy with his bed-ridden wife, played by Dorothy Tree, before leaving for a rendezvous with his girl of the moment.

Director John Huston.

double-cross. Doc suddenly tosses the satchel of gems in Brannon's face. At the same time, Dix draws his own gun. Two shots ring out. Brannon drops, mortally wounded from a bullet in the chest. Dix winces from a slug that slices through his side.

Dix turns to shoot Emmerich, but Doc realizes that they now hold a fortune in gems that is just so much junk if they can't trade it for cash. Therefore, he offers Emmerich a last chance to square himself by liquidating the jewels with the insurance company that underwrote the store's policy. "They'll listen to reason," Doc says. "This is a very bad jolt for them. And it's possible they'll be willing to buy the jewels back, no questions asked, for twenty-five percent of their worth."

Emmerich makes the contact and then prepares to leave the country with his mistress Angela. But the police have found Brannon's body and discovered the list of Emmerich's debtors in Brannon's pocket. At Emmerich's home, they ask his whereabouts at the time Brannon was killed. Emmerich says that he was with Angela, then quickly telephones her after the police leave.

However, his desperate alibi crumbles quickly. The police, recognizing the expert planning in the caper, have already linked the crime to Doc and

published his picture in the newspapers. A cab driver remembers taking Doc to Cobby's just after Doc got out of prison. Under tough questioning, Cobby breaks down and implicates Emmerich.

There is a subplot here that touches on one of the most realistic elements of the film. The confession is wrung out of Cobby by Lieutenant Dietrich (Barry Kelley), a precinct detective who has been on Cobby's payroll for years. But now with the pressure on from headquarters, the crooked cop must forget his friends and break the case to protect his own hide. Kelley's icy, under-played performance—along with superb acting by Calhern—is a high point of the film.

Police pay Emmerich a second visit—this time at Angela's apartment. It is immediately clear to Emmerich that his escape plan has failed. Angela also sees the handwriting on the wall. "What about my trip, Uncle Lon?" she coos. "Don't worry, baby," Emmerich replies, wearily giving her full figure the once-over, "you'll have plenty of trips." Under threat of criminal charges, Angela can no longer verify Emmerich's cover story. Trapped by his web of lies, Emmerich excuses himself to call his wife, goes into a den, and shoots himself.

Cobby's confession has also led to Gus' arrest.

24

That leaves only Doc and Dix at large. They barely escape from a beat patrolman who recognizes Doc from his picture. At their hideaway, Doc mutters about the incredibly bad breaks that have plagued them.

"Put in hours and hours of planning. Figure everything down to the last detail. Then what? Burglar alarms start going off all over the place for no sensible reason. A gun fires of its own accord and a man is shot. And a broken down old cop, no good for anything but chasing kids, has to trip over us. Blind accident. What can you do against blind accidents?

"One thing I ought to have figured and didn't was Emmerich. . . . It was the extra dough he promised. I got hungry. Greed made me blind."

Doc offers to split the gems with Dix. But Dix, not knowing how to cash them, shrugs and gives Doc his share. Then the old master criminal hires a taxi to take him to a distant city. Just outside of town, Doc lingers to watch a svelte teenager gyrate to juke box music. While he does, two cops spot him and take him into custody.

Only Dix remains free now. Weakened and still badly wounded, he gets a car and with the help of a girlfriend, a dim-witted B-girl named Doll (Jean Hagen), he takes off for Kentucky. "Our farm was in the family for generations," Dix muses. "One hundred sixty acres, thirty in blue grass and the rest in crops." He remembers the good old days when he was a boy riding a tall black colt named Corncracker. Then, the hard times came. The crops failed. His father died. His family lost the farm. "I'll never forget the day we left," Dix says. "Me and my brother swore we'd buy Hickorywood Farm back some day."

Toward the end of the journey, Dix, losing blood, lapses into unconsciousness and Doll stops at a country doctor's house. But Dix revives and rushes off with Doll when he overhears the doctor telephoning the police. Hours later, they pull up at the farm. Dix staggers from the car and falls exhausted and dying amid half a dozen colts roaming free over the blue grass meadows he dreamed of owning one day.

The Bad and the Beautiful

As the film opens, studio boss Harry Pebbel (Walter Pidgeon) calls in three former friends of producer Jonathan Shields to discuss a movie that is to be a comeback attempt for Shields. They are from left Barry Sullivan, Lana Turner, and Dick Powell.

The Bad and the Beautiful (1952)

Directed by Vincente Minnelli. Screenplay, Charles Schnee,* based on a story by George Bradshaw. Camera, Robert Surtees.* Editor, Conrad Nervig. Art directors, Cedric Gibbons,* Edward Carfagno.* Producer, John Houseman. Costume design, Helen Rose.* Released by Metro-Goldwyn-Mayer. 118 minutes.

Georgia Lorrison	*Lana Turner*
Jonathan Shields	*Kirk Douglas*
Harry Pebbel	*Walter Pidgeon*
James Lee Bartlow	*Dick Powell*
Fred Amiel	*Barry Sullivan*
Rosemary Bartlow	*Gloria Grahame**
Victor "Gaucho" Ribera	*Gilbert Roland*
Henry Whitfield	*Leo G. Carroll*
Kay Amiel	*Vanessa Brown*
Syd Murray	*Paul Stewart*
Von Ellstein	*Ivan Triesault*
Lila	*Elaine Stewart*
Gus	*Sammy White*
Miss March	*Kathleen Freeman*
Ida	*Marietta Canty*
McDill	*Robert Burton*
Eulogist	*Francis X. Bushman*
Wardrobe Man	*Ned Glass*
Little Girl	*Sandy Descher*
Singer	*Peggy King*
Leading Man	*Steve Forrest*
Secretary	*Perry Sheehan*

*Academy Award Winner.

Making the rounds at a Hollywood party are Kirk Douglas, Paul Stewart, Vanessa Brown, and Barry Sullivan. That's Gilbert Roland, on the couch, with the white dinner jacket.

Hollywood had made movies about itself before—*A Star Is Born* (1937), *Sullivan's Travels* (1941), *Sunset Boulevard* (1950)—and it would again—*The Goddess* (1958), *The Oscar* (1966), *The Day of the Locust* (1975). But none portrayed the naked ambition, sheer ruthlessness, and bankrupt morals of the people of the film industry as searchingly and as candidly as *The Bad and the Beautiful.*

If some of the characters were standard filmdom types and if they were more superficially rather than insightfully presented, the picture, nonetheless, came through as a vivid melodrama, limning their private and professional lives.

George Bradshaw's short story, "Tribute to a Bad Man,"* which chronicled the rise of a cynical heel in the theatre, was the basis for the movie. John Houseman, a former film associate of Orson Welles, thought that a film version would play

better with movie people, and so he changed it to a Hollywood setting. Houseman showed a first draft scenario to Vincente Minnelli, who had just finished *An American in Paris* (1951) and who had been chiefly noted for directing musicals. Minnelli, intrigued by the old Hollywood, was instantly hooked.

"All that one loved and hated about Hollywood was distilled in the screenplay," Minnelli said—"the ambition, the opportunities, and the power. . . . But it also told of triumphs against great odds and the respect people in the industry had for other talents."

The story centered around Jonathan Shields (Kirk Douglas), a calculating, double-crossing but gifted producer who uses the talents of a gaudy assortment of filmfolk on which to build his own career. There is a young, hard-working director (Barry Sullivan) whose picture Shields swipes; an alcoholic bit player (Lana Turner) whom he molds into a glamorous, confident star by pretending to love her; and a prize-winning novelist (Dick Powell) whom he gets to write his big movie by maneuver-

*That was also the film's original title. But since Lana Turner shared star billing with Kirk Douglas, the studio felt it was inappropriate. So they changed it to *The Bad* (Douglas) *and the Beautiful* (Turner).

29

ing the novelist's pretty but distracting wife into an affair.* Yet, in the end, they all come to realize that Shields had been largely responsible for their lucrative careers.

The Bad and the Beautiful has become something of a cult movie because many of the characters have been based on Hollywood legends. Shields was fashioned around several film personalities, most notably David O. Selznick. The actress brought Diana Barrymore to mind. And the director recalled Val Lewton, Selznick's story editor who became a talented, if neglected, producer of strikingly original low-budget horror films for RKO.

"There was a pitfall to avoid, I felt," Minnelli said. "The characters could become caricatures if not properly controlled. It was a challenge."

There was much debate at the time as to whether Minnelli met his self-imposed challenge. Hollis Alpert of *Saturday Review* said he did. Bosley Crowther of the *New York Times* felt he failed.

Looking at the film a quarter century later, my vote goes with Crowther. One is struck by the shallow, flimsy portrayal of some of the characters. Nearly all are stereotypes. (In fact, in the eyes of Pauline Kael, the picture was "a satire in spite of itself. . . .") And yet there is no denying that there are powerful scenes and that the picture plays.

It offers a fascinating peek at the people inside the movie industry who have made it big. And the backdrop of the Hollywood milieu seems authentically created.

If there was divided opinion over the movie, there was one thing most critics agreed on—Lana Turner's performance. Many felt it was the best of her long and uneven career, one that admittedly was based more on her image as a sex symbol than her ability as an actress. However, producer Houseman felt she was underrated. He told Minnelli that though she had never been capable of sustaining a good performance over an entire picture, she had been very good in spots. Minnelli decided to try to draw out these inspired sequences. In his book, *I Remember It Well*, Minnelli told how he was able to shoot a sequence over and over without

shaking her confidence in herself. In one scene, Miss Turner is living alone, drinking heavily in an apartment crowded with memorabilia of her famous father.

" 'That was good, Lana,' I told her after one of the early takes. 'But the sound men said they didn't quite pick up the last part of your speech. Let's try it again. This time, try to speak the lines with less emotion. More matter of fact. And, of course, you'll have to slur them again.'

"Another take was required due to trouble with the lighting. In fact, every retake was needed because it was somebody else's fault but Lana's. I finally got what I wanted, a brilliant reading by Lana.

"As she got more into the picture, her nervousness disappeared. She effectively made the character's transition from tramp to glamor queen, and proved what a fine actress she was along the way."

The picture opens as studio boss Harry Pebbel (Pidgeon) calls together three former friends of Jonathan Shields to see if they will work for him in a comeback effort. Shields, who is now in Paris, wants James Lee Bartlow (Powell) to write the scenario, Georgia Lorrison (Turner) to star in it, and Fred Amiel (Sullivan) to direct. All turn him down flatly. It's clear they all hold no love for the absent Shields (Douglas).

But Pebbel asks them to reconsider and puts through a transatlantic call to Shields. While they are waiting, Pebbel has a point to make, one that can only be perceived if they all take a retrospective look at their relationships with Shields. And so, in a narrative reminiscent of *Citizen Kane*, the story of Shields' life is seen through the eyes of three people who despise him.

First, director Amiel. He met Shields at the funeral of Shields' father, a movie pioneer. Amiel, then a jobless director, was hired to attend the ceremony along with a score of extras in mourners' clothes. The elder Shields was such a ruthless executive that he had virtually no friends when he died. Unbeknownst to Amiel, he stands next to the younger Shields during the graveside service. "A madman who almost wrecked it [the movie industry]," he mutters, "a butcher who stole everything but the pig's whistle."

When Amiel goes to pick up his fee, he is stunned to find his graveside companion doling out the cash. "You were paid to give a performance," the younger Shields says. "Eleven dollars to act like a mourner. You didn't do it. You don't get paid."

That afternoon, Amiel drives to Shields' house and apologizes. When Shields learns that Amiel is in the movie business, too, Shields invites him in.

*MGM originally wanted Powell to play the director. However, he related more to the writer and persuaded the studio to let him do that part. Another change came when Walter Pidgeon saw the script and asked for the role of Harry Pebbel. Pidgeon's rather stiff, sober-sided image didn't square with the studio's concept of a more rough-hewn, self-made type. "But Walter was adamant," Minnelli said. "He turned up one day at my office, his gray hair disguised by a crew-cut wig and in an ill-fitting suit to show me how he would look in the part. He convinced me." But not this writer. To my mind, Pidgeon was a poor choice who added little to the picture.

They soon find they have much in common—including the fact that they are both broke and out of work.

"What I aim to be is a director," Amiel says.

"What's stopping you?"

"I know I can direct better than most of the hacks I work for. Trouble is when it comes to selling myself—you know, telling people how great I am—I get tongue-tied."

A low profile was also one of the character traits of Val Lewton, Amiel's model to a large extent. Lewton, never fully appreciated by his superiors, lacked a forceful enough personality to get promoted to major productions or to quit and strike out on his own as an independent producer.

Shields and Amiel decide to pitch in together. They start by doing quickie poverty row Westerns. At night, they crash the best parties and rub elbows with stars and studio executives. At one of these free-wheeling parties, Shields spots Pebbel playing poker for big stakes. He knows his dad could beat Pebbel and Shields could beat his dad. So Shields gets Amiel and others to bankroll him and he joins

the game the next night. Not only does Shields blow the few hundred his friends put up for him, but he drops another $6,000 he doesn't have. However, this proves to be an inspired ploy. Shields offers to work off what he owes, and Pebbel, then a B-unit studio chief, feels he has no choice but to agree if he wants to see any of his money. He makes Shields a producer at $300 a week.

In the next few years, Shields learns his trade by producing eleven B-pictures for Pebbel. Amiel directs six of them. Then one day Pebbel assigns them to a sleazy horror movie called *The Doom of the Cat Men*. At first, they bemoan their fate. It doesn't help matters when the wardrobe man shows them some shoddy costumes of "cat people." But as they toss ideas around in a projection room, Shields gets a brainstorm.

"Put five men dressed like cats on the screen—what do they look like?" Shields asks.

"Like five men dressed like cats," Amiel says.

"When an audience pays to see a picture like this, what do they pay for?"

"To get the pants scared off them."

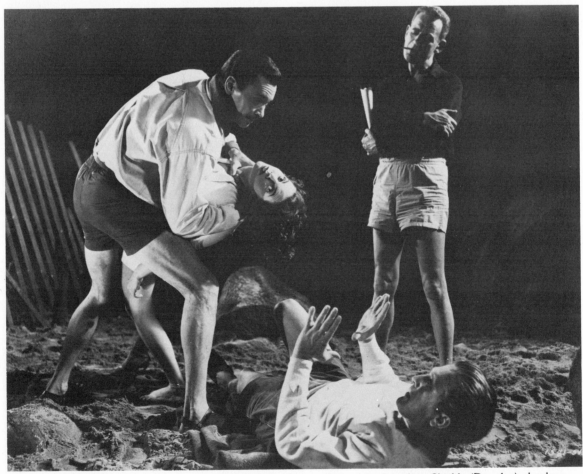

Director Amiel (Sullivan) assumes the position in a horror flick while Jonathan Shields (Douglas) checks a camera angle. Paul Stewart looks on. Vanessa Brown is the gal being garroted.

"And what scares the human race more than any other single thing?"

"The dark," says Amiel.

"Of course," says Shields. "Why? Because the dark has a life of its own. In the dark, all sorts of things come alive."

"Suppose we never do show the cat? Is that what you're thinking?"

"Exactly. . . . Now what can we put on the screen that will make the back of their necks crawl?"

"Two eyes shining in the dark . . . ," says Amiel. "A dog frightened, growling, showing its fangs. . . . A bird, its neck broken, feathers torn from its throat. . . . A little girl screaming, claw marks down her cheek."

The sequence is a good example of how Shields, who was primarily patterned after Selznick, was actually created as a composite type. It was one of Lewton's (not Selznick's) devices to test a screenplay on his staff by turning off the lights in the middle of his narrative and finishing it in darkness. Another of Lewton's techniques that run like a theme through his horror movies—*Cat People* (1942), *I Walked with a Zombie* (1943), *The Leopard Man* (1943), *The Curse of the Cat People* (1944)—was to suggest fright rather than show it. So although Amiel was modeled on Lewton, here we see Shields getting the idea to play to the audience's fear of the dark.

Their picture is a hit. However, instead of catapulting them out of poverty row, it only gives them another routine assignment in the same horror genre.

Amiel won't buy this. He feels they are more than ready to move into major productions and shows Shields an outline he has done of *The Faraway Mountain,* a sprawling major novel. No writer has yet been able to turn this best-selling book into a picture. Nevertheless, Shields asks Pebbel for a go-ahead and Pebbel, against his better judgment, finally gives Shields a tentative okay to at least do a script. Pebbel warns him he's going to fall flat on his face and then go back to doing B-movies for good.

For the next three weeks, Shields and Amiel work night and day writing, revising, and reshaping their scenario. Then comes the big decision day in Pebbel's office. Amiel waits outside, getting increasingly tense as the minutes fly by. Suddenly it's over. Shields rushes out ecstatic. Pebbel has gotten the front office to budget a million dollars for the picture, a Mexican location, a top-notch cameraman, and Von Ellstein (Ivan Triesault), a distinguished German filmmaker, to direct.

"Von Ellstein to direct?" says Amiel, startled.

"Oh, you're taken care of," Shields says. "It won't be a separate panel. But your name will be on the screen—assistant to the producer."

"Thanks," he says hoarsely.

"Fred, you're just not ready to direct a million dollar picture."

"But you're ready to produce one. . . . You're stealing my picture. It was my idea."

"Without me, it would have stayed an idea."

And so we return to the present to Pebbel's conference room, now knowing that Shields has launched his career by picking the brains of his colleague and then taking all the glory. "But look what it did for you, Fred," says Pebbel. "He brushed you off his coattails so you had to stand on your own two feet. And all you got in the world is one wife, six kids, and an Academy Award. And every studio in town after you."

Now Pebbel turns to Georgia and she recalls how far she was from fulfilling her talent as an actress when she met Shields. She had one line in a Shields movie, but he saw star potential in her screen presence. And so late one night he paid her an unannounced visit. He found her in an apartment turned into a memorial to her father, a famous thespian—pictures, news clippings, his pipes, recordings. Shields plays a record of her father doing Macbeth (the voice of Louis Calhern). She says she hates the sound of his voice and tells Shields to cut it off.

"Make up your mind," he says. "You hate him and you build this shrine to him. He died over ten years ago and you've been holding a private wake for him ever since. You can't be a star in a cemetery."

In love with the memory of her father, she has wallowed in self-pity, drink, and easy living. She had even tried suicide twice. "Because he drank, you're a drunk," Shields says. "Because he loved women, you're a tramp."

With that, he smashes the record, scrawls a moustache on her father's portrait, and leaves her sobbing. But Shields' visit has a profound effect. Georgia makes a clean break with the past, starts a new life, and resumes her career in earnest. Her first picture is a flop, but Shields is impressed with her performance. Against the advice of Pebbel, who now works for him, Shields decides to gamble on giving Georgia a starring role. "When you're on the screen, no matter whom you're with, whatever you're doing, the audience is looking at you," he tells her. "That's star quality."

Thrilled and swept away by Shields' faith in her, Georgia plunges into the production with all her ability. But as the shooting begins and the tension mounts, she finds she isn't up to the pressures of

Douglas gives some no-nonsense, hair-curling advice to actress Georgia Lorrison (Turner), who is washing out her career in alcohol.

the tight, demanding shooting schedule. She goes back to drinking and fails to show up on the set. When Shields finds her, she tells him that she ran away because she was afraid she would ruin his picture. She says she loves him and he returns her affection. But he tells her that right now he needs a star, not a wife. And he persuades her to give it another try.

On the set, in a fade-away shot similar to the famous opera sequence in *Citizen Kane,* a crane-mounted camera backs high away from a love scene Georgia is playing. And we see the absorbed looks of the director, crew, and technicians. But whereas in *Kane* the electrician high up on the catwalk held his nose to show his disdain for Susan Alexander's feeble voice, it is clear here that the behind-the-scenes people are captivated by Georgia's performance.

However, Georgia's love affair with Shields is short-lived. On the night of the cast party celebrating her triumph, she goes to Shields' house only to find him with a starlet.

"Maybe I like to be cheap once in a while,"

Shields roars, hurt and embarrassed. "Get out," he screams.

Georgia, now knowing their tender moments have really been empty ones, runs to her car and starts driving wildly in a raging rainstorm.

In the scene some feel is Turner's greatest single performance, she veers through traffic, crying hysterically. Minnelli plotted out the electrifying scene almost as if he were choreographing a ballet. "The car was on a turntable," he said. "I devised the camera's in and out movements, first zooming in on Lana's face, then on her foot as it pressed down on the accelerator, then on the back of her head so that the blurred image of the rain she had to drive through was suggested. When it was all laid out, I explained the scene to Lana. Her hysteria was to increase as the car speeded along, until that point where the car skids and Lana presses the brake, her whole countenance being dissolved— and somehow cleansed—by an avalanche of tears."

She came through with flying colors. "Lana went through the tortured scene with the technique and skill of the consummate actress," Minnelli said. "I was astonished and thrilled that she had come along so far in the picture . . . if only a director would take the time with her."

Now the camera returns once again to the present and Pebbel reminds Georgia that it was Shields who launched her acting career. Moreover, he let her tear up her contract and walk out on him. "I wanted to take you to court," Pebbel said. "But he said, 'No.' So you signed with A & L and made them the millions that we should have made. . . . Ah, yes. Jonathan sure fouled you up."

Finally, Pebbel turns to Bartlow, who was a professor at a small Virginia college when Shields called him one day to tell him he had just bought screen rights to Bartlow's first book. Then Shields invites him and his wife Rosemary (Gloria Grahame), a gushing Southern belle, to Hollywood. The movie capital overwhelms Rosemary. But Bartlow is cool and detached and, at first, turns down Shields' offer to write the script for his book. Nevertheless, two weeks later, Bartlow signs to write a treatment for his opus. So sure was Shields

that the professor would stay that he had Bartlow's typewriter and favorite writing chair flown out.

What Shields failed to count on was the constant distraction of Bartlow's flighty, breathless wife who drags him out to night spots where she flirts with dashing Latin star Victor "Gaucho" Ribera (Gilbert Roland). After the first week, Bartlow, jealous and exhausted, has written only half a page.

Eventually, Shields persuades Bartlow to spend a few days alone with him in his remote mountainside retreat. At the same time, Shields arranges for Gaucho to squire Rosemary around town. Away and uninterrupted, with his wife out of his hair, Bartlow starts producing. Aided by the craftsmanlike editing of Shields, he turns out a sparkling finished scenario in a week.

On their way back, tragedy strikes. At a gas station, they spot a newspaper headline that tells of the death of Gaucho and Rosemary in a small plane crash. The plane was en route to Mexico. At the crash scene, press agents fend off reporters asking if Rosemary and Gaucho were having an affair. However, Bartlow knows the truth.

Sullivan, Turner, and Powell eavesdrop on the conversation of Douglas, their former boss. They have all turned down his movie offer but can't resist the temptation of hearing his newest idea for a movie. This is the scene that ends the picture.

In the weeks that follow, Bartlow, trying to forget his loss, plunges himself into movie work. The picture does not go well. Shields fires the director, then takes on the job himself with even worse results. Discouraged and humiliated, he shelves the picture. To try to lift him out of his despondency, Bartlow invites him to a Lake Tahoe cabin where Bartlow plans to start a new book. Shields accepts the offer with gusto and starts packing immediately. As he does so, he glibly rambles on about Gaucho and lets slip the fact that he actually set up Gaucho's fatal trip, however innocently.

Bartlow, stunned, socks him. But Shields tells Bartlow that he's better off without Rosemary. "She was a fool. She got in your way. She interfered with your work. She wasted your time. She wasted you." Bartlow walks out.

Again, the camera returns to Pebbel's office where Pebbel is reminding Bartlow that he went on to write a best-seller on a Southern belle. "Yes, Jim, Jonathan sure destroyed you. You came out of it with nothing—nothing but a Pulitzer Prize novel and the highest salary of any writer in Hollywood.

"Look folks, you've got to give the devil his due. We all owe him something. And you know it."

Pebbel's call to Paris is ready and he asks them if they'll help Shields get started again. Each one shakes his head and they start to leave. Once out of the office, they can hear Pebbel responding to Jonathan's outline of the movie story. Georgia, curious, picks up the phone in the outer room. Bartlow and Amiel gather round to listen. The camera backs away and we see their ears pressed to the phone, fascinated. The movie ends here but we know that these people whom Shields has created, despite their bitter feelings for their old boss, will not be able to resist.

There were some interesting postscripts. First, the studio tried out the picture on preview audiences with encouraging results. They rated it "very good" to "outstanding." Still, many felt it was too long. So Minnelli and producer John Houseman cut twelve minutes, including a helicopter flight that Douglas and Powell took to find the crashed plane. It seemed like an anticlimax, they decided. Also dropped was the Paris room from which Douglas talked by telephone to Pebbel. Showing the Hollywood end of the conversation seemed enough.

On Oscar night, the picture came away with five Academy Awards, including best supporting actress for Gloria Grahame. Her prize was a surprise because her part was small and some thought she failed to play it with any degree of authenticity.

Finally, ten years later, *The Bad and the Beautiful* was resurrected in another Minnelli film about a faded actor who gets another chance—*Two Weeks in Another Town* (1962). In that film, the characters screen a movie they made in the past that had become their symbol of former glories, a yardstick by which others measured success.

"We'd wanted to use *Champion* (1949), Kirk's first big hit," Minnelli said. "But United Artists wanted too much money for us to use it. The only other important picture of Kirk's immediately available was *The Bad and the Beautiful*. In using it, we were accused, perhaps justly, of being immodest."

Ballad of
a Soldier

The moving climax of *Ballad of a Soldier*. Alyosha (Vladimir Ivashov) embraces his mother (Antonina Maximova) after his long cross-country trip from the front.

Ballad of a Soldier
(1959)

Directed by Grigori Chukhrai. Screenplay by Valentin Yoshov and Chukhrai. Camera, Vladimir Nikolayev and Era Saveleva. Music, Michael Siv. Directed by Chukhrai. A Mosfilm Production. 85 minutes.

Alyosha	*Vladimir Ivashov*
Shura	*Shanna Prokhorenko*
Alyosha's Mother	*Antonina Maximova*
General	*Nikolai Kruchkov*
Invalid	*Evgeni Urbanski*

Alyosha has knocked out two German tanks and his elated general (Nikolai Kruchkov) has summoned him to headquarters to grant him a favor. The young soldier asks for leave to see his mother.

A Russian peasant woman stands by an empty road. Seen in silhouette against an enormous cloud-filled sky, she is alone and seems to be searching for something in the vast emptiness.

"This is the road to town," a voice in the background says as the clouds scud by far above her. "Those who leave from our village and those who come home depart and return on this road. She is not waiting for anyone. The son she waited for, her son Alyosha, did not return from the war. He is buried far from his native land near a village with a foreign name.

"Early in spring, strangers lay flowers on his grave. They speak of him as the Russian soldier, a hero. For her, he was simply a son, her boy, about whom she knew everything from the day he was born until the day he went away along this road. He was our friend and we wanted to tell his story, a story that few people know—not even she, his mother."

So begins the absorbing film *Ballad of a Soldier,* a movie that many feel was the greatest picture to come out of Russia in the post-World War II period. Directed by the then young Soviet filmmaker Grigori Chukhrai, it marked a break in the Stalinist emphasis on dull propaganda and political films. *Ballad of a Soldier* is the simple story of a young soldier who accidentally performs a battlefield deed of heroism and wins a six-day pass to see his mother. The movie then traces his adventure-filled, interrupted journey home, reaching a climax as he arrives to greet his mother, then tears himself away in the same breath to go back to the front. The full poignancy of this tender moment rests on the knowledge that this boy—who is so young he has not yet learned to do anything but go to war—will die in battle.

"What we wanted to show was not how a man became a hero in war," said Chukhrai, "but what sort of a man he was and why he fought." Chukhrai was himself a paratrooper who fought from the center of Stalingrad to Vienna. He was wounded five times and lost many friends and relatives in the war. "I wanted to speak to those comrades, young men of my own age, who became soldiers when they left school."

What soon becomes obvious in this evocative and sensitive picture is that it is a war story without war scenes (if you forget the very beginning). The enemy is never seen, nor is the word "German"

39

ever used. There is no gunfire or bloodshed. It is all told in terms of behind-the-line scenes—in marked contrast to the stereotyped Hollywood front-lines approach to this genre.

"We decided," said Chukhrai, "that we would not use gigantic battle scenes or the usual accessories of war films. We looked for a way to condemn war that was simple and total."

Much of the film's success derives from the appealing and human performances of two student actors—Vladimir Ivashov as the soldier and Shanna Prokhorenko as the girl he meets on a train. Both were making their film debuts. Chukhrai searched long and carefully to cast them. Ivashov, a nineteen-year-old actor who studied at the Institute of Cinematography in Moscow, was the seventy-third actor interviewed for the role. Miss Prokhorenko, twenty, another Institute student, was the twentieth actress tested.

On a U.S. visit, she described her day in a Moscow acting school. "I go to the Institute six days a week," she said. "There are classes for all film workers—actors, writers, directors, cameramen, and so forth. We are students for four years. Then, we graduate and start working."

In 1959 she got $40 a week as a student, plus her own apartment. When she worked in a movie, she earned about $200 a week, as well as vacations in the Crimea and elsewhere. School was out from mid-June to September.

Ballad of a Soldier, only the second movie for Chukhrai,* catapulted him to international fame. The film won two minor awards in 1960 at the Cannes Festival and the prize for the best entry at the San Francisco Festival.** Chukhrai also won the San Francisco Festival's best director award. "This thirty-nine-year-old director is a poet in his medium," said Paul Beckley, critic for the *New York Herald-Tribune.*

As the years pass, *Ballad of a Soldier* and another Russian movie, *The Cranes Are Flying* (1958), remain among the finest foreign films

*His first, also a success, was *The Forty-First* (1956). After *Ballad of a Soldier* he went on to direct *Clear Skies* (1961), *People* (1966), and *The Battle of Stalingrad* (1970).

**Ivashov and Miss Prokhorenko came to San Francisco for the Festival and captivated American audiences. Said *Life:* "From the moment Shanna walked out on stage, giggled, and said, 'Good eve-ining. I cannot say something because—just a little English,' the two owned San Francisco." During the Festival week, they went shopping, toured vineyards, and sang Russian cowboy songs to Ivashov's balalaika music.

Alyosha and Shura (Shanna Prokhorenko), a girl he meets hitchhiking on a freight train, on their journey together. "I won't forget you," he tells her as they part.

emphasizing the uselessness and wastefulness of war.

As the movie opens, we are somewhere on the eastern front in Russia during World War II. Five German tanks, the vanguard of an attack force, are bearing down on a Soviet company. The lead tank lumbers over a bunker and comes upon a lone Soviet signalman. Its cannon pointed menacingly, the tank lurches on—ready to crush him like a beetle moving in to devour an ant.

The terrified young soldier runs, trips, and runs again. The camera follows him—slanting, tipping, and finally turning upside down—capturing the dizzy, disoriented feeling of the youth's helplessness as he scrambles for safety. The juggernaut keeps bearing down. But at the last instant, the fleeing soldier comes upon an anti-tank gun. Frantically, he grabs it, levels it, and fires. Miraculously, he hits the steel monster in a vulnerable spot. Up it goes in flames. The soldier, inspired by his daring deed, runs to an abandoned machine gun, opens up on the second tank, and sends it up in smoke, too. Suddenly, the other tanks slow, halt, then turn around. Singlehandedly, he has repulsed the enemy assault.

Hours later, the soldier is before his general (Nikolai Kruchkov) in a command post. The general says that he wants to decorate him but the prospect of a medal makes no impression on this homesick boy. "Comrade General," he says, "instead of giving me a citation, could you let me go home and see my mother?" It would give him time to fix her leaky roof, he says.

The general is, at first, irritated. "All of us would like to go home," he says. "But we've got a job to do up at the front." However, he takes another look at the youngster. The soldier's uniform cannot mask the boy's tender years. And so, in return for the morale boost the youth's heroic action has given his troops, the general relents. He gives the private a six-day furlough—two days to get home, two days to fix the roof, and two days to get back. The general asks only one thing—that the lad return on time.

"I promise you I won't overstay my leave," the overjoyed soldier says. "Not even one second." The general looks silently after him for a few long moments as the boy runs out exuberantly.

Now begins a series of strange incidents as Alyosha starts his trip home. On the way to the train station, he passes a platoon bound for the front. One of the infantrymen calls him, begging him to do him a favor. He asks Alyosha to take a present to his wife—two precious bars of soap. "I live on Chekov Street only a block from the

station," the infantryman says. "You have to change trains there anyway. Tell her you saw me. And I'm all right."

At the crowded depot, Alyosha meets a soldier on crutches (Evgeni Urbanski). His leg has been blown off. The amputee asks him to watch his suitcase while he sends a telegram. But when the train pulls in, he hasn't returned. Alyosha searches for him and finds him staring into space. "I wrote my wife, but I'm not going back," the one-legged man says bitterly. "Even before the war, I was pretty jealous. But now . . . I'm not going back to her like this. She's still a pretty girl. She'll do all right."

"What about you?" Alyosha asks. "Where will you go now?"

"It's a big country," he says.

Nevertheless, the despondent soldier finally climbs aboard the train and Alyosha tells him he will stay with him until his wife shows up at his hometown station. As they rattle through the broad, open countryside, an old man sits next to the wounded soldier. He tells him not to brood about his handicap but to learn to live with it. "I have a daughter," the old man says. "She's married only a month. She's already a widow."

At first it appears that there will be no one to meet the crippled soldier. Then a lovely, dark-haired girl calls his name. She rushes through the crowd and throws her arms around him.

"You're all right," she says, covering him with kisses.

"No," he says. "I was—"

"No, no, no," she cuts him off. "You've come back. That's all."

As the amputee's concern disappears, Alyosha slips away unnoticed. His train has long since pulled out so he sneaks on board a freight. In the boxcar he has climbed aboard, a young girl named Shura has also stowed away. Petrified at seeing Alyosha, she cries "Mama" and throws out her shawl holding her possessions. Then she tries to jump after them, but Alyosha stops her. After reassuring her, he sees that she is half-starved and he shares his food with her.

"Would you forgive me?" she says. "I was really silly."

"I guess I frightened you," he says. "So it was my fault, too."

And so begins a fleeting but tender relationship as the two experience one exciting incident after another. A sentry threatens to kick them off unless Alyosha gives him the cans of beef he is taking home for his mother. However, a tough lieutenant overhears the bribe attempt and puts the sentry under arrest.

A young girl holds up bars of soap, a wartime luxury that Alyosha has brought back from the front and given to a comrade's father.

At a stop, Alyosha leaves the train to get Shura some water. Before he can return, the train starts up with Shura aboard, but Alyosha finds her waiting for him at the next town. It turns out to be the hometown of the infantryman who gave him the bars of soap.

They go to his apartment, only to discover the soldier's wife with a lover. Angry and disillusioned, Alyosha rushes out. However, he learns that the soldier's father lives nearby in a shelter for bombed-out survivors, so he goes to the old man and gives him the soap. With the homeless residents of the shelter looking on, Alyosha tells the proud father that his son is a brave and exemplary soldier and remembers his father dearly.

Hours later, they reach Shura's hometown and there is an inevitable sad farewell. "I won't forget you," Alyosha shouts as his train pulls out. "I'll come back to you. Write me a letter."

Now Alyosha realizes that because he has not been indifferent to other people's problems, he has used up his own furlough. Four days of his leave are up. He barely has time to get home, greet his mother, and return to the front. And this is what we see at the moving climax to the film. It is a sequence that ranks with great scenes of any film made in the 1950s.

Alyosha has hitched a ride to his farming community. As the peasant women in the wheat fields see him, they call to Alyosha's widowed mother. The word spreads down the line until it reaches her. A handsome, earthy woman, she gets up from her field chores and starts running toward her boy. Trees and wheat stems sweep by in a blur as she rushes toward him, waiting on the road. "Alyosha," she cries and throws herself into his open arms. There is a long silence as they embrace.

"My son, you came back," she says, rapturously. The other women from the community crowd around.

"I'm in a hurry, mother," he can only sputter. "I got delayed. I used up all my time. I've got to go back now."

"Right away?" she asks incredulously, stunned, unable to believe that the flower of her life who has come back from the brink of death is now going to leave her in the very same instant.

"Yes, I'm sorry, Momma. Right away."

There is another silence as she peers into her son's clear, unlined face searchingly, as if trying to fix every inch of it indelibly in her memory.

"I won't let you go," she cries, trying to hold on to the one treasure left to her. "My little boy, Alyosha. Don't go."

"I'm sorry, Momma," he mutters. But the emotion of the moment is too much for him. He, too, breaks out in tears and begins to sob. Suddenly the mother sees that she is breaking her son's manly spirit. She cannot let him leave like this before all his friends and neighbors.

She stops crying and throws back her head proudly. "What's wrong?" she asks. "I'll be waiting for you. You must come right back to me. Your dad didn't return. But you will." She says the words strongly, full of confidence.

"I will, Momma," her son answers.

And so Alyosha leaves. And that is the whole story—simple, artless, like a fairy tale or a ballad. But, at the same time, it is moving and lyrical and deftly etched.

As Alyosha goes down the road, his mother stands watching him fade in the distance, riding out of her life, lost to her. Great clouds sweep by in the sky and the same deep voice in the background that started the film ends the movie:

"This is all we wanted to say about our friend Alyosha. He might have become a farmer, or a great doctor, or a wonderful father. Who knows what such a boy had it in him to be? But he was, and will remain forever in our memory—a soldier, a hero, and our friend."

Shura washes her legs at a whistlestop during her long train journey with Alyosha.

Alyosha meets a soldier who has lost his leg in battle and tries to convince him that his wife will want him back.

Ben-Hur

Charlton Heston as the Jewish prince Judah Ben-Hur in the 1959 MGM movie that won a record eleven Oscars.

Ben-Hur*
(1959)

Directed by William Wyler.* Screenplay by Karl Tunberg with Christopher Fry, S. N. Behrman, Gore Vidal, and Maxwell Anderson. Based on the novel by General Lew Wallace. Musical score, Miklos Rozsa.* Costume design, Elizabeth Haffenden.* Special effects, A. Arnold Gillespie,* Robert MacDonald,* and Milo Lory.* Sound effects, Franklin E. Milton.* Editors, Ralph E. Winters and John D. Dunning.* Camera, Robert L. Surtees.* Art and set decorators, William A. Horning, Edward Carfagno, and Hugh Hunt.* Second unit, Yakima Canutt, Andrew Marton, and Mario Soldati. Produced by Sam Zimbalist. An MGM Picture. 212 minutes.

Ben-Hur	*Charlton Heston**
Quintus Arrius	*Jack Hawkins*
Esther	*Haya Harareet*
Messala	*Stephen Boyd*
Sheik Ilderim	*Hugh Griffith**
Miriam	*Martha Scott*
Tirzah	*Cathy O'Donnell*
Simonides	*Sam Jaffe*
Balthasar	*Finlay Currie*
Pontius Pilate	*Frank Thring*
Drusus	*Terence Longdon*
Tiberius	*George Relph*
Sextus	*Andre Morell*
Flavia	*Marina Berti*
Tiberius' Aide	*Ralph Truman*
Mallauch	*Adi Berber*
Madonna	*Jose Greci*
Joseph	*Laurence Payne*
The Christ	*Claude Heater*
Gratus	*Mino Doro*

*Academy Award Winner.

Condemned to the galleys as a Roman slave, Ben-Hur survives to rise to glory in Rome and return to his native land.

It all started in 1876 on a train going to Indianapolis. Two riders turned their discussion to the subject of the hereafter. One of them was Robert Ingersoll, a famous lawyer and orator. The other was General Lew Wallace, a Civil War hero who had begun another career as a writer.*

"Is there a God?" asked Wallace. "Is there a Heaven and a Hell?"

"I don't know," said Ingersoll. "Do you?" Ingersoll's brilliant lectures assailing the evidence that there was an Eternal Being had earned him the title of "The Great Agnostic." Through eloquence, wit, and logic, he had shaken the faith of thousands. Now, he was reversing Wallace's question.

Ingersoll went on for two hours to state his doubts. He became so carried away that his ideas

flowed "like a heated river," said Wallace. "I sat spellbound."

Though Wallace was not even a church member himself, he came to regard Ingersoll's thesis as a challenge. Ingersoll had, in a sense, flung down the gauntlet, but Wallace did not try to answer him in their train meeting. Instead, he decided to convert an unfinished novel he was writing into his reply. That novel would become *Ben-Hur,* a book that would sell more copies in its time than any other work except the Bible.**

Wallace had never been to the Holy Land—a trip he would not make until he had finished the book. Therefore he went to the Library of Congress in

*In 1864, Wallace, leading 5,800 green troops, held off General Jubal Early's contingent of 28,000 Confederates at Monocacy, a delaying action that was credited as saving Washington from capture. After the war, Wallace returned to his law practice in Crawfordsville, Indiana, writing in his spare time. Thereafter, he was governor of the Territory of New Mexico (1878-1881), ambassador to Turkey (1881-1885), and then a popular lecturer and author until his death in 1905. His statue stands in the Hall of Statuary in Washington as one of the representatives of the state of Indiana.

**This is the popular story of the origin of *Ben-Hur,* an event Wallace himself wrote about in responding to questions about how he came to write his famous epic. However, in 1947, Wallace's biographer, Irving McKee, cast some doubt on the accuracy of Wallace's memory. McKee noted that even before meeting Ingersoll, Wallace was talking about his fictional Jewish hero. In a letter to his wife written in 1874, two years before the Ingersoll meeting, Wallace said, "Now for home and a Jewish boy whom I got into trouble, and must get out of it as best I can—all in my book." Nevertheless, if the Ingersoll encounter did not initiate the idea for *Ben-Hur,* it almost certainly added resolve to Wallace's seven-year writing chore.

Washington and reconstructed biblical history, geography, and color by poring over every book relating to Jews. He returned to his Crawfordsville, Indiana, home with bulky pages of notes and books and an immense relief map of Palestine.

Wallace wrote his lengthy 250,000-word masterwork during evenings, on Sundays, and during time stolen from his law practice and his tenure as territorial governor of New Mexico. Finally, one day in 1880, he submitted his handwritten novel to Harper and Brothers. He called it *Judah, A Tale of the Christ.* Judah Ben-Hur was the hero's full name. Ben, in Hebrew, means "son of." The publisher liked it right away but felt that Judah was too much like Judas. So Harper prevailed on Wallace to change the title to *Ben-Hur.* However, Wallace insisted that the subtitle, *A Tale of the Christ,* be kept.

Critics, in the main, ignored the book, but those who reviewed it generally panned it. They felt that its characters were stilted, its plot was lacking in dignity and grandeur, and its denouement was helped along by too many coincidences. The fact that Wallace was a soldier and politician did not help, for it stamped him as an amateur in the eye of critics of the day. "I protest," said one James Watson, "as a friend of Christ, that He has been crucified enough already, without having a Territorial Governor after Him."

But millions of readers were enthralled by the story of the impact of Christ on an aristocratic Jewish family, and particularly on Judah Ben-Hur, the son of that family. They were carried away by the sweeping adventures of the tough-fibered man who endured years as a galley slave and then rose again to glory in Rome, capital of the nation oppressing his people. Carl Van Doren later said that *Ben-Hur* did more to establish the popularity of the novel in this country than any other book.

No small spur to the book's appeal was the fact that Victorian America was going through a religious renaissance. After a slow start, sales doubled every year. By the end of the first decade, the public had bought an unprecedented 500,000 copies, and the demand was just beginning.* Interest was so widespread that it reached to the White House. General U. S. Grant, who hadn't read a novel in ten years, said that he couldn't put the book down. He read it in a twenty-four-hour period after staying up all night.

Offers to bring the novel to the stage besieged Wallace. He resisted them all until the late 1890s, when Abraham Erlanger, of Klaw and Erlanger, the

*There are no accurate figures on all-time total sale, but the best estimate is over 2,500,000 copies.

Broadway producers, went to Wallace's home and made him an offer.

"Mr. Erlanger," said the general, "do you believe in Jesus Christ?"

"Frankly," said Erlanger, who was a Jew, "I don't." Undaunted but fearful of seeing the whole project scuttled on the strength of this single response, he added: "My partner, Klaw, does. But he's up in Boston."

This *non sequitur* notwithstanding, the general finally agreed on the condition that the play would not show the face or figure of Christ. The drama, which used a shaft of light to indicate His Presence, opened in 1899 at the Old Broadway Theatre in New York City. It had vast choruses, elaborate crowd scenes, intricate lighting, and a breathless sea rescue—with stagehands in the wings shaking great lengths of cloth to simulate waves. Though critics complained that it was more circus than drama, it became as great a popular success as the novel. As the book introduced readers to the novel, so did the play serve to bring newcomers into the theatre. "To untutored thousands, *Ben-Hur* was a religious experience," said biographer McKee. "Tears coursed down their faces when the shaft of light appeared. They felt they were in the presence of the Son of God."

William S. Hart, later to become famous as a solemn-faced movie cowboy, was the original Messala. William Farnum, also destined for the silent screen, took over the title role in 1901.

Audiences marveled at the two chariots, their horses thundering on treadmills while a painted panorama of the Circus Maximus whirled behind them. They were the sensation of the stage presentation. Within six years, the chariots increased to eight. The play eventually went on tour and foreign rights were sold. Wherever it appeared, it was a gala occasion. At the London opening, first-nighters included Arthur Conan Doyle and Sir Henry Irving. King Edward and Queen Alexandria watched from a special box built in the center of the pit.

For the next twenty-one years, *Ben-Hur* never stopped running somewhere in the world. An estimated 20,000,000 people saw it, and every actor who played in it has his favorite anecdote. One of the most unusual stories came from Hart who told of the night in Boston when the treadmill machinery worked wrong and Messala won the race.

In 1907, when silent movies were in their infancy, the Kalem Company of New York made *Ben-Hur* into a one-reel film. Wallace had died two years earlier, having earned more in royalties for a single

Heston in the famous chariot race. It cost $1 million to film this memorable scene. Stuntmen did the long takes. Even so, handling the four race horses was so difficult, Heston had to train three months just for the closeups.

book than any author had ever done. However, his heirs sued on the grounds that they had not granted permission for the filming. Kalem fought the case all the way to the Supreme Court, but the judges ruled in favor of the author's heirs, and the film was withdrawn. The suit established the fact that authors had legal rights in the new field of motion pictures.

Then, in the mid-1920s, MGM bought the film rights for a million dollars, a sum without precedent at that time, and produced a picture that was even more lavish a production than the play. Under Fred Niblo's direction, the film company enacted the sea battle in the Mediterranean with 14 ships and 280 men. One ship caught fire during the shooting and some extras were lost when they leaped overboard in their armor. However, the studio managed to keep the incident quiet. The production included 10,000 actors, 198 horses, and a specially constructed grandstand that was 3,000 feet long. To film the chariot race, MGM used 42 cameras—one in an airplane.

Despite the colossal staging, many critics felt that the story was weak. They praised, instead, the scenery, and, of course, the exciting chariot race. However, even without critical accolades, it became a classic of the silent screen that was seen by worldwide audiences. Britain applauded it. King George and Queen Mary attended a special showing in Windsor Castle. Its lone international failure came in the Far East, where China banned it as pro-Christian propaganda. In 1931, a version with sound effects was issued. Audiences heard the thunder of hoofbeats, the roar of the crowd, the crack of the charioteers' whips, and the moans of the dying in battle.

But this version was to be outdone thirty years later by the third movie, which added color and wide-screen innovations. As it turned out, the 1959 Ben-Hur was the biggest roll of the dice that MGM ever made. When the studio added up all the cash it had laid out to make the biblical adventure, the sum threatened to drown MGM in a tide of red ink. The bottom line was $15 million, thus making it the most expensive film of its time. The tab for a single sequence—the chariot race which ran for fifteen minutes on the screen—was $1 million. That was more than the entire budget of most other movies.

Even the non-financial statistics were mind-boggling. Shot in the new big-screen process called Camera 65, the picture used 2,000,000 feet of film, 300 sets, and 25,000 extras and bit players. It ran six hours but was cut to a playing time of three hours and thirty-two minutes—fifteen minutes longer than Doctor Zhivago (1965) but seven min-utes shorter than Gone with the Wind (1939). (A re-released version I saw in 1975 ran only two hours and forty minutes and suffered from injudicious cutting.)

However, unlike many other pictures of the Great Era of Ancient Spectacles, it justified its studio's faith in the grandeur that was Rome. For a change, Ben-Hur got favorable reviews,* and it earned a whopping $37 million domestic gross.** The picture received a dozen Academy Award nominations, topped only by the fourteen that went to All About Eve in 1950. All but one nomination came through with an Oscar for Ben-Hur.†

Ironically, William Wyler, its director (who had served as a $10 a week assistant in the MGM version done in the 1920s), at first had no interest in the movie. He agreed to direct it only after unrelenting pressure from producer Sam Zimbalist who died while the movie was being made. Zimbalist had wanted to see the picture made since 1951 when he produced Quo Vadis. But when he approached Wyler, the director only shrugged. It wasn't his style, Wyler said. Wyler's previous films included Mrs. Miniver (1942) and The Best Years of Our Lives (1946), for which he won Oscars.

"That doesn't matter, Willy," Zimbalist said. "The spectacle will take care of itself. What we want is good, intelligent stuff. Intimacy is the meat of the story. The spectacle is, perhaps, one-tenth of the whole film."

Wyler read the script but still remained uncommitted. Zimbalist persisted and kept seeing him. Once, when Zimbalist showed him a layout of the chariot race, Wyler was intrigued enough to offer to direct that sequence, but nothing more.

---

*Notable exceptions were religious groups. Although the Catholic Legion of Decency gave it a top rating, Jesuits panned it because they said it portrayed Romans as stupid. The movie, they said, had all the subtlety of a third-class Western. The Christian Century was unhappy at its "distortion of the Bible"—to which director William Wyler replied that it was not a biblical film but first-century fiction. Other dissenters were Dwight MacDonald of Esquire who noted that the film shifted the blame for Christ's crucifixion from the Jews to the Romans. Still another detractor was British documentary filmmaker Basil Wright who said it was "not a patch on its [1925] predecessor."

**In 1978, it stood as the 23rd all-time biggest domestic (U.S.-Canada) grosser. Variety listed the top three as: Star Wars (1977), which grossed $127 million, Jaws (1975), $121 million, and The Godfather (1972), $86 million. Ben-Hur's domestic gross was $37 million, second only to C. B. DeMille's The Ten Commandments (1956)—which pulled in $43 million—as the domestic film rental earning champ of the 1950s.

†One of its eleven Academy Awards was for Miklos Rozsa's music. The longest film score ever composed, it took nine months to write. Some critics rank it among the best film scores of all time.

Once friends and now bitter rivals, the Roman tribune Messala (Stephen Boyd) and Ben-Hur battle in close quarters in the chariot race.

Then, one day, he read the novel, and it changed his mind. "The more I thought about it," Wyler said, "the more I saw the possibilities." Wyler felt the Wallace story did not have to be changed, merely edited and its dialogue sharpened. In addition, the job would rate a sizable salary and be a challenge as well. Although not a practicing Jew, Wyler also felt that the story would be appealing because it reminded him of the new nation of Israel fighting for its life.

The cast, as it turned out, was an international one. Charlton Heston, the noble, steely-eyed king of epics, was actually a second choice for the lead. Cesare Danova, an Italian actor with an Olympian physique, was the studio's original selection. However, his English was heavily accented, and Wyler prevailed on MGM to go with the 6'2" Heston as the Judean prince.

Jack Hawkins of England, after finishing *The Bridge on the River Kwai*, played Quintus Arrius, the Roman naval commander. For Messala, Ben-Hur's friendly enemy, the studio got relative newcomer Stephen Boyd of Ireland. From Israel came unknown Haya Harareet to portray Ben-Hur's sweetheart, Esther. MGM publicists said only that she was from the "Near East." That ploy failed to fool the United Arab Republic which, in protest over the casting of an Israeli actress, banned the picture even before it was made. Later, Moslem countries prohibited its showing because they said it was too favorable to Hebrews.

MGM didn't skimp on its production budget. In Rome, Wyler got a diplomat's villa and servants, plus a limousine and chauffeur. MGM had decided against making the picture in Hollywood because it required too many large sets that would have interfered with other productions. Therefore it leased the vast Cinecitta Studios, Europe's largest motion picture plant.

During the ten-month shooting schedule, 500 correspondents from all over the world showed up. Many of them wrote about taking a chariot ride on the massive set. One of the visitors was Ed Sullivan who presented on his television show a film clip of himself learning to ride a chariot.

But it was more than the publicity and the hoopla

that made the production a success. What set it apart from the run of DeMille spectacles was the tasteful, intelligent handling of its human story. "Not only is it not simple-minded, it is downright literate," said Arthur Knight in *Saturday Review*. "There are no erotic ballets in worship of some pagan sun goddess, no slinky sirens in diaphanous silks . . . and where there are scenes of spectacle— notably a stirring sea battle and the famous chariot race—they serve the story."

As the movie opens, the tribune Messala (Boyd), commander of the legion which precedes Jerusalem's new Roman governor, rides into the ancient city. Sextus (Andre Morell), whom Messala is relieving, tells him that the country is changing. It isn't just the reluctance of the people to pay Roman taxes. The roots of unrest lie deeper. There are strange spirits at work which Sextus attributes to a young carpenter's apprentice who is preaching that God is not a long way off—but in every man. Messala laughs this off, saying that he intends to enforce the Emperor's command that Judea be made into a more disciplined province.

Judah Ben-Hur (Heston), prince of one of the country's wealthiest families, arrives to pay his respects. The Roman soldiers are shocked to see their commander rush to greet a Jew, an enemy of Rome. But Messala has grown up in Judea, and he and Ben-Hur are old friends.

However, their conversation soon makes it clear that there is a chasm between them now. Messala, who has fought in Britain, Africa, and Spain, sees all life as a Roman world. He warns Ben-Hur that if he is to live in it, he must become part of it, and he urges him to reveal the identity of his country's underground leaders. Ben-Hur responds by saying that his allegiance is to his people.

Ben-Hur's mother, Miriam (Martha Scott), and his sister, Tirzah (Cathy O'Donnell), are saddened to hear of the change in Messala. But this sadness is trivial compared to what will follow. The next day, Gratus (Mino Doro), the new governor, parades triumphantly into Jerusalem. At the house of Ben-Hur, the family is on the rooftop, watching. Suddenly Tirzah, leaning over the rail to get a better view, accidentally loosens a tile. It falls and startles Gratus' horses, knocking the new governor to the ground. Messala and his troops, panicking at what seems to be an assassination attempt, invade the house and arrest Ben-Hur, his mother, and his sister.

Without a trial, Miriam and Tirzah are condemned to life imprisonment. Ben-Hur is then ordered to the galleys, and he is immediately thrown in with other prisoners on a forced march to the sea. "I pray that you live till I return," Ben-Hur says to Messala. "Return?" Messala replies, laughing. Under the Roman lash, many prisoners die along the way, dehydrated by the desert heat. When they pause in the village of Nazareth, the guards allow all except Ben-Hur to drink from a fountain. As he lies in the sand, a hand reaches to him with a gourd of water. His benefactor never speaks, nor is he identified—but we know it is Jesus.

Three years later, Ben-Hur, older but tougher, is number 41 among slaves rowing one of Rome's great sea galleys. "We keep you alive to serve the ship," the slaves are told. "Row well and live." Quintus Arrius (Jack Hawkins), the new commander of the force, is impressed with the slave's strength and nobility. He offers to take him to Rome and train him as a gladiator, but Ben-Hur answers that hate has kept him alive while other men have died like flies. He refuses the offer unless it means his freedom.

One day, pirate ships attack the fleet, closing in on the Roman warships and then boarding them. Arrius orders Ben-Hur's chains removed. As the pirates ram his ship, Ben-Hur sees Arrius battered overboard. He leaps into the sea and pulls the commander to a piece of debris. Days later, a Roman ship picks them up.

To film this sequence, MGM dug an artificial lake and put two full-size galleys in it for close shots. In all, they built more than forty ships for long shots of the battle. Heston remembered the galley scenes as among the most uncomfortable he worked in. "This damned slave galley is exactly that," he wrote in his diary. "Hottest set I've ever worked in." A week later, a cold spell suddenly descended and Heston found himself half-chilled to death on a wet bobbing raft.

Under director Wyler, who had a reputation as a hard taskmaster, Heston said the location shooting was grueling. "We often worked seven days a week," Heston said, "always twelve hours a day." However, Heston was proud of the final product. "Doing a picture for Willie Wyler is like getting the works in a Turkish bath," Heston said. "You damn near get drowned. But you come out smelling like a rose."

In Rome, the Emperor Tiberius (George Relph) grants Arrius' request that he be allowed to adopt Ben-Hur as a foster son. Ironically, as Ben-Hur and Messala have started as friends and grown to be enemies, Ben-Hur and Arrius have reversed this relationship. In time, Ben-Hur becomes Rome's most celebrated athlete. But even as he attains money, position, adulation, and Arrius' deep affection, he cannot forget his homeland and his family. One day he tells Arrius that he must go back.

Months later, traveling in Judea, Ben-Hur meets Balthasar (Finlay Currie), one of three men who some years ago followed a star to Bethlehem and laid gifts before a newborn boy. The older man introduces Ben-Hur to bearded Sheik Ilderim (Hugh Griffith), a wealthy Arabian sportsman who is training his horses for the chariot races.

Finally, Ben-Hur reaches Jerusalem where he is amazed to find Esther (Haya Harareet), the daughter of Hur's old steward (Sam Jaffe), living as a recluse with her father. He is now crippled from Roman torture.

The next day, Ben-Hur marches boldly to Messala's home and asks about his mother and sister. They are lepers who are held in solitary confinement, deep in the dungeons. Messala, however, denies knowing their whereabouts. Then, as soon as Ben-Hur leaves, he orders Miriam and Tirzah to the Valley of the Lepers, outside the city.

Believing his mother and sister to be dead, Ben-Hur returns to the sheik's encampment. When he learns that Messala will be in the chariot race, he agrees to drive the sheik's four white horses.

A huge throng turns out to see the races. Even the new governor, Pontius Pilate (Frank Thring), attends. There are drivers from Athens, Corinth, Syria, Cyprus, and Carthage, but all eyes are focused on two chariots, one drawn by Ben-Hur's beautiful white steeds, the other by Messala's four glistening black horses.

One after another, Messala knocks drivers out of the race when his spiked wheels shatter their chariots. Finally, the race reaches its climax when Messala tries to upset Ben-Hur. The wheels of their chariots lock. But it is Messala's which give way, wrenched from their axle by Ben-Hur's chariot. At breakneck speed, Messala is sent across the race course where the trailing chariots and horses unavoidably trample him.

The race set, which took a year to build, dominated the studio lot. Covering more than eighteen acres with a 1,500-foot straightaway in the center, it was the largest single movie set built. Atop a central divider strip, four statues stood thirty feet high. Overlooking the area, the grandstand rose five stories and seated 24,000.

MGM took almost three months to film the race, which many rate as one of the most exciting crowd scenes ever made.* It used six $100,000 camera

units. Craftsmen built eighteen chariots, at a cost of $1,200 each, and styled them to represent different nations. The studio scoured Europe and the Near East for finely bred horses—four per chariot—and taught them chariot racing in a training area the same size as the set.

Here, Hollywood's best stunt men practiced along with the stars. "Both Heston and Boyd spent every minute between shooting other scenes, practicing their chariot racing with (stunt man) Yakima Canutt," said Wyler. "This went on for three months before they actually shot the race. They both still have scars on their hands from the ordeal. And all they were trying to do was get good enough for the closeups. The longer shots were done by cowboys and trick riders."

Since both Boyd and Heston were blue-eyed, Wyler fitted Boyd with contact lenses to make him appear as a black-eyed Messala. The lenses bothered him, and scenes had to be switched to give his eyes a rest.

After the race, the narrative slackens as the plot moves from action to religious mysticism. Ben-Hur visits the dying Messala. The unrepentant Roman tells him that his mother and sister still live. "Look for them in the Valley of the Lepers," says Messala. "The race is not over." He dies feeling that he has had some revenge for his humiliating defeat.

Pontius Pilate tells Ben-Hur that the Emperor has made him a Roman citizen, but Ben-Hur says that he prefers to stay with his own people. In time, he finds Miriam and Tirzah scrounging for food in the leper colony, a sight so painful to him he cannot bear to speak to them.

Walking back to Jerusalem, Ben-Hur and Esther meet Balthasar, who leads them to the outskirts of a crowd to listen to Jesus of Nazareth speak. Esther, impressed when she learns of his miracles, persuades Miriam and Tirzah to accompany her to see the new preacher. Ben-Hur is also profoundly stirred.

But the events of history move quickly. Ben-Hur, returning to Jerusalem, arrives just in time to see Jesus, now a prisoner, bearing a cross on his back to Calvary. As Jesus once gave Ben-Hur water in Nazareth, so does Ben-Hur return the favor now. Later, when Jesus dies on the cross, there is a blinding rainstorm that miraculously washes away the leper sores of Ben-Hur's mother and sister.

The movie does not make Ben-Hur's adoption of Christianity explicit, but Wallace's book leaves no

*Other industry nominees for the most thrilling crowd scenes: the burning of Atlanta in *Gone with the Wind* (1939), the earthquake in *San Francisco* (1936), the tidal wave in *The Hurricane* (1937), the animal stampede in *King Solomon's Mines* (1950), the gladiators' revolt in *Spartacus* (1960), and the desert train attack in *Lawrence of Arabia* (1962). From other Heston films, there is also the circus train wreck from *The Greatest Show on Earth* (1952) and the parting of the Red Sea from *The Ten Commandments* (1956).

doubt. The novel's last paragraph speaks of his grave among the catacombs of Rome where the earliest Christians practiced their new religion.

And what of Wallace's own beliefs? The record is unclear. He said that the seven years he spent writing *Ben-Hur* changed him from a man of indifferent religious feelings to an "absolute believer in God and the divinity of Christ." Yet this may have been merely a public statement to support the sale of his book. Readers, who found their own religious convictions strengthened, obviously would have been disappointed to hear that *Ben-Hur* was no more than a rousing yarn to Wallace.

The fact is that biographer McKee says Wallace's letters bear out that he was never influenced by religious sentiment. Nor, apparently, had he any firm beliefs about formal religion. In 1882, on the eve of his son Henry's marriage, Wallace advised him to join whatever sect his bride belonged to. In 1888, eight years after *Ben-Hur*'s publication, Wallace told interviewers that he was not a lay member of any church.

The Blackboard Jungle

Glenn Ford as Richard Dadier, a new teacher who starts his career trying to teach slum youths in an inner-city high school.

The Blackboard Jungle (1955)

Directed by Richard Brooks. Screenplay by Brooks, based on Evan Hunter's novel. Art directors, Cedric Gibbons, Randall Duell. Musical adaptation, Charles Wolcott. Photography, Russell Harlan. Editor, Ferris Webster. Music, Bill Haley and the Comets, includes: "Rock Around the Clock," "The Jazz Me Blues," "Jungle E-Bop," "Don't Tell Me Lies," "Rick's Ballad," and "Invention for Guitar and Trumpet." Produced by Pandro Berman. An MGM Picture. 101 minutes.

Richard Dadier	Glenn Ford
Anne Dadier	Anne Francis
Jim Murdock	Louis Calhern
Lois Hammond	Margaret Hayes
Mr. Warnecke	John Hoyt
Josh Edwards	Richard Kiley
Mr. Halloran	Emile Meyer
Dr. Bradley	Warner Anderson
Prof. Kraal	Basil Ruysdael
Gregory Miller	Sidney Poitier
Artie West	Vic Morrow
Belazi	Dan Terranova
Pete Morales	Rafael Campos
Emmanuel Stoker	Paul Mazursky
Detective	Horace McMahon
Santini	Jameel Farah*
Miss Brady	Henny Backus

*Later Jamie Farr of TV's "M*A*S*H."

Dadier confronts student Gregory Miller (Sidney Poitier), a class leader who calls him "Teach."

Artie West (Vic Morrow), leader of a gang of hoodlums, flicks open his six-inch switchblade knife and advances toward his male teacher. One of his pals locks the classroom door, blocking off any escape. The rest of the kids are on their feet to see the battle royal.

West lunges at the teacher, missing his chest, but slicing open a gash in his hand. Despite his wound, the teacher stands his ground. Then he starts moving in on West, challenging him, calling his bluff, offering to fight him with bare hands. There is no turning back now. It is a match that will bring one of them down.

This is the climactic scene from *The Blackboard Jungle*, an uncompromisingly vivid picture that held up to America a mirror of troubled inner-city schools. The image was a harsh and unrelenting one that many turned away from. In Italy, judges dropped the film from the Venice Film Festival after Ambassador Clare Booth Luce protested its inclusion. In this country, some educators said that the movie projected a distorted picture of juvenile delinquency in the public schools.

"Is it a true and valid picture of conditions in any schools today?" asked Bosley Crowther, critic of the *New York Times*. "Are there any schools where pupils are so completely arrogant and out of hand? . . . If so, this picture is tragically justified and it is time for some drastic social action. But if it isn't—if the details in the film are 'stacked' and exaggerated . . . then it seems to us irresponsible and fraught with peril."

Readers responding to Crowther's column were mixed in their reaction. Some said the picture misrepresented and sensationalized. "Not more than one percent of the entire high school population might truly be considered either potential or actual juvenile delinquents," said C. Frederick Pertsch of the New York City Board of Education. Others said they felt the film had performed a public service. One viewer, Ervin Eatenson of New York City, said that even if conditions are exaggerated, "the purpose of such a movie is served well enough, indeed, if society is introduced—however starkly—to conditions such as those seen in *Blackboard Jungle*."

Of course, we know today that the school situation the movie exposed accurately delineated conditions in scores of our largest cities. As the years passed, more and more middle-class families deserted the cities for the suburbs—swelling the proportion of lower income and minority children in urban school systems. Eventually, there was a multitude of blackboard jungles.

And so today the movie plays not as a period piece from the 1950s but as a vivid, living drama, a relevant slice of social commentary that not only was prophetic but remains pertinent decades after it was made.

The movie opens with Bill Haley and the Comets belting out the rowdy jazz number "Rock Around the Clock," which began the rock 'n' roll era. Meanwhile, the camera follows quiet-spoken Navy veteran Richard Dadier (Glenn Ford) walking under a noisy el to his first teaching job. Dadier is starting at North Manual High School, a vocational school in a congested lower-class area of a large city.

"There is no discipline problem in this school, Mr. Dadier, as long as I'm principal," Dr. Bradley (Warner Anderson), an iron-willed educator, tells him. But Dadier hears different opinions when he meets his colleagues. "This is the garbage can of

the educational system," says Jim Murdock (Louis Calhern), the history teacher.

"Any tips for a rookie?" Dadier asks.

"Two," says the cynical Murdock. "Don't be a hero. And never turn your back on the class."

Murdock has been teaching for twelve years. All he's got to show for it, he says, are two purple hearts and no salary increases. "They hire fools like us with college degrees to sit on their garbage can—keep them in school—so women for a few hours a day can walk around the city."

"These kids," asks Dadier, "they can't *all* be bad. Can they?"

"No?" says Murdock. "Why?"

Dadier has come to North Manual because he needs a steady paycheck. With his wife (Anne Francis) only a few months away from having their first child, any job looks good. Nevertheless, he learns the wisdom of Murdock's advice during his very first day in school.

His class is a collection of lazy, undisciplined, brutish misfits. It is a dumping ground for teenagers who are not old enough to work in the eyes of the

Dadier comes home bruised and beaten when his kids waylay him and another teacher in an alley. His wife (Anne Francis) urges him to quit.

Dadier advances on Artie West (Vic Morrow), a hoodlum who has stabbed him with a switchblade knife.

law, but too young to get out of school. Restless and bored, the boys are merely marking time until they go into the service or get a job. Dadier has the almost impossible job of breaking the barrier of ignorance and rebellion and trying to kindle the first sparks of interest in education.

Led by Gregory Miller (Sidney Poitier),* a black whom Dadier thinks he can win over, and Artie West (Vic Morrow), a sadistic bully, Dadier's class quickly makes clear its contempt for authority. Surly and rude, they call him "Chief" and "Teach." They pay little attention to him, holding their own conversations or cracking jokes while he speaks. When humor fails, Dadier tries discipline, only to be taunted by West. "You ever try to fight thirty-five guys at one time, Teach?" West asks.

That afternoon, while Dadier is waiting for Lois Hammond (Margaret Hayes), an attractive new

teacher who has offered him a ride home, he hears a noise in a darkened library room. When he goes in, Dadier finds a youth wrestling Miss Hammond to the floor and tearing her blouse. Dadier subdues the boy and calls the police, an action later resented by the other students who hew to a code of silence. Days later, Dadier and a fellow teacher, Josh Edwards (Richard Kiley), are waylaid in an alley.

Anne, Dadier's wife, urges him to quit, but he says that now he is even more determined to stick it out. "I've been beaten up," he says, "but I'm not beaten. And I'm not quitting."

As the weeks go by, the students keep up their harassment. One of them keeps writing and phoning Dadier's wife, telling her that Dadier is having an affair with a teacher. Another tells the principal that Dadier is a bigot, falsely accusing Dadier of maligning his students. The other teachers are having their troubles, too. Murdock slaps a boy when his temper frays. Josh quits after his class, goaded on by West, destroys his prized collection of phonograph records.

Still, Dadier, idealistic and dedicated, persists. He scores a small victory when he is put in charge

*The first black superstar, Poitier had been in four previous movies with mixed success. His searing, sensitive performance in *Blackboard Jungle* established his credentials as a dramatic actor. From then on, when a part called for a tense, brooding young black, first call went to Poitier. His credits include *Edge of the City* (1957), *Lilies of the Field* (1963) for which he won an Oscar, *In the Heat of the Night* (1967), and *Guess Who's Coming to Dinner* (1967).

of the Christmas show and Miller organizes a singing group for the occasion.

Then there is a confrontation with West after school when the youth reveals some of his true feelings for just an instant. And West's thoughts anticipate some of the problems that were echoed by his contemporaries of the 1960s. Dadier has just seen Artie's gang steal a newspaper delivery truck. He warns West that that kind of action can lead to prison. West rejects his advice with this argument:

"You know, a year from now the army comes by and says—'OK, Artie West, you get in uniform, you be a soldier. You save the world and you get your lousy head blown off.' Well, maybe I get a year in jail and maybe the army don't want Artie West to be a soldier no more. Maybe what I get is out. . . ."

One day, Dadier walks Miller to his after-school job in a garage and urges him not to quit school. Miller will be old enough to make this decision at the end of the year.

"Mr. Dadier, you're pretty new at this," Miller says. "Soon you're going to be quitting yourself."

"I'll make a deal with you," Dadier says. "We'll have a sort of pact, you and I. Neither of us will quit. How about it?"

Miller doesn't answer.

Even while Dadier is talking with Miller, his wife, tormented and unnerved by the anonymous letters and phone calls, is rushed to the hospital where her baby is born prematurely. It isn't until three days later that Dadier learns his child will live, and his outrage over the school situation that threatened his baby's life suddenly breaks his resolve.

"Who cares about teachers anyway?" Dadier tells the history teacher, Murdock. "Teachers get two dollars an hour. A household cook gets more than we do. And they get room and board."

But Murdock asks Dadier to stay, saying that he has been getting through to his students. "You proved something," Murdock says. "The kids can be taught—if you don't stop trying."

Dadier does go back and walks right into the most frightening scene of his young career. During a test, West blatantly cheats by copying from another pupil's paper. After he is warned, he keeps right on. Then he refuses to obey Dadier's order to bring his paper to him.

When Dadier tells West he is going to take him to the principal, the youth whips out a switchblade and dares him to try. West's pals lock the door. One of them sneaks behind Dadier to trip him. Miller slugs the kid, then warns Dadier to back away.

"Take it easy, Chief. He's [West] crazy. He's high. He's floating on sneaky Pete wine."

Dadier has decided this is the showdown, his make-or-break challenge. If he can overcome West, he can win the respect of the class.

"Give me that knife, West."

"All you got to do is take it. Where do you want it? In the belly? How about in the face?"

Dadier advances slowly. As he does, West lashes out. The teacher sidesteps—enough to pull his body away from West's knife, but not his hand. Blood wells up from a gashing cut.

Dadier's resolve is unshaken. He keeps coming —and this begins to unsettle West. An unarmed man is standing up to him. The only way he can stop him is to kill him, and West isn't ready for that.

So West calls for his pals to jump Dadier, but no one moves. Dadier's raw courage has impressed them. They remain frozen to their places, waiting to see if their gang leader has the guts to do the job himself.

"You're not so tough without a gang to back you up," Dadier says. "But you were tough that night in the alley, weren't you? Seven to two . . . the gangup didn't work. Then you went to the principal with that story about race prejudice. You couldn't get rid of me that way. Then you started sending those foul letters to my wife."

Dadier now has West cornered. "End of the line, boy." Dadier moves in swiftly, sending the knife skidding to the floor with a sharp blow to West's wrist. As Dadier struggles to overcome West, a pal picks up the knife. But the class is now behind Dadier. They subdue the second boy, then help Dadier march the pair to the principal's office.

That afternoon, as Dadier leaves for home, Miller falls in alongside.

"There's talk about you quitting this school," Miller says. "Going someplace where there are nice obedient boys and girls."

"What do you think?"

"I figured it's just talk," Miller says. "You know the ropes around here pretty good now. Be a shame to waste all that. . . . See you tomorrow, Mr. Dadier?"

"I thought you were quitting at the end of the year. That right?"

Miller looks at Dadier and half smiles. Then he recalls the offer Dadier made at Miller's garage job, an offer he has never responded to.

"We have a pact," Miller says. "We wouldn't want to break that."

"No," Dadier says. "I guess we wouldn't."

"See you around," Miller says, moving on.

"See you around," Dadier replies.

Born
Yesterday

Judy Holliday as the prototype dumb blonde Billie Dawn, a part that won her an Oscar in her first starring role. With her are Broderick Crawford and William Holden.

Born Yesterday
(1950)

Directed by George Cukor. Screenplay by Albert Mannheimer, based on the play by Garson Kanin. Musical director, Morris Stoloff. Art director, Harry Horner. Photography, Joseph Walker. Editor, Charles Nelson. Produced by S. Sylvan Simon. A Columbia Picture. 103 minutes.

Billie Dawn	*Judy Holliday**
Harry Brock	*Broderick Crawford*
Paul Verrall	*William Holden*
Jim Devery	*Howard St. John*
Eddie	*Frank Otto*
Norval Hedges	*Larry Oliver*
Mrs. Hedges	*Barbara Brown*
Sanborn	*Grandon Rhodes*
Helen	*Claire Carleton*
Bootblack	*Smoki Whitfield*
Manicurist	*Helen Eby Rock*
Bellboy	*William Mays*
Barbara	*David Pardoll*
Elevator Operator	*Mike Mahoney*
Interpreter	*Paul Marion*
Native	*John L. Morley*
Policeman	*Charles Cane*

*Academy Award Winner.

62

Billie playing gin rummy, the favorite card game of sugar-daddy junk-dealer Harry Brock (Crawford). It is Brock who is the target of Billie's oft-quoted line, "Drop dead."

She had a voice like a wounded turtle, a look of unblinking vacantness, and hips that wiggled like revolving doors.

But it was her irreverent, rather ungenteel, frequently confused way of putting things that tickled movie audiences most: "Do me a favor, will ya, Harry? Drop dead." "Wanna wash your hands or something, honey?" "This country belongs to the people who inhibit it."

This was Billie Dawn of *Born Yesterday,* the dumbbell ex-chorine who outdimwitted such peroxide wonders of the 1950s as Adelaide of *Guys and Dolls,* Lorelei of *Gentlemen Prefer Blondes,* and Dagmar of late-night TV. So sensational was Judy Holliday in creating the role that she rocketed to stardom and won the Academy Award in her first starring role in a motion picture.

Ironically, in real life she was the antithesis of the gum-chewing, tinny-voiced moll she portrayed. Judy was highly intelligent (she had an IQ of 170 in high school) and spoke with a soft inflection. She had light-brown hair, and lived quietly in an old apartment in Greenwich Village and later in the famous mausoleum-like Dakota apartment house (where *Rosemary's Baby* was shot) off Central Park West.*

Judy was a shy person who thought herself plain and constantly battled a tendency toward overweight. An ardent student of drama, music, and literature, she yearned to break away from her typecast role as a whining, scatterbrained blonde —but to little avail.

Because she had no equal in the role, she was irrevocably linked to the part. Yet, incredibly, although it was she who created the role of Billie Dawn in the Broadway play, she was ignored for years while Columbia conducted an exhaustive search—rivaling only the marathon testing for Scarlett O'Hara—for someone to take the part. Those considered for the part included Rita Hayworth, Lucille Ball, Lana Turner, Ida Lupino, Paulette Goddard, Susan Hayward, Marie Wilson, Evelyn Keyes, and Celeste Holm. Actually tested were Gloria Grahame, Marie McDonald, Peggy Knudson, Jean Hagen (who went on to play the

*Her only marriage, to musician David Oppenheimer, ended in divorce in 1957. They had one child, a son, Jonathan.

part in a road company), Mary Healy, Cara Williams, Barbara Hale, Paula Hill, and Jan Sterling (who did the role in the Chicago Theatre company).

The reluctance to give the role to Miss Holliday was partly due to Hollywood's traditional view that it was unimaginative to use the stars of a play in the movie version. But it was also due to Columbia's rough-talking, strong-willed boss, Harry Cohn, who couldn't see her as a movie actress. He was unimpressed with her stage performance and called her "that fat Jewish broad."

Even after more perceptive heads finally prevailed, Cohn, in his first meeting with Judy, gave her a fast once-over and said, "Well, I've worked with fat asses before." (Despite the ungallantry of the remark, it had its effect. Judy, who had a predilection for overeating, took off fifteen pounds in three weeks.)*

Born Judith Tuvim in New York City in 1922, she pointed toward a stage career from earliest childhood. While other little girls were cutting out paper dolls, she was taking ballet and acting lessons. After graduating from high school at sixteen, she tried unsuccessfully to get into Yale's School of Drama to study playwriting and directing. Following a stint as switchboard operator at Orson Welles' Mercury Theatre, she teamed with a troupe of unknown performers, including Betty Comden and Adolph Green, to form a night club act called "The Revuers."

At this point, Judy changed her last name ("Tuvim" means "holy day" in Hebrew) to Holliday. Meanwhile, the group's satirical sketches became a hit at the Village Vanguard, the Rainbow Room, and other top clubs. Some bit parts in Hollywood followed. She appeared in *Winged Victory* (1944), *Greenwich Village* (1944), and *Something for the Boys* (1944).

Her big break came when she played a prostitute in a short-lived Broadway comedy called *Kiss Them for Me*. Her act stole the show, winning for her the $500 Clarence Derwent Prize for best supporting actress. It also won her the recognition of producer Max Gordon who was then rehearsing a Garson Kanin comedy called *Born Yesterday*.

When Jean Arthur took sick and dropped out of the production just before it was to open in Philadelphia, Gordon telephoned Judy. The call couldn't have come at a more opportune time. Since winning the prize, she had had no parts. She

had gone through, she recalled, "a whole terrible year of grubbing, with no rent money, no food money and having to eat at friends' houses." With only four days' notice, she took over the role of the wisecracking Billie and was an instant hit. The show ran for 1,643 performances on Broadway. Then, in 1949, she made a triumphant return to Hollywood—first in a supporting part in *Adam's Rib* (1949), then in the starring role in the movie version of *Born Yesterday*. The film has become a comedy classic and the character Judy created is one of the memorable celluloid figures of the 1950s.

The movie opens as Harry Brock (Broderick Crawford), a millionaire junkman who has made his fortune out of war-surplus metal, checks in at a ritzy Washington, D.C. hotel. He has reserved an entire wing for himself and his beautiful but dumb mistress, ex-chorus girl Billie Dawn.

"Mrs. Brock seems delighted with the arrangement," beams the hotel manager.

"It's not *Mrs.* Brock," thunders Brock. "There ain't no Mrs. Brock except my mother. And she's dead."

Brock reportedly was modeled after Columbia boss Harry Cohn, who became so infatuated with the play that he paid $1,000,000 for the movie rights. That was the highest purchase price up to that time for a screen property.

Crawford was not the original choice for the part. It was first offered to Paul Douglas, who played opposite Miss Holliday in the stage version. At first overlooked, Douglas turned the part down when it finally came his way because he felt that the movie script subordinated his role.

Unfortunately, Crawford's performance was disappointing. His Harry Brock was one-dimensional, and the tycoon junk dealer came across as merely brash and vulgar. Crawford's characterization lacked the charm and humor and hence the sympathy that Douglas gave to the role.

Brock has come to the capital to try to set up an international cartel in scrap. He wants to insure that no legislation is going to block his way. First, he takes time out to be interviewed by reporter Paul Verrall (William Holden), whose tough questions and cool manner impress Harry. The reporter turns down a proposition to go on Harry's payroll, but the junkman remembers him.

Later that day, Harry invites Congressman Norval Hedges (Larry Oliver) and his wife (Barbara Brown) to his posh suite. When he introduces Billie, Brock quickly sees that her ignorance of even the basic rules of etiquette and social graces could wreck his plans.

Making small talk, the congressman's wife says,

*Also recruited from the stage version were Frank Otto, who played Eddie Brock, the junkman's cousin, Howard St. John, the sleazy lawyer, and Larry Oliver, who played a senator not above bribery.

"Too bad the Supreme Court isn't in session. You'd love that."

"What is it?" Billie shrills. Before Mrs. Norval has recovered from that baffling response, Billie asks, "Wanna wash your hands or something, honey?"

"Every time she opens her kisser something wrong comes out," Brock laments later. He can't afford to kick her out because he has put ownership of most of his junk empire in her name. So to "smarten her up . . . to smooth the rough edges off," he asks reporter Verrall to coach her. Vaguely fascinated, Verrall agrees.

Up to now, Billie's education has covered only men and mink, but she is a quick learner. And the results of her tutoring turn out to be much different than Brock had figured.

Verrall, taking his job seriously, gets Billie to read books and the newspapers. Then he takes her on a tour of Washington's historic landmarks. Gradually he plants enough civic ideals and democratic principles in her mind for her to perceive that Brock's business dealings are crooked.

The next time she sees Congressman Hedges she berates the legislator for becoming a stooge to Brock. "If he pushes you around," Billie says, "he can push a few million people around."

When Brock's lawyer (Howard St. John) asks her to sign some more corporate papers, Billie balks. She says she won't sign anything else until she knows what it is. "I used to think you're a big man, Harry," she tells Brock. "I'm beginning to see you're not. . . . There's a better kind of life than the one I got. Or you've got."

Losing his patience, Harry slaps her and forces her to sign. When she calls him a "fascist," Harry looks quizzically at his lawyer. "I was born in Plainfield, New Jersey. She knows that," Harry shrugs. Then he asks, "Do you think we can find someone to make her dumb again?"

But there is no turning back for Billie now. "Will you do me a favor, Harry," she asks, setting up the movie's best remembered line.

"What?"

"Drop dead."

And she stomps out. But Verrall persuades her not to leave Harry—at least, not just yet. Instead,

Holden playing Paul Verrall, the bespectacled Washington newspaperman who becomes Billie's tutor, then her lover.

65

he suggests that they slip back into the apartment and take with them all the papers recording Harry's nefarious transactions.

That done, they return and threaten to expose Brock. Turning ugly, he warns them that he has too much at stake. If they want to stay alive, he says, they'll return the papers. "You ain't going to be telling nobody nothing pretty soon," Brock yells.

"Double negative," says the new Billie Dawn.

When Harry sees that they are sincere, he tries another tack. He offers them $100,000. To Brock's amazement, Paul turns down the money. "My girl wouldn't like it," he says, turning to Billie. "Legislation's not meant for buying and selling."

Billie adds: "This country and its institutions belong to the people who inhibit it."

Then Billie plays her trump card. She tells Harry she has all his corporation papers that have given her control of his business. She says she will agree to sign them all back to him—one at a time—on condition that he behave. Still blustering, Harry roars, "Dumb chump. Crazy broad," as they walk out.

But it is clear he is a beaten man. Brock's lawyer, acknowledging Billie and Verrall's victory, toasts them: "To all the dumb chumps and all the crazy broads, past, present, and future, who thirst for knowledge and search for truth . . . [and] make it so tough for crooks like you and me."

Born Yesterday was an immediate box office hit. Yet, ironically, one of its strengths—its virtually literal translation—proved to be a weakness. It played more like a stage comedy than a film. In his book *Cukor and Co.*, Gary Carey said that the movie was one of director George Cukor's least successful adaptations. "Frequently the film is as boring to watch as a TV show," Carey said, "for it is in large part a succession of medium shots and close-ups."

Nevertheless, audiences laughed loudly at the off-beat plot. The picture became one of Columbia's brightest comedy hits, and Judy's performance won glowing tributes. The *Christian Science Monitor* said that the film brought to the screen "the most raucous and most hair-raising talent for low comedy since Marie Dressler, Sophie Tucker, Mae West, Martha Raye, or (for that matter) W. C. Fields." She went on to win the Oscar against such tough competitors as Gloria Swanson (*Sunset Boulevard*) and Bette Davis (*All About Eve*).

The Billie Dawn role—or reasonable facsimiles thereof—was essentially the only movie part Judy was to play, much to her displeasure. They included such pictures as *The Marrying Kind* (1952), *It Should Happen to You* (1954), and *The Solid Gold Cadillac* (1956). She scored another Broadway success in *Bells Are Ringing* in 1956 and later made a movie version.

Then, in 1960, at the peak of her career, she learned that she had throat cancer. Removal of a tumor enabled her to continue performing for a while. But there were no more successes. An attempt at a straight role as Laurette Taylor in a play based on the actress' life failed. Philadelphia audiences booed her for mumbling her lines, not realizing that she was in the early stages of a fatal disease.

In 1963 she appeared in the short-lived musical *Hot Spot,* about the Peace Corps. Her illness progressed slowly until in 1965, at the age of forty-two, she died in New York's Mount Sinai Hospital. Though her death came on the day that the astronauts returned from their first space walk, her obituary appeared on the front page of the *New York Times*.

There were many tributes to her. Of them all, *Newsweek* gave probably the most perceptive assessment of her career. It said that the entertainment world had lost "an original in an age of replicas, a performer who transformed almost all her commonplace material she was generally burdened with. . . . [Her career showed] how little the American Theatre had to offer one of its most gifted performers."

The Brave Bulls

A matador slips away from a lunging bull while a capacity crowd applauds his graceful pass in Mexico City's famed Plaza Mexico.

The Brave Bulls
(1951)

Produced and directed by Robert Rossen. Screenplay, John Bright, based on a novel by Tom Lea. Camera, Floyd Crosby and James Wong Howe. Editor, Henry Batista. Art directors, Cary Odell and Frank Tuttle. Columbia Pictures. 106 minutes.

Luis Bello	*Mel Ferrer*
Linda de Calderon	*Miroslava*
Raul Fuentes	*Anthony Quinn*
Pepe Bello	*Eugene Iglesias*
Eladio Gomez	*Jose Torvay*
Raquelita	*Charlita*
Yank Delgado	*Jose Luis Vasquez*
Loco Ruiz	*Alfonso Alvirez*
Pancho Perez	*Alfredo Aguilar*
Monkey Garcia	*Francisco Balderas*
Jackdaw	*Felipe Mota*
Enrique	*Pepe Lopez*
Little White	*Jose Meza*
Goyo Salinas	*Vicente Cardenas*
Abundio de Lao	*Manuel Orozco*
Tacho	*Esteve Dominguez*
Policarpe Cana	*Silviano Sanchez*
Lara	*Francisco Reiguera*
Don Alberto Iriarte	*E. Arozamena*
Rufino Vega	*Luis Corona*
Senora Bello	*Esther Laquin*
Chona	*M. del P. Castillo*
Alfredo Bello	*Juan Assael*
Indio	*Delfino Morales*
Lala	*Rita Conde*
Don Tiburcio	
Balbuenna	*Ramon Diaz Meza*
Mamacita	*Fanny Schiller*
Don Felix Aldemas	*Fernando Del Valle*

Matador Luis Bello (Mel Ferrer) watches the action in the bullring as he waits his turn to do battle.

We are in the huge 50,000-seat Plaza Mexico, the famous bullring in Mexico City. The matador is waving his cape. The bull stamps the earth a couple of times, then lowers his head and rushes. The matador stands his ground, sweeping the cape as the sharp horns flash by inches from his abdomen.

This is a pass in the life and death drama of the bullring created so eloquently in the film *The Brave Bulls*. There have been other movies about toreadors—*Blood and Sand* (1922 and 1941) is one of the memorable ones—but none has set down the story of death in the afternoon as realistically.

"If Art is a total conception totally communicated," said *Newsweek* after *The Brave Bulls* opened, "then a motion picture released this week achieves the category of Art." It ranked the picture "squarely alongside such milestones of American moviemaking as *Citizen Kane* [1941]."

Where *The Brave Bulls* departed from other bullfighting movies was in its uncompromising decision to eschew romanticism and capture all the raw and lusty details of life in the arena. Once that decision was made, there could be no thought to making the picture in color.

Said James Wong Howe, the cameraman: "There are two types of photography: beautiful, romantic, well thought-out—*that* did not fit this picture. And realistic, sharp, good, black-and-white contrasts, so you can feel the sun, well-defined lines, almost like wood-cutting—*that* is what was required."

Producer-director Robert Rossen agreed wholeheartedly, despite efforts of the Mexican government to convince him to capture the splendid strong-hued pageantry of the bullfight in color. "Mexico did not pull the wool over my eyes," Rossen said. "I was not taken in by the lovely clouds. I tried my best to understand Mexico and bullfighting from the point of view of the Mexicans. And I believe the picture will truly reflect an important phase of Mexican life. But bullfighting is a grim, realistic business. I've filmed it so raw, it jumps right out of the screen at you."

Rossen, the man most responsible for bringing this taut, hard-hitting drama to the screen, was a director through whose movies run the common themes of violence and soul-searching. His credits include *Body and Soul* (1947), the searing John Garfield film about a prize-fighter battling his way

69

to the top; the Oscar-winning *All the King's Men* (1949), about the power-hungry Southern politician modeled after Huey Long; and later *The Hustler* (1961), a gripping portrait of a pool shark and his sleazy world.

"Typically, Rossen's searcher is a young man," says Alan Casty, author of *The Films of Robert Rossen*, "often rootless or socially dispossessed, with a certain inner force, someone who cannot fully identify or control his energy, this source of grace and power. Under the shaping pressures of a corrupt society, his élan turns aggressive, perverse, destructive."

In a way, Rossen was like the tortured hero of his movies. The grandson of a rabbi, he was born in 1908 on New York City's tough East Side. He was a boxer even while he studied creative writing at New York University. He gave up the ring to join the radical theatre of the depression 1930s—and it was here that he got his early training as a technician, actor, director, and writer.

His play *The Body Beautiful* lasted only four performances, but it led to a Hollywood contract as a screen writer. Among his many scenarios for Warner Brothers were *They Won't Forget* (1937), *The Roaring Twenties* (1939), *The Sea Wolf* (1941), and *The Edge of Darkness* (1943). However, he was never comfortable as a writer and grumbled about the way directors changed his dialogue.

One day Harry Cohn, the boss of Columbia Studios, gave him his chance. Cohn offered to let Rossen direct one of Rossen's own scripts, *Johnny O'Clock* (1947), a story of a gambler in trouble with the law. It was not a big hit, even with Dick Powell in the lead, but Rossen's talent showed through, and he never went back to the typewriter.

Nevertheless, his career as a director was nearly torpedoed before it was launched. During the investigation of Communists in Hollywood during the 1950s, Rossen took the Fifth Amendment when he appeared before the House Un-American Activities Committee. However, he was able to save face when he recanted, made a return appearance, and publicly admitted that he had belonged to the Communist Party from 1937 to 1947.

Rossen said that he had made sizable contributions to Communist Party causes during that time, and he named fifty-seven persons he had known in Hollywood as party members. He also told the committee that he had decided to testify because he had come to believe that no person should put his own individual morality above national security. His repentant appearance made him a controversial figure, but it opened the way for him to return to directing.

The film that had preceded his congressional troubles was *The Brave Bulls*, the fourth movie Rossen had directed. Rossen was fascinated with the possibilities of making Tom Lea's novel into a movie because he saw in its bullfighter, who doubts his courage, a projection of his vision of inner conflict. Moreover, there was in its Mexican locale an opportunity to bring vivid images of crowds and bullfighting to the screen.

The picture, which Rossen also produced, opens with a narrator's voice that immediately sets the tone of the movie. It tells us about bulls that are raised to go into the bullring. "They are born and bred to fight. There are men who are trained to fight these bulls. But, being men, they are not born to fight. And they cannot be bred to be without fear."

The film itself opens with three seemingly unrelated events. First, we see a tailless black bull named El Brujo seeking shade on one of the Mexican bull ranches.

Then the camera shifts to a bar in the little town of Cuenca where the owner of a small bullring sits over a tequila brooding about his dwindling crowds. In a rash moment, Eladio Gomez (Jose Torvay), the owner, promises two drinking companions "something special" for the town's biggest bullfight.

Who will fight the bull? "Luis Bello," he boasts. "The signed contract is in my office." In fact, there is no contract. Gomez has never met Bello. In any case, Bello's hefty fee of 30,000 pesos is much too rich for Gomez's wallet. But Gomez knows that he must produce now or be laughed out of town.

Hundreds of miles away, Bello (Mel Ferrer), who knows nothing of Gomez's boast, is fighting bulls at La Pascua. Thousands cheer his skilled cape passes. Then, unexpectedly, the bull drops his head and tosses Luis into the air. Though Luis returns to kill the bull, his leg wound sends him home to his mother's house in Cuerreras to recover.

The bullfighting scenes presented Rossen with a problem. Rossen shot them in Mexico where he made most of the film. But rules of the Johnston Office required a humane society representative to be on the set and forbade a director from staging the more brutal aspects of bullfighting, particularly the kill.

Rossen got around this restriction because the rules say nothing about photographing real bullfights. Rossen did this, and at the same time drew on Mexican newsreel coverage of these events.

However, the production code also prohibited showing scenes of animal killings. Thus, the American version of the movie did not include the climax of the bullfight. Nor did it show the dying bull, twisting in his death throes as flag-bedecked mules drag him from the arena.

At his peasant home, Luis is idolized by his kid brother Pepe (Eugene Iglesias), who wants to be a big-time matador like Luis. But Luis' rest is short-lived. His manager, Raul (Anthony Quinn), summons him to fight in the Plaza Mexico the following Sunday.

In Mexico City, Luis joins Raul and a party of socialites out for a night on the town. At one swank cafe, he meets a sultry blonde, Linda de Calderon. The matador is immediately attracted to the aristocratic beauty.

Linda is played by Miroslava, a Czech-born refugee from Hitler's Germany, who was picked over forty other candidates for her role. The actress, whose last name was Stern, escaped from her country via the Trans-Siberian railroad. She settled in Mexico, and then had a fling at Hollywood via an RKO contract. In eight months, how-ever, she had failed to appear in a single picture, so she returned south of the border where she made eleven movies and became a leading film star.

Sadly, her career was a short one. In 1955, four years after doing *The Brave Bulls*, she came back to the U.S. and appeared as Joel McCrea's leading lady in *Stranger on Horseback*. That same year, she died in Mexico City from an overdose of sleeping pills following an unhappy love affair with a real-life matador. She was twenty-five.

While Luis is out one night, he and his manager Raul are intercepted by Gomez, the bullring owner from Cuenca. "I'm asking to have my little plaza (bullring) honored by the great matador," he says. But Luis is not impressed. He has already turned down Gomez's offer several times.

"I fought for you once when I first started out," Luis says. "I fought in many places like yours. And they're all the same—dirty holes for infirmaries, butchers instead of doctors, oxen for bulls. Drunks throwing cushions and bottles. I fought in many places like yours, and I've got the scars to prove it."

Nevertheless, this time Luis finally agrees—on two conditions. His brother Pepe must share the

Bello is embraced by his girlfriend of the moment, played by Miroslava, a Czech-born actress. She took her life at age twenty-five after an unhappy romance with a real-life matador.

billing as a full matador, and Gomez must buy San Mateo bulls, the finest and costliest in Mexico.

Ferrer spent many hours studying cape work under the tutelage of Paco Rodriguez, his double. But Rossen would not risk letting Ferrer take any real chances in the bullring. Ferrer and Eugene Iglesias, who played Pepe, had no real encounters with a bull. Cameraman Howe created the illusion by mounting a bull's head high on a wheelbarrow-like contraption. A studio hand propelled the outfit to simulate charges and the camera focused in tightly on Ferrer and Iglesias to show only their raised arms and the plunging barbs.

To get close-up action of the bull, Howe had professional bullfighters work with cameras strapped to their waist. Said Howe: "The camera was fixed so the fighter automatically turned it as his body turned. You just see that bull go right by you, even under the cape and all."

Howe also shot from a wooden box sunk in the center of the bullring. In addition he dubbed in footage taken of public bullfights in the Plaza Mexico and newsreel clips.

As important as the authenticity of the bullfights to the film were the locales and the hundreds of native characters that Rossen cast on the spot. Notable among them were: Charlita, a six-year-old child discovered in a railway station; Manuel Orozco, an elevator boy magically turned into a bullfighter; and a whole mariachi band. Matadors of the Plaza, as well as picadors and banderilla throwers, played themselves or comprised the entourage of Ferrer and Iglesias.

One of the best of these bit players was a woman who played Ferrer's mother. Rossen was disappointed in the actress hired for the part, feeling that she appeared too stereotyped. To take her place, he found on the set an old peasant woman (Esther Laquin) who had come to accompany her daughter, one of the extras.

The woman's job was to listen to Bello scold her and the family for being "parasites" while he is home nursing his wounds. Ferrer, who speaks Spanish, said that she listened impassively when he told her what she had to do.

"It seemed as if she didn't register a word I was saying," he said. "Then, when we went before the cameras, she was perfect. She just stood and stared while I was pouring out my tirade. Tears came to her eyes. You could see that she understood her son and that, though she was hurt, she knew why he was acting as he was—that his rage at the family was activated by nerves and fear. It was a beautiful piece of natural emotional acting."

Much of the shooting was done in the old colo-nial town of San Miguel de Allende, 200 miles northeast of Mexico City, as well as in the bull breeding ranches of Piedras Negras and Santin. The ranch sequences show up in the picture when Raul takes Linda and Luis to a tienta, or testing of cows. They are tested because even the mothers of brave bulls must have courage. Bello points to a brave cow as horseback riders prance around to rile them up, but Linda has more on her mind.

"You know many beautiful girls?" she asks.

"None like you," Bello replies.

Meanwhile, Gomez is at the great breeding ranch of Don Tiburcio Balbuenna (Ramon Diaz Meza). "Here are my brave bulls," the old grandee says. "They are the result of fourteen generations of breeding for bravery alone. They are born to fight. They have no other reason for existence, no other use on earth except an instinctive desire to use their horns to kill whatever disturbs them. It is that desire that dies in them last of all. The strange thing about breeding bulls is that you never know how successful you've been until a few minutes before your bull dies. A man who has bred a brave bull has a quality without measure, a spirit that may be tested only in the destruction of it."

It turns out that Gomez cannot afford four San Mateo bulls, but Don Tiburcio accepts a lesser sum and throws in a great black bull with the tassel of his tail missing. He is El Brujo.

Their deal concluded, the two men go into the ranch house to hear the broadcast of the Mexico City bullfight. It is a bad day in the ring. Luis dedicates a bull to Linda, who is at her first bullfight. However, he fails to show his usual bravery. Instead, he backs off from the bull and the crowd jeers. He leaves the ring agonizing over his lack of courage. A few minutes later, another bull fatally gores Juan Salazar, a veteran matador whom Luis has idolized.

Moody after Salazar's death, and concerned about his own career, Luis talks only about seeing Linda again and restoring his honor. But the following Sunday at Guadalajara, Luis is not only clumsy. He is clearly afraid of the horns.

"Why do you do it, Luis?" Linda asks later. "How can you go on doing that Sunday after Sunday?"

"It's what I do," he answers. "Luis Bello without bulls—nothing going back to nothing. But you saw only the bad. There is something to it, something great about it sometimes." He is talking about bullfighting as many Mexicans and Spaniards see it—as an art of defying death with grace, showing the glory of courage.

Now Raul, also attracted by Linda and anxious to get her to break off with Luis "for his own good," takes her on a weekend fling. Before they leave, he upbraids her for bewitching Luis and urges her to drop him. "He won't even be a good matador any longer," Raul says. "Right now, he only doubts himself in the ring. Then, he'll doubt himself as a matador."

They never get to resolve the issue. On their way back they are in an auto crash, and both are killed. The news stuns Luis. He now realizes that his manager has betrayed him. As the days pass, Luis feels that death is coming for him, too. Nevertheless, because he knows that Pepe is eagerly awaiting his debut as a full matador, he decides to go through with the fight at Cuenca.

On the day of the event, thousands jam the arena. The matadors march in with their cuadrillas behind them, followed by the picadors on their padded horses. There is the stirring brassy music of "La Virgen de la Macarena" and the first bull enters the ring snorting. The small town crowd, thrilled by the splendid quality of a rarely seen San Mateo bull, applauds the ferocious beast. Their applause soon dies, for Luis fights like an amateur. He turns, runs, and finally jumps the fence, while seat cushions thud on the sand.

Then Pepe changes the spectators' ugly mood. Poised and graceful, he is brilliant fighting the second bull. The crowd applauds him as he bravely moves in for the kill. But the bull's horns suddenly catch Pepe, ripping his leg. As he is carried out unconscious, Luis snatches a muleta and sword and rushes into the ring. The crowd jeers, but Luis,

ignoring them, makes the kill swiftly.

The ring is empty for a minute. Then the gate opens and out charges El Brujo, the bull without a tail. Instead of cringing, Luis now feels new strength coursing through his body. Realizing that he feared only the act of dying, not death itself, he flashes the slim flame of cloth like his old self. Time and time again he executes brilliant passes, and again the crowd is cheering wildly. But Luis sees and hears only the bull. Finally, he must do what he has never done, and what few in his generation have done: *recibiendo*—receiving the charge planted on the sand. As the crowd becomes hushed, Luis whispers to the bull: "Brave bull, it's time for one of us. Let's do it now. Only we know—they don't—what it's like to stand here and look at death right in the eye. Let's do it now with courage and with style. Come on, death. Brujo!"

Luis' sword plunges between the bull's shoulder blades and El Brujo falls dead at his feet as the crowd roars. "Come on, Pepe," Luis shouts to his wounded brother, now back in the arena. They have locked arms and are smiling now. "Come on, kid," Luis says. "The whole world is ours. You and me. We'll live forever and get rich."*

*Because of Rossen's troubles with the House Committee on Un-American Activities, the movie, made in the spring of 1950, was not released for a year. Even with this delay, Columbia had troubles marketing it. The picture was not a big grosser, but it was a critical success, and it has stood the test of time. Today it remains one of the lesser-known but truly gripping classics of the 1950s.

The Bridge on the River Kwai

The resolute British Colonel Nicholson (Alec Guinness) remains at rigid attention after the equally resolute Japanese Colonel Saito (Sessue Hayakawa) slaps him with a copy of the Geneva Convention rules.

The Bridge on the River Kwai*
(1957)

Directed by David Lean.* Screenplay by Pierre Boulle,* based on his novel. Art director, Donald M. Ashton. Editor, Peter Taylor.* Photography, Jack Hildyard.* Music (scoring), Malcolm Arnold.* Technical adviser, Major General L. E. M. Perowne. Produced by Sam Spiegel. Columbia. CinemaScope and Technicolor. Filmed in Ceylon. 161 minutes.

Shears	*William Holden*
Colonel Nicholson	*Alec Guinness**
Major Warden	*Jack Hawkins*
Colonel Saito	*Sessue Hayakawa*
Major Clipton	*James Donald*
Lieutenant Joyce	*Geoffrey Horne*
Colonel Green	*Andre Morell*
Captain Reeves	*Peter Williams*
Major Hughes	*John Boxer*
Grogan	*Percy Herbert*
Baker	*Harold Goodwin*
Nurse	*Ann Sears*
Captain Kanematsu	*Henry Okawa*
Lieutenant Miura	*K. Katsumoto*
Yai	*M. R. B. Chakrabandhu*
Siamese Girls	*Vilaiwan Seeboonreaung*
	Ngamta Suphaphongs
	Javanart Punychoti
	Kannikar Bowklee

*Academy Award Winner.

Colonel Nicholson, "Commander" Shears (William Holden), and Major Warden (Jack Hawkins) before the bridge, hub of a struggle of iron wills.

The year—1943.

The scene—a Japanese prisoner-of-war camp in Thailand.

The action—a ragtag outfit of British POWs entering a prison camp. Their clothes are tattered. Their shoes are torn. But they are marching smartly—stomach in, shoulders back, head erect—as if they were changing the guard at Buckingham Palace. And they are whistling their spirited regimental song, "The Colonel Bogey March."

This is one of the memorable scenes in a picture of many memorable scenes. Columbia's *The Bridge on the River Kwai* was as instant a hit as a movie can be. Even before it opened, it was reaping lavish praise. *Life* predicted that it was "destined to become a classic" as an anti-war picture. *Cue* put it alongside *All Quiet on the Western Front* (1930). In the first sentence of his *New York World Telegram* review, Alton Cook said that the movie may rank as the "most rousing adventure film inspired by the last World War."

Its excellence stemmed from a happy interplay of forces—first-rate performances by an all-star

cast, magnificent photography, and an engrossing plot. The film is based on Frenchman Pierre Boulle's novel about the building of Japan's so-called "death railroad" from Bangkok, Thailand to Rangoon, Burma during World War II. The Japanese, who occupied Thailand, wanted the line to support their attack on Burma. Thousands of Allied POWs died laboring in the scorching heat of that malaria- and cholera-infested jungle.

The central theme of Boulle's book is that war is futile and insane—an insanity that grips conqueror and conquered alike and throws all values out of joint. British prisoners, proud of their workmanship, build a railway bridge for their Japanese captors, only to see the bridge blown up by their own comrades in arms on the very day it opens. All this goes on while the movie explores the fierce loyalty that British and Japanese officers have to their rigid military codes. In the prison camp setting, the blind adherence to these codes triggers a bitter confrontation.

To play in this cynical but powerful story, Columbia recruited an international cast headed by William Holden,* Alec Guinness, Jack Hawkins, and Sessue Hayakawa, a forgotten Japanese star of silent screen melodramas. Hayakawa, who had fallen on hard times after earning $7,500 a week in the 1920s, made a spectacular comeback as the brutal camp commander who matched wills with Guinness. He got an Oscar nomination, eventually losing out to Red Buttons who won for his *Sayonara* role.

Since so much depended on authenticity, producer Sam Spiegel decided to shoot the picture on location. He had made similar decisions for *The African Queen* (1951) and *On the Waterfront* (1954), and both movies had more than justified their added expense.

When Spiegel's production unit got to Thailand, they found that the River Kwai is actually two rivers—Khwae Noi (Little Kwai) and Khwae Yai (Big Kwai)—with the bridge located about two-thirds of the way from Bangkok to the Burmese border. When studio officials looked at this site, they decided that it wouldn't do. The area was too flat and desolate. They needed a lush, exotic jungle area that could be exploited to the fullest in Technicolor.

They located what they wanted in a picturesque river valley in Ceylon, sixty miles from the nearest big city. In fact, the setting was so breathtaking that the scenery had to be judiciously "toned down" to fit the picture's grim theme.

Using thirty-five elephants, the production crew took four months to put up the log bridge at a cost of $250,000. Native laborers cut down 1,200 giant trees from the surrounding forest to span the rushing 425-foot Kelani River. Taller than a six-story building and a third longer than a football field, the movie bridge was reported to be one of the finest such structures in all of Ceylon. Visitors from miles around came to look at its majestic dimensions during the ten months it stood.

Though it was built to be blown up—a matter which was to trigger some controversy—the labor was not entirely in vain, because from the outset of the picture it is clear that the bridge is the hub of the film.

As the movie opens, Colonel Nicholson (Guinness) leads his muddy but unbowed regiment into a sweltering Japanese prison camp, insolently whistling their parade march. An American POW, "Commander" Shears (Holden), looks on in

amazement as Nicholson confronts Colonel Saito (Hayakawa), the Japanese commandant, with a copy of the Geneva Convention. Saito's goal is to finish building a railroad bridge across the River Kwai in time to meet a deadline set by his superiors. Nicholson has no objection to having his troops work on the project, but he insists that his officers perform no manual labor according to the Convention's provisions. The stony-visaged Saito eyes Nicholson, but says nothing.

However, at formation the next morning, Saito orders the prisoners, including officers, to work. Defiantly, Nicholson tells them not to budge. When Nicholson pulls out his Geneva Convention rulebook, Saito slaps it across his face.

"What do you know of the soldier's code?" says Saito, contemptuously. Under Japanese military tradition, surrender is a disgrace. Rather than return home dishonored after the war, many Japanese officers commit hari-kiri. "You are unworthy of command," Saito says. He snatches Nicholson's swagger stick, breaks it over his knee and orders Nicholson into the "oven"—a windowless, kennel-sized hut of corrugated iron set out in the blazing sun. Saito throws the other officers into a cramped punishment hut.

That night, Shears and two British officers try to escape. Japanese bullets cut down the two Britons, but Shears makes it to the river and gets away.

As the days go by, the torturous conditions of the oven fail to break Nicholson's resolve. Meanwhile, the inefficiency of the Japanese engineers plus the deliberate clumsiness of the prisoners cause all sorts of snafus, and the work falls far behind schedule.

Fearing for Nicholson's health, Major Clipton (James Donald), the medical officer, pleads for his release. Nicholson is only trying to follow the rules, Clipton argues. "Don't speak to me of rules," Saito says. "This is war . . . not a game of cricket. He is mad, your colonel, quite mad."

But the next day, Saito sends Clipton to the oven to try to talk Nicholson into giving in. As they converse, Saito watches tensely with binoculars. Nicholson, despite his weakened condition, still won't retreat an inch. "If we give in," he says in stiff-upper-lip fashion, "there'll be no end to it. It's a matter of principle."

And so, reluctantly, it's Saito who yields. When Nicholson is released, his men carry him on their shoulders and cheer him wildly.

Once free of his prison, Nicholson proceeds to astound everyone. He insists that the bridge be finished at top speed. He wants to show that even as prisoners the British are superior. Prideful and

---

*Instead of getting a salary, Holden took a percentage of the profits. It worked out beyond all expectations. The picture did so well that Holden piled up earnings of more than $2 million, most of which was deferred to give him a tax break. The studio is paying him $50,000 a year for life.

oblivious to the aid he is giving the enemy, he insists on perfection to every detail. To rationalize his decision to his fellow officers, he points out that the enlisted men are badly in need of the sort of discipline that only hard work can provide. So zealous is Nicholson as the project gets under way that he orders them to work overtime, and he even calls for volunteers from the infirmary.

Meanwhile, hundreds of miles away, Shears has reached civilization. However, his hope of getting discharged is short-lived. Major Warden (Hawkins) of British Intelligence tells him that the British have gotten permission from the U.S. to use Shears on a commando raid to wipe out the River Kwai bridge. Shears, who is needed to help guide the raiding party, confesses that he is not really an officer. He says that he donned the uniform of a commander who had been killed so that he could get better treatment as a prisoner. Warden already knows this because he has seen Shears' dossier. And so Shears, realizing he is hooked, "volunteers."

After parachuting into the jungle, Warden, Shears, and several commandos join a group of peasants and start their push. A female touch in the movie takes place here as four Siamese women, all

beauties, accompany them as bearers. On the march they stumble on a Japanese patrol. The British kill them, but in the shoot-out Warden is wounded in the leg. Doggedly he insists on limping through the jungle. He struggles on until one day they come in sight of the bridge.

Wasting no time, that very night they set explosives under the bridge and run wire to a plunger concealed behind rocks near a sandbar. One man, Lieutenant Joyce (Geoffrey Horne), is stationed nearby to push the plunger when the first troop train crosses. Across the river, Shears and Warden watch from the jungle.

Then two unexpected things happen. First, by morning the level of the water has receded so much that the wires are exposed. The raiding party waits tensely as the minutes drag on.

Then Nicholson and Saito lead their troops onto the bridge for a flag-draped completion ceremony. They nail up a wooden plaque proclaiming that soldiers of the British army designed and built the bridge. Nicholson, savoring every minute, makes a last loving inspection of his beloved structure when suddenly he spots something in the water.

Puzzled, Nicholson suggests to Saito that they

Japanese soldiers lead an exhausted Nicholson out of the "oven," a windowless hut where he has successfully withstood Saito's efforts to break him.

Colonel Saito stands ready to cut a ribbon opening the bridge on the River Kwai as sentries fire a salute.

take another look around before the train comes. As the commandos watch agonizingly, Nicholson and Saito slowly trace the course of the wire through the river across the sandbar behind the rocks to the plunger. Just as Nicholson discovers that the bridge is mined, Lieutenant Joyce rushes out and plunges his knife into Saito. "Bandits," Nicholson yells, not realizing that he is raising the alarm against his own army.

Off in the distance, the train whistle bellows as Joyce frantically tells Nicholson that he is a commando and that he has orders to blow up the bridge.

Shocked that a British soldier could be sent to blow up his handiwork, Nicholson leaps on Joyce's back to prevent him from getting to the plunger. From the opposite bank, Shears, realizing that he cannot shoot without risking hitting Joyce, dives into the river and swims toward the struggling men. The train comes into sight. Joyce pulls free, but as he nears the plunger, Japanese bullets drop him.

Events start moving helter-skelter now. Warden puts a shell into his mortar. The train, with banners streaming, rumbles on, its passengers waving. Shears forges across the river, only to go down with a bullet in the leg. He gets up and lunges

futilely at Nicholson as another bullet thuds into him.

"You?" Nicholson exclaims. "You!" Shears replies between clenched teeth. He makes a feeble effort to stab Nicholson as his head falls heavily to the sand.

"What have I done?" Nicholson gasps, finally realizing that he is blocking his own army's operation. Before he can act, Warden's mortar thunders a few feet away. Mortally wounded, and with his head reeling, Nicholson staggers blindly for three or four steps and then falls to the ground on top of the detonator.

The blast, engineered by explosive experts, caused more than a few jitters among the production crew because it was obviously a one-time shot. Producer Spiegel was worried that the bridge was built so sturdily that the explosives might fail to bring it all down. To ensure its total demolition, he had dynamite put in every nook and cranny.

Columbia flew six special cameras in for the scene. They were placed in special shock-resistant beds to prevent them from vibrating. But when the cameras started turning as the train came into sight, the director blew his whistle—cutting the sequence. At the last minute, a nervous technician questioned whether the rail lines that wound through mountain passes on both sides might not break. If they did not, the bridge could have gone down, but the rails would have stayed put, suspending the train in mid-air.

Workmen made more preparations. Then the train started again. When it was a quarter of the way across, the stuntman-engineer swung from the cab and raced to safety—hidden from the cameras by the coaches. This time it was a "go."

A geyser mingled with sand and boulders shot up from the river. Then came a deep, hoarse rumble and the snapping of timber. The six-coach train trembled, buckled, and then plunged into the river as the bridge collapsed.

As smoke and dust drifted over the scene, Clipton looks over the desolation. "Madness, madness," he mutters. In the dark waters, Nicholson's proud plaque floats away. In the sky, a great bird soars.

Some critics objected to the ending, saying that it never made clear whether Nicholson intentionally tried to hit the plunger. But Spiegel said it would have been corny if Nicholson had deliberately gone to the plunger and set off the charge.

"He has awakened from his delusion that building the bridge was what he most wanted to do," says Spiegel. "Nicholson says: 'What have I done?' But he cannot bring himself to destroy the bridge. When it is destroyed, it happens like most things, as much through fate as through decision.

"In fact, the irony is that Warden aims the mortar at him and thus almost stops him from blowing up the bridge. Every possible force prevents him from doing the clear-cut thing."

Author Boulle also had misgivings about the ending. In his novel, Nicholson thwarted the commandos and prevented them from dynamiting the bridge. Boulle felt that the bridge's destruction wasn't necessary to make his point about war's futility. But the studio did not think that an audience would be happy sitting still for nearly three hours and expecting a big bang that didn't go off.

However, the most serious criticism about the movie came from those who felt that it misrepresented some major facts about the war. Some objected to the portrayed stupidity of the Japanese. The picture gave moviegoers the impression that the Japanese were so lacking in engineering skill that only the ingenuity of the British could get the bridge built. "It seemed to me," said critic Scott Young, "that the movie, by not allowing the Japanese a single saving grace of skill or intelligence, translated the Kwai story into a statement of white supremacy." The irony is that the Japanese had just beaten the Allies in a campaign in which building bridges and transportation was vitally important.

Former POWs also contended that the picture did not accurately depict what actually happened

Nicholson, shocked that a British commando (Geoffrey Horne) could be dispatched to blow up his bridge, leaps on his back to stop him from getting to the dynamite plunger.

A mortar shell spews up sand, water, and shrapnel, mortally wounding Nicholson.

behind the lines. In real life, there was a senior British officer, a Colonel Philip Toosey, whose men helped build the Kwai bridge and railway. However, his collaboration was undertaken not to prove he could build a better bridge but merely to make it possible for his men to survive with better rations, medical supplies, and working conditions. There was no choice but to work for the Japanese.

Under Toosey, most of the soldiers survived—unlike the indentured Asian coolies in nearby camps. On the Kwai railway, some 200,000 Asian laborers are estimated to have died. Only 18,000 POWs succumbed to the heat and disease.

Boulle, a planter in Malaya who joined the French forces in Indochina at the war's outbreak, never knew Toosey. He said that he based his story on two French colonels, and he added that he did not intend his book to be history. However, since he took the river's real name and based his story on real events, that story in time took on the aura of authenticity.

Today, tourists still go to see the real bridge on the River Kwai. The Japanese actually built two bridges. One was a temporary wooden structure that is gone. The other, a permanent iron trestle bridge on concrete piles, still stands. And it is this drab-looking structure that over the years has acquired all the trappings of a myth. On plaques at each corner of the bridge, the Japanese have engraved the legend, "In Memory of Deceased POWs."

Despite the literary license taken by Boulle, or perhaps because of it, the movie swept seven Oscars—including the awards for best picture, best actor (Guinness), best direction (David Lean), and best screenplay (Boulle).*

A decade later, its story continued to be enthralling. In 1966, when it played on television for the first time, it drew sixty million viewers—the largest TV audience recorded up to that time.

*Industry insiders say that Carl Foreman did the major part of the screenplay but couldn't be credited because he was then one of the blacklisted Hollywood Ten.

The Caine Mutiny

Humphrey Bogart playing paranoid navy skipper Captain Queeg in *The Caine Mutiny*. Others are Fred Mac-Murray, Robert Francis, and Van Johnson.

The Caine Mutiny
(1954)

Directed by Edward Dmytryk. Screenplay by Stanley Roberts. Additional dialogue by Michael Blankfort. Based on the Pulitzer Prize-winning novel by Herman Wouk. Photography director, Franz Planer. Musical score, Max Steiner. Songs: "I Can't Believe That You're in Love with Me" by Jimmy McHugh and Clarence Gaskill; "Yellowstain Blues" by Fred Karger and Wouk. Art director, Cary Odell. Film editors, William A. Lyon and Henry Batista. Special effects, Lawrence W. Butler. A Stanley Kramer Production released by Columbia Pictures. Technicolor. 123 minutes.

Captain Queeg	Humphrey Bogart
Lieutenant Barney Greenwald	Jose Ferrer
Lieutenant Steve Maryk	Van Johnson
Lieutenant Tom Keefer	Fred MacMurray
Ensign Willie Keith	Robert Francis
May Wynn	May Wynn
Captain DeVriess	Tom Tully
Lieutenant Commander Challee	E. G. Marshall
Lieutenant Paynter	Arthur Franz
Meatball	Lee Marvin
Captain Blakely	Warner Anderson
Horrible	Claude Akins
Mrs. Keith	Katherine Warren
Ensign Harding	Jerry Paris
Chief Budge	Steve Brodie
Stilwell	Todd Karns
Lieutenant Commander Dickson	Whit Bissell
Lieutenant Jorgenson	James Best
Ensign Carmody	Joe Haworth
Ensign Rabbit	Guy Anderson
Whittaker	James Edwards
Urban	Don Dubbins
Engstrand	David Alpert

Lieutenant Maryk (Johnson) relieves Queeg on the bridge during a typhoon, saying the captain is sick and not competent to command. Ensign Willie Keith (Francis), center, looks on.

Probably no movie of the 1950s created as much pre-production excitement.

For months, movie writers sprinkled their columns with suggestions for the parts. Readers had their own ideas and flooded Columbia Studios with letters lobbying for their favorites. Hardly a day would pass without an agent calling producer Stanley Kramer to promote his client.

In the end, the Pulitzer Prize-winning novel, *The Caine Mutiny,* went into production with some of Hollywood's biggest box office names alongside unknowns.

Humphrey Bogart got the key part as Captain Queeg, the Caine's psychotic skipper. Van Johnson moved out of his familiar comedy roles to play the confused but honest Lieutenant Steve Maryk, the man who wrested command from Queeg during a typhoon. Fred MacMurray was the glib Lieutenant Keefer who manipulated others to undertake the mutiny. And Jose Ferrer was the brilliant defense counsel, Barney Greenwald.

Then there was newcomer Robert Francis as young Ensign Willie Keith who won his sea legs on the *Caine.* Considered one of Hollywood's promising stars, the twenty-five-year-old Francis was killed a year later in the crash of a private plane near Burbank, California. Donna Lee Hickey, a Copacabana chorus cutie, made her screen debut, too, as Willie's girl, May Wynn. She adopted her name in the movie, but despite good looks and a serviceable performance, she quickly faded from the Hollywood scene.

Of all the choices, the selection of Bogart raised the most eyebrows. "When we announced that Bogart would play Captain Queeg," said Edward Dmytryk, the director, "it was argued that Queeg should be played by a younger man. Some said Bogart was too tough to be convincing. . . . But he was able to project superficial toughness and still show the captain as the frightened, terribly vulnerable neurotic who cowered under a hard-boiled veneer. In sequence after sequence, he managed to elicit both hate and pity."

Bogart asked for the part after reading the book. He felt that he understood the Caine's skipper, and so he resisted suggestions from Columbia executives to portray Queeg as a crazed officer or a pure martinet.

"I disagree with all people who call him a Captain Bligh," Bogart said. "Queeg was not a sadist, not a cruel man. He was a very sick man. His was a life of frustrations and insecurity. His victories were always small victories. He made the men stick their shirt-tails in and he cleaned up the ship. But when he was faced with a real problem—the typhoon, for example—he cracked up. . . . In peacetime, Queeg was a capable officer. But he couldn't stand the stress of war."

The movie went into production with a $2.5 million budget and a seventy-one day shooting schedule. By the time it reached the theatres, the book had been read by three million people and a play adaptation had toured the country and then scored a Broadway success.*

Its fame pre-sold the movie, but it also proved to be a handicap. The story was so well known that the filmmakers felt they had to reproduce the details of the plot exactly as the public remembered them. And that led to an overlong story with too much fat that could have better been trimmed away. Even so, the book's best-remembered scenes—the yellow stain incident, the strawberry caper, the typhoon, and the trial—are all vividly portrayed.

In producing the picture, Kramer, who had paid author Herman Wouk $65,000 for the movie rights, made a sharp departure from previous films. Earlier pictures—like *Champion* (1949) and *High Noon* (1952)—were based on off-beat, little-known stories with unusual castings and low budgets. With the deep inroads television was making on movie audiences, however, Kramer felt that blockbuster films using popular stories and casts with stars had a better chance of making money.

His biggest task was to convince the navy to lend him some ships so his crucial action scenes would have authenticity. The speculation was that the navy, proud of its record of never having had a mutiny, would not buy a picture about a ship revolt or a neurotic regular officer. But the speculation notwithstanding, Kramer had no trouble getting the service's wholehearted cooperation.

The navy supported the venture for three reasons. First, the feeling was that the day of rah-rah navy movies was over. Second, even though the story made Queeg a coward, that was balanced by Willie Keith's growth and development from a boy to a man during his naval service. Lastly, it was an intriguing story that even won the admiration of the navy's top brass. "It's a hell of a good yarn," said

*Called *The Caine Mutiny Court-Martial,* it starred Lloyd Nolan as Queeg, John Hodiak as Maryk, Henry Fonda as Greenwald, Robert Gist as Keefer, and Charles Nolte as Keith. The play had its first performance in Santa Barbara, California, on October 12, 1953, and opened in New York on January 20, 1954.

Admiral William F. Fechtler, chief of naval operations. "But I wonder how one naval reserve officer could have collected in two years on one ship all the screwballs I have known in my thirty years in the navy."

The movie opens as Willie Keith, a Princetonian, graduates to become an ensign in the naval reserve. The year is 1943, and Keith is quickly on his way to the Pacific after first having a wrenching farewell scene with his girl, a night club singer named May Wynn.

At Pearl Harbor, Keith reports on board the destroyer-minesweeper *Caine,* an unkempt, beaten-up bucket of bolts far from the sleek cruisers or aircraft carriers Keith had hoped for. "They're making a mistake scraping this ship," one sailor says, "The only thing keeping water out is the rust."

Sensing Keith's disappointment, the *Caine's* captain, Lieutenant Commander DeVriess (Tom Tully), lets Willie know right away that he doesn't take kindly to prima donnas. "I only hope you're good enough for the *Caine,*" DeVriess says.

As the weeks pass, DeVriess displays under his tough outer shell a high fitness for command and close rapport with his crew. But these qualities escape Keith who feels that the *Caine* is a slack ship whose decks "look like a Singapore junk." He yearns for a skipper like the ones he had heard about in midshipman class.

It doesn't take long before Keith gets his wish. One day DeVriess is unexpectedly transferred. The new skipper, Lieutenant Commander Philip Francis Queeg, a Naval Academy graduate, is a spit-and-polish officer. "I'm a book man," says Queeg. "I believe that everything in it was put there for a purpose. Deviate from the book and you'd better have half a dozen good reasons. And you'll still get an argument from me. And I don't lose arguments aboard my ship."

Queeg's first act is to tell his officers that he won't tolerate sailors going around with their shirt-tails out. "Shirt-tails outside trousers is the regulation uniform for bus boys," says Queeg, "not for sailors in the U.S. Navy."

Unfortunately, the next time Queeg notices this infraction occurs at the worst possible moment. While the *Caine* is engaged in towing a target for firing practice, Queeg spots a sailor with his shirt-tail out. Keith, as morale officer, is given a bawling out along with the sailor. Helmsman Stilwell (Todd Karns) interrupts to try to say that the *Caine* is turning in a slow circle. However, Queeg goes right on with his tirade, and the *Caine* passes over its own tow line, cutting the target adrift. However,

Lieutenant Commander Challee (E. G. Marshall) questions Queeg during the Caine mutiny court-martial.

Queeg refuses to acknowledge that his ship has cut the line. He sends a message to fleet headquarters saying that the line was defective.

On their next assignment, the *Caine* is ordered to the Kwajalein invasion to lead marine landing craft to shore. The closer the ship gets to the heavily fortified island, the more intense the shelling becomes. Queeg, apparently petrified, increases speed and steams several hundred yards ahead of the attack boats. He orders his men to drop a yellow dye marker, showing the landing boats the route through the reefs. Then the *Caine* turns tail, leaving the marines to make it to the beach on their own.

The incident does not go without notice. The men nickname Queeg "Old Yellowstain." One sailor composes a ballad called "Yellowstain Blues." However, in the wardroom, Queeg awkwardly appeals for understanding from his officers. "A command is a lonely job. Sometimes the captain of a ship needs help," Queeg says, taking out two steel balls and rolling them between his thumb and forefinger.* The men sit in stony silence.

Later, Lieutenant Steve Maryk, the executive officer, defends Queeg, saying that the captain is tired and his nerves are shot from his Atlantic wartime duty. Lieutenant Tom Keefer claims Queeg is unbalanced. "He has every symptom of acute paranoia," Keefer says. "It's just a question of time before he goes over the line."

Maryk threatens to report Keefer if he persists in his charges. However, inwardly Maryk has begun to have doubts of his own. Secretly, he starts a log on the captain. Meanwhile, Keefer takes advantage of every opportunity to try to convince his fellow officers that Queeg is mentally disturbed.

He doesn't have to wait long for the next incident. A few days later, Queeg becomes convinced that someone has filched frozen strawberries from the wardroom refrigerator. To find the culprit, he calls an officers' meeting at 1 A.M. and orders a shipboard search for a duplicate key to the refrigerator lock. Despite the fact that Queeg turns the ship upside down, the search yields no key.

*The balls were widely interpreted as a symbol of the masculinity that Queeg fears he has lost through his cowardice. The fictional device became so talked about in the 1950s that one toy manufacturer advertised "Queeg Balls" as a tongue-in-cheek present for paranoid friends.

Ensign Harding (Jerry Paris), who has orders back to the States, tells some of the officers as he leaves that the messboys ate the strawberries. He had told this to Queeg, Harding says, but the captain threatened to cancel Harding's orders if he informed anyone else.

The question of Queeg's mental state comes to a head when the *Caine* steams into a typhoon. The ship starts to roll and pitch fiercely, taking heavy waves across her bow. Maryk feels that the *Caine* must change course or risk capsizing, but Queeg seems frozen to inaction.

Again and again Maryk pleads with Queeg to change course, but Queeg refuses. Finally, Maryk, feeling he has no other choice, assumes command. "Captain, I'm sorry, but you're a sick man," Maryk says. "I'm relieving you as captain of this ship under article 184." That section of Navy Regulations permits a subordinate officer to relieve a commanding officer under extraordinary circumstances. Queeg tries to have Maryk placed under arrest, but Keith, the officer of the deck, backs up Maryk.

The navy had lent Columbia two destroyer-minesweepers—the USS *Thompson* and the USS *Doyle*. However, director Dmytryk did not shoot the crucial mutiny scene in the Pacific. "It would have been utter waste to go roving the Pacific in search of a storm," he said.

Instead, he created a typhoon on several Columbia sound stages and in a studio tank. Hundreds of gallons of water sluiced from vast containers down a chute over decks and cabins and the wheelhouse. An electric board controlled lighting simulations and a wind machine whipped rain-like blasts across the bridge. Workmen mounted the wheelhouse on wooden cradles and electrically-operated rockers.

Months later, Maryk and Keith face a court-martial board. Lieutenant Barney Greenwald, a former civilian attorney, is assigned to defend them. At first he is reluctant. "I think that what you've done stinks," Greenwald says. "Eight other officers have already turned it [the case] down." But when he perceives that Keefer was actually behind the action and now is free of any blame, he decides to stay on.

From the outset, the evidence is heavily weighted in Queeg's favor. The prosecutor (E. G. Marshall) points out that Queeg is a Naval Academy graduate with years of wartime experience, while Maryk and Keith were recently civilians.

But the worst blow comes when Keefer reverses his shipboard attitude and fails to support Maryk.

Q: Did you know Maryk suspected Queeg of being mentally ill?

Two of the Caine's long-suffering sailors— Horrible (Claude Akins) and Meatball (Lee Marvin).

Keefer: Yes, sir. Mr. Maryk showed me that medical log he was writing on Captain Queeg.

Q: Did you believe that log justified the relief of Captain Queeg?

Keefer: (Pause) No, sir.

Q: Were you surprised later when Mr. Maryk relieved the captain?

Keefer: I was flabbergasted.

Next, the prosecutor points out that three navy psychiatrists have pronounced Queeg completely rational. One of them, Dr Dickson (Whit Bissell), testifies that from a psychiatrist's standpoint, the defendants were not justified in relieving him.

On cross-examination, Dickson admits that Queeg had several symptoms adding up to a paranoid personality—feelings of persecution, a mania for perfection, unreasonable suspicion, and the neurotic certainty that he is always right. "But that [paranoia] is not a disabling illness," Dickson says. "There is a big difference between real mental illness and minor mental disturbances."

Maryk makes a poor impression as a witness in his own behalf when he concedes that he has had no training in psychiatry or medicine. He cannot even define "schizophrenia" or explain what a "manic depressive" is.

Then Queeg takes the stand to defend his actions. He says that he assumed command of a sloppy ship and was determined to bring it into line. On the crucial night, Queeg says that the *Caine* was riding well, far from foundering. "Lieutenant Maryk went into a panic and ran amuck," Queeg says. "He acted under the delusion that he, and he alone, could save the ship."

Then Queeg undergoes cross-examination. Under Greenwald's incisive but respectful questioning, Queeg is taken over the towing and the dye marker incidents. Gradually he begins to hedge and become nervous and confused. The questioning steps up in tempo and Queeg pulls out his steel balls, but they fail to compose him. Then when Greenwald asks about the strawberry incident and suggests calling Ensign Harding to testify, Queeg's defenses suddenly collapse.

Before the stunned court-martial board, he babbles on and on. "They were all disloyal," Queeg raves. "I wanted to run the ship properly. . . . They fought me at every turn. . . . Aha, the strawberries. That's where I had them. They laughed at me. But I proved beyond the shadow of a doubt and with geometric logic that a duplicate key to the wardroom icebox did exist. I'd have produced that key

if they didn't pull the *Caine* out of the action."*

That night, at a noisy celebration among the officers, Greenwald walks in drunk. He hasn't come to celebrate but to tell them what he really thinks of them. "I've got a guilty conscience," he says. To defend Maryk and Keith, he has had to torpedo Queeg, a career naval officer with an honorable record.

It is in this strange anticlimactic speech that the plot seems to become unhinged. With what appears like strained logic, Greenwald reminds the *Caine's* officers that they owe a great deal to Queeg. While they were living peaceful lives as civilians, men like Queeg were in the service standing guard over the country. Greenwald reminds them that after Kwajalein, Queeg had asked for their help, but they turned him down.

"If you had given Queeg the loyalty he needed," Greenwald asks, "do you think the whole issue would have come up in the typhoon?"

Then, turning to Keefer, he says: "And now we come to the man who should have stood trial. Queeg was sick. He couldn't help himself. But you, you're really healthy. Only you didn't have one-tenth the guts that he had. You managed to keep your skirts real starched and clean, even in the court-martial. For the rest of your life, you'll live with your conscience, if you have one. Here's to the real author of the *Caine* mutiny. Here's to you, Mr. Keefer." Then Greenwald contemptuously dashes his champagne in Keefer's face.

The movie made one major change in Greenwald. His religion never entered into his denunciation speech—a fact that always bothered Ferrer. Asked about this omission in a 1977 interview with *Newsday* reporter Al Cohn, Ferrer said: "I did identify deeply with the part of Barney Greenwald. And I was heartbroken because I felt that Greenwald's part was shortchanged in the movie. The novel gave a long—and, I think, important—background of Greenwald. [It brought out] the fact that he was a Jewish man who had gone into the navy, was discriminated against by the naval establishment, and left alone, kept out of the clubs. So when he came in to defend the fellow who had attacked Captain Queeg, Greenwald, in many ways, was attacking one of the pillars of the establishment."

Why was Greenwald's religion never mentioned? "In those days in pictures—with few excep-

---

*The movie was shown on television during the Watergate case and some saw a parallel between Queeg and former President Nixon. Both refused to recognize the truth of what they had done.

tions—you didn't say 'Jew' and you didn't say 'black,'" Ferrer said. "Everything always ended happily. And everybody was kind of attractive. It was all Bill Powell and Myrna Loy and Clark Gable, and don't make waves."

In the play, Greenwald explains his distaste for defending Maryk and Keith by saying: "Queeg deserved better at my hands. I owed him a favor, don't you see? He stopped Hermann Goering from washing his fat behind with my mother."

It may be that the peacetime navy plug was the price the service exacted for lending producer Kramer its ships. And it may be that Kramer felt it was not a very high price to pay.

Detective Story

Kirk Douglas playing a hard-driven, tough-minded cop and Eleanor Parker as his wife.

Detective Story
(1951)

Produced and directed by William Wyler. Screenplay by Philip Yordan and Robert Wyler, based on the play by Sidney Kingsley. Art directors, Hal Pereira and Earl Hedrick. Camera, Lee Garmes. Editor, Robert Swink. Released by Paramount. 105 minutes.

Detective James McLeod	*Kirk Douglas*
Mary McLeod	*Eleanor Parker*
Lieutenant Monaghan	*Horace McMahon*
Detective Lou Brody	*William Bendix*
Shoplifter	*Lee Grant*
Arthur Kindred	*Craig Hill*
Susan Carmichael	*Cathy O'Donnell*
Detective Dakis	*Bert Freed*
Detective Gallagher	*Frank Faylen*
Detective Callahan	*William Phillips*
Detective O'Brien	*Grandon Rhodes*
Karl Schneider	*George Macready*
Lewis Abbott	*Michael Strong*
Charlie Genini	*Joseph Wiseman*
Tami Giacopetti	*Gerald Mohr*
Endicott Sims	*Warner Anderson*
Miss Hatch	*Gladys George*
Police Reporter	*Luis Van Rooten*
Janitor	*Burt Mustin*
Mr. Pritchett	*James Maloney*
Taxi Driver	*Donald Kerr*

Detectives Lou Brody (William Bendix) and James McLeod (Douglas) question zoot-suited Charlie Genini (Joseph Wiseman), a four-time loser arrested for burglary.

He was born Issur Danielovitch in Amsterdam, N.Y., the only son among seven children of Russian immigrants. His father was a vegetable peddler. But even when Issur was earning $300,000 a year, he never forgot, or tried to hide, his humble origins.

"I had friends in New York who used to tell me their father kept horses. They meant race horses, for God's sake. And I'd tell them my father had a horse, too, and a cart, and a load of vegetables."

In between the time that "Issur Danielovitch" changed to "Kirk Douglas," he was a wrestler, a window washer, and a waiter. "My life has been like a B-movie," he was fond of saying. His trademarks were a cleft chin, dimples, and bright green eyes. However, he is best known for his intense, explosive personality which persists even when he is off camera. "Living with my husband," Anne Douglas, his second wife, once said, "is like sitting in a beautiful garden right next to a volcano that may erupt at any moment."

His fierce quicksilver temper has been both the be-all and the bane of his existence. It set him apart from dozens of other leading men, but at the same time it tended to make his characterizations one-dimensional.

"His personality has no elasticity," said David Shipman in his book *The Great Movie Stars*. "He is at his best as a driving egotist, propelled on some inner motor." Said Pauline Kael: "Douglas is maybe the least relaxed of enduring screen stars. He's *on* all the time. He holds your attention without really interesting you."

He was constantly compared to Burt Lancaster, a comparison he resented. They came up at about the same time, and even did pictures together. But Douglas always played secondary parts in those films. And, in the end, he never reached the heights that Lancaster did.

Nevertheless, Douglas achieved stardom in a single performance, stayed in the front-ranks of Hollywood performers for decades, and became an accomplished actor in his own right.

If he was a hard-working actor, he had lots of practice in his youth. As a teenager, Douglas worked as a department store clerk to earn money to pay for his college education. At various times he sold newspapers, washed windows, bellhopped, ushered at movies, and worked as a parking lot attendant.

At St. Lawrence College in Canton, N.Y., he also kept busy. He was on the wrestling team (and became an intercollegiate champion), a student body officer, vice president of the German Club, and president of the Mummers, the college dramatics group. In his spare time he wrestled in carnivals to meet some of his expenses.

It was his acting experience, though, that turned out to be most meaningful to him. After graduation in 1939, he enrolled at Manhattan's American Academy of Dramatic Arts. He attended class for two years, supporting himself with a waiter's job at Schrafft's.

One day his ebullient personality and ankle-length overcoat, a castoff from a college chum, caught the eye of a fellow student, Lauren Bacall. She thought the coat was an affectation until she realized that he couldn't afford to buy one. She remembered him and the coat years later when she was in Hollywood and Douglas was playing minor Broadway roles. Eventually she suggested to producer Hal Wallis—who was always looking for bright, unknown prospects—that he might find one in Douglas.

His first part was in *The Strange Love of Martha Ivers* (1946), starring Barbara Stanwyck. He went on to minor roles in a half-dozen other pictures until he was offered the lead part of an ambitious, unscrupulous fighter in *Champion* (1949). It was a low-budget movie and his agent suggested that he turn it down because MGM wanted him for *The Great Sinner* with Gregory Peck and Ava Gardner. That role would have paid him $50,000—the most money he'd ever been offered.

However, Douglas was impressed by the young producer of *Champion*, Stanley Kramer, and he agreed to do it for $15,000 and a percentage of the gross. He was an overnight hit, winning wide critical acclaim and an Academy Award nomination—his first of three, although he has never won an Oscar.*

Suddenly all the studios wanted him. He went on to score impressive notices in such films as *The Glass Menagerie* (1950), *Spartacus* (1960), and *Seven Days in May* (1964). With his distinctive dimpled chin and eagle face, he played tough gunfighters, crusty soldiers, predatory lovers, and egotistical heels. They called him "the man you love to hate." Said Douglas: "I've always enjoyed playing bastards because they're more interesting." He later formed his own company, Bryna Productions, named after his mother, and bought the rights to *One Flew over the Cuckoo's Nest* which swept all the major Oscars in 1975.

Ironically, Douglas' father never could accept his profession. "I went back to Amsterdam to visit a couple of times," Douglas said. "And my father would take me around to the saloons and introduce me to his buddies. But he'd never tell them what I did for a living. I'd ask him if he saw this picture or that picture and he'd say, 'Yeah, yeah,' and change the subject."

In his career that has spanned almost four decades, Douglas has made over fifty pictures. But for me the quintessential Kirk Douglas movie, the one that makes best use of his blistering personality and one that solidified his career, will always be *Detective Story*.

As the movie opens, a trembling shoplifter (Lee Grant) is being booked at the ramshackle 21st Precinct House in New York City.**

She is one of a host of minor characters that police will haul into the cluttered stationhouse during the course of the six-hour period that the picture covers. Each one will be a vignette, a mini-portrait of a human crisis. There is the pathetic young man who has embezzled from his employer to impress a model. There are the two bickering burglars, one of them a fourth offender, who are caught redhanded. And there is the unlicensed physician who delivers illegitimate babies in his farmhouse.

Central to all of them is Detective First Class James McLeod (Douglas), a tough, unforgiving cop who shows no mercy to the people who pass through the squad room.

At the outset, McLeod is booking embezzler Arthur Kindred (Craig Hill). Even though it is the young clerk's first offense, McLeod urges his boss (James Maloney) to press charges.

Meanwhile, the lawyer (Warner Anderson) of the unfrocked doctor is in the office of McLeod's immediate superior, Lieutenant Monaghan (Horace McMahon), to ask that his client, Dr. Karl Schneider (George Macready), be allowed to surrender himself to Monaghan rather than McLeod.

"Why?" Monaghan asks.

"Because I don't want any rubber hoses used on him," the lawyer says. A few minutes later McLeod steps into Monaghan's office and the lawyer demands to know why he has made his client's life a living nightmare.

"Because I'm annoyed by criminals who get away with murder," McLeod says.

The lawyer hints that there are other reasons, but, for the moment, he stops short of giving details. However, he does leave a set of nude pictures

---

*Other nominations were for *The Bad and the Beautiful* (1952) and *Lust for Life* (1956).

**Miss Grant got an Oscar nomination for supporting actress, as did Eleanor Parker for best actress. Grant, who was in her early twenties, was making her film debut.

of Dr. Schneider to show that there are no bruise marks on his body.

"[You're] a one-man army against crime," Monaghan tells McLeod. "What's eatin' you?"

"I hate criminals," says McLeod, whose father, we later learn, was one. "I don't believe in coddling them."

"What do you want to do, put Schneider on the rack?"

"No. I want to put him in the electric chair, where he belongs. And pull the switch myself."

Now we are introduced to the burglars. There is a great hubbub on the stairs as cops lug in zoot-suited Lewis Abbott (Michael Strong) and sharpie Charlie Genini (Joseph Wiseman). Even though they've been caught with $1,400 in burglary loot, Charlie swears that he is innocent. He says he's never been arrested before.

But McLeod instinctively recognizes him as a professional. "You're a cat burglar," McLeod says. "A real killer." It will turn out that this is Charlie's fourth offense, which means that a conviction will give him a mandatory life term.

Douglas prepared himself for the role by watching detectives interrogate and fingerprint prisoners, and then by appearing in the part on stage. He played eight performances in the Sidney Kingsley

play in Phoenix, Arizona before director William Wyler called his cast to the studio. Douglas and five other actors who appeared in the original 1949 Broadway production of the play were letter-perfect in their roles long before the cameras rolled.*

When Dr. Schneider is brought in, McLeod puts him in a lineup, but a witness, a nurse (Gladys George) who had assisted in his illegal deliveries, fails to pick him out.** She is wearing a fur stole and it's obvious to McLeod how she got it. "All right, you've earned your fur piece," McLeod says. "I hope you enjoy it."

McLeod's only other witness is an unwed mother, a victim of Schneider's butchery, who is in critical condition at Bellevue Hospital. McLeod puts Schneider in a police wagon and starts taking the doctor to the hospital to be identified, but on the way, the police radio reports that the witness

*They were McMahon, Wiseman, Miss Grant, Strong, and James Maloney who played Mr. Pritchett, the embezzling clerk's boss. Douglas replaced Ralph Bellamy and Eleanor Parker took Meg Mundy's role as McLeod's wife.

**Schneider was an abortionist in the play, which was written before abortion was declared legal. But in the movie he became an unlicensed doctor who delivered illicit children. The change was made to comply with the Breen Office's standards.

McLeod, losing his temper in the paddy wagon, manhandles Dr. Karl Schneider (George Macready), an unlicensed physician charged with illegally delivering the babies of unwed mothers.

died two hours ago. "Congratulations, Karl," McLeod says, his case destroyed. "You knew she was dead all the time. Then you bought off Miss 'Fur Piece' and turned yourself in. . . . I ought to fall on you like the sword of God. . . ."

"That sword has two edges," the doctor says, unfazed. "You could cut your own throat."

Schneider warns him that he has plenty of friends downtown. McLeod, losing his cool, turns on him savagely. He cuffs and manhandles the doctor until he collapses in pain. When the police wagon returns to the precinct house, Schneider is nearly unconscious.

"You lunatic," Monaghan says to McLeod. "Didn't I just get through warning you to lay off?"

Schneider, groaning, mumbles the name "Tami Giacopetti."

"Who is Giacopetti?" the lieutenant asks.

"Never heard of him," McLeod says.

"Giacopetti? I know him," one cop says. "He runs a horse room in the Village."

Monaghan orders his men to bring in Giacopetti. Then, unbeknownst to McLeod, he calls McLeod's wife to his office.

While we are awaiting this mysterious confrontation, the camera moves to another part of the station house. Arthur Pritchett, the boss of the young clerk, has come in to press charges. At the same time, Susan Carmichael (Cathy O'Donnell), a young neighbor who has a long-standing crush on the young clerk, comes to the station with almost enough money to pay back his boss. She begs him to give the clerk another chance.

"We don't run a collection agency here," McLeod complains, butting in. "We're here to prosecute criminals."

"But if it's a first offense . . ." Pritchett says.

"It's never a first offense," McLeod says. "It's just the first time they get caught."

The camera cuts back to Lieutenant Monaghan's office where we see Mrs. McLeod (Eleanor Parker) undergoing questioning. At first she denies knowing anything about Dr. Schneider. But the truth soon comes to light when Monaghan calls in Giacopetti (Gerald Mohr).

The two, it turns out, were once lovers. She became pregnant and went to Schneider. The baby was born dead. Mrs. McLeod has told her husband nothing, but now she is forced to reveal her past. However, when they are alone, instead of being understanding and offering compassion, McLeod is enraged. He rejects her coldly.

"My immaculate wife," he says as if he were spitting the words out. "I thought you were everything good and pure. I'd rather go to jail for twenty years than find out my wife was a tramp."

"Don't judge me, Jim," she says. "Try to understand. I was on my own, first time in a big city. I thought I was in love."

But McLeod is such a zealot that he cannot forgive a single misstep, even of someone who has really been true to him and whom he really loves. "What's there to understand? You went with him, a pig like that. You had a child by him. You went to that butcher Schneider. Everything I hate. What's left to understand?"

This scene is the heart of the movie. Yet, despite its high drama, it is the very reason that some critics said the film was more skillful than profound. "The moral, if any, in this film," said Bosley M. Crowther in the *New York Times*, "is that sometimes the most inhuman people are those with a passion to do good. Sometimes the most heartless creatures are those who assume themselves to be the champions of justice and virtue, without a measure of justice and virtue in their souls. But what makes such people so rigid? What conflicts drive them to become not only dangerous individuals but the spoilers of the very things they love? We have to know fully the reasons for a person's mania to understand."

And that is where Kingsley has let down the audience. McLeod has said his father was a criminal. He hates them because his father was one. But it is one thing to merely write in a character's motivation and quite another to show us scenes from his past to explain why he reacts so strongly. Without this insight, it is difficult to understand why McLeod is unable to overlook his young wife's transgression, or to be moved by the dissolution of their marriage.

McLeod makes one feeble attempt to reconcile himself with his wife. But it fails, and she tells him she is leaving him. Abandoned, seething in inner torment, and haunted by remorse, he stumbles into the squad room where an explosive situation erupts before his startled eyes. One of the burglars, Charlie, snatches a gun from a cop's holster. He warns all in the room to stay where they are and then starts toward the stairs. McLeod, unarmed, walks toward him and tells the burglar to put down his gun. Charlie, in turn, warns McLeod to stop, but McLeod keeps advancing. Everyone in the room stands motionless, frozen to inaction, watching the confrontation.

"Give me that gun," McLeod says, coming on.

Suddenly, Charlie, frightened and confused, opens up. Point blank, he fires two bullets into

McLeod's mid-section, dropping the detective on the spot.

Cops then rush in and grab the gunman, but McLeod lies mortally wounded. In a failing voice he tells his partner (William Bendix) to let the clerk go and to ask his wife to forgive him.

Then with his last breath, he begins mumbling the opening phrases of the Act of Contrition:

"In the name of the Father and the Son and the Holy Ghost. O my God, I am heartily sorry for having offended Thee. And I detest all my sins because I dread the loss of heaven and the pains of hell. . . ."

"But most of all because they have offended Thee, my Lord," says his partner, finishing the prayer, "who art all-good and deserving of all my love. And I firmly resolve with the help of Thy grace to confess my sins, do penance, and amend my life."

In the background, a police reporter (Luis Van Rooten) phones his story to a rewrite man on the copy desk: "Get this, Harry. Detective First Grade James McLeod, 21st Squad, shot and killed in the line of duty. . . ."

Five Fingers

James Mason as the suave, resourceful spy who hires himself out to the Germans and becomes known under the code name of "Cicero." The 1956 thriller is based on a real war exploit.

Five Fingers
(1952)

Directed by Joseph L. Mankiewicz. Screenplay by Michael Wilson, based on the book *Operation Cicero* by L. C. Moyzisch. Art directors, Lyle Wheeler and George W. Davis. Music, Bernard Herrmann. Cinematographer, Norbert Brodine. Editor, James B. Clark. Produced by Otto Lang for 20th Century-Fox. 108 minutes.

Cicero	*James Mason*
Countess Anna Steviska	*Danielle Darrieux*
George Travers	*Michael Rennie*
Sir Frederic	*Walter Hampden*
Moyzisch	*Oscar Karlweis*
Colonel Von Richter	*Herbert Berghof*
Von Papen	*John Wengraf*
Siebert	*Ben Astar*
MacFadden	*Roger Plowden*
Morrison	*Michael Pate*
Steuben	*Ivan Triesault*
Von Papen's Secretary	*Hannelore Axman*
Da Costa	*David Wolfe*
Santos	*Larry Dobkin*
Turkish Ambassador	*Nestor Paiva*
Italian Ambassador	*Antonio Filauri*
Japanese Ambassador	*Richard Loo*
Charwoman	*Jeroma Moshan*
Pullman Porter	*Otto Waldis*
Banker	*Marc Snow*
German Singer	*Faith Kruger*

Cicero, the valet to the British ambassador in Turkey, offers his services to skeptical Herr Moyzisch (Oscar Karlweis), a German embassy official.

James Mason, playing the valet of the British ambassador to neutral Turkey in World War II, steals into the ambassador's richly appointed office and quietly opens his safe. Quickly, but coolly, he sifts through top secret papers and then begins photographing them one by one.

Mason has temporarily disarmed the safe alarm by removing one of the house fuses. But unbeknownst to him, a cleaning woman has just replaced the missing fuse, and, to his horror, it goes off. There is a sharp, chilling clang. Within moments the embassy is alive with security men.

This is one of a series of highly charged suspense scenes from *Five Fingers*, a largely overlooked 1952 thriller that superbly recreated the real-life story of one of the war's most daring and highly paid spies.

Mason played the agent with the code name Cicero. His exploits were revealed in the book *Operation Cicero* by L. C. Moyzisch, who dealt with Cicero as a member of the German embassy staff in Ankara. The book was a best-seller and formed the basis for the screen play by Michael Wilson,* his next after writing the scenario for *A Place in the Sun* (1951).

*Joseph L. Mankiewicz thought so much of Wilson's scenario that he agreed to direct the film without taking any part in the script's preparation. Previously Mankiewicz had either written or collaborated with writers of other movies—*All About Eve* (1950), *No Way Out* (1950), *People Will Talk* (1951).

Interest in the master spy started when Britain's Prime Minister Ernest Bevan stated in the House of Commons that "only Providence saved the world when Moyzisch sent Von Ribbentrop the most amazing set of photostats in history." They revealed plans the Allies had made for the last years of World War II—including the time and place of the Normandy invasion. However, the Germans failed to make use of them because they suspected them to be a deliberate decoy. Although their agent Moyzisch had paid $300,000 for them, the Nazis' Von Ribbentrop threw them in the wastebasket.

Script writer Wilson saved the other great irony of this fascinating espionage case for the film's final twist. The movie, which in some ways embellished the real-life Cicero's adventures, is a gripping, highly stylized, urbane picture from start to finish. Unlike most spy stories, there are no killings or gunplay. Instead, it is a subtle cat-and-mouse melodrama.

In the Joseph L. Mankiewicz tradition, much of its action is revealed in cleverly written scenes highlighted by acerbic verbal exchanges. The picture works because Mason mesmerizes the audience with his polished manners, devilishly clever airs, and magnificent poise under pressure. One cannot help rooting for him, although, in a conventional telling of this tale, he would be the villain. He is aided by a highly professional cast featuring

Danielle Darrieux as the cunning Polish countess, Michael Rennie as the dogged British counter-espionage agent,* and Walter Hampden, famed for his stage role as Cyrano de Bergerac, as the dignified ambassador.

The story opens during a reception in the British embassy in Ankara in 1944. World War II is raging in Europe but all is peace and tranquility in neutral Turkey. We meet Von Papen (John Wengraf), the German ambassador, but only briefly. He exits by pre-arrangement when the British ambassador (Hampden) arrives in the middle of the party. Shuttling between them, unsuccessfully trying to interest them in setting her up in lavish quarters where she can wine and dine diplomats and hopefully pick up a military secret or two, is the beautiful but impoverished Countess Anna Steviska (Darrieux). It's clear that she is attracted to those with access to big money. When one middle-echelon attaché tries to flirt with her, she quickly puts him in his place. "Herr Moyzisch," she says, "please do not look at me as if you had a source of income other than your salary."

That night when Moyzisch (Oscar Karlweis) goes to his embassy quarters, he finds an unexpected visitor. The man (Mason) does not identify himself but urges Moyzisch not to call for help. "I have brought you the opportunity of your lifetime," the intruder says. "You can be the envy of the German foreign office." The stranger claims to have top secret British military and political documents, and offers them for sale for $50,000.

Moyzisch plays his cards close to the vest. He says that the Germans have never paid that much for any information. In any case, he says, the stranger impresses him as an amateur, and he is not interested.

The intruder is unfazed. "It appears that I must think for both of us," he sighs. The stranger instructs Moyzisch to inform Von Papen of his offer. He will have three days to consider it. Then the stranger will telephone Moyzisch and ask if he has received a letter. If the answer is "yes," the stranger will return with two rolls of film containing photos of the documents.

"If you approve of my first delivery, you can have more," the stranger says.

When Moyzisch asks for more information, the man clicks off an impressive array of material. He says he has photos of minutes of secret talks between Britain and Turkey regarding Turkey's pos-

sible participation in the war, as well as the latest Allied timetable of Balkan bombing raids, and secret minutes of the Teheran Conference.

"Destiny has held out his hand to you tonight," the stranger says as he steps out a side door. "Take it and hold on."

Moyzisch does, and he convinces his superiors to accept the deal. In Berlin, where the ultimate decision is made, high officials assign Moyzisch's contact the code name "Cicero."

Over the next several weeks, Cicero sells the Germans dozens of photos of secret British documents without revealing his identity. All he tells Moyzisch is that he works in the British embassy. It is only the audience who learns who Cicero is as the camera follows him through the teeming streets of Ankara to the embassy where he attends the British ambassador.

But while his position as a valet has gotten him into otherwise inaccessible rooms, it has also created a problem. Cicero has amassed a small fortune, and he is apprehensive that the money, if discovered, would expose him.

One evening he pays a call on the destitute Countess Steviska, whose husband he had once served as a butler. Cicero discloses his activities and offers her a part of his profits if she helps him. Her role would be to safeguard his money and rent a plush home that he could use as a meeting place for his German contacts.

The scene shows off Mankiewicz's conversation style at its best. With French songs playing on a phonograph in her shabby apartment, the two thrust and parry until they at last reach a compromise.

South America is Cicero's eventual goal, he tells his former employer. It would mean a new life, a new name, he says. "That, of course, would require passports, visas, letters of credit. You could be of great help."

"That's quite a trust you put in me," the countess says, putting Cicero on his guard. "If I were to be indiscreet, it could ruin everything for you."

"And for you, too. It is said that no man is a hero to his valet. It's also true that no woman is a mystery to her husband's valet."

"You know me that well?" she says, showing surprise.

"The source of your money has never concerned you any more than the source of your electric light. They become worrisome only when they are turned off."

"But there is pride," the countess reminds him. "I have pride."

"A great deal," Cicero concedes. "I depend on

*In a scheduling quirk, Miss Darrieux and Rennie not only never played a scene together but never met. As soon as her scenes were finished, she flew to Paris. Rennie, busy on another Fox picture, started his work on the day she left.

your pride. You'd find it intolerable to know that your wealth is the gift of a servant. Madam, you'll keep your mouth shut tight."

They drink to their new partnership, and Cicero proposes that she go with him to South America.

"It would be right for us now," he says, "because now, at last, we are equals."

Suddenly she slaps him. He looks back, stunned. "You made me a business proposition," she explains coolly. "I agree to that part of it. As for the rest of the proposition, it's not an impossibility. It's merely an improbability, and, above all, an impertinence."

"Because I addressed you as an equal?"

"No. Because you addressed me as a servant. Because in the manner of an inferior, you tried to buy something you didn't think you merited on your own. Now let's get down to the details of business."

"As Madam wishes," Cicero says.

And yet, the countess feels that Cicero has not quite gotten the point. She prefers a more informal relationship under the new circumstances. "My name is 'Anna,'" she says softly.

As time passes, the British suspect that there is a leak in their intelligence network and that its source is in Ankara. The foreign office dispatches George Travers (Rennie), a counter-agent. At the same time, the Germans send Colonel Von Richter (Herbert Berghof) to try to determine the authenticity of Cicero's documents. Von Richter's suspicions are put to the test when Cicero offers to sell him his most important secret—the time and place of the planned Allied invasion of Europe.

Why, Von Richter asks, does Cicero insist on being paid in British money if he is selling the Allies' key war secrets? Of what value would the money be if Germany wins?

"By informing a man about to be hanged of the exact size and location and strength of the rope," Cicero says dryly, "you do not remove either the hangman or the certainty of his being hanged."

In fact, the Germans are informed of every secret word that the British ambassador puts to paper, every secret conference, every secret pact. And yet, despite the unerring accuracy of the information Cicero gives them, German intelligence refuses to act. The German brass is convinced that Cicero is a British plant.

As for the British, they fail to find any breach in the embassy's security—that is, until one day Travers hooks up the ambassador's safe to an

At the story's end, police bring some bad news to Cicero in his plush hotel suite in Rio de Janeiro. At right is Larry Dobkin, later a director of B-movies.

103

alarm. Despite the risk, Cicero has to chance opening it. The Germans are pressing him for the invasion plans, offering him $100,000. But it isn't the Germans as much as the countess that forces his hand. Fearing that he will fail in this daring venture, she runs off to Switzerland, taking all of Cicero's money, and she leaves behind a letter to the British ambassador exposing Cicero.

It happens that the ambassador is away for the weekend. Therefore, taking advantage of the ambassador's absence, Cicero disconnects a fuse hooked to wires running to the safe alarm. Then he steals into the ambassador's office and opens the safe. But while he is photographing the top secret invasion plans, a chambermaid, trying to vacuum a hallway rug, fails to get any power. She searches for the source of the trouble, finds the missing fuse, and replaces it.

Suddenly the alarm is jangling. His cover blown, Cicero races out of the embassy. Travers is behind him and a wild chase ensues through the streets of Ankara. Cicero manages to give Travers the slip, arranges a meeting with the Germans in Istanbul, and, with both German and British agents on his trail, delivers the film and somehow emerges safely with the money in Rio de Janeiro.

And so in the film's windup, we see Cicero ensconced in a grand hilltop house in Rio with a magnificent view of the city's harbor. The ending is a gem of irony. First, the camera takes us to Berlin where we find that the Germans have also gotten a letter from the countess. This one names Cicero as a British spy.

"I have always believed it," shouts one Nazi general, tearing up Cicero's documents that accurately named Normandy as the site of the second front. "From the first I told you so. I know the British and their childish tricks."

"But the earlier documents," Moyzisch says, "they were genuine."

"Of course, they had to be," the general roars, "so that we would swallow the big lie. I knew it. I knew it all along."

Then the camera takes us to Rio where Cicero, in an elegant white dinner jacket, has his butler show in three visitors—a banker and two police officials.

The banker regretfully informs Cicero that there seems to be something irregular about his account. The money Cicero has deposited is counterfeit, the banker says. It is the most skillful counterfeit he has ever seen but, nonetheless, counterfeit. The banker adds that the bills have been forged in Germany and similar forgeries have also been confiscated in Switzerland. There they turned up in the possession of a Polish lady who is a political refugee.

"Anna," Cicero says, laughing. "Poor Anna."

"Believe me, Señor," a police offical says. "This is no laughing matter. It is my unhappy duty to tell you that you are under arrest."

But Cicero, realizing that he has been betrayed by both the countess and the Germans, can only giggle hysterically. He goes to his tree-lined balcony overlooking Rio's bright lights far below and scatters to the wind scores of bills, laughing all the while.

The real Cicero, an Albanian named Elyesa Bazna, was dogged with bad luck even after his spy venture. After the war he went broke in the import-export business, and then ran into trouble with creditors in Istanbul after starting a concert career as a baritone. When 20th Century-Fox announced that it was making a picture based on his exploits, he met with Mankiewicz and studio officials. But Cicero failed to get any work in the production even as a technical adviser. Less high-flown than his movie counterpart, Cicero married a chambermaid.*

*In fact, his life as a spy was really much more drab than portrayed in the movie. The countess was actually a Hollywood creation. In I Was Cicero, a book that Bazna wrote in 1962, he told of collaborating with a nursemaid at the embassy and later with his niece.

Friendly Persuasion

Gary Cooper, playing an Indiana Quaker, clutches his rifle as he lies wounded next to his neighbor, Sam Jordan (Robert Middleton).

Friendly Persuasion
(1956)

Produced and directed by William Wyler. From the book *The Friendly Persuasion* by Jessamyn West. Associate producer, Robert Wyler. Camera, Ellsworth Fredrick. Editors, Robert Swink, Edward Biery, Jr., Robert Belcher. Music, Dmitri Tiomkin. Songs, Tiomkin and Paul Francis Webster. Songs: "Mocking Bird in a Willow Tree," "Marry Me, Marry Me," "Indiana Holiday," "Coax Me a Little." Title song sung by Pat Boone. Allied Artists. 137 minutes.

Jess Birdwell	*Gary Cooper*
Eliza Birdwell	*Dorothy McGuire*
Widow Hudspeth	*Marjorie Main*
Josh Birdwell	*Anthony Perkins*
Little Jess	*Richard Eyer*
Sam Jordan	*Robert Middleton*
Mattie Birdwell	*Phyllis Love*
Gard Jordan	*Mark Richman*
Professor Quigley	*Walter Catlett*
Purdy	*Richard Hale*
Enoch	*Joel Fluellen*
Army Major	*Theodore Newton*
Caleb	*John Smith*
Quaker Woman	*Mary Carr*
Widow Hudspeth's Daughters	*Edna Skinner*
	Marjorie Durant
	Frances Farwell
Elders	*Russell Simpson*
	Charles Halton
	Everett Glass
Shell Game Operator	*Frank Jenks*
Bushwacker	*Richard Garland*
The Goose	*Samantha*

Dorothy McGuire, playing Cooper's wife, is scandalized as he and Professor Quigley (Walter Catlett) try to bring an organ into the strictly non-musical Quaker household.

In the mid 1940s, Paramount bought the rights to Jessamyn West's book about a Quaker family living in southern Indiana during the Civil War. In essence, the book was a series of short stories that told of West's great-grandparents as remembered by her mother.

Frank Capra thought it would make a warm and entertaining family-type picture. He was also struck by the drama inherent in the conflict between the Quakers' scruples against war and their duty to country. And so he persuaded Paramount to buy the movie rights.

Months passed, and for one reason or another, nothing happened. Eventually the studio dropped its plans for making the film, and producer-director William Wyler, who had won Oscars for *The Best Years of Our Lives* (1946) and *Mrs. Miniver* (1942), acquired the rights.

West was already well embarked on writing another book when Wyler's office called to tell her of Wyler's plans. Thus her thoughts were far from Hollywood or *Friendly Persuasion*, and that was part of the reason she failed to place the movie notable. "Who is Mr. Wyler?" West asked, taking Wyler's assistant somewhat aback. She would never have to ask that question again. But it took seven more years before she would start working on the movie script.

Wyler thought that Gary Cooper would be ideal for the part of Jess Birdwell, the Quaker father who guides his family through a turbulent period. Cooper, at first, didn't seem interested. "I ain't ever played a pappy yet, and I ain't aiming to now," he told Wyler.

But Wyler was persistent and persuasive, and Cooper finally agreed. There remained one major problem. Cooper already had a host of film commitments. Still, Wyler felt no one but Cooper could give the role the firm but gentle touch it needed. Instead of getting another actor, Wyler patiently waited seven years until Cooper was free. It was a decision he never regretted.

In picking his cast, Wyler selected some other tried and tested players. They included Marjorie Main as a widow with three unmarriageable daughters, and Dorothy McGuire as Eliza, Cooper's wife. Eliza had just as important and complex a role as Cooper. "Eliza will wear the pants if Jess doesn't look out," Wyler said. "[At the same time] she won't love Jess if she does."

West, who wrote about the making of the film in her book *To See the Dream*, thought of Katharine Hepburn, but she was unavailable. She also thought that Olivia de Havilland or Jane Wyman would be good. Ingrid Bergman and Maureen O'Hara were considered, too. So was Mary Martin, but, West said, she was said to be too hard to photograph. Vivien Leigh was too English, and Eva Marie Saint was too young. So McGuire was the final choice.

New faces included Anthony Perkins, Phyllis Love, and Mark Richman. Perkins, the son of Osgood Perkins, a famous stage star of the 1920s and 1930s, had made his film debut in *The Actress* (1953), and then gone to Broadway to replace John Kerr opposite Deborah Kerr in the play *Tea and Sympathy*. His sensitive performance as Cooper's oldest son would establish him as a coming star.

When Wyler finally got ready for production, he hired West as technical adviser and script writer. Others worked on the script, too. Nevertheless, when the movie was released, it carried no writing credit, saying only that the film was based on West's book.

If West felt slighted, she never let on publicly. After the shooting was finished, she had only nice things to say. She told Wyler that movie-making seemed like a twentieth-century version of what cathedral building was all about in the Middle Ages—a team effort. An author writes a book, but it takes a director, a cast, a film editor, and many others to turn it into a successful picture.

The movie opens with a lighthearted treatment of the Quaker family ways. On a beautiful Sunday, fun-loving, soft-spoken Jess Birdwell (Cooper) takes his wife and four children to meeting (church service). On the way, Birdwell ignores his wife's stern admonitions and races the family buggy against that of neighbor Sam Jordan (Robert Middleton) and loses, as usual, in the friendly rivalry.

Jordan attends a large, white-steepled Methodist Church which stands near the squat, plain-looking Quaker meeting house. The two church congregations contrast just as sharply. The Quakers wear simple, unadorned clothing, play no music or sing, and segregate men from women during their service. Instead of a sermon by a minister, the Quakers allow anyone to speak when he or she feels moved by the Spirit of God.

The Quakers, whose formal name is Society of Friends, say "thou" and "thy" or "thee" instead of "you" (because "you" was originally used as a form of honor for persons of high rank). Perhaps their most notable tenet is a strong belief in the Commandment "Thou shalt not kill."

Despite their maverick ways, the Quakers have lived in harmony with their neighbors for years. However, danger for both congregations looms on the horizon, for the Civil War is moving closer every day.

During their meeting, Major Harvey (Theodore Newton), a Union army officer, comes to urge the young Quaker men to join the war. He gets a cool reception.

"We are opposed to slavery," says Jess' wife, Eliza Birdwell (McGuire). "But we do not believe it right to kill one man to free another."

"Ma'am, it's not going to be a question of fighting for freedom or principle," the major says, "but of protecting our towns, our own homes from attack. Would you men stand by and see others die to protect you?" There is a silence. The major looks at Josh Birdwell (Perkins) and asks if he is afraid to fight.

"I don't know," Josh says.

"Here, at last, is an honest answer," the major says. "I don't want to offend. But how many of you are hiding behind your church to protect your skins? Do you think it's right for others to do the fighting for you?"

One of the bearded Quaker elders rises. "Nothing could ever induce me to bear arms against my fellow man," he thunders.

Jess Birdwell is on his feet with a less equivocal answer. "I doubt any of us here could say with surety just what we would do in case of attack."

West took both Cooper and McGuire to a real Quaker meeting so they could see one firsthand. They reacted quite differently. Cooper went as if he were a member of the congregation. "He became a Quaker," West said. "He didn't look about at all, but centered down into the silence." McGuire went to see. She became an observer, noting how the people worshiped.

"I understand Cooper's way better," West said. "I must become the character I write about, not put a set of observations on paper."

After the meeting, young Josh is troubled by some of the issues the major raised. Though fighting is against his family's beliefs, Josh fears that he may really be staying out of the war because he is not man enough to be a soldier. He wonders if he should join the army to prove his courage.

When the family returns home, Gard Jordan (Mark Richman), who is on leave from the service, calls on pretty Mattie Birdwell (Phyllis Love). He invites them all to go to the county fair. Eliza is at first opposed because there will be music, dancing, and other worldly activities. Eventually she relents, but her misgivings turn out to be well-founded. In the picture's most colorful scene, we see Mattie, carried away by the fun, dancing joyfully with Gard. Young Josh gets embroiled in a fight. Little Jess (Richard Eyer) turns out to be a whiz at the old shell game. Most wicked of all, Jess gives in to his love for music and buys an organ.

Soon after the fair, Jess and Josh go on a trip to sell their nursery stock. At the farm of the widow Hudspeth (Main), young Josh does a lot of squirming to keep at arm's length from her three aggressive, Amazon-like daughters (Frances Farwell, Edna Skinner, and Marjorie Durant). This is the one scene that West couldn't stomach. She felt that the man-hungry girls were portrayed too crudely. "There is no humor without humanity," West said. "And these girls are inhuman."

Meanwhile, Jess trades his horse for "Lady," a miserable-looking animal, but one that can run like a deer.

When Jess and Josh return to the farm, they find that the organ is being delivered. Eliza is shocked, regarding it as an instrument far too profane to install in a proper home. Either it goes or she goes, she tells Jess. When Jess opts for the organ, she marches off in a huff to the barn.

Later, Jess joins Eliza, announcing that he, too, will live in the barn. After a night together, one that recalls their honeymoon, they compromise. They will keep the organ but it must stay out of sight in the attic.

The following Sunday, Jess wins another great victory. Lady, despite her mangy appearance, shows her heels to Sam Jordan's horse.

Meanwhile, Confederate raiders are drawing closer, looting, burning, and killing. Neighbors plan to make a stand at a nearby river, and Josh decides that he must join the home guard. Eliza, a devout humanitarian who believes with all her heart that no man must harm another, pleads with Jess to stop their son. But Jess realizes that Josh must find his own way in life.

"I'm just his father, not his conscience," Jess says. "A man's life ain't worth a hill of beans—except he lives up to his conscience. I've got to give Josh his chance."

The battle scene was the film's climax. West urged Wyler to drop one sequence that had Cooper wreck Confederate cannons, thus sending the rebel soldiers in retreat. No such scene was in the book. Wyler argued that Cooper wasn't firing a shot. West responded that it would change the very nature of Cooper's character.

"Jess wasn't just a Quaker in the picture," she said. "He's Quakerdom itself . . . . If Jess fights, the picture is either tragic or an attack on Quakerism." In the end, Wyler saw it her way.

Anthony Perkins, playing Cooper's son, is surrounded by the three man-starved Hudspeth girls. They are played by Edna Skinner, Marjorie Durant, and Francis Farwell. This was one scene that author Jessamyn West couldn't abide. She said she couldn't "stomach" it because the girls' aggressiveness was too crude. But audiences liked it.

The raiders are beaten off in a bloody battle, but Josh is wounded. When Lady returns to the farm riderless, Jess, despite his beliefs, takes his rifle and goes to find him. On his way, Jess finds his friend Sam Jordan dying from a Confederate bushwhacker's bullet. The bushwhacker is lurking in the shrubs and wounds Jess. But Jess disarms him, grabs his rifle and turns it on the man. Then, with his finger on the trigger, Jess realizes that he cannot kill, and he lets him go.

Moments later, Jess finds Josh on the ground, lying sobbing and bleeding next to a raider he has killed. He takes Josh home and the boy, convinced now that he is not a coward, recovers.

The movie ends, as it began, with the Birdwells on their way to meeting—but there is one less person along. Mattie, soon to be married to Gard, rides in Gard's buggy. In the background, Pat Boone's voice trails off with the lyrics to the lovely title song.

From Here
to Eternity

Deborah Kerr and Burt Lancaster during a torrid (for the 1950s) love scene. A picture of them embracing in the surf became one of the most widely used stills from this era.

From Here to Eternity*
(1953)

Directed by Fred Zinnemann.* Screenplay by Daniel Taradash,* based on the novel by James Jones. Musical director, Morris Stoloff. Photography director, Burnett Guffey.* Art director, Cary Odell. Film editor, William Lyon.* Orchestrations by Arthur Morton. Song: "Reenlistment Blues" by James Jones. Music by George Duning. Produced by Buddy Adler. A Columbia Picture. 118 minutes.

Sergeant Milton Warden	*Burt Lancaster*
Robert E. Lee Prewitt	*Montgomery Clift*
Karen Holmes	*Deborah Kerr*
Angelo Maggio	*Frank Sinatra**
Alma (Lorene)	*Donna Reed**
Captain Dana Holmes	*Philip Ober*
Sergeant Leva	*Mickey Shaughnessy*
Mazzioli	*Harry Bellaver*
Sergeant "Fatso" Judson	*Ernest Borgnine*
Corporal Buckley	*Jack Warden*
Sergeant Ike Galovitch	*John Dennis*
Sal Anderson	*Merle Travis*
Sergeant Pete Karelsen	*Tim Ryan*
Treadwell	*Arthur Keegan*
Mrs. Kipfer	*Barbara Morrison*
Annette	*Jean Willes*
Sergeant Baldy Dhom	*Claude Akins*
Sergeant Turp Thornhill	*Robert Karnes*
Sergeant Henderson	*Robert Wilke*
Corporal Champ Wilson	*Douglas Henderson*
Sergeant Maylon Stark	*George Reeves*
Friday Clark	*Don Dubbins*
Corporal Paluso	*John Cason*
Georgette	*Kristine Miller*
Captain Ross	*John Bryant*

*Academy Award Winner.

Lancaster, as Master Sergeant Milton Warden, breaks up a fight between knife-wielding bully Sergeant Fatso Judson (Ernest Borgnine) and Private Angelo Maggio (Frank Sinatra). Others in the picture are: Jack Warden (extreme left), Claude Akins (second left, partially obscured), and Mickey Shaughnessy (with the corporal stripes).

Let's start with an anecdote that attempts to debunk one of the most famous behind-the-scenes stories in Hollywood.

It has to do with Frank Sinatra. If you remember, Mario Puzo's best-selling novel, *The Godfather*, has a character modeled after Sinatra (Johnny Fontaine). The crooner tells Mafia boss Don Corleone that he has a chance at a movie part that could launch his acting career. But, Fontaine says, the producer hates him. He won't even let him be considered for the role. In a few days, the producer wakes up in bed next to the severed head of one of his prize stallions. Not unexpectedly, that chilling experience prompts a sudden appreciation for Fontaine's talents.

The movie supposedly implied by the book was *From Here to Eternity*, which did, in fact, give Sinatra his first chance at a serious film role, and so well did he respond that his performance as Maggio rekindled his movie career.

The colorful tale from *The Godfather* makes good reading. Ah, but is it more fact than fiction? Definitely, says Fred Zinnemann, who directed the picture. "There was no horse's head," Zinnemann says. "What happened was that Sinatra read the James Jones novel and identified with the character. He lobbied for it by sending Harry Cohn and myself telegrams and signing them 'Maggio.'"

Zinnemann's choice was Eli Wallach. The trouble was that Wallach already had a commitment to appear in Tennessee Williams' play *Camino Real.*

"So we called Sinatra, who was in Africa with Ava Gardner," said Zinnemann. "He flew back to test at his own expense. [Cohn was a tough man with a buck.] His [Sinatra's] test was good and I saw no reason why he shouldn't do it. But there was no pressure. If I hadn't wanted him, he wouldn't have done it."

This is the story according to Zinnemann who, admittedly, has a kind of vested interest in the tale. So it may never be known whether Zinnemann's or Puzo's version is the true tale.

However, no one disputes the story of "Cohn's Folly." That's the term that used to be bantered about Hollywood parties when people discussed

Cohn's purchase of Jones' 868-page, 430,000-word novel. Nobody thought any studio could make a movie of the sprawling, gutsy book filled with obscenities, sex, brutality, and sadism. But nobody was figuring on an obscure screen writer to turn in a lean, tautly organized scenario that was a model of condensation.

That writer was Daniel Taradash, a pre-Pearl Harbor draftee himself, who was so taken by Jones' novel that he went to Columbia and asked for a crack at making it into a screenplay. Jones had previously turned in a film treatment. However, it departed from the book too much to suit the studio. And since no writer had been assigned a follow-up effort, producer Buddy Adler gave Taradash his chance.

The first thing he did was to reread the novel. After three-and-a-half months, Taradash said he boiled down the work to 900 pages of single-spaced notes. In another five months, he turned out a 135-page treatment. After three more months, he completed the first draft of the screenplay. It took another six months—for a total of nearly one year—to revise and polish the script into its final version.

Taradash, to be sure, took some liberties with the story. "The stockade brutality, I felt, could be more effective if suggested rather than literally depicted," Taradash said. "The blowing of the bugle, which had great meaning in the characterization of Prewitt, was shifted to make it a 'climax,' so to speak, of the 'second act' of the screenplay. And I had the notion of intercutting the two love stories—the first sergeant with the captain's wife and the private with his girl from the New Congress—to give a feeling of the unconscious interrelation of their lives."

There were other changes, too. The New Congress Hotel, a house of prostitution, became the New Congress Club, a social establishment like a USO, to placate the Breen Office, Hollywood's self-censoring organization. And, to win the army's cooperation in shooting the film, the cruelty of Captain Dana Holmes was made to seem an individual aberration (for which he was punished, unlike the book's outcome) rather than a general commentary on officer harshness.

But, by and large, Taradash did a faithful job. He had some candid and unpleasant things to say about the army, and he felt that his script retained the two major themes of Jones' novel—the story of a man fighting against a group and the story of a soldier killed by something he loves, the army.

The script won Columbia's immediate and enthusiastic acceptance and director Zinnemann set

to work casting the film. That turned out to be almost as challenging a task as Taradash's script work.

Cohn wanted a hardy, rough-hewn type like Aldo Ray to play Prewitt, but Zinnemann held out for Montgomery Clift. He pointed out that on the first page of the book, Jones describes Prewitt as a "very neat and deceptively slim young man." Zinnemann thought that a wiry, rawboned actor would underscore Prewitt's resiliency and strength of character as he stands up to "the treatment."

This same unorthodox approach to casting resulted in Deborah Kerr's selection. Joan Crawford was the studio's pick to play the seductive Karen Holmes. But Buddy Ehrenberg, Miss Kerr's agent, was then trying to rejuvenate the fading career of the Scottish-born actress. The epitome of British decorum, Miss Kerr had been imported by Louis B. Mayer in 1946 to become another Greer Garson. She was an accomplished professional, but she had created little attention playing white-gloved, high-minded ladies. Ehrenberg turned her liability into an asset by convincing Harry Cohn that Miss Kerr's bloodless gentility would give poignancy and depth to the character of a woman driven to promiscuity by a loveless marriage.

Zinnemann later said he opted for this unusual casting because he felt that it would add freshness to the film. It meant the actors could not fall back on their standard screen personalities to see them through the picture. Instead, they had to understand their roles thoroughly and then portray their characters so convincingly that audiences would forget their traditional typecasting. This was no easy task.

But Zinnemann was convinced that it was the right course, and his gamble paid off handsomely. "The cast seems so perfect for their roles," said *Variety*, "it would be hard to imagine anyone else playing the characters even though some of the assignments are off-beat to the extreme." *

From Here to Eternity won eight Oscars, including awards for best picture, best supporting actor and actress (Sinatra and Miss Reed), best director (Zinnemann), and best screenplay (Taradash). In

*One writer who took exception to the casting accolades was John Baxter. "Donna Reed is a prissy, dance-hall girl rather than Jones' original lacquered snobbish whore," Baxter said in his book *Sixty Years in Hollywood*. "Montgomery Clift lacks the intellectual self-esteem that makes Prewitt not so much an indomitable individualist as a stubborn drop-out. And Deborah Kerr, though effective as the bored, amoral captain's wife having an affair with a virile sergeant, seldom rises above miscasting." Nor did Baxter think much of Taradash's screen adaptation. "Twenty-four scripts were produced before finding one acceptable to all concerned," said Baxter, "and the result, understandably, is only a shadow of the original."

addition, Miss Kerr, Lancaster, and Clift got nominations for best actor and actress.

From the standpoint of box office, the movie was one of Columbia's biggest bonanzas of the 1950s (and the 1960s as well). The picture, which cost $2.4 million, made $19 million on its first release. So great was the demand to see it that the Capitol Theatre in New York City stayed open almost twenty-four hours a day. It closed briefly in the wee hours of the morning to let the janitors clean up.

The movie opens in 1941, in the summer before the Pearl Harbor assault. Robert E. Lee Prewitt (Clift), a "thirty-year-man" who has made soldiering his profession, arrives at Schofield Barracks, Honolulu. His pride hurt, he has left his old company after protesting the appointment of another soldier as head bugler above him. His protest has cost him a demotion from corporal to private.

But his expectation for fair treatment in his new company gets an immediate setback. From Prewitt's service record, the company commander, Captain Dana Holmes (Philip Ober), learns that Prewitt was a top boxer for his former outfit. It happens that the captain is coach of the regimental boxing squad and he urges Prewitt to join. In the back of his mind, Captain Holmes feels that a championship won't hurt his chances for promotion.

However, Prewitt, haunted by the memory of blinding a pal while sparring, wants no part of fighting anymore. He flatly rejects his commander's offer, an action that was unacceptable in the pre-World War II army where rank had its privilege. The army has no regulations that say a man must box, but there are ways to make him change his mind. The captain passes the word and the other boxers in the company see that Prewitt gets increasingly loathsome duties.

The company's top-kick, tough but fair First Sergeant Warden (Lancaster), advises Prewitt not to make trouble. Warden, a career soldier who despises weak, arrogant officers like the captain, is a realist. He believes that a smart soldier goes along with the system. But Prewitt is an uncompromising individualist and non-conformist whose philosophy is: "A man who don't go his own way is nothing." And so, day after day, he endures the "treatment," putting in long hours doing extra marching and working the garbage detail. The only one who offers him friendship is Private Angelo Maggio

Montgomery Clift, as the stubborn Pvt. Robert E. Lee Prewitt, cuts loose with some bugle riffs between beers at the New Congress Club. Sinatra lends an ear.

(Sinatra), a brash, little guy who respects Prewitt's courage.

While all this is going on, the captain is usually away from the post, womanizing or drinking at the officers' club, leaving his frustrated wife Karen (Miss Kerr) to play out a lonely life. Over the years she has gained a reputation for being a loose woman.

One day Warden calls on her and they begin a relationship that grows into a passionate romance. As he gets to know Karen, the sergeant learns that she has stayed with Holmes only because he has refused to divorce her for fear of jeopardizing his military career.

The weeks go by, and their clandestine meetings become more frequent. On one occasion, they go swimming on a deserted beach and lie locked in a tight embrace while the sea churns up white-capped breakers and the surf rolls over them. This famous love scene—shot at Blowhole Beach on the Island of Oahu—was so meticulously rehearsed that it took three days' shooting time.

The Breen Office thought it was too torrid and particularly objected to the sea washing over them. But it stayed in and has become the single most remembered scene from the movie. It has been satirized time and time again—most notably on television on Sid Caesar's "Show of Shows" and in the movies in *The Seven Year Itch* (1955) with Tom Ewell making love to Roxanne Arlen in a daydream sequence.

Meanwhile, Prewitt and Maggio have their own high time drinking and romancing on weekend passes. Maggio takes Prewitt to the New Congress Club in Honolulu. At the outset, the rules of the club are clearly spelled out for the benefit of Hollywood's censor. "Members are entitled to all privileges of the club, which includes dancing, snack bar, soft drink bar, and gentlemanly relaxation with the opposite gender—so long as they are gentlemen—and no liquor is permitted." The rules, of course, don't prevent GIs from smuggling whiskey under their loose-fitting sport shirts.

Prewitt's introduction to the club is almost a disaster. He and Maggio get into a bitter argument with Fatso Judson (Ernest Borgnine), the cruel sergeant of the stockade. Warden stops the melee after Fatso pulls a knife. But the stockade sergeant warns them he will not forget the incident. "Guys like you end up in the stockade sooner or later," Fatso says. "I'll be waiting."

However, the evening is not entirely wasted.

Clift and Lancaster share some booze as they get drunk together on a weekend pass.

Donna Reed as Alma, a prostitute who falls in love with Prewitt. She won a supporting Oscar.

Prewitt meets Lorene (Miss Reed), a "hostess" the other girls dub "The Princess" because of her aloofness. They hit it off and their association quickly reaches the point of intimacy. She gives Prewitt the run of her home on the hills overlooking the city, and it is here that he finds his only real escape from the treatment.

Later, when he proposes, she turns him down. She tells him that she plans to save enough to return to the States.

"I want to be proper," she says. "[I want to] meet the proper man with the proper position and make a proper wife and raise proper children."

The best Prewitt can offer is the wife of an army non-com. He tells her that he will even box so he can eventually make sergeant. But Alma rejects his offer.

Then, one night, Maggio gets drunk, starts a fight with two military police, and gets tossed in the stockade. There he becomes a target for Fatso Judson, who specializes in torturing prisoners. All this goes on off-camera, but we see the terrible abuse Maggio has endured when, a month later, he breaks out to find Prewitt. A physical wreck, and bleeding internally, Maggio dies in Prewitt's arms.

That night Prewitt goes to the company parade grounds and blows taps for Maggio. As the clear, soulful notes float through the hushed summer air, the camera wanders through the barracks and focuses on the somber faces of Maggio's GI pals.

Even after this tragedy, the treatment continues under Holmes' approving eye. One day, hulking Sgt. Ike Galovitch (John Dennis), Prewitt's worst tormentor, needles him to the breaking point. They go at each other in front of the company and Prewitt whips Galovitch in a savage brawl.

The fight proves to be Holmes' undoing. Some senior officers see it, find out what caused it, and make a report to the inspector general. Within days, Holmes is forced to resign to avoid court-martial. (In the book, Holmes is promoted to major, adding irony to the fortunes of army life. But the movie change was made as another concession to gain the army's support.)

Prewitt has not forgotten Maggio. He goes looking for Fatso one weekend, finds him in town, and challenges him to a fight in a shadowy alley. Fatso pulls a knife. Prewitt, anticipating this, draws one of his own. The camera pulls away from the fight and in the next sequence we see Fatso reeling out of the alley. Mortally wounded he sags to the ground and dies. Prewitt, cut badly, staggers to Lorene's house and goes AWOL while his wounds heal.

Things are going badly for Warden, too. He wants Karen to divorce Holmes, but she will marry Warden only if he becomes an officer. That's something he finds, in the end, that he cannot do. Like Prewitt, he is a confirmed thirty-year-man. He cannot identify with the officer class and he won't compromise. "You're already married," says Karen. "To the army."

When the Japanese launch their attack on Pearl Harbor, Prewitt, not yet recovered from his wounds, tells Lorene that he must rejoin his buddies. She pleads with him to stay, but that's not possible for Prewitt. His country is at war. "I'm a soldier," Prewitt says.

That night, as he tries to return to the barracks, a guard unit mistakes him for a saboteur and guns him down.

And so as the war begins, Prewitt and Maggio lie dead at the hands of their own army. Warden is gearing for combat. And Karen and Lorene are returning to the States to try to pick up the pieces of their broken lives.

On the deck of their passenger ship, they watch the island slowly slide away. They are as different as they are alike. They come from opposite ends of the social spectrum, but they both are unhappy women who have ended the love affair of their life. And they both have been done in by their inability to break away from conventionality. Karen would not marry anyone who was not an officer, and Lorene insisted on marrying a man of means to prove she is not really a trollop. Moreover, it is clear that Lorene will continue to play out her fantasy.

As the movie closes, Lorene introduces herself to Karen and tells her that her fiancé was a bomber pilot killed in the Pearl Harbor attack. "Maybe you read about it in the papers? He was awarded the Silver Star," Lorene says, clutching his bugle mouthpiece. "He was named after a general—Robert E. Lee Prewitt. Isn't that a silly old name?"

Karen tosses a lei into the sea. The legend is that if it floats back to shore, you will see Hawaii again. It doesn't.

General
della Rovere

"Good morning, Signorina. Here is something really terrific—an Oriental sapphire," says "Colonel" Grimaldi (Vittorio de Sica), trying to pawn off a fake jewel in war-torn Italy.

General della Rovere
(1959)

Directed by Roberto Rossellini. Story and screenplay by Sergio Amidei, Diego Fabri, Indro Montanelli. From an incident suggested by Montanelli. Photography, Carlo Carlini. Music, Renzo Rossellini. Executive producer, Morris Ergas. Released by Continental Distributing Inc. 160 minutes.

Bardone (Grimaldi)	*Vittorio de Sica*
Colonel Mueller	*Hannes Messemer*
Banchelli	*Vittorio Caprioli*
Fabrizio	*Giuseppe Rossetti*
Olga	*Sandra Milo*
Valeria	*Giovanna Ralli*
Mrs. Fassio	*Anne Vernon*
Contessa della Rovere	*Baronessa Barzani*
German Officer	*Kurt Polter*
Schrantz	*Kurt Selge*
The Madam	*Mary Greco*
The Prostitute	*Lucia Modugno*
German Attendant	*Linda Veras*

"Good morning, Signorina. Here is something really terrific—an Oriental sapphire that belonged to my mother. A unique stone. And only 100,000 lire will buy it."

This is Vittorio de Sica trying to pawn off another fake jewel as an incorrigible con-man in the Italian movie *General della Rovere*. A long and absorbing film, the picture is not only memorable for de Sica's poignant performance, but also for establishing the comeback of Roberto Rossellini.

The renowned Italian director, who became even more famous for his affair with Ingrid Bergman,* is credited with creating neo-realism (new realism)—a whole different style in filmmaking. Instead of working in a studio, Rossellini took his units to real locations—shooting in streets, alleys, and shabby apartments. He used available light and mostly non-professional players. His low-budget movies—*Open City* (1945) and *Paisan* (1946), which dealt with the rootless in war-torn Italy—centered around strong, socially conscious themes.

Rossellini improvised scenes as he went along and shot sequences unrehearsed. As time passed, the more his pictures became successful, the more he became conscious of his art. Gradually, his films lost their truth and beauty. And, beginning with the ill-fated *Stromboli* (1950), disaster after disaster plagued him.

Then came *General della Rovere*, which ended his losing streak. It gave him a share of the first prize at the Venice Film Festival and restored him to the front rank of international filmmakers.

For de Sica, the movie was yet another milestone in a long and remarkable career. A tall, handsome figure with pure white hair and a brilliant smile, he was Italy's highest paid actor and a matinee idol in the true sense of the term. Adoring women followed him. He was called "the model of suave and urban Roman sophistication."

"Brides left their husbands on their wedding nights to pursue me," de Sica once said. "Even young girls threw themselves at me. . . . I threw them out." He was also a gambler and addicted to roulette. He reportedly lost as much as $10,000 one night at Monte Carlo.

His international acclaim was primarily for his directing ability. In sharp contrast to his private life, his movies focused on the grim, harsh problems of the poor. It was in the lives of the poor, de Sica said, that the real drama of life could be found. "I love poor people," he said. "After all, if you exclude

adultery, what drama is there in the bourgeoisie?" With Rossellini, he became a leader in the neo-realist movement.

Shoeshine (1944) and *The Bicycle Thief* (1949) were de Sica's first big successes. They, along with *Yesterday, Today and Tomorrow* (1964) and *The Garden of the Finzi-Continis* (1971), won Oscars for the best foreign films.** His own favorite was *Umberto D* (1955), a somber story of an old man trying to maintain his dignity on a meager pension.

Ironically, though these pictures won international acclaim, they brought him little financial success. Even most of his commercial, less artistic movies were box office flops.

For money, he relied on his acting talent. "I have lost money on all the films I have made myself," de Sica said, "although they cost only a fraction of what a major Hollywood film costs to make. I found that nobody wants to finance my films. So I have to finance them myself. I do this by selling my services as an actor. By appearing in five films, I can make enough money to support myself and my family and to make one film of my own."

De Sica made his acting debut in 1923 and appeared in some 200 roles until his death in 1974. He played in many light comedies, films far from the sharp realism of his own work. An exception was *General della Rovere*, a moving story that combined his acting brilliance with the directorial genius of Rossellini. Many critics hailed it as a near masterpiece.

The picture opens on a bleak, gray dawn in World War II Italy. Bardone (de Sica), a Genovese gambler and small-time chiseler, is scurrying home past buildings scarred from the war.

Posing as "Colonel" Grimaldi, he scratches out a living by collecting money from relatives of captured Italian partisans. He is supposed to use the funds to bribe German authorities to buy the prisoners' freedom.

"Put your trust in me," Bardone tells one distraught father. "No stone will be left unturned. Your boy means so much to me. He's like my own."

Bardone's immediate concern is to raise 50,000 lire. He needs the money to meet the demands of a German bureaucrat who has the power to assign prisoners to war zone work camps or keep them in home front camps. Then, too, there are Bardone's mounting gambling debts.

When his mistress refuses to lend him the money he needs, Bardone goes to German headquarters.

---

*The two created an international scandal in the early 1950s when they had a son out of wedlock. They subsequently were married, had twin daughters, and then broke up.

**Technically, *Shoeshine* and *The Bicycle Thief* won "special" Oscars. Academy Awards for best foreign language film were not given out as such until 1956.

There, in lieu of money, he offers a bogus precious stone to his Nazi contact. "I brought a ring . . . a marvelous ring. Look, a sapphire. And it has a platinum mounting. Precious stones are an investment. A good sapphire is always a sapphire."

"I want it all in cash," says the bureaucrat, unimpressed.

Outside, Bardone spots a beautiful young woman who has just pleaded unsuccessfully with German authorities to release her partisan husband. Bardone tells her he has inside connections and that he might be able to help her husband. She offers him money for her husband's liberty, and they make an appointment to meet again. "I hope I'll have good news," Bardone says, tipping his hat.

A few days later, when he goes to meet the lady, he finds German police there to arrest him. The prisoner whom Bardone has promised to get released has been shot by a firing squad. Brought before the German commander, Colonel Mueller (Hannes Messemer), Bardone insists that his intentions were pure. "It all started with Senora Demenache. When they were arresting her son, well, I said, 'If I could, I'd do something.' Soon, there were other poor souls, suffering. I meant to do them a favor. But they were enticed by that. 'Please find out if our boy is living.' 'Do what you can to see our boy isn't sent to Germany.' It was done out of kindness. What would you have done?"

The colonel is not sympathetic. However, instead of sending Bardone to his execution, Mueller offers him an alternative. He asks Bardone to impersonate an Italian general, who has been killed, in a prison where partisans are being held. The partisan resistance leader is suspected of being held there. Bardone's job is to lure the partisan chief to make contact and identify himself so that the Germans can seize him.

When Bardone is imprisoned, the word is quickly passed: "General della Rovere is here." Taken to his sparse cell, Bardone reads on the cell wall the messages of the men who have preceded him. "It is all over for me. Life is a small thing. I'm to be shot by a firing squad. I go out to death without fear. I never thought it would be so easy to die."

At first, Bardone plays his part well. He inspires other prisoners with his concern for them and the toughness he shows his German captors. "This is General della Rovere," he tells the men via the cell-to-cell communications network. "Have courage."

One night, Allied bombers raid the area, dropping explosives close to the prison. Fearing that they will be trapped, some prisoners begin to panic, pleading to be let out of their cells. Bardone demands to be released and goes from cell to cell reassuring everyone. "Listen, you men," he shouts. "Face death with dignity. No faltering now. Show you are real men. We must show these wretched dogs that we are not afraid to die. Our victory is much nearer now. And so is our rescue."

One day, when the prison barber passes a message to him, Bardone informs Colonel Mueller. A few days later, the Germans torture the barber. Afterward he kills himself rather than face a second interrogation.

Torn by guilt and grief, Bardone rages at the colonel. He says that his cover is blown and the prisoners will now see through his masquerade. "They'll kill me," Bardone says.

The colonel has another plan. "They'll see that you've been a victim yourself," he says. "Then you'll be a hero." So Bardone gets a taste of torture, too, and this sets in motion a strange metamorphosis. He becomes the man he is portraying —the brave soldier willing to die before he would betray his men.

The end comes quickly. Nine partisans are called to appear before a firing squad. Bardone chooses to go with them rather than give the Germans the leader they are hunting. He leaves behind a letter for the real general's wife. "My last thoughts were of you," it says.

Just before the firing squad opens up, Bardone shouts to the doomed partisans: "Gentlemen. At this last moment, let us turn our thoughts to our comrades, our beloved country, and to his majesty, the King. Long live Italy."

There is a burst of rifle fire. The nine partisans and Bardone slump to the ground. A few moments later, a functionary mumbles to Colonel Mueller: "Sir, I think there has been a mistake. We were to shoot only nine."

The colonel pauses. "It's my own mistake, Lieutenant," he replies, realizing how badly he has misjudged the petty swindler who has tried to redeem his sordid life through courage and honor.

High Noon

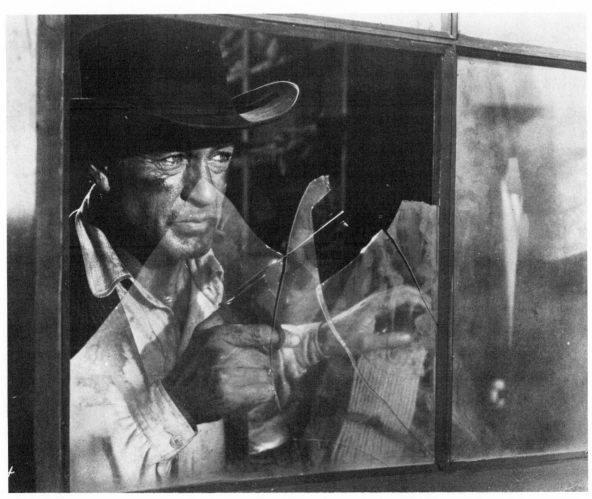

Gary Cooper, the lawman dedicated to his job, duels three desperadoes in *High Noon*, a movie many critics rate as the all-time best Western.

High Noon
(1952)

Directed by Fred Zinnemann. Assistant director, Emmett Emerson. Screenplay by Carl Foreman, based on the short story "The Tin Star" by John W. Cunningham. Music composed and directed by Dmitri Tiomkin.* Song, "Do Not Forsake Me, Oh My Darlin' " by Tiomkin* (music) and Ned Washington* (words). Sung by Tex Ritter. Photography, Floyd Crosby. Art director, Rudolph Sternad. Editors, Elmo Williams* and Harry Gerstad.* Sound, Jean Speak. Produced by Stanley Kramer. Released through United Artists. 84 minutes.

Will Kane	Gary Cooper*
Jonas Henderson	Thomas Mitchell
Harvey Pell	Lloyd Bridges
Helen Ramirez	Katy Jurado
Amy Kane	Grace Kelly
Percy Mettrick	Otto Kruger
Matt Howe	Lon Chaney, Jr.
Sam Fuller	Henry (Harry) Morgan
Frank Miller	Ian MacDonald
Mildred Fuller	Eve McVeagh
Cooper	Harry Shannon
Jack Colby	Lee Van Cleef
James Pierce	Bob Wilke
Ben Miller	Sheb Woolley
Sam	Tom London
Station Master	Ted Stanhope
Gillis	Larry Blake
Barber	William "Bill" Phillips
Mrs. Henderson	Jeanne Blackford
Baker	James Millican
Weaver	Cliff Clark
Johnny	Ralph Reed
Drunk (Jimmy)	William Newell
Bartender	Lucien Prival
Fred	Guy Beach
Hotel Clerk	Howland Chamberlin
Minister	Morgan Farley
Mrs. Simpson	Virginia Farmer
Charlie	Jack Elam
Scott	Paul Dubov
Coy	Harry Harvey
Sawyer	Tim Graham
Lewis	Nolan Leary
Ezra	Tom Greenway
Kibbee	Dick Elliott
Trumbull	John Doucette

*Academy Award Winner.

Cooper and his bride (Grace Kelly) have just started on their honeymoon when the conscience-stricken marshal reins up and turns around.

The noon train rumbles into the tiny frontier town of Hadleyville, its shrill whistle piercing the still prairie air. Off steps a tall, rough-hewn man whose dark, gun-metal eyes flicker over the flat landscape.

He is Frank Miller, a convict on his way to settle an old score. Miller has just been pardoned from prison. He has come here for a showdown with Marshal Will Kane, the man who put him behind bars five years ago.

Three members of Miller's old gang are at the station. They flock to him like cubs to a mother wolf, but the meeting is devoid of affection.

"Everything ready?" Miller asks icily.

"Just the way you want it, Frank," one henchman says.

Miller slaps on his gunbelt. He looks down the dusty main street, baking in the shimmering summer heat. "Let's get started then."

Thus begins the climax of a movie that ranks with the classic Westerns of modern times. It takes place alongside such stalwarts as *Stagecoach* (1939), *The Gunfighter* (1950), and *Shane* (1953). These pictures took major steps toward fulfilling the promise of a genre that began in 1903 with the modest, ten-minute film, *The Great Train Robbery*. But of them all, *High Noon* comes closest to being the truest fulfillment of its type.

"*High Noon*," says film historian Jon Tuska, "is the most perfect embodiment we have ever had of the kind of Western William S. Hart* so loved to make. It is a psychological Western. . . . Perhaps no other performance by an actor equals Gary Cooper's role—a tragic one, the realization of a man alone against all the forces of the universe."

In fact, the picture was so skillfully filmed that it seemed we were seeing less a movie than a slice of real life. Said Bosley Crowther, then the *New York Times* film critic: "This is no storybook Western. This seems a replica of actuality."

How real a portrait the events of *High Noon* paint of the true West can be debated, but its theme is certainly one that transcends the screen. There are those who, noting that the film was made during the McCarthy era, say that it was intended as an allegory of what they regard as the public spinelessness of that period.

John Wayne, whose reputation as a super patriot is well known, deplored the picture, and

*During his eleven-year career from 1914-1925, Hart expanded the Western's scope from a one-dimensional action picture to one with realism and depth. A Shakespearean actor who nevertheless had a firsthand knowledge of frontier life, Hart began the so-called adult Western—one that subordinates action to the development of a serious theme. He also presented the cowboy as a man of character, and he added romanticism and visual reality to the genre.

thought that its theme was alien to the American way of life. He summed up the plot in this way:

"Four guys come in to gun down the sheriff. He goes to the church and asks for help. And the guys go 'Oh well, oh gee.' And the women stand up and say, 'You're rats. You're rats. You're rats.' It's the most un-American thing I've ever seen in my whole life. The last thing in the picture is Coop putting the U.S. marshal's badge under his foot and stepping on it. I'll never regret having helped run (screenwriter Carl) Foreman out of this country."

Although Wayne said he meant this oath figuratively, it is true that Foreman got no more assignments after *High Noon*. He became a victim of studio blacklisting that stemmed from the McCarthyera investigations.*

However, director Fred Zinnemann maintains that the movie's main intention was merely to show to what length a man would go to defend his own convictions. "It so happened, at that time the film came out," Zinnemann said, "that McCarthy had intimidated large sections of the population. And many people who were innocent were afraid of saying what they thought. So the film seemed to have a bearing in showing a man who was not afraid of doing or saying what he thought was right. But people reacted to it primarily as drama. The other inference was secondary."

Whether *High Noon* was intended to operate on more than one level, it is nonetheless true that the theme of courage has been a concern of Zinnemann's most important pictures. Consider, for example, *The Men* (1950), *From Here to Eternity* (1953), and *A Man for All Seasons* (1966).

For Zinnemann, the highest courage was not displaying the most bravery in battle. His characters were not intrinsically heroic. Instead, they were ordinary people, wracked by self-doubts and inner conflict, who nevertheless had the moral fiber to rise to the occasion and confront danger. And, by so doing, they earned the right to their own self-respect and dignity.

There are, of course, others who contributed to the picture's success. Gary Cooper's sparse, underplayed performance did much to help make the picture into the classic that it is. No one could walk deserted streets of a Western town gunning for outlaws with more authority than the rawboned, stone-faced Cooper. (The movie repaid Cooper in kind. The Oscar he won, his second, served to re-

charge a career that had slipped into mediocrity.)

Adding to the film's myth-like quality was the plaintive ballad "Do Not Forsake Me, Oh My Darlin'," which became a popular hit. The song and the film score were written by Dmitri Tiomkin, a veteran composer of movie background music.** According to producer Stanley Kramer, the lyrics were originally used no less than eleven times throughout the film as "bridges" each time Cooper took a walk. This turned out to be a kind of musical overkill. A preview audience broke out in giggles the fifth time the singing occurred, and the giggles later exploded into laughter. "I finally took out seven of those renditions," Kramer said, "not including what was at the beginning and the end." That apparently did the trick. In director Zinnemann's estimation, the ballad gave a focus and direction to the picture, exceeding anything that he and his associates had anticipated during the filming.

Tex Ritter, a star of B-Westerns of the 1930s and 1940s, sang the lyrics. He did not appear in the movie, but his voice crooned hauntingly throughout the film during long stretches where the tight-lipped Cooper strode across the sun-parched streets toward his moment of truth.

There was, in addition, the graphic camera of Floyd Crosby and the skillful editing of Elmo Williams and Harry Gerstad, building suspense as they cross-cut from the depot, to the still streets, to the tense faces of men waiting in church, to the three outlaws at the station, to the tracks, and to the grim face of the marshal.

High Noon, then, was no single person's masterpiece. It was the happy result of a harmony of many inputs.

The movie opens quietly. As Ritter's voice sings sadly in the background, the screen shows a man on horseback waiting near a gnarled prairie tree. The sun is high in a clear blue sky. In the distance, another rider appears.

Now the titles flash on. Behind them, the rider reaches the waiting man. The two recognize each other, nod briefly, then wait together. The distant bell of a church tolls. From another angle, a third

*Foreman, nevertheless, did quite well afterward. He moved to England where he worked on the screenplay for *The Bridge on the River Kwai* (1957). He later wrote and produced *The Key* (1958) and *Born Free* (1965), and produced *Young Winston* (1963), among other films.

**A Russian-born *wunderkind* who gave piano recitals in Carnegie Hall when in his twenties, Tiomkin went to Hollywood in 1930 to become its highest-paid composer-conductor. He scored over 150 pictures, winning four Oscars. In addition to his two from *High Noon* (for best film score and song), he won one for *The High and the Mighty* (1954) and one for *The Old Man and the Sea* (1958). An exuberant, colorful personality, Tiomkin's major complaint as a Hollywood composer is against the practice of calling in a composer *after* a picture is finished—as was done in *High Noon*. But that is par for the course. Music, he says, is usually an afterthought in film productions.

126

rider gallops toward the two horsemen. When he reaches them, the first man takes out his watch. While he checks the time, the camera takes us closer and we see that the riders are travel-weary, rough-looking, and grim. The first man snaps his watch-case shut. He puts it away and motions quickly to the others. They spur their horses on.

The camera cuts to the tiny prairie town of Hadleyville. The three riders are cantering down its main street to the tiny railroad station. One of the riders, a whiskered cowboy, dismounts and goes up to the station master.

"Noon train on time?" he asks, wiping his forehead with his sleeve.

"Yes sir."

The cowboy looks at the station clock. One hour and thirty minutes to go. Hot and tired, he and his companions take their ease on a bench, reach for tobacco, and wait. The tracks trail off into a bleak, table-flat landscape.*

Meanwhile, in the nearby courtroom of Judge Percy Mettrick (Otto Kruger), town marshal Will Kane (Cooper) is performing his last act in office. He is giving up his job to marry Amy Fowler (Grace Kelly), a beautiful Quaker girl. They plan to move to another town and open a general store.

No sooner have they taken their vows than the station master (Ted Stanhope) rushes in with a telegram. As Kane reads it, his face becomes expressionless. "They've pardoned Frank Miller," he says. A hush falls over the wedding party. It was Kane who broke up Miller's gang and sent him to prison. The station master tells Kane that Miller's brother Ben (Sheb Wooley) and two more cohorts—James Pierce (Bob Wilke) and Jack Colby (Lee Van Cleef)—are at the depot and that they have asked about the noon train.

"Will," says Jonas Henderson (Thomas Mitchell), the town's senior member of its board of selectmen, "you get out of town."

"I think I ought to stay," Kane says.

*The scene of the empty station and railroad tracks running off in the distance under the vast cloudless sky is a recurrent one and a deliberate one. Zinnemann said that he tried to make the camera record a conflicting flow of visual patterns. "In most Westerns," Zinnemann said, "beautiful cloud formations are considered *de rigueur*. But we wanted to emphasize the flatness and emptiness of the land and the inertia of everybody and everything. To contrast all that with the movements of the marshal, we dressed Cooper all in black so that when his lonely figure issued forth into the stark, bright stillness, his destiny seemed even more poignant."

Another device to heighten the tension was the clocks—in the depot, the courtroom, the marshal's office. They constantly reminded the audience of the minutes before noon. Film time and real time did not coincide precisely. Early scenes were telescoped to allow for dramatic lengthening of later sequences. But the running time—84 minutes—corresponded roughly to the time the action would have taken in real life.

"Are you crazy? Think of Amy."

Before Kane can answer, his friends have bundled him and his new wife onto their horse and buggy, and off they ride out of town. However, no sooner does the little town fade in the distance than Kane has second thoughts. He stops his wagon. Running away, he realizes, is a false solution.

"It's no good," Kane says. "I've got to go back, Amy."

"I don't understand."

"I haven't got time to tell you," he says, turning his horses around.

"Then don't go back, Will."

"I've got to," he says simply. "That's the whole thing."

This scene, says critic Richard Griffiths, is a pivotal one in the film. "From this moment," Griffiths says, "we are not merely involved with the marshal: we sit in his seat, we see with his eyes, we are afflicted with his doubts and fears as he abandons an obvious course of action for one with unknown consequences."

Later in his office as he checks out his guns, Kane tries to explain to Amy the reason he is compelled to return. "I sent a man up five years ago for murder," Kane says. "He was supposed to hang. But up North, they commuted it to life. Now, he's free. I don't know how. Anyway, he's coming back."

Miller has sworn to kill Kane. He doesn't tell Amy this. Kane says only: "He was always wild, kind of crazy. He'll probably make trouble."

"That's no concern of yours," Amy pleads.

"I'm the one who sent him up."

"That was part of your job," Amy says. "That's finished now. They've got a new marshal."

"Won't be here until tomorrow. Seems to me I've got to stay. Anyway, I'm the same man with or without this." Kane points to his badge.

Amy will still not accept his explanation, so Kane tries to justify his return strictly on the common sense odds of survival. He tells her that he is no hero, but the danger she wants to avoid simply will not go away. If they flee, Kane tells her, Miller will stalk him wherever he goes. There will be a showdown sooner or later. It's in Kane's favor to have it in Hadleyville where Kane's friends can add their numbers to his cause, rather than in some lonely prairie town where no one knows him.

But Amy, whose religion has committed her to a life of non-violence, recoils from the bloody consequences of any shoot-out. If Kane won't go with her now, she tells him, she will be on the noon train. He looks at his wife of less than half an hour without speaking. Then he says: "I've got to stay."

Cooper plants a right on the jaw of the saloonkeeper (Larry J. Blake).

So with his bride about to leave him, Kane begins the task of rounding up a posse. He pays his first call on the town's leading citizen, Judge Mettrick, the man who has just performed the marriage ceremony.

However, it is clear that the judge wants no part of Miller and his gunmen. Kane finds him hurriedly packing his belongings.

"Have you forgotten I'm the man who passed sentence on Frank Miller? You shouldn't have come back, Will. It's stupid."

"I figured I have to. I have to stay."

"You figured wrong."

"I can deputize a posse. Ten to twelve guns is all I need."

"My intuition tells me otherwise," the judge says.

Then, while he wraps up his American flag and packs his gavel, law books, and scales of justice, the judge recounts an anecdote that will prove prophetic. In the fifth century B.C., the judge says, the citizens of Athens managed to throw out a tyrant under whom they had suffered grievously. However, when he came back years later with an army of mercenaries, these same citizens not only opened their gates for him, but stood by while he executed members of the League of Government.

In case Kane thinks this is just a fable, the judge

adds another anecdote, this one from personal experience. "A similar thing happened about eight years ago in a town called Indian Falls. I escaped death only through the intervention of a lady of somewhat dubious reputation—and, uh, the cost of a very handsome ring which once belonged to my mother." He shrugs. "Unfortunately, I have no more rings."

As Kane's wife could not fathom Kane's actions, neither can Kane understand the judge's. After all, he is a man of the bench. The weight of that position should carry with it certain unwavering obligations—even under the gravest of circumstances.

"You're a judge," Kane exclaims.

"I've been a judge many times in many towns," replies the practical older man who believes discretion is the better part of valor. "I hope to live to be a judge again."

Nothing Kane can say will change the other man's mind, Kane realizes. It's something inside that pushes a man to moral commitment. "I can't tell you what to do," Kane says.

And, with the hands of the clock edging closer to noon, Kane goes out to find his posse. Here's what happens:

Harvey Pell (Lloyd Bridges), Kane's ambitious assistant, says that he will stand by him, but he

128

wants something in return. Harvey is sore because he wasn't named Kane's successor. "You want me to stick? You put the word in for me." Replies Kane: "Sure I want you to stick. But I'm not buying you." Harvey tosses in his badge.

Next Kane calls on Helen Ramirez (Katy Jurado), the fiery, half-Mexican saloon owner who used to be his mistress. Kane has come to warn her that Miller is due on the noon train. She had left Miller for Kane, and Kane thinks that Miller's vengeance will not stop with him. She tells Kane she is getting out. "If you're smart," she adds, "you'll get out, too." Kane says, "I can't." "I know," says Mrs. Ramirez, who understands the marshal better than his new wife.

Kane's third stop is the Ramirez saloon where he overhears the saloon keeper, Gillis (Larry Blake), offer to cover bets that Miller will cut down Kane within minutes after the train comes in. Kane blows his cool and slugs him. Then he makes an appeal for deputies: "I'll need all I can get." There are no takers. "Some of you were special deputies when we broke this bunch," Kane says. "I need you again now." Silence. Things were different then, one man tells Kane. Then Kane had six top guns. Now he has none. Laughter swells up behind him as he leaves the saloon.

At the home of Sam Fuller (Henry Morgan), Fuller's wife tells Kane that her husband is at church.

Kane suspects she is lying since they always go to church together, but he says nothing. After he leaves, Mrs. Fuller looks contemptuously at her husband. "Do you want me to get killed?" he asks. "Do you want to be a widow?"

On the street, Jimmy, the town drunk (William Newell), a one-eyed man, offers to join forces with Kane, but it's more to prove himself than anything else. "It's a chance, see," Jimmy says. "It's what I need." Kane turns him down. Another volunteer—whom he also rejects—is a hero-worshiping sixteen-year-old.

And so, down to this last chance, he enters the church. "I need help," he says, interrupting the service. "Frank Miller's coming back on the noon train. I need all the special deputies I can get."

What are we waiting for, one man says. Hold on, says another. This dispute is something personal between Miller and Kane. It's not the town's business.

"You all ought to be ashamed of yourself," a woman cries. "It ain't his trouble. It's ours. I tell you if we don't do what's right, there'll be plenty of trouble."

And so the debate goes back and forth. The church seems split down the middle. Even the pastor (Morgan Farley) can't make a clear decision. On the one hand, he says, the commandments say "Thou Shalt Not Kill." Yet, we hire men to kill for us. In this situation, the right and wrong seem clear. "But," he says, "if you're asking me to tell my people to kill, and maybe get themselves killed, I'm sorry. I don't know what to say."

In the end, it is Henderson, the senior selectman, who makes the decisive speech. First, he pays tribute to Kane—"the best marshal we've ever had. Maybe the best we'll ever have." Second, he concedes that Miller is the town's concern, not Kane's. "It's our problem because this is our town. . . . If we want to keep it decent, keep it growing, we got to think mighty clear today."

But Henderson is, above all, a prudent businessman, and his sense of business outweighs his sense of right. He points up what a bad image a shoot-out would give Hadleyville in the North. It is there that the town gets its money to finance its growth. "If they're going to read about shooting in the streets, what are they going to think then? I'll tell you. They're going to think this is just another wide-open town. And everything we've worked for will be wiped out. In one day this town will be set back five years."

So Henderson asks Kane to leave. "It's better for you," Henderson says, "and better for us."

Even while Kane is leaving the church, the noon train is pulling in. Miller gets off and is immediately joined by three former henchmen. He slips on his gunbelt and sets right out to hunt down Kane.

Meanwhile, Kane's bride has sought out Mrs. Ramirez in her hotel room. She asks Kane's former mistress if Kane has come back to her. Isn't that the real reason he is staying? Mrs. Ramirez denies this. Then why has Kane returned, Amy asks.

"If you don't know," Mrs. Ramirez says coldly, "I can't explain it to you." Then, suddenly, Mrs. Ramirez lashes out. "What kind of woman are you? How can you leave him now?"

Quietly Amy replies that she saw her father and brother shot down. "They were on the right side," she says. "But that didn't help them." And that is why she became a Quaker.

Nevertheless, Mrs. Ramirez points out, it is her husband who is out there. He is putting his life on the line. He is all alone. "If Kane was my man," she says, "I'd never leave him. I'd get a gun and fight."

Kane, confused and shaken, seeks out Matt Howe (Lon Chaney, Jr.), the town's old marshal. Aged and arthritic, Howe gives him no solace. The public doesn't give a damn about integrity, he says. A town that won't defend itself deserves no help.

Grace Kelly avoids looking at Cooper as she waits for her train after she and her husband of less than an hour have had a bitter falling out. The hotel clerk (Howland Chamberlin) sets the clock, one of the many reminders of the time running out on Cooper.

"Get out, Will," Howe says. "It's all for nothing, Will."

Kane does go down to the town's livery stable. Harvey, his former assistant, sees him enter and taunts him. When Kane wavers, Harvey tries to knock him out and put him on his horse. But Kane fights back, overcomes Harvey, and walks outside for the showdown with Miller and his gunslingers.

Alone and silent, Kane walks apprehensively down the deserted streets. In high-heeled boots, his tin star pinned on his vest, he is the eternal sheriff facing down the eternal bad guys. Through a store window he catches a glimpse of the foursome down a side street. He comes up behind them and calls, "Miller." They go for their guns. But Kane gets off the first shot. Down goes Ben Miller, a bullet through the heart.

Unperturbed, the other three open up a barrage that drives Kane into the stable. He scrambles into the hayloft and, from that secure vantage point, drills a second desperado, Jack Colby, when he runs in with two guns blazing.

Pierce and Frank Miller regroup to consider the situation. They decide to smoke Kane out and they toss a kerosene lamp into the barn. It quickly bursts into flame. Kane, thinking fast, releases the horses and rides out on the last one, clinging to its side. But the outlaws lay down a hail of gunfire. A slug rips through Kane's arm and topples him. Quickly, he takes refuge in a store.

The two gunmen split up. Miller holds Kane's attention by firing from the street while Pierce slips behind the store and steals down an alleyway. But even before he can get a bead on Kane through a window, there is a gunblast from behind. A slug tears into his back from point-blank range. Amy has come to the scene, entered the marshal's office next door, and taken a gun.

The battle is still not over. Miller rushes into the

130

office, grabs Amy, and pushes her out in front of him. "Come out, Kane. Or your friend will get it the same way Pierce did."

Kane hesitates, but only for a second. He starts walking out slowly. Suddenly, Amy lurches, twists in Miller's arms, and jams her hand in his face. In that instant, Kane's hand flashes to his holster. Miller goes for his own gun, but too late. Kane has fired and sent a bullet ripping through his chest.

Not a word is spoken as Kane and Amy embrace. While they hold each other, the townspeople start filtering out and filling the street. But Kane's eyes look past the people who have abandoned him in his hour of need. He reaches for his badge, takes it from his vest and drops it into the dust. Silently, without even a good-bye, he and Amy climb aboard their buggy and drive off until they disappear in the distant prairie.

The Incredible
Shrinking Man

Director Jack Arnold's storyboard showing Scott fleeing from his pet cat.

The Incredible Shrinking Man (1957)

Directed by Jack Arnold. Screenplay by Richard Matheson from his novel. Camera, Ellis W. Carter. Editor, Al Joseph. Music supervision, Joseph Gershenson. Produced by Albert Zugsmith. Released by Universal Pictures. 81 minutes.

Scott Carey	*Grant Williams*
Louise Carey	*Randy Stuart*
Clarice	*April Kent*
Charlie Carey	*Paul Langton*
Dr. Thomas Silver	*Raymond Bailey*
Dr. Arthur Bramson	*William Schallert*
Barker	*Frank Scannell*
Nurse	*Helene Marshall*
Nurse	*Diana Darrin*
Midget	*Billy Curtis*

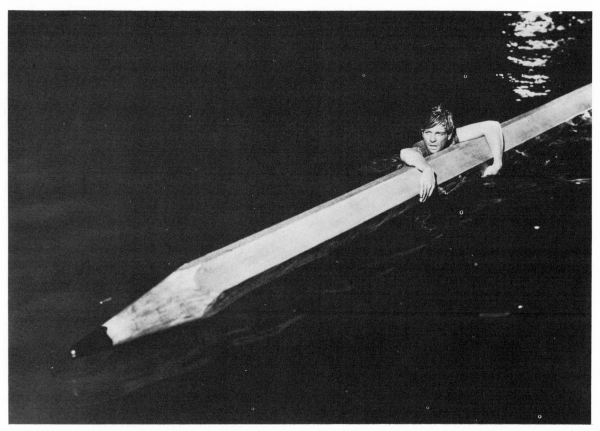

Williams holds on to a pencil to save himself from a flood in his cellar. The pencil was really 21 feet long.

The weird, almost supernatural saga of Scott Carey begins on a splendid summer day off the western coast of the United States. He and his wife are sunning themselves on the deck of their pleasure cruiser when Carey asks her to get him a beer.

While she is below, a strange white mist sweeps over the horizon and passes over their boat. It vanishes as suddenly as it appears, but from that moment on, Carey is a marked man.

Six months later, he notices his clothes hanging on him. His pants are loose at the waist; his cuffs drag; his sleeves flap over his wrists. Slowly, but inexorably, he is getting smaller, and there is nothing he can do to stop the curious and frightening process.

The Incredible Shrinking Man, though it lacked a star-studded cast or a name director or a big budget, has become one of Hollywood's memorable science-fiction pictures.

The 1950s, more than any other decade, was the golden era of science-fiction films. It began with *Destination Moon* (1950) and ended with *Have Rocket, Will Travel* (1959), a Three Stooges romp into space. In between, it produced such genre classics as *The Thing* (1951), *Forbidden Planet*

(1956), and *Invasion of the Body Snatchers* (1956).

But the distinguishing feature of the era's sci-fi pictures was the number of movies inspired by the atomic bomb. Its development and use in World War II gave screen writers ideas about the insidious effects of radiation. And so began a spate of mutation films—*Them* (1954—about twelve-foot ants), *It Came from Beneath the Sea* (1955—a giant octopus), *Attack of the Crab Monsters* (1957), *The Amazing Colossal Man* (1957), *Earth vs. the Spider* (1958), *I Married a Monster from Outer Space* (1958), and *Attack of the 50-Foot Woman* (1958).*

One of the most forgettable films of this genre was a Japanese goodie called *Godzilla, King of*

*The all-time spoof of sci-fi mutation films came from John Cashman, who does the capsule television movie reviews for *Newsday,* the Long Island daily. Cashman ran this entry among the TV listings on April Fool's Day, 1973:
****THE CLAM THAT ATE PITTSBURGH (Fantasy, 1969)
An immense bivalve mollusk goes berserk after drinking the Monongahela River and criminally assaults Three Rivers Stadium before being turned to stone by Mr. Rogers, who has a magic horseradish. Interesting, if you check the calendar. Dubbed. Sonny Tufts, Martin Kosleck, George Zucco, Lionel Atwill, Wild Bill Elliott, Sabu, Mark Damon, Iron Eyes Cody, ZaSu Pitts, and the entire Pirates' bullpen. (2 hrs.)

Monsters (1956). The movie, which starred Raymond Burr in an all-Oriental cast, told how H-bomb tests resurrected a prehistoric creature as tall as a thirty-story building. Godzilla, who apparently had been peacefully hibernating for centuries on the bottom of the sea, looked like a dinosaur misplaced from an episode of "The Flintstones." Still, Japan's top scientist regretted his nation's efforts to do him in. "Godzilla should not be destroyed," the scientist said. "He should be studied." But the truth was that the fire-breathing Godzilla had none of the affecting virtues of King Kong.

Tanks, cannon shells, and even high voltage lines failed to stop this bimbo. He turned Tokyo into a sea of flames; but, in the end, Godzilla met the fate of all monsters. A diabolical invention—an "oxygen destroyer" that kills all oxygen in water—wiped him out in his undersea home. "The menace is gone," says Burr. "The whole world can wake up and live again."

Of course, neither Godzilla nor any of these other pictures came to grips with the real problem of nuclear fission—the danger of atomic war. Also, these movies, while long on imagination, were short on technical effects. Often, instead of scaring an audience, they touched off gales of laughter.

There was at least one notable exception to this silly cycle—*The Incredible Shrinking Man*. Ironically, the movie reversed the mutation process, in that the hero got smaller instead of bigger.

Richard Matheson, who wrote the screenplay from his own book, said he got the idea from seeing a comedy film with Ray Milland and Aldo Ray. "There was a scene where Milland picks up Aldo's hat by mistake and puts it on," Matheson said in an interview with the author in 1976. "It fell over his ears. I got to thinking, 'What if a man, instead of finding out he has on the wrong hat, finds out his head had shrunk? And then he goes to the doctor and finds he is shrinking all over.' "*

It was an intriguing idea, and Matheson handled it resourcefully. But the movie worked not only because its story was unique, but because its special effects were handled imaginatively. To create the illusion of a man fading away to inches, director Jack Arnold built props on a gigantic scale so that a normal-size actor would look tiny against them.

*Matheson, who has since written the script for the first-rate TV vampire movie *The Night Stalker* (1972) as well as such pictures as *Duel* (1973) with Dennis Weaver and *The Morning After* (1974) with Dick Van Dyke, originally was disappointed in the movie version of *The Incredible Shrinking Man*. Like his book, his original script did the movie as a flashback, starting with the spider scene in the cellar. The studio made him rewrite it chronologically. "I thought the picture came to life only after the doll house scene," Matheson said. "And it left out a lot of values." But, he said, he changed his mind after seeing the picture at a film museum in Los Angeles with his older son. "He pointed out how unusual the picture was for its period. It was a picaresque story, going from incident to incident. And its special effects were really well done."

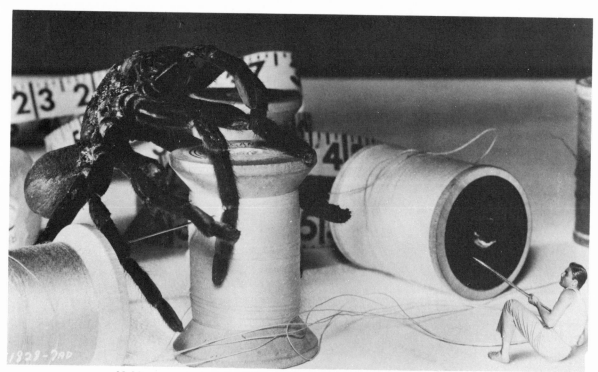

Holding a sewing needle, Williams braces to take on a menacing spider.

Every time the hero shrank, a new set had to be built and bigger props created.

Cecil B. DeMille was considered the king of the Hollywood spectacular with his huge casts, thousands of extras, and towering sets. But Arnold felt that he achieved something quite monumental, too, with a cast of less than a dozen and sets that included old paint cans and a piece of cake.

"It's all a matter of relative size," Arnold said. "A man standing next to the Great Pyramid in Egypt is dwarfed by it. But a man standing beside an orange crate can make the crate seem almost as large as the pyramid—if the man appears to be two inches tall."

To create this effect, Arnold doubled some objects in size. He built others twenty-five times as large. He constructed a few on a scale of one hundred to one. A paint can was fifty-five feet high. A wedge of stale sponge cake was eighteen feet high. A pencil, used by the hero as a spar to grasp in his flooded cellar, was twenty-one feet long.

Most of the special effects were done on a set reproducing the basement of the shrunken man's home. For a long sequence, the set had to be extended over nine sound stages. Had it been put together over a single unit, it would have measured over a mile long and nearly three-quarters of a mile wide.

There was one effect that confounded Arnold for a long time—how to produce huge drops of water. While the shrinking man was living in the cellar, drops from a leaking water unit were supposed to fall on his matchbox home, and the scene was to end with a flood. "We tried everything," Arnold said. "We got up on the top of the sound stage and rigged a device that released water a small amount at a time. But the water would spread out on the way down and look useless."

Then Arnold remembered a childhood joke he used to play with rubber condom contraceptives. "I discovered that they made dandy bombs when you fill them with water," Arnold said. "I used to drop them on top of people from windows. And I remember that they used to hold a tear-shaped form on their way down."

So Arnold filled one with water and had one of his technicians drop it from the top of the set. Sure enough, it fell in just the right shape and proportion. He ordered one hundred gross of them and set up a treadmill that released them at an increasing rate. At the end of the scene, gates of a tank were opened to release thousands of gallons of water on Grant Williams, the actor who played the shrinking man.

Weeks later, the production office called to question one item of Arnold's expense sheet. Did he really order one hundred gross of contraceptives? "I said: 'Fellows, it was such a hard picture, and we all worked so hard that we decided to have a big party at the end of it.'"

For Williams, the role of the shrinking man was a unique challenge. Much of the film was silent, and the movie depended on his ability to make outrageous situations look realistic. At the same time, there was a good deal of boredom for him to overcome as he acted out the part. Day after day, William played his big scenes in pantomime alone in front of a black velvet sheet. Later, his image was reduced and processed into scenes already shot with, for example, a cat or a spider. The effect was to give the animal and insect the illusion of great height.

"It was lonely and frustrating," said Williams, who was playing his first leading role. "On a good day we got a few seconds of usable film. Some of my best work went into it. And when it was released, I wasn't even the star. The story was."*

But that was just how it should have been, in the mind of director Arnold. A former actor, he had come to the set of The Incredible Shrinking Man after establishing himself as a craftsman in the science-fiction field.

In his book Science-Fiction Films in the Cinema, John Baxter calls Arnold "the greatest genius of American fantasy film." From 1953 to 1958, the key years of the sci-fi boom, Arnold directed such stalwart sci-fi movies as It Came from Outer Space (1953), The Creature from the Black Lagoon (1954), Tarantula (1955), and The Space Children (1958).

The most remarkable of these was The Creature from the Black Lagoon which introduced the Gill Man, a dragon-like being from another era that rises from underwater depths. Even though this was a low-budget picture, so well conceived and portrayed was this primal manfish that some fan-

*A native New Yorker, Williams started his acting career at the Barter Theatre in Abingdon, Virginia, then moved up to dramatic parts on Broadway and television. He was called to Hollywood to test for a proposed TV series to be called "The Sword." It never came into being. But Universal signed him to a long-term contract and he appeared in Showdown at Abilene (1956) and Four Girls in Town (1957) before getting his big break in Shrinking Man. However, instead of going on to greater glory, Williams faded from the scene in the 1960s after television roles in "Bonanza" and as a hard-boiled Sam Spade-type private eye. What kept him from stardom? "His looks weren't in vogue in the 1950s," Arnold said. "Grant was blond and blue-eyed, kind of too pretty to be a character actor, but not quite the picture book Rock Hudson or Robert Taylor type that Hollywood wanted at the time. He was short-changed. He never got the right parts."

137

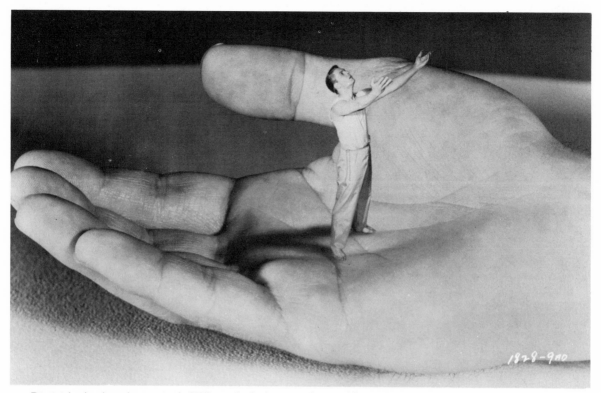

Diminished to less than an inch, Williams finds the everyday world a frightening experience. This scene contrasting him with a hand was not in the film.

tasy aficionados compared him to pantheon horror figures like Frankenstein's monster, Dracula, and the Wolf Man.

Arnold did a less-rewarding sequel—*Revenge of the Creature* (1955)—and then faded from the scene as the sci-fi period ended. He did go on to direct some good Westerns and the successful Peter Sellers film *The Mouse That Roared* (1959) and stayed active through the 1960s as an independent director-producer. But, unquestionably, this relatively obscure but specialized artist will be remembered best for *The Incredible Shrinking Man*. It is, says Baxter, "a fantasy that for intelligence and sophistication has few equals. This film is the finest Arnold made and arguably the peak of science-fiction films in its long history. . . .[It] is Arnold's masterpiece."

As the movie opens, Scott Carey (Williams), once a six-footer, is concerned and puzzled by his slowly shrinking stature following his boating trip. At first, his wife Louise (Randy Stuart)* passes it off as simply a weight loss. Then, one day, Carey asks her to kiss him. When she does, he points out that

she no longer has to stretch to reach him. "I'm getting smaller, Lou, every day," Carey says.

His physician, Dr. Thomas Silver (Ray Bailey), at first skeptical, eventually traces Scott's problem to his exposure to what apparently was a radioactive fog. Somehow, the radioactivity has reversed his chemical growth processes. There is no precedent for this, the doctor says. No matter where Scott goes for help or what specialist he sees, medical science is baffled.

Soon Scott has become less than five feet tall. Sensitive about his diminishing height, he stays home from his job, then quits altogether. Out of work and short of cash, he sells his story to a magazine. Within weeks he becomes known to the nation as a freak celebrity. Headline writers name him "The Incredible Shrinking Man." Reporters besiege him, and TV crews and crowds surround his house, trying to get a glimpse of Carey, now only four feet tall.

His wife tries to stick by him, but it is obvious that their marriage is gradually deteriorating. This is conveyed symbolically when Carey's wedding ring slips off his diminishing finger. There is a ray of hope when doctors give him what they think is an antidote, and Scott finds brief happiness with a circus midget. However, he leaves her when he starts shrinking again.

*Miss Stuart, the "Hubba Hubba Girl" on Jack Carson's radio show, had supporting roles in *I Was a Male War Bride* (1949), *Dancing in the Dark* (1949), and *Stella* (1950). She later went into television, appearing in hundreds of shows including the popular series "This Is the Life" and "Biff Baker, USA."

SC ⑬ PAN SCOTT OVER TO WATER HEATER

SC ⑬ SCOTT AT BASE OF WATER HEATER

WATER DROP →

SC ⑭ SCOTT CATCHES WATER AS IT DROPS DOWN

Director Jack Arnold's storyboard showing Scott Carey reduced to insect size, crossing his basement to a leaking water heater which threatens to flood him out.

Back at home, and tormented by his plight, Scott finds solace only in his loyal house cat. Then, a day comes when the cat becomes something more than a pet. Down to a few inches in height, Scott starts living in a doll's house. When his wife is out shopping, the cat tilts it over, tries to catch Scott and drives him into the cellar. When Louise returns, she finds the wrecked doll's house and shreds of Scott's clothes, and she assumes that the cat has eaten him.

In the basement, trapped by stairs that rise like sheer canyon walls, Scott is in another world. His voice is now too small to attract his wife's attention. And so, like Robinson Crusoe, he resigns himself to keeping alive with whatever resources he can find.

No desert island castaway ever faced so bleak an environment. A water leak nearly drowns him, and a hungry black spider, looking as big as a dinosaur, attacks him. But, using a straight-pin for a lance

and an enormous pair of scissors, Scott fights for his life and wins.

As the weeks pass, he survives by making a home in a matchbox and eating a huge leftover piece of cake.

The shrinking goes on inexorably. Now, down to the size of a mite, Carey is so small that he crawls through the basement mesh window screen. In the outside world, Carey looks up at the stars, swallowed up amidst the standing forest-like grass.

As the picture ends in a long and moving monologue, it is apparent that despite his Job-like suffering, he has gradually reconciled himself to his fate. The least of God's creatures is important in the infinite scheme of things. Nothing—no matter how small—is created to live a meaningless life.

A newspaper ad for *The Incredible Shrinking Man* shows Grant Williams battling his pet house cat with a sewing needle.

139

The final scene has become one of the most discussed sequences of all science-fiction films. Walking out into the vast reaches of his unknown world, Carey says: "What was I? Still a human being? Or the man of the future? If there were other bursts of radiation, other clouds drifting across seas and continents, would other beings follow me into this vast new world. [I was] so close to the infinitesimal and the infinite.

"But, suddenly, I knew they were really the two ends of the same concept. The unbelievably small and the unbelievably vast eventually meet—like the closing of a gigantic circle. I looked up as if somehow I would grasp the heavens, the universe, worlds beyond number. God's silver tapestry spread across the night. And in that moment, I knew the answer to the riddle of the infinite. I had thought in terms of man's own limited dimension. I had presumed on nature. That existence begins and ends is man's conception, not nature's.

"And I felt my body dwindling, melting, becoming nothing. My fears melted away. And in their place came acceptance. All this vast majesty of creation, it had to mean something. And then I meant something, too. Yes, smaller than the smallest, I meant something too. To God, there is no zero. I still existed."

Some critics felt unprepared for the metaphysical finale. They expected the movie to end with the discovery of an antidote that would restore the shrinking man to his normal height. Said one: "A curious pseudo-poetical, semi-religious ending is a shock, a frustrating evasion of the solution that the strange little film demands." Another said the picture had a "very contrived ending."

How does screenwriter Matheson answer that?

"You had to do something with the hero," he said. "You couldn't let him just disappear. That would be nothing. I wanted to say, 'There are universes within universes.' And I don't think that was inconsistent with the story."

But, in fact, it was director Arnold who wrote that soliloquy. In a 1978 interview with the author, Arnold said that the studio wanted an upbeat ending. To achieve it, executives wanted the shrinking man to grow up.

But Arnold said he told them "if you do that, you may as well throw the picture away."

"Well," they said, "you can't let him die."

So, they accepted a compromise—the closing speech that Arnold said he wrote. "I felt it was an upbeat ending. . . . He [the shrinking man] had taken on an almost Christlike appearance. And it seemed an almost religious atmosphere. . . . [He was saying that] all life is in the eyes of the beholder. There is no difference between the finite and the infinite. Life is a circle. It completes itself in a whole."

My own feeling is that the ending is somewhat jarring. Nothing in the movie leads up to such a philosophical monologue. Yet it is a moving and touching sequence, and, despite its lack of connection with the rest of the story, it works.

Matheson said that *The Incredible Shrinking Man* was a box office hit. "It made more money for Universal than *To Hell and Back* (1955) and *Away All Boats* (1956)," he said. These were the studio's previous big-time moneymakers of the 1950s.

"They had a lot of expensive sets left over and they asked me to write a sequel. I did and they called it *The Fantastic Little Girl*. It told about his wife getting small and going down to join her husband. But for some reason, it was never made."

140

Invasion of the Body Snatchers

Newspaper ad for *Invasion of the Body Snatchers*, a B-movie that has become a science-fiction classic.

Invasion of the Body Snatchers (1956)

Directed by Don Siegel. Screenplay by Daniel Mainwaring, based on a novel by Jack Finney serialized in *Collier's* magazine. Camera, Ellsworth Fredericks. Editor, Robert S. Eisen. Music, Carmen Dragon. Art director, Ted Haworth. Produced by Walter Wanger. Released by Allied Artists. 80 minutes.

Dr. Miles Bennell	*Kevin McCarthy*
Becky Driscoll	*Dana Wynter*
Dr. Dan Kaufman	*Larry Gates*
Theodora Velichec	*Carolyn Jones*
Jack Velichec	*King Donovan*
Nick Grivett	*Ralph Dumke*
Sally	*Jean Willes*
Wilma Lentz	*Virginia Christine*
Ira Lentz	*Tom Fadden*
Grandma Grimaldi	*Beatrice Maude*
Jimmy Grimaldi	*Bobby Clark*
Charlie Buckholtz	*Sam Peckinpah*
Dr. Harvey Bassitt	*Richard Deacon*
Dr. Hill	*Whit Bissell*
Policeman	*Guy Way*

(United Artists released a new version of the film in 1978. Directed by Phillip Kaufman, it starred Donald Sutherland, playing a health inspector instead of a doctor, and Brooke Adams as his assistant. Leonard Nimoy had the role of the psychiatrist. The picture's locale was San Francisco instead of rural and small-town California.)

Kevin McCarthy (right) and King Donovan (second right) are caught in the act as they break into a house to search for mind-sapping seed pods in a basement. Larry Gates, playing a doctor, is at left. The actor with the rifle is not identified.

In the middle of the night, a psychiatrist hurries to a hospital emergency room in the fictitious town of Santa Mira, California. Nurses take him to a disheveled and distraught patient who has been raving. "I'm not crazy," he shouts. "Make them listen to me before it's too late."

The psychiatrist orders attendants to release the man. The patient says he is a physician, too—Dr. Miles Bennell (Kevin McCarthy). Then he calms down and begins explaining the weird series of events that brought him to the hospital.

"It started—for me, it started—last Thursday.... I hurried home from a medical convention I was attending. At first glance, everything looked the same. It wasn't. Something evil had taken possession of the town. . . ."

So begins *Invasion of the Body Snatchers,* an unheralded B-movie that many serious film critics, including Andrew Sarris and Peter Bogdanovich, have come to rate as one of the few authentic science-fiction classics. "A catch-penny title," said Leslie Halliwell in his encyclopedic book, *The Film-goer's Companion,* "obscures the most subtle film in the science-fiction cycle."

The picture was produced in a decade that had such first-rate sci-fi fantasies as *The Thing* (1951), *It Came from Outer Space* (1953), *Forbidden Planet* (1956), and *The Incredible Shrinking Man* (1957). But *Invasion of the Body Snatchers* achieved the greatest latter-day success not only because its plot exists on two levels—as do some of the others—but because its insights directly relate to a contemporary era in America.

On the surface, the movie tells the story of giant seed pods, strange plants that appear mysteriously on earth with the power to drain all emotional life from people. The plants take over the mind and destroy individual feeling until each person becomes the soulless carbon copy of his neighbor.

Since the film came out in the midst of the McCarthy era, many interpreted it as a commentary on the insidious spread of communism. European as well as American film writers subscribed to this theory. One Italian critic, Ernesto G. Laura, wrote that the plants represented the idea of "communism which gradually takes possession of a normal person, leaving him outwardly unchanged but transformed within."

143

But director Don Siegel had a much broader idea in mind.* To Siegel, the film was saying that the "majority of people, unfortunately, are pods, existing without any intellectual aspirations and incapable of love." Given that state of mind, the masses lack the courage and strength to combat any popular movement, however evil.

Because of the defeatism inherent in the theme, Siegel had to fight the studio, Allied Artists, to produce the picture. He won, but not without compromising by adding a prologue (already cited) and epilogue to give the story a happy ending. In the original version, Siegel's ending had Dr. Bennell running onto the highway trying to get help. No one will stop because he seems like a drunk or a madman. That, of course, left the audience with an uneasy feeling that the pod people would inevitably take over the country, and eventually the world.

However, in the final version, the doctor's story is finally verified, and police start fanning out to contain the hostile invaders.

The problem, as Siegel recalled it, was that the studio misunderstood the audiences' reaction at three sneak previews. "They reacted in an extraordinary way, just as I'd hoped," Siegel said. "They started out by laughing. But then the tension increased and they ended up thoroughly scared. . . . Having heard the audiences laugh, the studio thought that the public was reacting against the film, and didn't realize what the laughter really meant.

"I was opposed to making any changes. But [producer] Walter Wanger, who was on my side, persuaded me that it was better to do them myself in the same spirit as the rest of the film. Someone was going to make the changes anyway, and they might very well compromise what we'd already planned and shot. So I decided to add the prologue and epilogue."

Even with the artificial ending, the film still has a chilling impact. Unfortunately, its critical reception was almost nil. Few movie critics then paid attention to pictures made on skimpy budgets without top stars and released with little publicity. Siegel, who wanted to call the film simply *Sleep No More,*** also felt that its hyped-up title did not help attract serious attention. Nevertheless, as the years passed, it started to interest movie buffs and student groups until, by its own sheer momentum, it won recognition.

*Other Siegel directing credits include *Riot in Cell Block 11* (1954), *The Killers* (1964), *Madigan* (1968), and *Dirty Harry* (1971).

**From Hamlet's "To be or not to be" soliloquy. The line is: "To die: to sleep; no more."

But back to the movie.

As Dr. Bennell recounts his story, he recalls how his nurse Sally (Jean Willes) had called him back to town because of what appeared to be a curious epidemic. She tells him he has an office full of patients.

"What's the matter?" the doctor asks curiously.

"They wouldn't say," the nurse says, as puzzled as he is. "Usually people can't talk enough."

On the way to town, they nearly hit young Jimmy Grimaldi (Bobby Clark) running away from his farm house. Sally says that his grandmother had been in to see Dr. Bennell last week. At the office, they find, oddly, that nearly all appointments have been cancelled.

But Bennell is at last cheered by a visit by Becky Driscoll (Dana Wynter), his former sweetheart who is now divorced as he is himself. "I guess that makes us lodge brothers now," Miles quips. "Except that I'm paying dues while you collect them." However, Becky has come on business. She tells him her cousin Wilma Lentz seems to be having a delusion. "You know her uncle Ira?" Becky asks. "She's got herself thinking he isn't her uncle. She thinks he's an imposter."

McCarthy, who made his film debut in the movie adaptation of *Death of a Salesman* (1952), was playing what would become his most famous role. Miss Wynter, a dark-haired British beauty with a cool, aristocratic air, was a worthy co-star.

Back at his office, Miles finds that Jimmy Grimaldi's grandmother (Beatrice Maude) has brought in the boy because he has become agitated and upset. "It's my daughter-in-law," the grandmother says. "He's got the crazy idea she isn't his mother."

After Miles gives him a sedative, he goes to see Becky's cousin, Wilma (Virginia Christine). She says her uncle looks and talks the way he used to, but there's something missing. "There's no emotion," she says, "just the pretense of it."

Outwardly Miles does not appear alarmed. He tells Wilma that no one could possibly impersonate her uncle without many people—including himself—recognizing differences. "The trouble is inside you," Miles says.

But behind his professional veneer, Miles is troubled. "Sick people who couldn't wait to see me, then suddenly were all right," he mutters to himself. "A boy who said his mother wasn't his mother. A woman who said her uncle wasn't her uncle."

Later, when Miles takes Becky to dinner, they run into Dr. Dan Kaufman (Larry Gates), a psychiatrist who says he has encountered the same

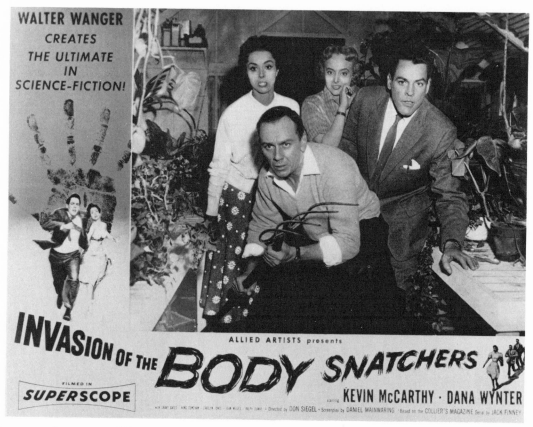

WALTER WANGER CREATES THE ULTIMATE IN SCIENCE-FICTION!

ALLIED ARTISTS presents

INVASION OF THE BODY SNATCHERS

FILMED IN SUPERSCOPE

KEVIN McCARTHY · DANA WYNTER

Directed by DON SIEGEL · Screenplay by DANIEL MAINWARING · Based on the COLLIER'S MAGAZINE Serial by JACK FINNEY

Donovan advances carefully on a budding pod ripening in his greenhouse. He destroys it with a pitchfork but another soon crops up to take its place. In the rear are: Dana Wynter, Carolyn Jones, and Kevin McCarthy.

cases. However, Kaufman doesn't seem concerned. He ascribes them to a kind of freak neurosis, perhaps a mass hysteria, possibly caused by worry about what's going on in the world.

Jokingly, Miles tells Becky that he hopes they don't catch whatever it is going around. "I'd hate to wake up some morning and find that you weren't you," he quips. His words will prove to be prophetic.

Their dinner is interrupted by an emergency call from Jack Velichec (King Donovan), a close friend. At Jack's house, he shows Miles and Becky a strange corpse-like figure—its smooth mannequin face only half-formed. It has all the features of a human, but no details. "It's like the first impression that's stamped in a coin," Jack says. "It isn't finished."

Miles suggests that Jack leave the corpse alone until morning and see what changes, if any, occur. He drops off Becky, then goes home. But before he gets to bed, he hears Jack and his wife (Carolyn Jones) pounding at his door, nearly hysterical. They say the corpse has turned into Jack's double right down to a cut in his hand. Miles quickly calls Dr. Kaufman, and then remembers that Becky's

father had acted strangely as he emerged from the cellar earlier that night. Miles drops everything, speeds to Becky's home, and creeps into the cellar. There he finds her half-formed double.

Upstairs in Becky's bedroom, Miles is unable to awaken her, so he carries her off to his own home where she revives. Dr. Kaufman has arrived but is skeptical of the story. Then they all go together to Jack's house—only to find the corpse gone. The same thing happens at Becky's home. "Now you see it, now you don't," says Dr. Kaufman jokingly.

The weird goings-on seem a little less spooky when a cop comes by and describes finding a male body in a burning haystack with its fingerprints burnt off by acid. Kaufman feels that all their minds, influenced by mass hysteria, have simply played tricks on them.

The next day, Miles gets some peace of mind. He finds that Jimmy Grimaldi's and Wilma Lentz's troubles have vanished. For a while, Miles, Becky, and Jack and his wife forget their collective nightmare. But during a cookout at Miles' home, they discover two giant seed pods in the hothouse. The pods open and out sprout two blank corpses.

They slowly begin forming the features of Miles and Becky.

This is one of the few instances in the picture where director Siegel has used special effects—usually a predominant element in science-fiction movies. In fact, Siegel deliberately steered clear of this overused sci-fi device. This is one reason why his movie is so fresh and engrossing decades after it was made.

Another reason that it stands up is its expertly orchestrated pace. The action never slows down. It begins slowly, and then, like a train building steam, rushes on breathlessly—ending in an enthralling chase sequence.

"When they're finished, what will happen to our bodies?" Becky asks.

There must be a difference, Miles says. Wilma and Jimmy had noticed that difference. Becky admits she did, too—her father. "That's what he was doing in the cellar, placing one of them," Miles says.

But where do they come from? So much has been discovered recently, Miles theorizes, that anything is possible. "Maybe they're the result of atomic radiation on plant life or animal life. Some weird alien organism—a mutation of some kind. . . .

Whatever it is, whatever intelligence or instinct it is that governs the forming of human flesh and blood out of thin air, is fantastically powerful. . . . All that body in your cellar needed was a mind."

"They have to be destroyed," Jack's wife says.

"They will be—every one of them," Miles says. "We're going to have to search every house in town."

He rushes to the phone to call the FBI. Curiously, the operator says that there is no answer. Since Miles knows that the FBI is open day and night, he realizes this can only mean that the telephone office has been taken over.

Their only hope is to get out of town, and so they split up. Miles and Becky drive off in one car. Jack and his wife leave in another. At a gas station, Miles notices the attendant closing the trunk. He stops further down the road and finds that the man has planted two seed pods in the trunk.

Hopeful that his nurse Sally can be rescued, too, he pulls up at her house—only to find her putting a pod next to her baby's crib. Back on the road again, they find that police have put out an all-points alarm for their car. In desperation, they drive to Miles' office to hide, hoping that Jack has gotten through.

Wynter and McCarthy walk slowly as they cross the street, trying to appear like pod people who have lost all emotion. But when a dog darts in front of a car, Wynter screams.

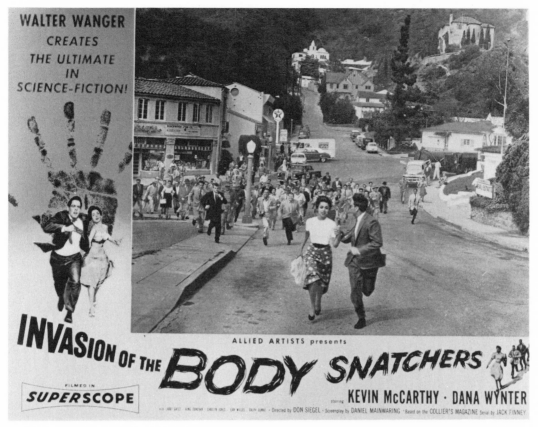

Wynter and McCarthy run for their lives chased by the townspeople, whose minds have been taken over by the seed pods.

As the hours slowly pass, they take stimulants to stay awake. They know their minds will be changed in their least resistant state—while they sleep. Outside at daybreak, they see trucks loading up pods, apparently freshly harvested, to distribute them to distant towns. "It's like a malignant disease spreading through the whole country," Miles says.

Now Miles realizes that there is no one left he can trust except Becky. The whole town has been taken over. It is a chilling feeling, but not something totally new.

"In my practice, I've seen how people have allowed their humanity to draw away," Miles says. "Only it happens slowly instead of all at once. They don't seem to mind. All of us—we harden our hearts, grow callous. Only when we have to fight to stay human do we realize how precious it is, how dear."

Suddenly they hear Jack's voice in the hall. He and Dr. Kaufman enter the office. Miles can immediately sense something wrong. Both have changed over. "Once you understand, you'll be grateful," says Jack. While they talk, a policeman is putting pods in the next room to grow into duplicates of Miles and Becky.

Kaufman explains that it's all for the best. "Less than a month ago, Santa Mira was like any other town—people with nothing but problems. Then out of the sky came a solution. Seeds drifting through space for years took root in a farmer's field. From the seeds came pods which had the power to reproduce themselves in the exact likeness of any form of life. There's no pain. Suddenly, while you're asleep, they'll absorb your minds, your memories. And you'll be reborn into an untroubled world."

"Where everyone's the same?" Miles asks.

"Exactly."

Miles also learns that the new beings have no need for love. They have no emotions or feelings, only the instinct to survive. "Desire, ambition, faith—without them life is so simple," Dr. Kaufman says.

But Miles is still determined to fight for his freedom. He pushes Jack and Dr. Kaufman to the floor and jabs them with a hypodermic filled with a strong sedative. A cop bursts in while they are struggling. Becky plunges another needle into him. Now the way to the street is clear.

Miles' plan is to try to make it to the main high-

McCarthy reels from car to car on the highway, trying to warn drivers of the pod menace. Director Don Siegel wanted to end the film here with McCarthy turning to the camera, pointing to the audience and saying, "You're next." But studio heads opted for a happy ending.

way. "Keep your eyes wide and blank," he cautions Becky as they begin walking slowly amidst the pod people outside. "Show no interest or excitement." At first, they attract no attention. But then a dog darts in front of a car, and Becky can't avoid screaming.

Miles grabs Becky's hand and starts running out of town, heading up into a hilly wooded area, with police and scores of townspeople following them. In the distance, the town's siren blasts menacingly.

Weary and exhausted, Miles and Becky finally come upon an abandoned mine. They find some loose floor boards in a passageway and hide beneath them until the mob has passed. In the dark, Becky can't keep her eyes open any longer. She falls asleep ever so briefly. Even so, the lapse is death to her soul. When Miles kisses her, he draws away from her unresponsive lips. A memorable closeup shows Miles' look of utter fright.* "He's in here," Becky, his sweetheart of a moment ago,

screams like a harridan. "Get him!"

Now Miles is running again. Suddenly there is a break in the woods and he finds himself on a crowded highway. The mob stops short as Miles threads his way between the lines of traffic. "Wait. Let him go," says one man (Sam Peckinpah, later to be a famous director). "No one will believe him."

Reeling between the cars, and with headlights streaming in his face, Miles shouts: "Help! Wait! Stop and listen to me! These people who're coming after me are not human." Motorists take him for a drunk and keep going.

Miles jumps on the back of one truck, only to find it is hauling seed pods. He jumps back on the highway, again trying to summon help. "Look, you fools. You're in danger. Can't you see? They're after you. They're after all of us. Our wives, our children, everyone. . . ."

Then, turning and pointing directly into the camera, Miles cries: "You're next!"

This is the stunning finale to Siegel's version.**

*Director Siegel took particular pride in this sequence. "What I thought was quite delicious was our playing with the fact that as a pod you don't feel any passion," Siegel said. "So when he tries to kiss her in a non-pod way, and she is a limp fish, he knows immediately she is a pod."

**Many TV stations and student film groups end the movie here, cutting out the tacked-on finale as well as the added opening sequence.

But, intent on an upbeat ending, the studio added another scene that took the movie back into the emergency room. There, after hearing Miles' fantastic tale, the psychiatrist steps out into the hallway.

"Will psychiatry help?" another doctor asks. "He's as mad as a March hare."

The psychiatrist starts to go back to the emergency area. But as he does, an accident victim is carried in. "We had to dig him out from under the most peculiar thing I ever saw," the attendant says.

"What thing?" the psychiatrist stops and turns.

"They looked like great big seed pods."

"Where was the truck coming from?"

"Santa Mira."

Without another word, the psychiatrist rushes into the emergency room. He orders the two policemen there to sound an all-points alarm to block all highways. Then he picks up the phone. "Operator. Get me the FBI. . . . Yes, it's an emergency." As he talks excitedly, the camera focuses on Miles. He is leaning against the wall, drained of all strength, but relieved that his story has at last been vindicated.

I Want to Live!

Susan Hayward as the party girl and convicted murderer Barbara Graham, whose execution raised questions about the cruelty of capital punishment. Hayward's performance won an Oscar.

I Want to Live!
(1958)

Directed by Robert Wise. Screenplay by Nelson Gidding and Don Mankiewicz, based on newspaper articles by Ed Montgomery and letters of Barbara Graham. Music by John Mandel. Camera, Lionel Lindon. Editor, William Hornbeck. Jazz played by Gerry Mulligan, Shelly Manne, Art Farmer, Bud Shank, Red Mitchell, Frank Rosolino, Pete Jolly. Producer, Walter Wanger. A Figaro Production released by United Artists. 120 minutes.

Barbara Graham	Susan Hayward*
Ed Montgomery	Simon Oakland
Peg	Virginia Vincent
Carl Palmberg	Theodore Bikel
Henry Graham	Wesley Lau
Emmet Perkins	Philip Coolidge
Jack Santo	Lou Krugman
Bruce King	James Philbrook
District Attorney	Bartlett Robinson
Richard G. Tibrow	Gage Clark
Al Matthews	Joe De Santis
Father Devers	John Marley
San Quentin Warden	Raymond Bailey
Nurse	Alice Backes
Matron	Gertrude Flynn
Sergeant	Russell Thorson
Captain	Dabbs Greer
Sergeant	Stafford Repp
Lieutenant	Gavin MacLeod
Corona Warden	Olive Blakeney
Ben Miranda	Peter Breck
Rita	Marion Marshall

*Academy Award Winner.

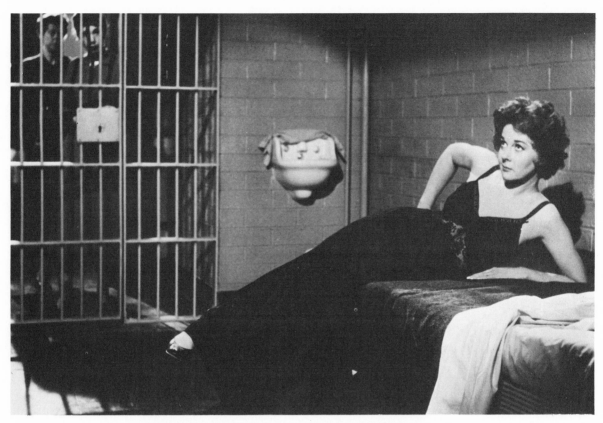

Hayward in a familiar place (for Barbara Graham)—a jail cell.

In San Quentin's gas chamber, a prison guard straps thirty-two-year-old Barbara Graham into the execution chair. A sleep mask hides her eyes from a dozen witnesses who have come to see the sulphur-tongued party girl's last moments. Two agonizing stays of execution have jangled her nerves but they have not broken her spirit.

"Take a deep breath," the guard whispers. "It's easier that way." The woman looks up scornfully. "How would you know?"

This is the next-to-last sequence from *I Want to Live!,* the most impassioned film about capital punishment to come out of Hollywood. The 1950s was the ideal decade for such a picture. The case of Caryl Chessman, who languished on death row for eleven years while he unsuccessfully fought his death sentence through the courts, focused national attention on the death penalty. But producer Walter Wanger felt that a woman's battle for life would more clearly dramatize the horror of a state execution.

Wanger was drawn to the Barbara Graham case by a series of newspaper articles by Ed Montgomery. As a reporter for the *San Francisco Examiner,* Montgomery said that he had heard key parts of the testimony although he had not covered the trial. He was convinced of Mrs. Graham's guilt

then, but subsequent evidence and death row interviews with her changed his mind.

The crime for which she and two male hoodlums were tried was a brutal one. Mrs. Mabel Monahan, a widow whose nephew was a Las Vegas gambler, was thought to have a big money cache hidden in her suburban Los Angeles home. The gang— composed of Mrs. Graham, Jack Santo, Emmett Perkins, and a third man—broke in to get it. According to testimony at the trial, while the men ransacked the house, Mrs. Graham stuffed Mrs. Monahan's head into a shopping bag and pistol-whipped her to death. Mrs. Graham maintained that she was innocent, but one member of the gang turned state's evidence and named her as the slayer.

What made the film stand out above all previous death house movies was its unrelenting portrayal of Mrs. Graham's death. Nothing was spared to show every detail of the execution, from the preparation of the gas chamber with cyanide pellets to the cloud of lethal gas sweeping through the air-tight room.

The movie even showed how the prison doctor examines the condemned before ordering the gas blown from the chamber. From outside the chamber, he listens for heartbeats through a special extension stethoscope hooked up to a vest worn under the condemned person's clothing. The eleventh-hour postponements made the death ritual even more gripping. The last stay came minutes before Mrs. Graham was to die as she was about to enter the gas chamber.

In the end, despite the cruel nature of the crime, everyone involved in her death—the warden, the prison guards, the nurse, the priest—sympathized with the hard-boiled brunette and hoped for a reprieve. And that is exactly the effect the picture had on movie audiences.

Barbara's alleged innocence was a matter that became more controversial after her death. Nevertheless, so grim was the gas chamber scene that the British Board of Censors refused to allow details of the execution to be shown. The board said that an execution was not fit material for entertainment.

However, the movie had more than sharp realism going for it. It also had the searing performance of Susan Hayward, a fiery redhead who had gotten four Academy Award nominations but no Oscars.* Born Edythe Marrener in Brooklyn, she first gained Hollywood's attention after she appeared on a *Saturday Evening Post* cover.

David O. Selznick spotted her picture and invited her to Hollywood. His studio gave Miss Hayward several screen tests, including one for the role of Scarlett O'Hara in *Gone with the Wind* (1939). She was the right age for the part—only nineteen—and resembled Vivien Leigh. But there was already a veneer of toughness in her screen presence.

Instead, she appeared in a number of minor roles, including a small part in *Beau Geste* (1939), starring Gary Cooper. Her first acclaim came two years later in a character role in *Adam Had Four Sons.*

Then she went on to do more than fifty films, ranging from *Reap the Wild Wind* (1942) to *The Hairy Ape* (1944) and *The Snows of Kilimanjaro* (1952). Though she went on to stardom, she never achieved the stature of other female heavies like Bette Davis and Barbara Stanwyck. This may have been because although she was aggressive and gutsy, she at the same time lacked a distinctive and individualized personality.

Nevertheless, she got her share of strong, sym-

*Deborah Kerr holds the dubious distinction of being the only six-time Oscar nominee who came up empty-handed in every competition. Champion nominees are Katharine Hepburn (eleven) and Bette Davis (ten). Hepburn won three times. Davis won twice. Greer Garson and Norma Shearer each had six nominations, and each went on to win one Academy Award. Deadlocked at five nominations each are Ingrid Bergman, Olivia de Havilland, Jennifer Jones, and Irene Dunne. All but Miss Dunne eventually won an Oscar.

pathetic leading roles. Her Oscar nominations came for her performance as an alcoholic in *Smash-Up* (1947); in the romantic drama *My Foolish Heart* (1949); as Jane Froman, the singer, in *With a Song in My Heart* (1952); and as Lillian Roth, the singer-actress who overcame alcoholism, in *I'll Cry Tomorrow* (1955). Her also-ran Oscar status finally ended with yet another real-life part, the Graham role.

As the movie opens, Barbara Graham is working as a prostitute in San Francisco's tenderloin district. From the outset, the film makes no effort to gloss over Barbara's lurid lifestyle. In real life, she was an amoral person who would not hesitate to indulge in any form of crime or vice as long as it was exciting. Some said it was easier to say what she was not. She was not a drug addict, and, according to a psychologist, she was not capable of physical violence.

In San Francisco, her sordid life brings her into contact with small-time gangsters. She soon is convicted of perjury for providing a false alibi for two hoods who had robbed a delicatessen. Her sentence was part of a long record that traced back to reform school.

After her release, she joins an unsavory pair of gamblers—Perkins (Philip Coolidge) and Santo (Lou Krugman). Her job is to steer likely looking prospects into card games, a ploy that quickly fattens her bankroll. One day Barbara breaks away from her underworld life to take a handsome bartender, Henry Graham (Wesley Lau), as her fourth husband. But Graham has a weakness—narcotics —and after a child is born, their marriage goes on the rocks. One day he demands their last $10 for a fix. Barbara flings the money at him and tells him to get out. Broke and desperate, and with bill collectors pounding at her door, Barbara rejoins Santo and Perkins.

It is here that the picture is at its weakest in terms of its documentary nature. Graham resumes her underworld life, but the movie fails to show any of it. Nor does it contain a single sequence of the Monahan slaying. Instead, we see the cops tail Barbara one night on her way to the gang's hideout. When she goes in, floodlights illuminate the house and a police loudspeaker orders them all to come out with their hands up. Barbara walks out last, defiantly waving her baby son's toy tiger. She swaggers into the glare of the lights and growls for the benefit of the crowd. Newspapers dub her "The Tiger Woman." Later they call her "Bloody Babs."

At a San Francisco police precinct, she learns that the police have charged her and her companions with the Monahan slaying. The arrest is a

Charged with murder, Hayward tells her lawyer (Gage Clark) that she has an airtight alibi. It turns out that she has badly miscalculated.

turning point in Barbara's life. Bruce King (James Philbrook), a third man accused of being in on the crime, turns state's evidence and names Barbara as the killer. Her alibi is that she was home when the murder occurred. But that alibi is flimsy because only her husband can verify it, and since he is a dope addict, his testimony is virtually worthless.

In despair, Barbara agrees to "buy" an alibi from a friend of a cellmate. The friend visits her in jail. However, before agreeing to the deal, he insists that she tell him where she really was on the night of the murder. When she says that she was at home, he accuses her of lying and starts balking on the deal. She offers to double his money, but he turns her down. Finally, seeing no other way out, she tells him she was at the Monahan house.

As the trial begins, the evidence piles up against Barbara. King testifies that Barbara battered Mrs. Monahan with a gun butt while he, Santo, and Perkins searched the house. Barbara is relying entirely on her purchased alibi, but when the man appears on the stand, she is shocked to learn that he is really a policeman. The cop, Police Officer Miranda (Peter Breck), testifies that Barbara admitted to him that she was at the scene of the crime.

With her case in shambles, Barbara is led crying from the courtroom. "Have you anything to say for TV?" a newsman asks. "I'm innocent," she says. "What about the testimony of Bruce King and Police Officer Miranda?" "I'm completely innocent," she cries. "I was home with my family that night. They'll all die violently—the spies, the liars, all the ones who want me dead. I'm innocent." (Ironically, in real life, within three years after her execution, four principals in the trial were dead—the man who turned state's evidence, the D.A. who prosecuted her, the judge who passed sentence on her, and the warden who carried out her execution.)

After nearly six hours of deliberation, the jury comes in with the verdict—guilty as charged. It makes no recommendation for mercy.

Remanded to the women's prison at Corona, Barbara begins the long wait for the gas chamber. Meanwhile, her lawyer starts her appeal. He also brings noted psychologist Carl Palmberg (Theodore Bikel) into the case. Palmberg examines her and diagnoses her as a compulsive liar with no regard for law and order, but he is convinced that she cannot kill. He feels that the strategy of Santo and Perkins was to "keep her out front and say that she did it," thinking that the state would not execute a

Wesley Lau, playing Barbara Graham's heroin-addicted husband, begs for money for a fix. Hayward gives him her last dollar, then tells him not to come back.

woman, and if the state would not send the actual killer to the gas chamber, their lives would also be spared.

Palmberg also finds that Barbara is left-handed, although King testified that she hit Mrs. Monahan with a gun in her right hand. Palmberg's findings are beginning to rally forces to her defense. Even reporter Montgomery changes his mind and joins a campaign to free her.

When her state appeal eventually fails, her attorneys take the case to the U.S. Supreme Court. But then Barbara gets a double setback. First, Palmberg, her chief defender, dies suddenly. Then, the high court refuses to review her case.

The final scenes are the movie's most memorable. She is shackled and taken from Corona to the death house at San Quentin. There, while guards prepare the gas chamber, a priest hears her confession and gives Extreme Unction to her in her small cell.

Barbara seems reconciled to her fate, but her calmness is shattered when her lawyer's last-ditch court efforts to save her causes her execution to be postponed once, and then again. At one point, a

phone rings calling off the execution as she is being led into the chamber. "Why do they torture me?" she cries in anguish.

But nothing can stop the execution. In the cramped gas chamber, guards strap Barbara in the execution chair. Moments later, glass pellets containing cyanide drop behind her from beneath the chair and break in a chamber of sulfuric acid. The two chemicals mix and form lethal hydrocyanic acid gas. Barbara struggles as the deadly clouds swirl around her. Then her head lolls and she loses consciousness. Death comes within minutes.

Some critics felt that Hayward's performance, however intense, was monotonous and one-dimensional, but it made a profound impression on the public and it won her her only Oscar.

That same year, *Cavalier* magazine called the movie a Hollywood "hoax." It said that the film turned Barbara into a "celluloid Joan of Arc," leaving the impression that she was innocent. In fact, it printed a deposition from a deputy district attorney in Los Angeles who said that the lawyer in Barbara's appeal tried to persuade Wanger to show that Barbara was truly guilty according to the

Hayward screams defiantly as she is led to her prison cell following her murder conviction.

evidence at her trial, but Wanger would not agree. The article also said that the movie left out the testimony of two prominent characters whose appearance at the trial played an important part in convicting her.

"What emerges from the silver screen," *Cavalier* said, "is a carefully loaded series of arguments, scenes, and progressively shocking sequences. But it is completely one-sided in arguing that she was completely innocent of any complicity in the brutal murder and that she was framed and perjured and entrapped into the gas chamber, that the penalty was far worse than the crime it punished, a crime the viewer will seriously doubt she committed."

Nevertheless, the movie unquestionably contributed to the public's awareness of capital punishment and made a strong case to put an end to state executions.

La Strada

Giulietta Masina, wife of director Federico Fellini, as the simple-minded Gelsomina.

La Strada* (The Road)
(1956)

Directed by Federico Fellini. Story and screenplay by Fellini and Tullio Pinelli. Director of photography, Otello Martelli. Editors, Leo Cattozzo and Lina Caterini. Music, Nino Rota. Produced by Dino De Laurentiis and Carlo Ponti. A Trans-Lux Release. 115 minutes.

Zampano	*Anthony Quinn*
Gelsomina	*Giulietta Masina*
Matto (The Fool)	*Richard Basehart*
Colombaioni	*Aldo Silvani*

and
Marcella Rovere
Livia Venturini

*Academy Award Winner for Best Foreign Language Film and grand prize winner at the Venice International Film Festival.

The strongman Zampano (Anthony Quinn) buys Gelsomina from her poor family to assist him in his traveling act. Here, he shows trinkets to Gelsomina's brother and sister while she waits with her mother.

A traveling strongman comes to a seaside town to find a replacement for his female assistant who has died. From her poverty-stricken mother, he buys a second daughter, a happy but half-witted girl. She becomes his slave, serving as cook and concubine. He also teaches her some clown routines to dress up his pitiful act, and off they go on the road.

So begins *La Strada*, a movie as profound and unique as it is simple and poignant.

If the film seems to exist on many levels, it is not surprising, for its director, Federico Fellini, is a man of many qualities. Basically, he is an open and direct filmmaker. When he did *La Strada*, he had no office of his own, nor did he even have a room in his apartment that could serve as one. Instead, he used his car—in which he frequently took long solitary drives.

Yet his reputation is that of a multifaceted thinker, and the meaning of his movies is often veiled in mystery. Like Bergman, he has originated his own symbolism, and his self-conscious flamboyance makes his creative efforts doubly difficult.

However, Fellini says that whether an audience understands his intentions is not the most important thing to him.

"How can I worry about something completely unknown?" Fellini asks. "Anyway, what does that word 'audience' mean? Who are they? It is a monster without any collective conscience or identity. And so it is impossible to be conditioned by their wants. . . . I don't make a film with Anita Ekberg because they like her in the U.S.A. . . . I just say something that I like to say. And because I am a normal man, I think that my problems and dislikes, my fears and hopes, should interest other normal people."

Actually, the episodes in his pictures usually come out of his own life. *The White Sheik* (1951), one of his early films, stems from his short career as a cartoonist. *La Strada* came out of his travels with a circus. And Fellini says that the newspaperman hero of *La Dolce Vita* (1960) was a projection of himself. "I'm just a story-teller," Fellini says. "The cinema happens to be my medium."

Because he is so much at home in his medium,

161

he is able to go on a set without being bound by a detailed shooting script. His penchant for improvisation—shooting movies off the top of his head—is legendary. In an interview with *Newsday* reporter Bill Kaufman, Anthony Quinn described Fellini's *modus operandi* like this:

> Fellini had a script, sure. But it wasn't really used by actors during the filming in the way that actors usually use a script. We didn't refer to it daily. Rather, the scenes were blocked out by the director. We knew the general direction our lines were to be in. But the script was far away from our minds. If, in a scene, something occurred to us, we just extemporized it.

Yet, Fellini pooh-poohs this, saying he merely takes advantage of opportunities that arise on the day of the shooting. In a *Playboy* magazine interview, he put it this way:

> If I wanted to commit artistic and economic suicide, that would be a beautiful and spectacular way to go. But since I don't, I arrive on the set with a script in hand—though it doesn't really mean that much, except as a pacifier for actors who fear improvisation, and for producers who crave reassurance that the structure for a film story has been created. What *does* matter is that I have a very precise idea of where I want to go in the film and how I want to get there long before the camera starts to roll. Once it does, of course, I try to remain flexible enough to amend and adorn the action as the need arises—rather than adhere to the original scenario as though it were Holy Scripture.

> You might conceive of a scene in a park. . . . But when you get there, you realize that your actor with his face would not have spoken that way in a park. Or, the actress wears a dress that prevents her from saying a certain line. Also, instead of filming two actors talking, you may discover while you're filming that a close-up of a fountain or a panning shot of the rare furnishings of a drawing room will say more than the entire ten pages of dialogue. In this sense, I make myself available to adaptation. But I do not extemporize.

Despite his adaptability to circumstances, Fellini is at heart a meticulous craftsman. "For every film," he says, "I audition 3,000 or 4,000 faces." Quinn recalls the care that Fellini took in *La Strada* to find a simple box that Quinn used to carry cigarette butts. "I remember that the property man brought about one hundred boxes," Quinn said. "Federico wasn't satisfied with any. As far as I was concerned, any of those boxes would have done to carry the butts in. But Federico had a very specific idea. And I think that finally—after we must have seen five hundred boxes—finally, he selected one that had a meaning for him."

So true is Fellini to the cinema that he refuses to make pictures outside his native Italy. "Many years ago," Quinn continued, "when Federico came to Hollywood and he was given all sorts of offers from the various studios to come here and make pictures, he said: 'I couldn't because I couldn't tell if an American actor was holding a cigarette correctly or not.' And what he meant was that he has to say something about his own time, in his own world."

Nothing in Fellini's background suggested his future career. He was born in 1920 in Rimini on northern Italy's Adriatic coast, the son of a well-to-do grocer and wine wholesaler. At the age of twelve Fellini left home to join a circus as an apprentice clown. He was back home a few months later, growing up in the Romagna region, where, one writer says, "ideas flow freely and words come easily."

Still restless, young Fellini left home again at seventeen. Drifting from Florence to Milan to Rome, he turned a talent he had developed for sketching into a modest job as a newspaper cartoonist. Then came World War II. When Fellini reached draft age, he managed to avoid the army by pleading temporary ill health. Later, during the Allied occupation, he eked out a living as a street corner artist, doing quick caricatures of American GIs.

His stand was along sidewalk cafes on the Via Veneto, one of the haunts for show business people. One day, Roberto Rossellini happened by and chatted with him. From that conversation a friendship began, and Rossellini, then a young filmmaker, invited Fellini to collaborate with him. Fellini did, and the result was *Open City* (1946), a milestone in the cinema. Fellini became a regular member of Rossellini's screen writing team and helped to turn out *Paisan* (1946), another international hit.

Then, in the early 1950s, Fellini branched off on his own. "I don't think I chose the career of a film director with any premeditation," Fellini said. "Working in films as a writer, I was never satisfied at the way directors carried out the work. Suddenly, one day, I accepted a rash offer from a producer friend of mine and decided that I would do a film from a script I had written. That's how I became a director."

His first two pictures were only moderate successes, but his third, *I Vitelloni* (1953), won widespread acclaim and launched his career. He was then thirty-three. As the years passed, he became known as one of the more poetic neo-realists (those filmmakers who showed life uncompromisingly, "the way things are"), and there followed such other films as *La Strada, Nights of Cabiria* (1958), *La Dolce Vita* (1960), and *8½* (1963).

All of them helped to mold the character that has come to be known as a Fellini film. His personality dominates the picture from start to finish. He designs the sets and the costumes. The story idea is always his. The characterizations and symbolism are his. The dialogue, in the end, is mostly his. And the plot lines seem to weave about one central theme—people seeking human warmth but usually from the wrong persons, or people searching for their own identity but usually in the wrong places. No picture expressed this persistent theme better than *La Strada*, the movie that allowed him to blossom to the full flower of his creative ability.

Fellini reportedly wrote the movie for his wife, Giulietta Masina, who, as the simple-minded Gelsomina, established herself as a Chaplinesque pantomimist of depth and pathos. At first he could not find a producer. Two of them offered to back the film, but only if Fellini cast Burt Lancaster and Silvano Mangano. He refused.

Then one day, while he was picking up Miss Masina at a studio in Rome, he ran across Anthony Quinn. The hulking American actor was starring in *Attila the Hun*. Fellini immediately saw him as the circus strongman Zampano. Quinn, at first, balked at playing the role, but when he saw Fellini's *I Vitelloni*, he recognized his genius and agreed. With Quinn in the cast, Fellini had no trouble getting funding.

As the story opens, Zampano has bought

Her face painted like a clown, Gelsomina finds great delight in helping Zampano with his act. Its climax comes when he snaps a chain by expanding his barrel chest.

Gelsomina becomes Zampano's dedicated servant but he repays her devotion with only grumpiness and indifference.

Gelsomina, the most useless member of her family, and made the peasant girl part of his traveling act. Frightened at first, Gelsomina soon begins to find a great delight in wearing a clown's costume, sounding a trumpet, banging a drum, and dancing a step or two to attract street-corner audiences. For them, Zampano performs his *tour de force*— breaking a chain by expanding his barrel-like chest.

As they travel from village to village in Zampano's ramshackle trailer, the warm-hearted Gelsomina becomes attached to the giant, but he responds with rocklike indifference. He takes no pleasure, as she does, in the wonders, delights, and sorrows that cross their path as life unfolds on the road, nor does he give her a kind word. When she tries to run away, he finds her and beats her.

For the winter, Zampano joins a small circus outside Rome. There, an acrobatic clown, Matto the Fool (Richard Basehart), takes great satisfaction in needling and teasing the strongman. At first Matto implies that he holds Zampano's mistreatment responsible for Gelsomina's sister's death. Then he makes fun of Zampano's pathetic act. Finally he

enrages Zampano with a punning slur on his manliness. Zampano pulls a knife and warns Matto not to goad him any more. But, like a man possessed by a devil, the clown cannot hold his tongue. When they come to blows, Zampano winds up in jail.

Free from her master, Gelsomina talks to Matto and tells him how much she resents her insignificant life. "I'm just no good to anyone," she says. Matto persuades her that she is of use to Zampano, whether he realizes it or not. "Everything in this world serves some purpose," Matto says.

Then he urges her to leave Zampano and come into his act, but Gelsomina turns him down. However, Matto has opened a new vista for her. She begins to believe that as long as she is of use to her master, he will recognize her one day and things will get better.

Freed in the morning, Zampano leaves the circus with Gelsomina and they resume their dreary rounds. "Why do you keep me with you?" Gelsomina asks as they sleep in a stable one night.

Zampano does not answer.

"Would you feel very bad if I died?"

"What are you bothering me for with this nonsense?" Zampano says.

"Zampano, do you like me a little?"

But he is sleeping.

After a hard winter, they come upon Matto in a chance meeting on the road. When the clown baits the strongman again, Zampano becomes enraged, beats Matto, and, in a fury, kills him.

As the days pass, Gelsomina can't get Matto out of her mind. His death haunts her. "The Fool . . . won't laugh anymore," she says. She goes into a decline, weeping and screaming in her sleep. She has become the voice of Zampano's conscience.

Sick of her melancholy, Zampano abandons her one night while she is sleeping by the side of a road. He joins another circus and resumes his act. The years pass, but Zampano cannot blot Gelsomina from his memory.

One day in a seaside town, he hears a girl humming the tune that Gelsomina played. He asks where she heard it and learns that Gelsomina has died. "My father found her over there on the beach," the girl says. "She was ill, poor thing. . . . We took her to our house. She never said anything. She just made little crying noises. When she felt better, she would sit in the sun and play on her trumpet. And then one morning, she just didn't wake up."

The news has a striking effect. Grief-stricken, Zampano drinks himself into a stupor. "I don't need anybody," he mumbles. "Just me alone." But he knows he is lying. He staggers blindly down to the ocean, wades into the surf, and then sinks to his knees on the beach.

An isolated figure against the immense sea and sky, he sobs in the helpless realization of his clumsy brutality and his utter solitude. As Gelsomina has found that everything in life has a purpose, Zampano has discovered that life can be tragic and that loneliness is the bitterest tragedy of all.

Les Diaboliques

Through the crossboards of stairs, we see the sensitive, placid features of Vera Clouzot (wife of director Henri-Georges Clouzot).

Les Diaboliques
(1955)

Produced and directed by Henri-Georges Clouzot. Screenplay by Clouzot and G. Geronimi, based on a novel by Pierre Boileau and Thomas Narcejac. Music, Georges van Parys. Editor, Madeleine Guy. A United Nations Picture Organization release. 110 minutes.

Nicole Horner	*Simone Signoret*
Christine Delasalle	*Vera Clouzot*
Michel Delasalle	*Paul Meurisse*
Inspector Fichet	*Charles Vanel*
M. Herboux	*Noel Roquevert*
Mme. Herboux	*Therese Dorny*
M. Drain	*Pierre Larquey*
M. Raymond	*Michel Serrault*
Handyman	*Jean Brochard*
Dr. Loisy	*Georges Chamarat*
Prof. Bridoux	*Jacques Varennes*

(In 1974, ABC presented a TV movie version of *Les Diaboliques* called *Reflections of Murder*. It starred Tuesday Weld, Joan Hackett, and Sam Waterston.)

Simone Signoret carefully squeezes the drops of a deadly drug into a wine bottle that Vera Clouzot will offer to their intended victim. The New York Film Critics named *Les Diaboliques* the best foreign film of 1955.

If you have never seen *Les Diaboliques* (1955), read no more. The only way to feel the tightening suspense of this remarkable French thriller is to see it knowing nothing about its denouement.

If, however, you have already watched this macabre film, you will, like me, never forget its final reel. Who can forget that scene when the headmaster's body appears in the bathtub? Fully clothed, the dead man begins rising from his watery grave, his eyeballs rolled back in his head.

This was director Henri-Georges Clouzot at his Grand Guignol best. Clouzot was so ingenious at making the hackles rise that he became known as the French Hitchcock. But his success was a long time in coming, and it was not easily achieved.

Born in 1907, Clouzot was no stranger to adversity. Myopia (near-sightedness) cost him a chance at a naval officer's career, and a reversal in his par-

ents' financial situation ended his law studies. Undaunted, he started a new career. He became a film cutter and a script adapter. Then he went to Berlin and worked with Anatole Litvak. But just as he was coming into his own, he fell ill and spent the next five years in a sanitorium.

When he recovered, he went back to script writing, and finally, during World War II, he got a chance to direct his first film. It was called *L'Assassin Habite du 21* ("The Killer Lives at No. 21") (1942). His first widely acclaimed picture was *Le Corbeau* ("The Raven") (1943), a black study that tells how poison pen letters, all signed "Le Corbeau," tear apart a small French town.

Then came *Quai des Orfèvres* (literally "Dock of the Workers," but changed to "Jenny Lamour" for U.S. release) (1947), a tough police movie, *Marion* (1948), and the highly rated *Le Salaire de la Peur*

("The Wages of Sin") (1953), a tension-filled story of four men driving lorries loaded with TNT across Central America. But his masterpiece came a year later when he filmed *Les Diaboliques* ("The Diabolical Ones"), a film taken from the novel *Celle Qui N'Etait Plus* ("The One Who Is No More") by Pierre Boileau and Thomas Narcejac.

Critics hailed it as a classic horror film. "It is a pip of a murder thriller, a ghost story and a character film rolled into one," said Bosley Crowther of the *New York Times*. It was an immediate sensation in the United States as well as in France. Crowds lined up outside theatres for hours, even in the rain, waiting to see the picture. Once the film started, no one was admitted, and the distributor asked audiences not to reveal its double twist ending.

The picture revolves around the efforts of two ladies to do away with a cruel, tyrannical headmaster (Paul Meurisse) at a French boarding school for boys. One of them, Christine (Vera Clouzot, the director's wife), a delicate, sickly but beautiful woman, is married to the headmaster. She is an heiress and owns the school.

The other is a new teacher, Nicole (Simone Signoret), the headmaster's mistress, a cold-blooded, assertive, handsome woman. She has grown to hate him because he is a bully and a boor. He has recently blackened her eye.

One day she suggests to the wife, who has also been cuffed about by the heel, that they join forces and get rid of their common problem. Together they work out what appears to be a perfect crime.

Nicole and Christine leave for a weekend together at Nicole's apartment. Once there, Christine calls her husband and tells him she has decided to divorce him. Panicked by the thought that his wife's fortune will now slip through his fingers, he orders her to do nothing and rushes over to persuade her to change her mind.

Little does he know that he is playing right into the ladies' diabolical plan. When he arrives, Christine gives him a glass of drugged wine. Then, though her heart is fluttering, she helps Nicole drag the doped man to the bathtub, put him in, and fill it. As he tries to struggle to the surface, Nicole weighs him down by putting a heavy ornament on his chest. Then they cover the top of the bathtub with a sheet and leave him there overnight.

The plan is only half over. The next morning, they put the body in a huge laundry basket and carry it to the car. A neighbor helps them and Christine shivers as the top pops open. However, Nicole keeps her wits. She quickly shuts it and ties it down with a rope before their nefarious deed can

be discovered. Then they drive to school and, when it is dark, dump the body in the school's pool.

The slaying and the disposal of the body are carried out in such awkward, breathless style that we, the audience, seem as relieved as are the ladies when the body slides into the pool's dark waters. This is why the murder stands out in the mind. "The entire murder sequence is a clumsy, stumbling, panting scene of horror," said Ivan Butler in his book *The Horror Film*. "It is all ghastly, and all done without any hint of the sadistic reveling in violent death which makes many routine films so repellent."

The plotting of the murder scene is one reason that critics have compared Clouzot to Hitchcock. "In some degree, it resembles the killing in Hitchcock's *Torn Curtain*, in which he has stated his intention of showing just how difficult it is to deprive a man of his life," Butler said. "It is, when one considers it, a more salutary, a fundamentally less indecent method of presentation than the balletic deaths of a Western or the technicolored glamorized slayings in historical or romantic 'epics,' where murder appears as simple or aesthetically satisfying. Killing is a difficult and filthy business, Clouzot and Hitchcock say, and should appear as such."

But more tension awaits us. When the pool is drained, the body is gone, and in the next few days the headmaster's corpse seems to be stalking the school. The cleaner returns his suit, pressed and clean. A pupil says he has seen the headmaster on the grounds. Then Christine reads that an unidentified body has been pulled from the Seine. She goes to the morgue but it is not he. However, a shabby, retired detective (Charles Vanel) sees her there, gets interested in the case, and persuades her to let him try to solve the mystery.

Then Nicole, a bundle of nerves, departs, leaving Christine alone in the school. That night Christine goes to bed and hears footsteps down the creaky, dimly lit hall. Quivering, she goes out to find out who's there.

The picture rises to a chilling climax as she wanders through the dark passageways in her white nightgown. Hearing someone at the typewriter, she goes into the room and sees her husband's hat and gloves on the table. But the room is empty.

A hand turns the knob slowly. A light flickers. Terrified, Christine runs to the bathroom and there she confronts a truly chilling sight. In the bathtub, underwater, lies the body of her husband—just as it did when she and Nicole drowned him. Suddenly he slowly starts to stand, his eyelids opening on blank white eyes.

170

Christine, shocked to the marrow, staggers backward. Her breath starts coming in gasps, then not at all. A strangled cry comes from her throat. She falls back on the wall, then slides down slowly, her head at an awkward angle, and slumps to the floor, dead.

Now the mystery begins to unfold. The headmaster removes false whites from his eyes and Nicole emerges from one of the darkened rooms.

"Have we done it this time?" Nicole asks, embracing her lover.

"She was a tough nut, the witch," the headmaster says. "And she said she had a weak heart."

"Poor darling," Nicole says to the headmaster. "You're soaked."

"When I think of that bath," the headmaster says, "it took me an hour to crawl out. And that trip in the basket."

"How you must have suffered."

"And that dip in the pool."

"The things she made us do. I got scared myself. But it was worth it. Now, we're rich. All told, what do you think we'll get?"

Their rejoicing is short-lived. Out of the shadows steps the detective who convinced Christine to let him investigate the case. "Fifteen to twenty years hard labor," he says. "Depends on your lawyer."

Despite the acclaim the picture received, Signoret said she worked under a great deal of tension. She found both Vera Clouzot and Clouzot himself difficult to get along with. And she felt her performance was disappointing to the director. "I had a tendency to play her [Nicole] as guilty, whereas the suspense relied on the fact that the audience should believe her innocent until the last two minutes of the film."

Clouzot still has one more surprise left. A few days later, when the school is closing, the same pupil who had reported seeing the missing headmaster now has had another strange encounter. He tells the disbelieving teachers that he has seen the dead Christine on the grounds of the school.

"The headmistress gave me a slingshot," he says. "She said, 'Go and play, dear. Have a good time.' "

The teachers scoff at him and order him to stand in a corner for punishment. "I saw her," the pupil says. "I know I saw her."

Some have criticized Clouzot for this fanciful ending, saying that it takes away from the credibility of the story and the character relationships he has so carefully built up. But others feel that it works as a shock finale that tantalizes the moviegoer and makes the movie linger in the mind.

"Clouzot was not, after all, setting out to study the interaction of human characters (though they have more individuality and depth than many he found in more pretentious and serious films), but to raise our hackles," says Butler. "And raise them he undeniably does."*

---

*Alfred Hitchcock tells his tongue-in-cheek story about a bizarre effect suspense movies had on one moviegoer. Hitchcock got a letter from a man saying that his daughter was so frightened after seeing *Les Diaboliques* that she wouldn't take a bath. A few years later, *Psycho* shocked her so badly that she wouldn't take a shower. It's getting unpleasant to be around her now, the man said. What should he do? Hitchcock said he wrote back: "Send her to the dry cleaners."

Limelight

Chaplin as the vaudeville comedian Calvero in *Limelight,* the last movie he made in the United States and his favorite.

Limelight
(1952)

Produced and directed by Charles Chaplin. Music and screenplay by Chaplin. Camera, Karl Struss. Production manager, Lonnie D'Orsa. Assistant director, Robert Aldrich. Editor, Joe Inge. Musical assistant, Roy Rasch. United Artists. 135 minutes.

Calvero	*Charles Chaplin*
Terry	*Claire Bloom*
Neville	*Sydney Chaplin*
Harlequin	*Andre Eglevsky*
Columbine	*Melissa Hayden*
Clowns	*Chaplin*
	Charles Chaplin, Jr.
	Wheeler Dryden
	Nigel Bruce
	Norman Lloyd
	Buster Keaton
	Marjorie Bennett
Children	*Geraldine, Michael, and Victoria Chaplin*

Calvero facing the reality of his advancing years. His career is fading while that of his protégée, Terry, the ballerina (Claire Bloom), is just starting.

They would shoot a comedy sequence. It wouldn't go right. So they would do it over, and then once again. After a while, a voice from behind the camera would quietly say, "That was a gem." Sometimes Chaplin would agree. More often, he would ask for another take.

Then he and his fellow actors would take their places, and the camera would whirl again. Finally the camera would stop, and Chaplin would thrust his hands in his pocket, cock his head, and walk across the arc lights. "That one was good," Chaplin, the director, would say.

"Print it."

In *Limelight*, as in most of his major films, Chaplin had virtually *every* key role in the making of the picture. He was not only its star and director, but its producer, author, composer, choreographer, and editor.

Yet even with Chaplin's tight control, *Limelight* is a flawed movie. Chaplin has never been at his best in a serious film. More to the point, *Limelight* is too long, too sentimental, too talky. Even so, it has become one of Chaplin's classics. Its bittersweet love story has warm and poignant moments. One

cannot help leaving the theatre emotionally spent, if not in tears. And some of Chaplin's slapstick routines, especially the one with Buston Keaton, are hilarious.

Limelight, the last picture Chaplin made in America, was a turning point in his life. Just after the film's release, the British-born Chaplin went on a world tour to promote the movie. While he was abroad, U.S. Attorney General James P. McGranery canceled Chaplin's re-entry permit. McGranery accused Chaplin of associating with communists because of Chaplin's alleged Red sympathies, and of moral turpitude because his personal life scandalized some people. (Chaplin's first two wives were sixteen when he married them and he later was named in a paternity suit by aspiring actress Joan Barry.)*

Chaplin moved to Switzerland and began a lifelong exile, broken only by a brief but triumphant return in 1972 for a special Academy Award and a New York Film Festival tribute. By this time, the

*Blood tests showed that Chaplin was not the child's father. Even so, a jury found against him and the court ordered him to support the baby.

175

once effervescent Chaplin had aged into senility. He died at his thirty-eight-acre estate near Vevey, Switzerland on Christmas Day, 1977.

Ironically, in 1973, *Limelight* won an Oscar for best musical score—Chaplin's—in a dramatic movie. This came about because when the film was originally released, pressure from the American Legion prompted many movie houses to stop running the movie or to cancel its run altogether. It was never shown in Los Angeles, and under the Academy's rules a movie must be seen in that city to qualify for a nomination. Two decades later, *Limelight* met that requirement.

If it took twenty years for *Limelight* to earn an Oscar, its creation also took a marathon-like effort. Chaplin needed two and a half years to write the script. The story repeated the theme of loneliness that pervaded his silent films. It also borrowed something from Chaplin's own music hall background, although he had another explanation for its origin. In his biography, Chaplin said he got the idea from watching comedian Frank Tinney in New York's old Winter Garden Theatre. Several years later, Chaplin saw him again and was shocked.

"The comic muse had left him," Chaplin said. "He was so self-conscious that I could not believe it was the same man. . . . I wanted to know why he had lost his spirit and assurance."

In *Limelight*, the comic's name is Calvero and age was his undoing. "Calvero grew old and introspective and acquired a feeling of dignity," Chaplin said. "And this divided him from all the intimacies with the audience."

Chaplin had his own way of producing the script. He would write several pages, then cut out whole paragraphs, tape them to other excised sections and finally give the whole patchwork manuscript to his secretary to be typed. When finished, it totaled 750 pages.

Chaplin wrote full biographies of all the main characters, but it turned out that he was able to use very little of this material. "Yet," he said, "I was able to build my characterizations on those pages thrown away."

Chaplin once said that *Limelight* was his favorite of all his own movies, and it is not hard to see why, given his early life. Born in London in 1889, Chaplin was the son of struggling variety actors. His mother, a music hall soubrette, lost her voice and then her reason, while his father found refuge in alcohol. So like a Dickens waif, Chaplin spent his childhood in the workhouse and in homes for orphans and destitute children. As a teenager he took to the streets of London where he begged and

danced for pennies. He later became a juvenile actor. At twenty-one, he came to the United States with a traveling music hall troupe—that included Stan Laurel—and joined the infant movie industry.

It was here that Chaplin found himself. He created the famous tramp character—the little fellow with baggy pants, outsize shoes, and bamboo cane—and made dozens of two-reel comedies, directing and writing many of them. In 1917 he signed the first motion picture contract for an annual million-dollar salary. Two years later, he joined with Mary Pickford, Douglas Fairbanks, Sr., and director D. W. Griffith to form United Artists Corporation. Now that Chaplin had his own studio, he started producing his own pictures as well.

He continued this policy over the years—writing, directing, starring in his films, and later, when sound came, writing the music. In 1921, Chaplin topped all previous successes with the picture *The Kid*, which introduced Jackie Coogan. There followed such hits as *The Gold Rush* (1925), *City Lights* (1931), *Modern Times* (1936), *The Great Dictator* (1940), *Monsieur Verdoux* (1947), and *Limelight* (1952).

Of all his films, *Limelight* produced the most mixed reaction among critics. Norman Nadel was among those who felt that Chaplin fell far short of his potential. He found the film "self-conscious, maudlin, overrated, inexcusably banal, dull." Said Nadel: "The serious dialogue could be burlesqued by Imogene Coca and Sid Caesar on television and everybody would laugh."

Others found the story moving and sensitive—particularly when they saw it years later. Andrew Sarris says that the picture was infinitely more impressive when he watched it in 1964 than when he went to see it at the time of its original release. "Twelve years and thousands of films later . . . *Limelight* dwarfs most of its competition," said Sarris.

It is the summer of 1914 as the picture opens. A young woman lies breathing her last in her dreary London flat, the air filled with gas from her stove. Outside, a vaudeville comic, Calvero, returning to his room, slightly tipsy, smells the escaping gas. He breaks down the door, rescues the girl, and carries her to his room.

"Why didn't you let me die?" she says when she revives.

"What's your hurry?" he replies.

Her name is Terry and she is a dancer. She tells Calvero that her health has brought her to a desperate state. Rheumatic fever hospitalized her,

Calvero puts on his stage makeup alongside his cohort, played by Buster Keaton. The hilarious two-man act was a highlight of the film.

left her penniless, and ended her career as a ballerina. However, when she talks about the futility of living and the meaninglessness of her existence, Calvero cuts her short.

"The trouble is you won't fight," he says. "You've given up. But there's something just as inevitable as death. And that's life. Think of the power of the universe—turning the earth, growing the trees. That's the same power within you—if you'll only have the courage and the will to use it."

But the suicide attempt has traumatized Terry, and she can't use her legs. Day after day she lies helplessly in bed. Thus begins a friendship. While she is recovering, Calvero lets her share his apartment—he sleeps on the couch—and the two get to know each other.

One day Terry tells him that she once fell in love with a man she has never known. She worked in a music shop and became fond of a poor but handsome composer who regularly bought sheet music with his last few shillings at the store. Now he has become famous and she feels that she will never meet him.

Calvero reassures her. He tells Terry that she will find him eventually. "You'll be at the height of your success," he says. "And he'll call on you. He'll tell you he's composed a ballet for you. He'll tell you that he loves you and that he has always loved you."

Soon Terry sees that Calvero is going through a crisis, too. His career is on the skids, and she asks what has happened.

He shrugs, saying that he drinks too much. "As a man gets on in years . . . a feeling of sad meanness comes upon him. And that's fatal for a comic," he explains. "I lost contact with the audience. And that's what started me drinking. I had to have it before I went on. I couldn't be funny without it. The more I drank—it became a vicious circle. Then, I had a heart attack. I almost died."

The next day a telegram comes from Calvero's agent. He has an engagement for him. "This is the turning point," Calvero says, enthused. But he's in for a disappointment at his agent's office.

When he wants to know what the terms and billings are, the agent tells him not to ask. "Your name is poison," the agent says. "They're doing this as a favor to me."

177

At the music hall Calvero's act is a flop, and he shuffles disconsolately back to the flat. "They walked out on me," he says. "They haven't done that since I was a beginner. The cycle is complete."

Terry tries to cheer him up. "You can't expect too much from your first performance. When you go back, it will be different."

"I'm not going back," he says. "They've terminated the contract."

Now she assumes the mentor's role. She tells him that he can't give up, that he has to fight. Her voice rises, and as she goes on talking, she is on her feet. She is walking again.

In a few weeks Terry not only has a job in the chorus of a ballet company, but also a clown's part for Calvero. Then a lead role opens for a new ballet and she auditions. Playing the piano is the young composer she met in the music store. His name is Neville (Sydney Chaplin).

In an empty theatre, she dances superbly to Chaplin's lovely theme music. When she is finished, the impresario (Nigel Bruce) goes over to her. "Allow me to congratulate the next prima ballerina of the Empire Theatre," he says. Calvero sits alone in the darkened theatre as Terry, Neville, and the impresario all go off together. Her star is rising while his has faded. But in a moment, Terry dashes back. "I've waited for this moment," she tells him. "I love you. Please, Calvero, marry me."

He only laughs. "What nonsense, my dear. I'm an old man."

The next day, Terry has lunch with Neville and the love affair that Calvero predicted has its beginning.

Weeks later, the ballet opens and Terry has a momentary relapse. She gets the jitters halfway through the performance and becomes hysterical. Offstage, she tells Calvero that she can't go on. "My legs are paralyzed," she screams. He slaps her flush on the face. She is so stunned that she forgets her fright, rushes out on stage, and dances sublimely. When the curtain comes down, she gets a standing ovation.

Things don't go as smoothly for Calvero. He runs into an old crony who tells him he's gotten a chance to play a clown with a ballet company. Not knowing Calvero is that clown, he says that he's heard the fellow who has the part isn't any good. Wounded, Calvero walks out, leaves Terry, and strikes out on his own. He joins a group of strolling musicians who play for loose change at saloons.

But he and Terry don't stay apart for long. Months later she runs into him and pleads with him to come back. At first he begs off. However, she

Chaplin as he looked in the act he performed with Keaton.

persuades him to try a comeback at a gala vaudeville engagement in which she is dancing. He admits that he has been working on an act with a fellow comic (Buster Keaton), and finally he agrees.

The night of the opening, the ballet impresario tells Calvero that he will make all the performers look like amateurs. "That's all we are—amateurs," Calvero says philosophically. "We don't live long enough to be anything else."

Calvero goes on and does a riotously funny musical act. Keaton plays an awkward pianist accompanying Calvero, who appears as a violinist. Still, bad luck plagues Calvero. He ends by falling into a bass drum in the orchestra. It is part of the act, but he is unable to pull himself erect.

"I must have hurt my spine," he says backstage. It isn't his spine. Calvero has had a heart attack. Terry rushes over to him, but he minimizes his pain and tells her they will both go on to glory now. "I'll tour the world," he says. "You'll do the ballet and me the comedy."

When Terry goes on, Calvero asks some stagehands to carry him to the wings. He dies there as Terry spins and turns and whirls in the limelight.

The Man in the White Suit

Alec Guinness as the embattled man in the white suit.

The Man in the White Suit
(1952)

Directed by Alexander Mackendrick. Screenplay by Roger MacDougall, John Dighton, and Mackendrick. Adapted from an unpublished play by MacDougall. Photography, Douglas Slocombe. Editor, Bernard Gribble. Sound, Stephen Dalby. Scientific adviser, Geoffrey Myers. Art director, Jim Morahan. Music by Benjamin Frankel. Produced by Michael Balcon. A J. Arthur Rank Organization Presentation. An Ealing Studios Production released by Universal-International. 85 minutes.

Sidney Stratton	*Alec Guinness*
Daphne Birnley	*Joan Greenwood*
Alan Birnley	*Cecil Parker*
Michael Corland	*Michael Gough*
Sir John Kierlaw	*Ernest Thesiger*
Cranford	*Howard Marion Crawford*
Hoskins	*Henry Mollison*
Bertha	*Vida Hope*
Frank	*Patric Doonan*
Harry	*Duncan Lamont*
Wilkins	*Harold Goodwin*
Hill	*Colin Gordon*
Miss Johnson	*Joan Harben*
Roberts	*Arthur Howard*
Green	*Roddy Hughes*
Mrs. Watson	*Edie Martin*
The Lodger	*George Benson*

Sidney Stratton (Guinness), an eccentric scientist, creates turmoil in Britain's textile industry when he invents an artificial fabric that will never stain and never wear out. Here, one of his unauthorized experiments has been found out.

If you wanted to nickname him, you could have called him the actor least likely to succeed.

When he was twelve, his headmaster rejected his bid for a part in the school play. "You wouldn't be any good at acting," he was told.

When he left school at eighteen and took dramatic lessons, his teacher gave him his money back after weeks of coaching. "I'm afraid you're wasting your time," she said sadly.

Even after a promising stage career, when he tested for the movies, a producer told him, "I don't think you're quite the type for a film actor."

Alec Guinness lived down these rebuffs to become one of the great actors of this century: first as a stage performer—he played the classics in the Old Vic Company; then as a screen star—he appeared in a spectacular array of parts. A master of disguise, a comedian with a deft and subtle humor, a character actor with uncanny range and imagination, he grew to rank with Olivier, Gielgud, and Richardson in the pantheon of British acting.

Yet this giant of the thespian world is in private life so retiring and so painfully shy that a magazine writer once called him a "one-man Tibet." He is

said to run out of a store if he is recognized.

In interviews he talks about himself only reluctantly, and then unpretentiously. He often refers to himself in the third person—using the impersonal pronoun "one." Reporters say that his look is indirect, and he often covers his mouth when he laughs.

He is sensitive about his baldness, but he refuses to wear a wig. He speaks so softly that visitors often have to strain to hear him and they soon find themselves imitating his hushed voice.

He walks as quietly as he talks. "He is usually at your elbow before you know he is there," a colleague says. "Sort of materializes like a Cheshire cat." Guinness, says British critic Kenneth Tynan, has no face other than the one he assumes for the role. "He is a master," says Tynan, "but a master of anonymity."

Those who do penetrate the Guinness reserve report that he has made some perceptive observations about his craft. He once said that the key to his success was the way he imitated a character's walk. Whether he is playing an old English mum, a ramrod career army officer, or an eccentric scientist, Guinness says that the secret of capturing the role is developing the gait because it is the mark of the person.

"I'm never happy over any characterization until I start from the feet up," Guinness says. "This is my personal idiosyncracy. Until I have decided how the character walks, nothing happens. This is a hangover from my student days when I didn't have much money. I spent spare time following people to see how they walked. And as I began to imitate their walk, I fancied I was beginning to know something about the person."

Guinness often surprises fellow actors with what seems to be a phenomenal ability to memorize dialogue. In *The Mudlark* (1951), in which he starred with Irene Dunne, he played Disraeli, and in one scene he made an eight-minute speech which was shot word-perfect in one take. Actually, it's a technique he mastered in his many years in the theatre. He writes out his lines in a notebook, and then he reads them over and over. If he misses as much as a word or a line, he rewrites it until it stays indelibly in his mind.

Guinness has had ample opportunity to put this talent to use. Beginning with *Great Expectations* (1947), he has appeared in thirty-six pictures. He once played eight speaking parts in a single movie—*Kind Hearts and Coronets* (1949).

Still, the theatre remains his first love. "I don't think an actor's life in films is remotely interesting," he says. "It can be enjoyable, I suppose, to do your bit. But the bit is rarely more than two or three minutes a day."

"I've made some pretty lousy films," Guinness added, "partly due to having contracts to fulfill, and you think, 'Well, I don't know, it isn't terribly good. But the next one might be even worse. So I'd better do this.' It's a great mistake, this frightened thing of seeking security by saying, 'Fine, I'll have a big contract for four pictures.'

"Basically, I like being my own master. In films, you're on the cutting room floor. You have no final control over your performance. In the cinema, I've been so often caught out by something disappearing from a performance which I was relying on, that I'd have played the whole thing differently if I'd known that particular thing was going to go."

Nevertheless, his film career brought him an Oscar and contributed in no small way to his knighthood. But Sir Alec had to come a long way to gain those accolades. "My success, such as it is," Guinness says, "is all due to lack of food and to severe disappointments."

He was born in London in 1914 but rarely speaks of his early years. In fact, there is no mention of his parents' names in his listing in the British *Who's Who*. However, his biographies generally report that he was the only child of Andrew Guinness, a bank executive, and Agnes Guinness. Young Alex was raised by his mother. His father left him a small trust fund after he died when Alec was fourteen, but there seems to have been little contact between the two during his lifetime.

At six, Alex was sent off to a middle-class boarding school called Pembroke Lodge. He was, by his own words, an "unprepossessing" child. Quiet, lonely, ungainly, awkward in sports, he got more than his share of ragging. But even at this early age, he felt a love for acting. "I would tell stories after lights went out in the dormitories," Guinness said. "When everyone else was fast asleep, I was still droning on." At the age of twelve he transferred to Roxborough, where the dramatic society specialized in Gilbert and Sullivan. Unfortunately, Guinness could not carry a tune, and his bid for a part left his headmaster sadly shaking his head.

Guinness graduated near the top of his class, but he did not have enough money to afford dramatic school. Therefore, when he was eighteen, he took a job as an ad writer in London. Before two years were up, he left and decided to consult with his idol, John Gielgud. Guinness had won a Shakespeare reading contest, and Gielgud, one of the judges, still remembered him. Sympathetic, Gielgud sent the young hopeful to study with actress Martita Hunt. After twelve lessons, she despaired of his ever making a career in the theatre and handed back to Guinness the small fee she had charged him. (She would later continue the lessons and appear with him in his first movie, *Great Expectations,* in 1947.)

Undaunted, Guinness got a scholarship with the Fay Compton Studio of Dramatic Art. The scholarship covered tuition but provided no living expenses. He lived a spartan existence in an attic room on one meal a day—usually baked beans on toast—and walked everywhere. He stuffed his shoes with paper, and to save his paper-thin soles he took to walking barefoot when the weather was warm.

When his scholarship ran out, he went back to Gielgud who got him several tryouts, but each time the parts had been awarded before Guinness got there. Then one day, Guinness, frail and thin, passed a theatre on the way home. "I must have been quite light-headed from lack of food," Guinness said, "because instead of going to the stage door to apply for a job, I went to the box office." His arrival coincided with that of the stage manager who happened to be looking for an actor. Guinness got the job—a triple-duty part. He played a Chinese coolie in the first act, a French pirate in the second, and a British sailor in the third. The play was *Queer Cargo,* a thriller about a ship in the Far East, and Guinness' salary was three pounds (about $7.20) a week.

This was enough to allow him to eat regularly and go to the Old Vic on his days off. There, some weeks later, Gielgud saw him in the lobby. "Where have you been?" Gielgud asked. "Next week I start rehearsals of *Hamlet* and I want you in it." Guinness got a minor role, Osric, "the admirable popinjay of a courtier." The play ran 155 performances, and Guinness was singled out for special mention. He was never out of a job again.

Guinness spent the next five years doing the classics, shuttling between Gielgud and Tyrone Guthrie. "I always found myself playing old men," he said. "Clearly, I was never a beauty."

When Guinness was twenty-four, Guthrie gave him a chance to play Hamlet in a modern dress version. It was one of his few failures.

After time out for World War II service in the navy, Guinness launched his movie career. But first he had to endure a third rebuff when he made no impression in a tryout at Riverside Studios near his London home. As a result, Guinness went to director David Lean who signed him for the role of "Pocket" in Dickens' *Great Expectations,* a movie that won wide acclaim. But it was his next role as Fagan—with putty nose, bushy whiskers, and menacing eyebrows—in *Oliver Twist* (1948) that really launched his career.

"I count that moment [the making of *Oliver Twist*] when the man in the street began to recognize me," Guinness said, "starting, of course, with London taxi drivers, many of whom are cockney Jewish. The word 'Jew' is never heard in the film. But there was an outcry in America, and, interestingly, in Russia when the film came out. I was accused of being anti-Semitic, which is absurd, since I married into a Jewish family."*

Guinness, a convert to Catholicism, reached a

*He is married to Merrita Salaman, an English actress. They have one child, a son, who overcame polio to follow his parents into the theatre.

Stratton proudly shows off his indestructible suit to textile workers (Vida Hope, Patric Doonan, Duncan Lamont). All they see is a lot of unemployment ahead.

Stratton and the boss' daughter (Joan Greenwood).

peak of popularity with a string of droll comedies, starting with his third film *Kind Hearts and Coronets,* followed by *The Lavender Hill Mob* (1951), *The Promoter* (1952), *Captain's Paradise* (1953), *The Ladykillers* (1955), and *The Horse's Mouth* (1959). His Oscar came for a dramatic role—that of the resolute British officer in *The Bridge on the River Kwai* (1957). Knighthood followed in 1959. In the 1960s and 1970s Guinness had only mixed success, but he continued to enhance his career with such performances as the callous Scotch colonel in *Tunes of Glory* (1960), the crafty King Feisal in *Lawrence of Arabia* (1962), and the title role in *Hitler: The Last 10 Days* (1973).

However, his comedy parts established Guinness' reputation, and it is for these roles—in which he played ordinary men at odds with society—that he will be best remembered. One of his great performances was as the eccentric scientist in *The Man in the White Suit,* a picture that had deep social implications as well.

The movie opens as Sidney Stratton (Guinness), a young idealistic scientist, is fired from a janitor's job at a British textile mill. Stratton, a brilliant self-educated chemist, has taken the position so he can secretly use the mill's research laboratory. He is obsessed with the notion that he can develop an artificial fabric that will never stain and never wear out.

The implications of such a material boggle the mind. Imagine an indestructible suit that would always stay clean. A man could buy one suit and wear it for a lifetime. The super fabric could save a person a small fortune.

But Stratton has already been fired from a succession of textile labs where he had unsuccessfully tried to bootleg his experiment, and this day his luck is no better. Industrialist Alan Birnley (Cecil Parker) is touring the mill. When he goes through its research lab, he is struck by the strange-looking apparatus Stratton has set up off in a corner. Even stranger is the weird cacaphony of sounds—gurgling, bubbling, belching noises—that issue forth from a jungle of Stratton's test tubes and beakers.*

"What's this?" Birnley asks, eyebrows raised.

Nobody has the slightest idea. A hectic search quickly begins to uncover the source of the unauthorized experiment. Eventually, the firm discovers that purchases totalling $10,000 in heavy hydrogen and other unapproved chemicals have been made. Even before the finger points at him, Stratton quietly takes his leave for what he hopes will be a greener pasture.

He finds it at Birnley's own mill, which has a fancier research lab and an opening for a laborer. One day Stratton helps move a new ten-foot-high electron microscope into the lab, and, as luck would have it, he falls into an extraordinary opportunity. Stratton so impresses the lab director with his intimate knowledge of the delicate instrument that the director, mistaking Stratton for a manufacturer's representative, invites him to stay on and help set up the instrument. Thus the groundwork is laid for another "unofficial" experiment.

Inevitably, his undercover work here, too, is spotted, and the discoverer is none other than Daphne Birnley (Joan Greenwood), the mill owner's daughter. Stratton begs her not to give him away.

"I'm going to astound the world," he tells her, and he tries to get her to keep his secret by explaining just what he is attempting to do. It's quite a mouthful.

"Look, you know about the problem of polymerizing amino acid residues?" She blinks. "Look, you know what a long chain of molecules is?" Another blank look. "Do you know what a molecule is?" Something like an atom, she ventures.

"That's it," he cries. "Atoms stuck together like a long chain. Now, cotton and silk and every natural fiber are made of these chains. And recently we've learned to make artificial fibers with an even longer chain—such as rayon and nylon. Well, I think I've succeeded in a co-polymerization of amino acid

residues and carbohydrate molecules, both containing ionic groups. It's perfectly simple. I believe I've got the right catalyst to promote interaction between the reactive groups at the end of the peptide chains and the carbohydrate combinations where the charges of the ionic groups will cross-link the chains and confer valuable elastic properties. . . ."

By the time he has finished, Stratton has won a convert. She agrees to keep his secret, and his experiments go on. At first he is unsuccessful, but, undaunted, he works on until one day—Eureka—he finally hits on the right formula.

When he presents his discovery to Birnley, the industrialist, after some prompting by his daughter, shrewdly perceives how quickly such a revolutionary fiber would propel him to the forefront of the industry. He gives Stratton all the lab equipment he needs.

Within weeks, Birnley's mill has turned out the first prototype suit, a luminous all-white garment. Birnley plans to go into immediate production. Says Daphne to Stratton: "Millions of people all over the world fighting an endless losing battle against shabbiness and dirt—you've set them free. The whole world is going to bless you."

It turns out that she is far off the mark. Instead, the miracle suit seems a threat to the whole economic structure. Stratton has mounted an attack on a sacred cow that someone once called "planned obsolescence."

In our economy, everything is programmed to wear out. Cars won't last more than three or four years without major repairs—nor will television sets, radios, or refrigerators. Therefore we trade them in on a new model. We take for granted, too, that women's stockings will develop a run in a week or less, and that a pair of shoes won't last more than six months without running down at the heels. So accustomed are we to rapid replacements that women blithely accept the fact that this year's fashions will rarely be in vogue in a year.

Stratton's discovery would end all this nonsense—at least in the garment industry. The only trouble is that it would also shut down the entire textile industry and put thousands of mill workers and retail store employees out of jobs. Stratton is unwittingly headed on a collision course with both management and labor.

The mill owners are the first to organize. Sir John Kierlaw (Ernest Thesiger), an aged tycoon, leads an entourage of manufacturers to Birnley's home. "Some fool has invented an indestructible cloth," Kierlaw says. "How much does he want [to step out of the picture]?"

*The sound effect came to be called the "guggle." It was concocted by Mary Habberfield, sound editor at Ealing Studios, with the help of a tuba and a bassoon. Coral Records later put the sounds to rhythm and issued the results on a platter called "The White Suit Samba."

Birnley, at first, will have none of this. He says that he fully intends to manufacture the cloth and market it.

"Are you mad?" says one mill owner. "It will knock the bottom out of everything."

"What about the sheep farmers and the cattle growers?" says another. "And the importers and the middlemen? It will ruin all of them."

"I'll admit some individuals will suffer—temporarily," says Birnley. "But I'll not stand in the way of progress. The welfare of the community must come first."

"You're not likely to suffer much," one says acidly.

These are pretty sober and deep ideas that are being kicked around. But the reason the movie works is that all this is going on within the context of a droll comedy.

While the manufacturers are trying to get Birnley to change his mind, members of the working class have learned of the invention and are trying to convince Stratton that his hopes that his fabric will be produced are just a pipedream.

"What did you think happened to all the other things [inventions]?" a laborer says. "The razor blade that never gets blunt. The car that runs on water. They'll never let your stuff on the market."

It's not like that at all, Stratton insists. Birnley is holding a press conference soon, and then he is going right ahead with production.

That press conference must be stopped, another working-class man says. "If the stuff never wears out, we'll only have one lot to make. . . . Six pence of work and that will be the lot. Every mill in the country will be laid off."

Actually, the workers have nothing to worry about. At Birnley's house, his fellow industrialists have succeeded in pressuring him to cancel production plans. When Stratton shows up to sign contracts, the platoon of manufacturers surround him and offer him $500,000 to suppress his work. Shocked, he tries to bolt from the room. The captains of industry stop him, but only temporarily. With the aid of Daphne, he slips out a window to try to tell the world of his invention. Downstairs a group of workers have gathered after striking in protest over the rumor of the impending start of production of the new fabric.

When Stratton's absence is noticed, the manufacturers and union men join in pursuit of their fleeing common enemy. Stratton tries to hide in a working-class neighborhood. There, an old woman asks him: "Why can't you scientists leave things alone? What about my bit of washing when there's no washing to do?"

Eventually, trapped and cornered like a hunted animal, Stratton awaits his fate resignedly as the mob closes in. Someone grabs his lapel. Instead of yanking Stratton into the air, off comes a huge hunk of fabric. Another man pulls at the garment. He comes away with a handful of cloth.* Alas, there's a technical flaw in the material.

"It's coming to pieces," one man yells. The crowd howls with gleeful laughter that echoes into the night.

The camera cuts to the entrance to the Birnley mill. It is a bright, sunny day. Everything is normal now. The crisis is over.

Stratton is leaving the plant. A sad, lonely figure, he walks slowly down the street, distracted in thought. Suddenly he stops. "I see," he mutters to himself. It's as if someone has turned on a light. He straightens up, and his labored stride becomes sprightly. As he walks away, there is in his gait the zest and bounce of a scientist on the track of a new discovery.

*The studio made special suits for this scene from paper tissue. It had to have nine in all for all the retakes. During the rest of the picture, Guinness wore a more permanent suit made from a form of acetate rayon.

186

The Man with the Golden Arm

On the set of *The Man with the Golden Arm* are Kim Novak, Mrs. Arnold Stang, Eleanor Parker, and Arnold Stang.

The Man with the Golden Arm
(1955)

Produced and directed by Otto Preminger. Screenplay by Walter Newman and Lewis Meltzer, from the novel by Nelson Algren. Camera, Sam Leavitt. Editor, Louis R. Loeffler. Music, Elmer Bernstein. Jazz by Shorty Rogers and his Giants with Shelly Manne. Poker technical adviser, Jack Entratter (then a director of the Sands Hotel in Las Vegas). Distributed by United Artists. 119 minutes.

Frankie Machine	*Frank Sinatra*
Zosh	*Eleanor Parker*
Molly	*Kim Novak*
Sparrow	*Arnold Stang*
Louie	*Darren McGavin*
Schwiefka	*Robert Strauss*
Drunky	*John Conte*
Vi	*Doro Merande*
Markette	*George E. Stone*
Williams	*George Mathews*
Dominowski	*Leonid Kinskey*
Bednar	*Emile Meyer*
Shorty Rogers	*Himself*
Shelly Manne	*Himself*
Piggy	*Frank Richards*
Lane	*Will Wright*
Kvorka	*Tommy Hart*
Antek	*Frank Marlowe*

George Mathews has caught Frank Sinatra red-handed as Sinatra palms a card in their high stakes poker game. At left is Robert Strauss.

"You know what you're letting yourself in for? It ain't pretty. And it could be dangerous."

Frankie Machine, a heroin addict, has decided to try to kick the habit "cold turkey." Molly, his girl-friend, has offered to help him through the tor-turous days of drug denial. But Frankie warns her of the risk she is taking.

"Sometimes a junkie will kill to get away from the treatment. . . . So, if you have any knives or scissors in the house, we got to put them away for a while. And don't let me out of the room—no matter what I say, or promise, or how I beg. Because if I get out, it will only be to get out and find a fix. . . . Just lock me in the room. And if I try to make a break for it, stop me any way you know how."

This is a key scene from Otto Preminger's memorable picture, *The Man with the Golden Arm.* Looking back on the film today, it is hard to understand how a movie that tells us that taking dope is bad could have had so much trouble with censors, but trouble it had. And it was only due to Preminger's determination to defy the Production Code of the Motion Picture Association of America that the movie was made and then got shown with-out cuts.*

The Code no longer exists. In its place are rat-ings showing a picture's suitability for various age groups. But for several decades it was as much a part of the motion picture industry as the Oscar. No producer made a picture without first consider-ing how it would stack up against the Code's restrictions.

The original purpose of the Code, which traced back to the 1920s, was to head off protests from the Catholic Legion of Decency, other religious, frater-nal, and educational groups, and state and munici-pal censors. To avoid confrontations with these groups, Hollywood opted for self-regulation.

Self-regulation worked like this: The Motion Pic-ture Association appointed a Code review board. Its job was to look over scripts before movies were made and make sure that they followed certain moral standards. To set moral standards, the board published a Production Code that listed

*The Association was often referred to as the "Hays Office" after Will H. Hays, its president from 1922-1946. Hays had been President Harding's campaign manager and U.S. Postmaster-General. Eric Johnston, Joseph I. Breen, and Geoffrey M. Shurlock succeeded Hays. Shurlock, the last of the Code chiefs, retired in 1969 when the Code became defunct.

taboos about crime, sex, obscenity, profanity, and vulgarity.

The following are some examples of Code violations:

—Turning the audience's sympathy to the side of crime, wrongdoing, evil, or sin.

—Justifying or glorifying suicide or using it to defeat the ends of justice.

—Showing law-enforcement officers dying at the hands of criminals, unless such scenes are absolutely necessary to the plot.

—Making mercy killing seem right or permissible.

—Showing scenes implying that casual or promiscuous sex relationships are the accepted or common thing.

—Showing open-mouth kissing and lustful embraces.

—Using the word "abortion."

—Using sex hygiene and venereal diseases as subject matter.

—Using vulgar expressions and double meanings—including such words as "chippie, fairy, goose, nuts, pansy, S.O.B., son-of-a."

—Showing complete nudity, in fact or in silhouette.

—Portraying ministers of religion, or persons posing as such, as comic characters or as villains.

—Producing a picture that tends to incite bigotry or hatred among people of different races, religions, or national origins, or using such words as "Chink, Dago, Frog, Greaser, Hunkie, Kike, Nigger, Spig (sic), Wop, Yid."

Pictures that conformed to the Code received a seal of approval. Some 4,000 to 5,000 theatres throughout the country voluntarily agreed to show only those films with a seal.

So all-pervasive was the Code that *every* director has his recollection of some encounter he had with the board.

Henry Koster was unable to keep a sequence in *It Started with Eve* (1941) that had a doctor (Walter Catlett) come into Charles Laughton's sick room. He pulls a cigar out of Laughton's mouth, walks into the bathroom, and flushes it down the toilet. "We do not permit the sound of a toilet in a picture," said Geoffrey Shurlock.

In *Music for Millions* (1944), Koster said, Margaret O'Brien asks a nurse whether June Allyson's baby is a boy or a girl. "Why don't you come in and see?" the nurse suggests. The Breen office ordered the sequence cut.

David O. Selznick was able to keep Rhett Butler's famous parting line, "Frankly, my dear, I don't

give a damn," in *Gone with the Wind* (1939), but only after arguing tenaciously and then agreeing to pay a $5,000 fine.

Some directors adopted ingenious ways to circumvent the censors. In *A Place in the Sun* (1951), George Stevens had a scene where Shelley Winters asks a doctor for an abortion. The Code prohibited use of the word. But Stevens managed to do the sequence without mentioning "abortion," yet making the point. The film passed.

Alfred Hitchcock had his own method of handling censors in Britain, where he began his career as a director. "In the early days of the English cinema, we were able to sit with the British Board of Film Censors as our films were reviewed," Hitchcock said. "There was one old boy—his name was Wilkinson—who wore glasses which had one opaque lens. One was able to sit beside him in the viewing room. And whenever the offending piece of film approached, I said, 'Mr. Wilkinson. . . .' He turned his head toward me. And the objectionable scene went by on the screen without his seeing it."

Outright defiance of the Code did not begin until 1953 when Otto Preminger produced *The Moon Is Blue,* an adult sex comedy. The chief problem was the picture's moral tone. The plot had to do with the proposed seduction of a young lady, and it bandied around the idea of free love. The censors felt it violated the Code's clause that said: "Pictures should not infer that low forms of sex relationships are the accepted or common thing."

Preminger argued that no seduction ever occurs. In the end, the young lady wins her man precisely because she is decent. Therefore, goodness and innocence triumph.

Unable to get the censors' approval, Preminger released the picture without a seal. Theatre owners, aware that publicity about the row had made the public curious, decided to run it anyway. *The Moon Is Blue* became a major box office hit and provided the first damaging blow to the Code's authority.

Preminger turned to the drug scene next. He was impressed by Nelson Algren's powerful novel on addiction. Dope was a growing social problem, but nobody was making movies about it anymore. The Code had temporarily lifted its ban on films dealing with narcotics use in 1946, but the decision turned out to be short-lived. H. J. Anslinger, chief of the U.S. Narcotics Bureau, said that in the period of the relaxed Code, the Bureau had found positive evidence that youngsters' curiosity had been aroused by the pictures they had seen.

It was Anslinger's condemnation of movies

showing drug traffic that led to a new ban. It now wasn't enough to present drugs in an unfavorable light. Narcotics were not to be presented at all.

The blanket denial notwithstanding, Preminger believed that once the censors saw his picture, they would modify the Code. He felt that *The Man with the Golden Arm* was an extremely moral film. It contained no sex and no off-color scenes, and it portrayed drug addiction without glamour or attractiveness. Drug traffic was shown, but only as it realistically occurred—as a sordid business where the pusher baits his victim to get him hooked, then gradually raises his price. No one who saw the movie, Preminger thought, could come away wanting to try drugs for kicks.

He was right, but even so the board was not moved to grant a seal. Preminger had taken a calculated risk and failed. However, judging from *The Moon Is Blue* experience, it was obvious that loss of the seal would not damage any picture's box office appeal. If anything, it would have precisely the opposite effect.

Preminger's course of action was clear. In a great huff, he and United Artists, the distributor, resigned from the Motion Picture Association. The walkout brought the expected controversy and headlines. Over 1,000 theatre owners, contemplating ringing cash registers and long lines outside their houses, agreed to show the movie—seal or no seal. State by state, the barriers fell. The movie became a major hit.

Preminger's victory dealt a mortal blow to the Production Code. Though it was to remain in force for another decade, it was clear that its creators, the major studios, would not abide by it when they felt it stood in the way of big profits.

The movie that put the second nail in the Code's coffin takes place in Chicago. Frankie Machine (Frank Sinatra) is returning to his squalid neighborhood haunts after six months in the federal narcotics hospital in Lexington, Kentucky.* Frankie, a small-time poker dealer who is so good they call

*Marlon Brando was also considered for the part. Preminger sent the first thirty pages of the script to both Brando's and Sinatra's agents. Sinatra was so taken with the story that his agent called the very next day and accepted the role without even seeing the rest of the story. When Preminger told Brando's agent that an actor had already been chosen for the part, Brando's agent couldn't believe it. "He thought I was bluffing," Preminger said. The casting choice, I think, was a mistake. Sinatra gave a fine performance, one of his best. But the part, I think, was written for Brando. He would have been outstanding, and the picture would have gained enormously from his presence.

Sinatra pours out his troubles to Novak in the bar where she works.

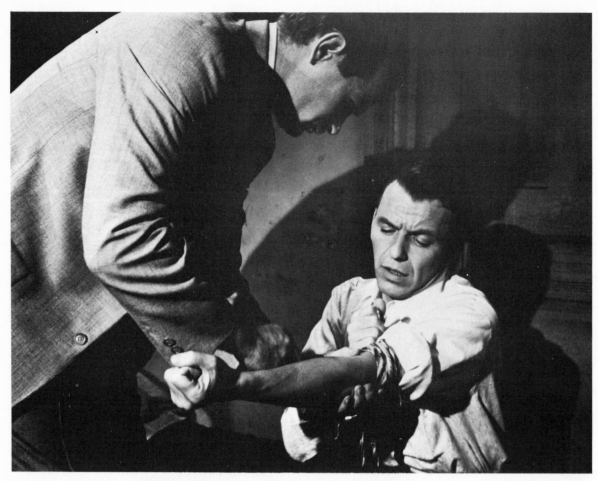

Louie the peddler (Darren McGavin) gives Frankie a heroin fix.

him "the man with the golden arm," has kicked the heroin habit. Or, as Frankie puts it he's gotten a "forty-pound monkey off my back." Frankie has sworn off cards. In their place, he has learned to play the drums, hoping this will give him a new start in life.

But within hours after he steps off the bus, the old pressures start impinging on him—Schwiefka (Robert Strauss) who wants him back in the dealer's slot; an ailing, nagging wife; and a dope peddler who welcomes him by offering him a free fix.

At Antek's bar, Frankie is greeted by barflies and friends, including old sidekick Sparrow (Arnold Stang), a little punk who specializes in assorted petty crimes like swiping "lost" dogs (and then returning them to their owner for the reward). Louie the peddler (Darren McGavin) is there too, but Frankie turns down his needle.

"I'll be around," Louie says.

Uncertainly, Frankie returns to his cramped, ugly apartment and his wife, Zosh (Eleanor Parker), a petulant woman in a wheelchair. She has

been unable to walk since, as she puts it, Frankie got drunk and "crippled" her in a car accident. Frankie tells Zosh that he's going to try to join a big band. Zosh argues against it. She wants things to be as they were before.

"You're the best dealer in the business," she says.

"No more. I'm a drummer," Frankie tells her. When he leaves with Sparrow, wearing a suit his pal has stolen, Zosh walks to the window to watch them.

However, Schwiefka is not letting go. When the police pick up Frankie and Sparrow, charging them both with shoplifting, it's no secret who the informer was. Schwiefka shows up to post bail on condition that Frankie deal for him again.

Back in the slot, Frankie plays poker deftly until his hands start shaking, and he steps outside for some air. Louie, the drug peddler, follows him and suggests a fix. Frankie declines again, this time less firmly, and crosses to the Sahara Club, a striptease joint where his old flame, Molly (Kim Novak), works. They renew acquaintances, and it is ob-

Zosh (Eleanor Parker),
Frankie's "invalid" wife.

vious that it would not take much to rekindle the spark. But Frankie says that as long as Zosh is in a wheelchair, he won't be around anymore. "You can't make a fool out of somebody who loves you and they're so helpless."

As the weeks pass, Zosh, jealous and unhappy over his new ambitions, badgers him at home while he practices. One day, when she complains about the noise, she yells, "Take the drums down to your girlfriend if you gotta practice." Confused and guilt-ridden, Frankie seeks out Louie for a fix.

"Monkey's never dead," Louie says. "And monkey never dies. You kick him off. He just hides in a corner waiting his turn." Frankie says it's his last shot. But we know that one shot will lead to another.

At Antek's, Molly senses Frankie's struggle. She gets him to call for an audition date and agrees to let him practice drumming at her apartment. Frankie quickly sharpens his touch. But before he can go for his tryout, Schwiefka prevails on him to deal just one more night against a pair of well-heeled gamblers, and Louie persuades him to have one more fix.

"Here we go. Down and dirty," Frankie says as the big poker game starts. It goes on all night. Frankie runs up a big winning streak until at day-break he pleads exhaustion. When Schwiefka takes over the slot, the game starts going against the house and Frankie, reluctantly, has to return.

With everything at stake, Louie urges Frankie to "make sure" of a winning hand. That proves to be Frankie's undoing. One of the players spots him palming a card. Suddenly, the table is upended. The gamblers, enraged, thrash him. And then the game is over, and everyone is gone.

His nerves frayed, Frankie follows Louie to his room, pleading for a fix. When the peddler holds out on him, Frankie hits him with a chair and knocks him out.

Then, suddenly, remembering his audition date, Frankie rushes to the band rehearsal. But the dope takes its toll and he fails miserably. Desperate for money, he goes home to buy a fix, narrowly avoid-ing Louie who comes in and finds Zosh on her feet. "You can walk," Louie says, astonished. "What's the angle?"

The angle, although Louie doesn't realize it, is that Zosh has been feigning this handicap to hold onto Frankie. When Louie threatens to give her secret away, she follows him to the stairs, lunges at him frantically and accidentally pushes Louie over a railing to his death.

Meanwhile, Frankie, ready to steal or beg to get relief from his pain, goes to Molly's apartment. There he learns that the cops think he has killed Louie. He pleads for a fix but Molly shows him no pity. "Why should you hurt like other people hurt? Just roll up your pain into one big hurt, and then flatten it with a fix. All that you're gonna need is another and another."

She urges him to kick the habit "cold turkey." Shamed, Frankie finally agrees if she will stand by him. For three bitter days, Frankie suffers, weeps, perspires, and throws furniture around in a locked room in Molly's apartment. Once she has to pull him from an open window where he stands ready to jump. He pleads, then threatens her, then begs her to kill him to end his agony. Finally he passes out. Hours later, he wakes up weak and haggard, but triumphant. He has beaten the habit.

When he has recovered his strength, Frankie goes to tell Zosh that he is leaving. He tells her he has to save himself and that he will send her money to take care of her. When he turns to leave, Zosh jumps up frantically and follows Frankie into the hallway. "Don't leave me," she screams.

The cops have been told that Frankie has come home and have followed him to Zosh's apartment to arrest him. When Zosh rushes out, she runs into them. Frightened now that her secret is revealed, she runs out in panic, slips down a stairway, and falls to an alley below. Zosh dies with Frankie at her side. Then he walks away, followed by Molly, as Sparrow watches them go.

Preminger felt the movie had to have a hopeful ending, but it contrasts with a downbeat finale in the original version. In Algren's book, Frankie never does get the monkey off his back.

Marty

Marty (Ernest Borgnine) and his pals, Kid (Walter Kelley) and Joe (Robin Morse), scan the latest pinups in a girlie magazine.

Marty*
(1955)

Directed by Delbert Mann.* Screenplay and story by Paddy Chayefsky.* Photography, Joseph LaShelle. Music, Roy Webb. Song, "Hey, Marty," by Harry Warren. Editor, Alan Crosland, Jr. Produced by Harold Hecht. Presented by Hecht and Burt Lancaster. Filmed in the Bronx. United Artists. 99 minutes.

Marty Pilletti	*Ernest Borgnine**
Clara Snyder	*Betsy Blair*
Mrs. Pilletti	*Esther Minciotti*
Catherine	*Augusta Ciolli*
Angie	*Joe Mantell*
Virginia	*Karen Steele*
Thomas	*Jerry Paris*
Ralph	*Frank Sutton*
The Kid	*Walter Kelley*
Joe	*Robin Morse*

*Academy Award Winner.

Marty, a wallflower at the dance, looks over the field. The film gave Borgnine his first big non-heavy role and became the major jumping-off point of his career.

"Marty, why don't you go to the Starlight Ballroom tonight?" Mrs. Pilletti is talking to her stout, thirty-four-year-old son. She is beginning her weekly ritual—urging him to find a nice Catholic girl and settle down.

Marty keeps his attention on his spaghetti. But his mother persists.

"Ma, when you gonna give up?" Marty finally asks. "You got a bachelor on your hands. I ain't never gonna get married. Whatever it is that women like, I ain't got it. . . . I'm a fat, little man. . . . All that ever happened to me was girls made me feel like I was a bug."

Then, his rage expended, Marty pats his mother consolingly on the arm.

The first television play to be made into a successful movie,* Marty told the modest story of a lonely Bronx butcher who despairs of finding a

---

*The TV play starred Rod Steiger. Its author, Paddy Chayefsky, was a native New Yorker who rose to prominence with such other TV scripts as Bachelor Party, Middle of the Night, and The Catered Affair. Many later were made into movies. Chayefsky's first original screenplay, The Goddess (1958), won the Critics' Prize at the Brussels Film Festival.

sweetheart. Produced for a mere $300,000, it won glowing reviews and even achieved international fame when it was sent to the Soviet Union in 1959 as part of a cultural exchange program during a thaw in the cold war.

The Russians shipped us The Cranes Are Flying (1959), a poignant movie that captivated American audiences. Marty was also warmly received. At its Moscow premiere, more than 1,000 Russians laughed loudly and wept quietly. At the end, many clapped, an unusual tribute in a Soviet movie house.

The Russian triumph was the crowning touch to Marty's amazing success story. Four years earlier, it had won the grand prize at the Cannes Film Festival. It also had taken four Oscars—best picture, best actor (Ernest Borgnine), best director (Delbert Mann), and best screenplay (Paddy Chayefsky).

How did this low-budget movie, without a single star, go so far so fast? First, its interest in plain and awkward people—an unusual theme for its time— made it emerge as a picture of rare compassion. It showed that a love story did not have to be made about beautiful people.

Second, in a decade of wide-screen extravaganzas, its simple story stood out by its understatement.

Last, its casting was superb. Betsy Blair created a human portrait of a shy, ugly-duckling school teacher deserted on the dance floor. A little-known actress then, she was actually a dark-haired beauty. A child model, Miss Blair studied dancing before becoming a Diamond Horseshoe chorus girl in New York. From there she stepped into the dance line of the Broadway musical *Panama Hattie,* where she met and married Gene Kelly. After scoring a hit in the lead of William Saroyan's play *The Beautiful People,* she went to Hollywood with Kelly. She was in such films as *The Snake Pit* (1948) and *Kind Lady* (1951) before she got her first major role in *Marty.**

*Despite the fact that her performance in *Marty* won critical plaudits and a supporting Oscar nomination, Miss Blair soon faded from sight. She was blacklisted for her radical political views. A bleak period of no movie offers and a divorce followed. Later, she moved to Europe where she married Karel Reisz, director of such films as *Saturday Night and Sunday Morning* (1961), *Morgan* (1966), and *Isadora* (1968). She has since limited her appearances to the British stage, some TV plays, and a few foreign films.

Borgnine's appearance also represented a character change. The burly actor had previously played heavies like the sadistic Fatso in *From Here to Eternity* (1953) and the murderous cowhand in *Bad Day at Black Rock* (1954). Born in Hamden, Connecticut, Borgnine (his real name) served in the navy for ten years before his mother suggested that he try an acting career. He went to school on the GI Bill. Summer stock, television, and stage roles followed. Then he got a chance to work in movies. His Oscar-winning performance came only four years after his film debut in *China Corsair* (1951).**

Marty, then, was a jumping-off point for its leading players, and it remains a movie that retains much of its original poignancy decades after it was made.

The picture opens with a group of young bachelors hanging out in a street corner cafe in the Bronx on another aimless Saturday night. Dateless and

**After *Marty,* Borgnine became best known for his TV series "McHale's Navy," and for his marriages. His wives included Mexican actress Katy Jurado (1959-1964) and singer Ethel Merman (1964). He also was able to break away from the stereotype villain roles and play a variety of leading parts in such pictures as *Jubal* (1956), *The Catered Affair* (1956), *The Dirty Dozen* (1967), and *The Poseidon Adventure* (1972).

Marty offers Clara (Betsy Blair) a soda from a vending machine. Once married to Gene Kelly, Blair's career stopped abruptly after she was blacklisted during the McCarthy era.

Marty tells his pal Angie (Joe Mantell) about his terrific date last night. But Angie sees her only as a rival and calls her a "plain Jane."

bored, they banter about sex—conquests, girlie magazines, and likely prospects.

"What do you wanna do tonight?" asks Angie (Joe Mantell).

"I dunno, Angie. What do you wanna do?"

They are neighborhood pals in their twenties and thirties, living dull, provincial lives in the same city blocks where they were born. Of them all, the one who seems to have reached the dreariest dead end is Marty. He is a decent, kind-hearted sort, but he is portly, homely, and unpolished, lacking confidence in the social graces. Nothing has ever come of the dates his pals have gotten him.

"Let's go down to 72nd Street," Angie says. "You have to beat them (girls) off with clubs."

In the end, Marty joins the stag line at the crowded Stardust Ballroom. There he gets more rebuffs. "Care to dance?" he asks one girl. She glances at him. "I don't care to dance just yet," she says.

Marty is about to call it quits when another fellow comes over and offers him five dollars to take his blind date off his hands. He's met an old flame and wants to spend the evening with her. Marty turns

him down. But the young man eventually finds another male wallflower who takes him up on the offer.

A few minutes later, Marty spots the brushed-off girl rushing from the dance hall in tears. She has refused the stag's offer. Marty goes after her, finds her on the roof, and lets her cry on his shoulder. Skinny and shy, her name is Clara (Miss Blair). She is a young teacher, and like Marty she is awkward and plain. She has endured a lifetime of slights and has all but given up on romance.

"I cry a lot, too," says Marty. "I'm a big crier. I know exactly how you feel."

Later when they dance, a magical thing starts happening. They both blossom from their shells, and all their pent-up emotions burst forth. Marty is overwhelmed to meet a girl who does not find him repulsive—who, in fact, listens, engrossed, as he talks about himself. He talks about his war service and his high school days. He tells her that math and German were his best subjects, that he had an 82 average, and was accepted at City College, but he had to go to work because his father died. That was seventeen years ago, Marty exclaims.

"Boy, am I talking," Marty says. "I never talked so much in my life. Most of the time when I'm with a girl I don't have a word to say." Marty pauses. Then he says: "You know, you got a real nice face, really, a nice face."

"Thank you," Clara says.

By the end of the evening, a bond has been forged between them. They stop at Marty's home on the way to her apartment. While they are waiting to meet his mother, Marty tries to kiss Clara. Surprised by his sudden approach, Clara moves away. When she sees that Marty has misunderstood her shyness and seems hurt, she tells him: "I want very much to see you again."

They turn slowly to each other, meeting in a long, tender kiss. Marty is touched. Tears flood his eyes.

When Marty's mother (Esther Minciotti) comes home, she greets Clara with old world hospitality. However, it soon becomes apparent that she feels threatened by Clara. Mrs. Pilletti tells Clara about her sister, Catherine (Augusta Ciolli), who has become an unwelcome presence in her younger son's home now that he is married. When Clara leaves, Marty's mother tells him how disappointed she is in Marty's choice of a girlfriend. Clara isn't Italian, Mrs. Pilletti says. She's a college girl, and all college girls are tramps.

Later, even Marty's pal Angie talks Clara down. He rates her a "plain Jane . . . a dog . . . a real nothing." Angie resents her because he sees she is going to come between him and Marty.

"I don't think she was so bad looking," Marty says.

"Well, she must have kept you in the shadows," Angie says.

The next day, Sunday, Marty goes to his old neighborhood haunt. His pals are absorbed in the usual dreary conversation. They talk about what to do to pass the night—picking up some girls; cards; a movie; a burlesque show.

"What do you feel like doing, Angie?"

"I dunno."

Suddenly, Marty comes alive.

"'What are you doing tonight?'" Marty shouts, mimicking their conversation. "'I dunno. What are you doing tonight?' The burlesque. Loew's Paradise. Miserable and lonely. Miserable and lonely and stupid. What am I, crazy? I got something good here. What am I hanging around with you guys for?"

"What's the matter, Marty?" asks Angie, dumbfounded.

"You don't like her [Clara]. My mother don't like her. She's a dog. And I'm a fat, ugly man," says Marty. "Well, all I know is I had a good time last night. I'm going to have a good time tonight. If we have enough good times together, I'm going to get down on my knees and beg that girl to marry me. . . . You don't like it, that's too bad."

Marty rushes to a phone booth, leaving his chums speechless. He drops in a coin and dials. "Hello," he says. "Hello, Clara."

On the Waterfront

Marlon Brando as the troubled ex-prizefighter Terry Malloy who testifies against mobsters in his waterfront local.

On the Waterfront*
(1954)

Directed by Elia Kazan.* Screenplay by Budd Schulberg,* from his story suggested by articles by Malcolm Johnson. Director of photography, Boris Kaufman.* Art director, Richard Day.* Assistant to producer, Sam Rheiner. Film editor, Gene Milford.* Music by Leonard Bernstein. Produced by Sam Spiegel. Filmed in New York City and Hoboken, New Jersey. Columbia Pictures. 108 minutes.

Terry Malloy	*Marlon Brando**
Father Barry	*Karl Malden*
Johnny Friendly	*Lee J. Cobb*
Charley Malloy	*Rod Steiger*
Kayo Dugan	*Pat Henning*
Edie Doyle	*Eva Marie Saint**
Glover	*Leif Erickson*
Big Mac	*Tony Galento*
Truck	*Tami Mauriello*
Pop Doyle	*John Hamilton*
Mott	*John Heldabrand*
Moose	*Rudy Bond*
Luke	*Don Blackman*
Jimmy	*Arthur Keegan*
Barney	*Abe Simon*
J. P.	*Barry Macollum*
Specs	*Mike O'Dowd*
Gillette	*Marty Balsam*
Slim	*Fred Gwynne*
Bad Girl	*Joyce Lear*
Tommy	*Thomas Handley*
Mrs. Collins	*Anne Hegira*
Driver	*Nehemiah Persoff*

*Academy Award Winner.

At the shape-up, Terry holds a working tab behind his back, teasing Edie Doyle (Eva Marie Saint), who desperately wants it so her father can get work.

"I coulda had class. I coulda been a contender. I coulda been somebody. Instead of a bum—which is what I am."

—Terry Malloy in *On the Waterfront*

In 1973, director Elia Kazan and screenwriter Budd Schulberg made a sentimental journey to Hoboken. Twenty years earlier, the two had taken a film crew to the New Jersey port to shoot a movie on mob control of the docks. That movie, *On the Waterfront,* went on to win eight Oscars. It marked what many feel was the finest performance of Marlon Brando. It has since become an American classic.

Now Kazan and Schulberg had come back for another look at the one-mile-square city and its sleazy dockside streets teeming with longshoremen. Though much of Hoboken had been torn down as part of a major renovation project, the trip still brought back memories.

"This is it," Kazan said when he turned into a narrow cobbled alley. "This is where we shot the scene where the mob tries to run Brando down.

We made this scene off the cuff, all of a sudden. It hasn't changed." Nor had the wharf with a barge and a little shack where Brando and the pier gang boss, played by Lee J. Cobb, have a knock-down, drag-out fight.

"I think it was the right way to make a picture," Schulberg said. "It took nine weeks to shoot. We made it by walking around the city. . . . We never could have done the film in a studio. Even the interiors were done in actual apartments here and in the [St. Peter and Paul] church. I think what comes through in the film is that we cared about what we were saying."

Later, in a clam house, Schulberg sat with his wife, actress Geraldine Brooks, and talked with a beer stein in his hand. "The movie wasn't the story of one person," Schulberg said. "It was about everybody who stood up to the mob. You know, I saw it again a few years ago. It still grabbed me."

The idea to do a movie on a dull-witted but well-intentioned dock worker who finds the courage to expose his racketeer-dominated union traces back to 1947. It was in that year that Malcolm Johnson wrote his Pulitzer Prize-winning newspaper series "Crime on the Waterfront." The *New York Sun* reporter's stories told how union bosses teamed with racketeers to dominate the waterfront locals. Terrorizing union membership, they controlled jobs and skimmed rich windfalls off the top. The series led to an investigation and hearings by the State Crime Commission. Eventually, there were indictments and jail terms.

Kazan thought there was a film here and asked Arthur Miller to do a screenplay. Miller turned Kazan down, but for reasons other than the story idea itself. Kazan had made an appearance before the House Un-American Activities Committee—testifying about what he knew about communist activities in the theatre and in Hollywood—and reportedly had some damaging things to say about Miller. In his book *Brando,* author Gary Carey wrote: "Though the director's [Kazan's] testimony was never made public, it apparently put Miller in a baby-pink spotlight."

Kazan then got in touch with Schulberg. He, on the other hand, was not at all deterred by Kazan's HUAC appearance. "Like Kazan," Carey wrote, "Schulberg had also named names for HUAC. And his script became a justification of 'stool-pigeoning' on one's buddies."

For the next several months, Schulberg plunged into the project. He read and reread Johnson's long series, haunted the Hoboken piers, and talked with stevedores, union officials, and priests who had inside knowledge of the corrupt dealings. Karl Malden's role, for example, was based on Father John M. Corridan's fight to end the unfair shape-up (an arbitrary daily hiring practice) and racketeering infiltration. Corridan's most widely presented sermon was called "Christ Goes to the Shape-Up."*

After months of hard work, Schulberg showed his finished script to Kazan, but they found no backers. Darryl F. Zanuck felt the story wasn't right for CinemaScope, which he was readying as his answer to television. Other producers turned it down because they thought the stark social realism of the film made it too controversial. There was also a question as to whether they could ever shoot it on location. Many felt that waterfront elements

would never let production equipment get on the piers, or that there would be labor troubles, or reprisals against the company.

Eventually, however, they were able to persuade Sam Spiegel, an independent producer fresh from his triumph with *The African Queen* (1951), to back the project. Spiegel at first masked his identity with the name S. P. Eagle, but he soon joined the operation with enthusiasm. He, Kazan, and Schulberg began reshaping the story. Their goal was to create a gripping documentary-style movie à la Kazan's *Boomerang* (1947) and *Panic in the Streets* (1950), or in the style of Spiegel's *The Stranger* (1946) and *The Prowler* (1951), or Schulberg's best-seller *The Disenchanted.*

Weeks later, when they were finally ready, they picked Hoboken for their locale. Then, with fingers crossed, they began production. "Things were awfully hot around the harbor," said Schulberg. "'Gadge' (Elia Kazan) had a bodyguard. There were some threats. But in the end, nothing serious happened."

Realism was uppermost in Kazan's mind. He had picked Hoboken because it offered a certain visceral quality. He wanted to show its vacant lots, grimy waterfront and dirty brick walls.

Filming went on in the bitterest part of winter, and icy winds swept across the wharf. "Working conditions were murderous," Kazan said. "We shot film every day, regardless of the weather. We worked through November and December rain, January and February snow, sleet, slush, and smog. We shot in freezing damp warehouses, on ice-caked piers, in back streets and alleys, on tenement rooftops, in flats, in churches and parks."**

To capture the dock's bleak, wintry atmosphere, he hired the innovative cameraman Boris Kaufman. For further authenticity, to play union goons he got the former prizefighters Tony (Two-Ton) Galento, Abe Simon, and Tami Mauriello, all of whom had battled heavyweight champion Joe Louis. All three lost.

The picture also introduced two talented personalities to movie audiences. One was composer-conductor Leonard Bernstein, who wrote his first cinema score. The other was Eva Marie Saint,

*Another real-life character reportedly portrayed in the film was Anthony (Tony Mike) De Vincenzo, who was a real-life witness against waterfront crime bosses. He said he was the model for Terry Malloy, the tough stevedore played by Brando. De Vincenzo was hired in an advisory capacity for the picture. But he ended up suing for $1,000,000, charging that the studio had violated his privacy. He reportedly collected about $25,000 in an out-of-court settlement.

**The on-location shooting gave producer Spiegel some of his biggest headaches. He rented five adjacent tenement rooftops until the landlord of building number three decided he wanted more money. They tried shooting around it, but ended up paying the loot. Later, Spiegel rented a saloon for $150 a night. Then the owner wanted $1,000 a night and Spiegel, already committed to the set, had to pay it. The word got around that Spiegel was an easy touch and a parade of grafters started moving onto the set. In all, Spiegel handed out an extra $30,000 to get "cooperation."

making her film debut as the convent-schooled girl who falls in love with Brando.

Playing Claudia on television's "One Man's Family," Miss Saint had become one of TV's best known performers. One writer had called the blonde actress "the Helen Hayes of television." Another, Ernest Havemann of *Life,* had extravagantly predicted that her name "may someday be a household word like Bankhead, Bergman, or Berle."

Her portrayal in *On the Waterfront* was a sensitive and moving one, and she won an Oscar for best supporting actress. But she made only a dozen more pictures through the 1950s and 1960s, mostly in highly forgettable movies, and fell far short of fulfilling Havemann's lofty prophecy.

The key to the movie's success, though, was the casting of waterfront ruffian Terry Malloy. Spiegel wanted Frank Sinatra, who had just launched a comeback in *From Here to Eternity* (1953). But Kazan's choice was Brando, then at the height of his young career, and Kazan's judgment prevailed.* Kazan never regretted the decision. "It

*Sinatra reportedly stopped talking to Spiegel when he learned he had failed to get the role. Moreover, he sued Spiegel—unsuccessfully—for $500,000 for allegedly backing out of the deal.

was maybe the best performance he ever gave," Kazan said.

The movie opens with a murder. Terry Malloy calls up to the tenement apartment of Joey Doyle, a young dockworker who has broken the waterfront's unwritten D and D (deaf and dumb) code. Joey has decided to cooperate with state investigators and testify against labor boss Johnny Friendly (Cobb).

"Joey," Terry shouts. "Hey, I got one of your birds. He flew in my coop. You want him?" Raising pigeons is one of the neighborhood hobbies. The bird-fanciers keep their pets in rooftop coops.

The camera pans to two shadowy figures waiting for Joey. Minutes later, his body hurtles down to the pavement below.

"I thought they was going to talk to him and get him to dummy up," Terry says later. He realizes that he has been the bait in a murder trap. "I figured the worst they would do is lean on him a little."

"A canary," scoffs Truck (Tami Mauriello), one of Johnny Friendly's plug-uglies.

"Maybe he could sing," laughs Big Mac (Tony Galento), another Friendly roughneck. "But he couldn't fly."

Terry, as tough and hard as he seems, can't

Terry shows Edie his pigeon hutch on the roof of his tenement. "One thing about them [pigeons]," Terry says. "They're very faithful. They get married just like people." Looking on is Thomas Handley.

The famous taxi scene. Terry's brother Charley (Rod Steiger) has pulled a gun, imploring his brother not to testify against the union bosses. The much-quoted line, "I coulda been a contender," comes from this sequence.

shake the unsettling feeling that he has helped kill a friend. His sullenness is noticed.

"I know what's eatin' yuh," says labor boss Friendly. Then he points out that Joey was threatening the whole existence of the local. "We got the fattest piers in the fattest harbor in the world," Friendly says. "Everything that moves in and out, we take our cut. You don't think I can afford to be boxed out of a deal like this?"

"Hey," says Terry's brother, Charley (Rod Steiger), the local's lawyer, "you got a real friend here. Don't forget it."

At the shape-up the next day, Pop Doyle (John Hamilton), Joey's father, shows up for a job. The hiring boss passes him up but then scatters the last few working tabs on the wharf. Longshoremen scramble for them and Doyle's daughter, Edie (Eva Marie Saint), jumps into the melee to try to grab one for her father. Terry snatches the last one and teases the girl by holding it just out of her reach. When someone tells him it's Joey's sister, he stops abruptly, gives the tab to her, then walks off.

Meanwhile, Father Barry (Karl Malden) has been watching all this. He tells the longshoremen who have failed to get work that they shouldn't

stand for this shabby treatment, and he organizes a meeting in his church.

Friendly sends Terry to find out what's going on. "Who killed Joey Doyle?" Father Barry asks. "You know who the pistols are. Are you going to keep still till they cut you down one by one?"

Suddenly an army of hoodlums storms the meeting. Terry grabs Edie and guides her to safety. Then he walks her home.

"Which side are you with?" Edie asks.

"Me? I'm with me—Terry."

As they stroll through a playground, Miss Saint accidentally drops one of her white gloves. Instead of stopping the sequence, Brando picks it up and, in an inspired bit of business, begins pulling it on his own hand. They sit by the swings and Terry reminisces about school days.

"You don't remember me, do you?" Terry asks.

"I remembered you the first moment I saw you," she says.

"By the nose, huh?" Terry laughs. "Some people just got faces that stick in your mind."

The next day, Edie goes up to the roof and finds Terry taking care of Joey's pigeon hutch.

"I wouldn't have thought you were so interested in pigeons," Edie says.

206

"Yeah. I just go for it," Terry says. And then he tells her about the precarious life of a pigeon in New York. "Yuh know this city's full of hawks. That's a fact. They hang around on the big hotels. And they spot a pigeon in the park. And—swoosh—right down on him. . . . One thing about them [pigeons]. They're very faithful. They get married just like people. And they stay that way until one of them dies."

Gradually, Edie has discovered a sensitivity beneath Terry's tough outer shell. And so later, when he invites her out for a beer, she accepts. But Joey's name keeps coming up and Edie eventually begs Terry to help find his killer. "Edie, I'd like to help," Terry says. "But there's nothing I can do."

On his way home, a car nearly sideswipes Terry. Out steps Johnny Friendly.

"I thought you were going to keep your eyes on that church meeting," Friendly growls.

"I was there," Terry says. "There was nothing happening."

Infuriated, Friendly tells Terry that Kayo Dugan (Pat Henning), one of the longshoremen at the meeting, has given a thirty-nine-page deposition to the crime commission. "Thirty-nine pages of our operation," Friendly roars.

The next day a load of cargo crashes down on Dugan, killing him, as he is working in the hold of a ship. (For this shot, Kazan put a camera inside an iron cage and positioned it lens-up on the bottom of the hold. It gave the audience the same chilling view of the falling sling of cargo that Dugan had in his last moments.)

Now Terry is determined to tell all he knows to the authorities. He confesses to Father Barry that he was the one who set up Joey Doyle, and he also tells this to Edie. But before he is scheduled to appear before the commission, a taxi sweeps up beside him and his brother, Charley, asks him to get in.

The cab scene is a real grabber. To me, it ranks as one of the finest sequences filmed in the 1950s. Charley tells Terry that the mob is willing to give him an easy loft job worth up to $400 a week.

"I get all that dough for not doing nothing?"

"You don't *do* anything. And you don't *say* anything."

Terry balks. "There's a lot more to this than I thought, Charley."

"Listen, Terry," Charley says, losing his temper. "You know how much those piers are worth that we control through the local? You think we're going to jeopardize the whole setup for one rubber-lipped ex-tanker?" Charley suddenly pulls a gun

and implores Terry to take the job. Astonished, Terry pushes the gun away. "Oh, Charley," he says, unable to believe his brother would point a gun at him, let alone shoot him. "Wow."

There is a long pause. Then Charley brushes some tears away and reminisces.

Charley: When you weighed 168 pounds, you were beautiful. You coulda been another Billy Conn. That skunk we got you for a manager, he brought you along too fast.

Terry: It wasn't him, Charley. It was you. Remember that night in the Garden. You came down my dressing room and said, "Kid, this ain't your night. We're going for the price on Wilson." You remember that? "This ain't your night." My night! I coulda taken Wilson apart. So what happens? He gets the title shot outdoors in the ball park. And what do I get? A one-way ticket to Palookaville. You was my brother, Charley. You shoulda looked out for me a little bit. You shoulda taken care of me a little bit so I wouldn't have to take those dives for the short-end money.

Charley: I had some bets down for you. You saw some money.

Terry: (Yelling) You don't understand—I coulda had class. (Voice gradually subsiding) I coulda been a contender. I coulda been somebody. Instead of a bum—which is what I am. Let's face it. (Long pause, then, without rancor—softly, almost tenderly) It was *you,* Charley.

Terry has bared his soul, facing up to the fact that he has made nothing of his life. But if this is so, then Charley is the worse offender, for he helped turn his brother into a driftless hulk, sacrificing his potentially brilliant boxing career to satisfy the greed of the mob.

In the 1950s, "I coulda been a con-ten-der" became a catch phrase. Youngsters everywhere aped Brando's poignant lament, mimicking his dock worker's accent. The word "contender" rings with all the bitter irony of lost aspiration.

Reflecting on that unforgettable sequence in 1965, *Newsday* columnist Mike McGrady wrote: "Today, ten years after *Waterfront,* the scene remains fresh. One recalls clearly the inflections, the pauses, the reaching out, the attaining of mood and meaning. A stumblebum's moment of truth and all the emotions—regret, anger, forgiveness, affection, reproachfulness—fused in a moment of memorable poignancy, a picture of a man coming to grips with himself."

Brando and Steiger reportedly had problems doing the scene. Seven takes were made. Brando, at first, could not remember his lines. Then, Steiger was moved to tears. "Steiger's one of those actors who loves to cry," Brando said. Later, in the screening room, Brando thought his performance was so bad he walked out without saying anything to Kazan. But some say Brando was really embarrassed because the film revealed so much of his true personality.

That night, Terry finds Charley's body swinging from a baling hook in a back alley. Bent on vengeance, Terry gets a gun and goes after Johnny Friendly, but Father Barry catches up to him and urges Terry to go, instead, to the crime commission.

"If you really want to finish Johnny Friendly," the priest says, "don't fight him like a hoodlum down here in the jungle. He'll hit you in the head and plead self-defense. You fight him in the courtroom tomorrow with the truth."

Terry does just that. He takes the stand and testifies that it was Friendly who got rid of Dugan to maintain control of waterfront locals. The hearings are being televised and the camera shifts to a plush apartment where a fat man with a cigar angrily orders a servant to switch off his set. "If Mr. Friendly calls, I'm out," the fat man says. "If he calls ever, I'm out."

Some critics have said this scene points up a weakness in the picture. It's not clear if this Mr. Big is a politician, a shipping magnate, or a labor union executive. And so the film fails to show the full extent of the roots of corruption. But this would only diffuse what is now the taut, finely etched drama. The source of union power is another story for another movie.

"You've just dug your own grave," Friendly tells Terry. "You're dead on this waterfront. You don't drive a truck or a cab. You don't push a baggage rack. You don't work no place. You're dead."

The days drag on for the now unemployed Terry. Friends shun him. Neighbors call him a "canary." Kids kill his pigeons.

One day, Terry, growing more frustrated with each day, heads for a showdown. He tells Edie he's going down to the shape-up.

"I'm just going to go down there and get my rights," he says.

On the waterfront, a murmur ripples through the crowd of longshoremen as Terry appears. The foreman, loyal to Friendly, hires everyone but

The savage waterfront battle with local boss Johnny Friendly (Lee J. Cobb). Terry has evaded an overhand right and is getting set to uncork a punch of his own.

After the fierce struggle, a bruised Friendly emerges roaring to his longshoremen to get back to work. Those are former heavyweight boxers Tami Mauriello (hatless to the right of Cobb) and Abe Simon (extreme left with fur collar). They both fought Joe Louis and lost.

Terry. Undeterred, Terry walks over to the pier shack that Friendly uses as his headquarters. The longshoremen follow.

"Hey, Friendly," Terry shouts. "Come out of there."

Friendly steps out, seething with anger, and tells Terry to get lost, but Terry won't go away. Instead, standing up to Friendly before his own local, Terry yells: "You take them heaters away from you and you're nothing. You take away the kickbacks and the shakedown cabbage and them pistoleros and you're nothing."

"Come on," Friendly roars, daring Terry to challenge him.

"You give it to Joey. You give it to Dugan. You give it to Charley, who was one of your own. You think you're God almighty. But you know what you are?"

"Come on," Friendly calls, impatiently.

"You're a cheap . . . lousy . . . dirty . . . stinkin' . . . mug. And I'm glad what I done to you."

Terry dives at Friendly and they tear savagely at each other. It is soon apparent that the old union boss is no match for the ex-fighter. With explosive force, Terry plants a hook on Friendly's jaw, doubles him up with a wallop to the stomach, and sends him crashing against the shack. Friendly yells for help, and two of his goons pull Terry behind the shack. Tough as he is, he cannot overcome their numbers. Along with Friendly, they beat him unmercifully.

"They'll kill him," one longshoreman cries. Two more henchmen quickly move out to see to it that no longshoremen break through to help Terry.

Minutes later, Friendly, cut and exhausted, steps out. Terry remains behind in a crumpled heap. "Just let him lay there," Friendly says. Then he turns to the crowd of dock workers and orders them back on the job, but they don't move. They have seen one beating too many.

"Terry don't work," some brave soul says. "We don't work."

Numb and in pain, Terry is ministered to by Father Barry (Karl Malden) and Edie after the fight. He struggles to his feet and leads the longshoremen back to work.

"Work?" Friendly bellows. "He can't even walk."

The father of the murdered Kayo Dugan steps forward, and in a sudden act of courage he shoves Friendly off the pier. A roar of laughter rises up from the longshoremen as the big union boss splashes in the freezing river.

Father Barry and Edie rush to the shack area where Terry lies. Blood gushes from his nose and mouth. He clutches his ribs. He can barely talk.

On the pier, one longshoreman says: "Terry walks in, we walk in with him."

"Do you hear that, Terry?" Father Barry says. "You lost a battle. But you have a chance to win the war."

"Get me on my feet," Terry says. Slowly, agonizingly, he staggers toward the pier shed. Then he stops, weakened by the pain. He knows, though, that if he can reach the shipping boss at the loading pier, the men will follow him. And if that happens, the chances are that the longshoremen will take no more orders from Friendly.

"Finish what you started," the priest whispers. Terry pushes his tortured body ahead, grimacing, reeling, eyes rolling. But he goes on. Suddenly, scores of stevedores are rushing after him.

Left behind is the once-imposing but now forlorn, dripping wet figure of Johnny Friendly. Angry and blustering, he yells: "Where you guys going? Wait a minute. I'll remember this. I'll remember every one of you. I'll be back. Don't you forget that. I'll be back."

But his words are like ashes in the wind. He remains a lonely and pathetic figure in defeat.

Paths of
Glory

Kirk Douglas as the idealistic French colonel who tries to save his court-martialed soldiers from a firing squad.

Paths of Glory
(1957)

Directed by Stanley Kubrick. Screenplay by Kubrick, Calder Willingham, and Jim Thompson, based on a novel by Humphrey Cobb. Photography, George Krause. Music, Gerald Fried. Editor, Eva Kroll. Special effects, Erwin Lange. Produced by James B. Harris. A Bryna Production released through United Artists. 87 minutes.

Colonel Dax	*Kirk Douglas*
Corporal Paris	*Ralph Meeker*
General Broulard	*Adolphe Menjou*
General Mireau	*George Macready*
Lieutenant Roget	*Wayne Morris*
Major Saint-Auban	*Richard Anderson*
Private Arnaud	*Joseph Turkel*
Private Ferol	*Timothy Carey*
Colonel Judge	*Peter Capell*
German Girl	*Suzanne Christian*
Sergeant Boulanger	*Bert Freed*
Priest	*Emile Meyer*
Private Lejeune	*Kem Dibbs*
Private Meyer	*Jerry Hausner*
Shell-Shocked Soldier	*Frederick Bell*
Major Gouderc	*Paul Boes*
Colonel de Guerville	*Wally Friedrichs*
Cafe Owner	*Roger Vagnoid*
Captain Nichols	*Harold Benedict*
Captain Rousseau	*John Stein*
Captain Renouart	*Ira Moore*
Captain Sancy	*Leon Briggs*
Private Duval	*Marshall Rainer*
Doctor	*Halder Hanson*
K.P.	*Rolf Kralovitz*

Adolphe Menjou as the wily, practical General Broulard who misreads Douglas' motives.

There are moments that cannot be forgotten, scenes that remain etched in memory.

One remembers the withering trench fire and the futile attack on the German fortification called the Ant Hill.

There is the French general's frantic order to shell his own men who have stopped advancing.

And Kirk Douglas' impassioned, but unsuccessful, defense of his three court-martialed soldiers. And their death before a firing squad.

Most of all, one remembers the last scene. French infantrymen get a break from the war and drink at a nondescript cafe near the front. The owner drags out a frightened German girl to sing before her country's enemies. At first the soldiers laugh at her futile attempts. But gradually they are struck by her innocence in the midst of a cruel and inhumane war. Suddenly, they become hushed, silent, until her tiny voice is the only sound in the cafe. Then, one by one, they join in. A sad chorus fills the room, while tears well in the eyes of seasoned, battle-hardened veterans.

Paths of Glory is a classic that claims a place among the great anti-war pictures of all-time. Yet, as in the case of many outstanding films, it had to wage an uphill struggle to be made. And even after

it was released, authorities in France and other European countries prohibited movie theaters from showing it.* As late as the 1970s, the picture had not been screened in France.

It all started when James Harris and Stanley Kubrick, two cinema *wunderkinds*, decided to team up. In 1956, the young producer-director duo had just won critical acclaim with their first effort, *The Killing*, a melodrama about a racetrack robbery that starred Sterling Hayden. They wanted to keep the combination going, but they had not been able to find another property. The two had been searching for the right story for months when one day Kubrick recalled a novel that had moved him as a teenager. It was *Paths of Glory*, a 1935 bestseller by Humphrey Cobb that later became a Broadway play. When Harris read the book, he be-

*In 1958, the film was withdrawn from the Brussels Film Festival after French war veterans and Belgian spectators booed it. But it was later resubmitted (and won the Grand Prix) with a foreword to smooth French pride. It said, in part: "This episode of the 1914-1918 war . . . constitutes an isolated case in total contrast with the historical gallantry of the vast majority of French soldiers." In Switzerland, a ban against the movie remained until 1970. When it was first imposed, Swiss authorities said that they feared the film, which they characterized as "subversive propaganda," might offend French pride and thereby impair relations with a "friendly neighbor."

came enthusiastic, too, and immediately acquired film rights. However, that was as far as the project went for a while. No one in Hollywood would touch it.

Studio moguls acknowledged that it had a powerful theme. But they thought it would never make it commercially—first, because its plot was too grim, and, second, because it lacked a love story. Some of the big studios were willing to release it if changes were made to write in the character of a beautiful girl and cut some of the combat scenes.

Harris and Kubrick refused to compromise. "We felt the story was more than strong enough to stand on its own without the addition of the stereotyped Hollywood standbys—actresses with sex appeal and triangles," Kubrick said.

And so the two went ahead on their own. However, they changed tactics. To sell their movie, they decided that they would first have to sign a star. Kubrick had helped write a film script of the book. He and Harris showed it to Kirk Douglas, who, without hesitation, agreed to do it. With such a name actor signed, United Artists accepted the package deal.*

Now the wheels were rolling again. At first they picked France for the site of the film. But when they got overseas, they found that Munich had better location prerequisites—spacious plains for the spectacular battle sequences, an accessible medieval chateau to serve as the general's headquarters, and the vast Geiselgesteig Studios, one of the largest and best-equipped in Europe.

Much of the filming—the movie was to take ten weeks to do at a cost of about $1 million—was shot outside Munich in a country pasture that Harris and Kubrick rented from a farmer. "We employed approximately 800 men, all German police," Kubrick said. At that time the German police went through three years of military training, and Kubrick felt they would be as good as regular soldiers for purposes of the picture.

It took sixty men, working in day and night shifts, to create the battlefield. First, they had to demolish barns, buildings, and sheds. Next, they shredded trees with shellfire and withered spring foliage to no-man's-land gray. Then, using cranes to tear crater holes and trenches, workmen transformed

*The script the studio eventually approved had one key change. It saved the court-martialed soldiers at the last moment—contrary to the novel's ending. Kubrick felt uncomfortable about this. When Douglas asked how he planned to resolve the situation, Kubrick said, "Hell, let's shoot them." Executives at UA learned of the switch only after seeing the first finished print, but they were so impressed with the film that no one said a word.

the farm site into a western front setting. They set up barbed wire and littered the area with old World War I shell casings and abandoned war equipment. In one section, they "crashed" a 1915 warplane into the mutilated earth. Finally, an army of electricians strung up miles of wire to detonate explosives, smoke bombs, and fireworks.

Kubrick, a stickler for detail, made only one concession to realism. He enlarged the trenches to a width of about six feet to make room for tracking cameras. The French World War I trenches were narrower. But Kubrick was intent on getting rolling head-on shots of Douglas and George Macready, who played Douglas' commanding officer, walking through the trenches, and this was the only way he could film such sequences.

Kubrick had been concerned with realism even before his movie days. The son of a Bronx doctor, he was a less than spectacular high school student who graduated with a 67 average. However, school became a passing interest after his father bought him a Graflex camera. He became fascinated with photography. Just after his high school graduation, he snapped a picture of a newsdealer weeping as he sold papers announcing FDR's death. *Look* magazine bought it, and shortly thereafter Kubrick became the magazine's youngest photographer.

Despite his subsequent success as a photojournalist, Kubrick became increasingly interested in movies, but it was years before he had even a modicum of success. When he was twenty-one, the 5' 8", dark-haired Kubrick made his first picture, *Day of the Fight* (1951), a 15-minute documentary of middleweight Walter Cartier during the tension-packed hours before he entered the ring. It barely made a profit, costing $3,900 and selling for $4,000. But despite its commercial failure, Kubrick never forgot the thrill he felt when he saw it playing as a short at the Paramount Theatre in New York. "I knew I was absolutely hooked," he said.

After another financial flop—a documentary called *Flying Padre* (1952) about a New Mexico priest who flew a Piper Cub to minister to his widely dispersed flock—Kubrick decided to try his hand at a feature-length film. He quit his job at *Look*, raised $50,000, mostly from his family, and shot a picture called *Fear and Desire* (1953). The movie, the story of four soldiers lost behind enemy lines, was hardly noticed. His next opus, *Killer's Kiss* (1955), about a prizefighter and a floozy, fared just as poorly.

Years later, in a retrospect of his work at New York's Museum of Modern Art, Kubrick refused to let either of these films be shown. Nevertheless, they enabled him to learn his craft without having to go through a long apprenticeship in other studio jobs.

Then his luck changed when he met James Harris, a young millionaire television distributor. Together they produced *The Killing* (1956), a movie that impressed critics. *Time* and *Saturday Review* rated it as one of the ten best films of 1956. It has since become a cult classic. Yet, even though it was made for only $320,000, it too failed at the box office.

Undaunted, Kubrick went on to do *Paths of Glory* (1957). That was the turning point. Film critics hailed it as a work of art. It was sparsely done and so filled with crackling action and dialogue that there did not seem to be an inch of wasted footage.

There was no stopping Kubrick now. After directing *Spartacus* (1960) at Kirk Douglas' request, he turned out one of 1962's biggest commercial hits—*Lolita*. Even before the rave reviews for that picture were in, he began working on *Dr. Strangelove* (1964), an irreverent, black-humored film about nuclear holocaust. Stanley Kauffmann called it "the best American picture that I can remember since Chaplin's *Monsieur Verdoux* (1947) and Huston's *The Treasure of the Sierra Madre* (1948)."

Four years later, in 1968, his soaring career spun to even loftier heights with the release of his three-year, $11 million metaphysical, science-fiction epic *2001: A Space Odyssey*. At first attacked by some befuddled critics, it became acknowledged as a *tour de force* of cinematic imagination. Three years later, Kubrick scored again with *A Clockwork Orange* (1971), a sobering vision of behavior control in a future dominated by street gangs. Then, in 1975, he did *Barry Lyndon*, an impressionistic, exquisitely photographed adaptation of Thackeray's first novel, which got mixed reviews.*

The success of Kubrick stems from many things. At the forefront, certainly, are his assured camera technique (which emphasizes natural lighting wherever possible), his ability to inspire great performances, and his deft choice of stories. "I wait till I think I've got to make this [picture] if I never make another," Kubrick says. "This gives you the patience to attend to the thousands of details to get them just right."

Kubrick, reluctant to delegate authority, insists on supervising every aspect of his film, from casting to editing. He even takes over the camera when he

*Unlike many other directors, each of Kubrick's films seems totally different in concept. It is as if each time he sets out to do a movie, he wants to make a complete break from the past.

can. When *2001* was screened for New York critics, Kubrick was in the projection booth. Archer Winsten of the *New York Post* once summed up Kubrick's formula: "Spend months deciding on a target and your feelings for it. Use infinite care in taking aim. Fire only when you are triply certain. Attend to every detail after the shot. Leave nothing to chance. And take your time, all the time in the world, as people do when they are truly obsessed."

Only time will tell what Kubrick's final place will be in cinema history. But nothing can diminish the power of the best of his works—particularly *Paths of Glory*, his first major movie.

The screen version of Humphrey Cobb's grisly and bitter war novel opens on the bleak western front of 1916. The virtually impregnable fortifications zigzag 500 miles from the English Channel to the Swiss frontier. Successful attacks are measured in hundreds of yards and are paid for in hundreds of thousands of lives.

For political reasons, the French general staff has decided to try to take the Ant Hill fortification, a key element the Germans have held tenaciously for a year. General Broulard (Adolphe Menjou) goes to the chateau headquarters of General Mireau (George Macready) to tell him of the plan. The attack has been ordered in forty-eight hours. "That comes pretty close to being ridiculous," Mireau says. "My division has been cut to pieces. What's left is in no position to hold the Ant Hill, let alone take it."

Gauging his younger colleague cannily, Broulard shifts his approach. He tells Mireau that there is a good chance of promotion if the position is taken. "We might do it," Mireau mutters, pacing, pounding his fists into his palm. "We might do it."

Within hours he is at the front, breaking the news to his stunned regimental commander, Colonel Dax (Douglas). Formerly a lawyer in civilian life, Dax thinks the scheme is suicidal. Even Mireau concedes that more than half the men will be killed in the attempt, but he won't waver. And Dax, in true-blue military style, follows orders.

Hopeless from the start, the attack fails disastrously. German machine guns cut down one company even before it can reach its own barbed wire. Another company is pinned down midway through no-man's land.

In the rear, livid with rage and humiliation, General Mireau orders his artillery to open fire on his own troops. Twice his artillery officer refuses. Half-insane after the failed charge, Mireau orders Dax to pick men from each company to stand trial for

George Macready playing a general who sacrifices his troops in a hopeless attack because he stands to gain personal glory. His aide, played by Richard Anderson, looks on as the general orders his artillery to fire on his own men in a fruitless attempt to stop their retreat.

cowardice. "If those little sweethearts won't face German bullets," the frustrated Mireau says, "they'll face French ones."

Nothing Dax can say will dissuade Mireau from changing his order. So three men—scapegoats for their superior officer's ambition—are brought to trial. The first is picked by lot, the second because his sergeant despises him, and the third because he has been considered an undesirable in civilian life.

Dax is permitted to act as defense counsel at the court-martial. It turns out to be a farce. No stenographic records are kept. No character witnesses are permitted. No indictment is read.

In the immaculate, elegant, high-ceilinged ballroom of an ancient French chateau—which contrasts sharply with the grimy trenches—the prosecutor gets the three men to admit that they retreated under fire. He argues that this cowardice constitutes a stain on the flag of France. As his polished boots click and echo on the castle's stone floor, he adds: "It is to us that the sad, distressing, repellent duty falls to find the accused guilty. . . ."

Dax, in an impassioned rebuttal, says that the attack was no blot on the honor of France. Rather, it is the court-martial that is the disgrace. Then, turning to the military panel, he says: "To find these

men guilty will be a crime to haunt each of you to the day you die." Nevertheless, the panel returns a guilty verdict and sentences the men to be shot at dawn.

At a somber last meal in their cell, the three men mull over their fate. "You see that cockroach," says Corporal Paris (Ralph Meeker). "Tomorrow morning we'll be dead and he'll be alive. It will have more contact with my wife and child than I will."

Under the pressure, one of the condemned suddenly loses control and starts raving. To stop him, Corporal Paris punches him. The soldier topples to the stone floor and strikes his head so sharply that he fractures his skull and sinks into unconsciousness. Despite his condition, General Mireau refuses to postpone his execution.

So important was the execution scene to Kubrick that he shot it an unheard-of fifty-six times to get it just the way he wanted it. "You have to live with a film the rest of your life," he explained later. "If there's some shortcoming in a film that was brought about by your failure to face a problem—you didn't want to hurt somebody's feelings or you wanted to avoid conflict—it's still your film to live with the rest of your life."

Hours before the scheduled execution, Dax calls

Emile Meyer as a priest giving the last rites to Timothy Carey, chosen for execution only because his commander considers him a social undesirable. A gawky, sad-faced simpleton, he goes whimpering to his death.

General Broulard from a dress ball to make one last plea for his men. The general is unmoved, although he concedes the heavy casualties Dax's men have taken. On the other hand, he figures that the execution will have beneficial effects.

"This execution will be a perfect tonic for the entire division," Broulard says. "There are few things more fundamentally encouraging and stimulating than seeing someone else die. You see, Colonel, troops are like children. Just as a child wants his father to be firm, troops crave discipline. And one way to maintain discipline is to shoot a man now and then."

Then Dax plays what he thinks will be his trump card. The colonel tells Broulard that General Mireau had ordered his own battery commander to fire on his own soldiers during the attack. This all happened before witnesses, Dax says, and he has sworn statements to prove it.

"What has all this got to do with the charges against the condemned prisoners?" the general asks.

Dax counters by asking if it wasn't the same General Mireau who ordered the court-martial to atone for his frustrations. "General, what would your newspapers and politicians do with that?"

Broulard does not reply. Impassive, he merely excuses himself without indicating what action, if any, he will take.

The next morning, the prisoners are marched to an open area near the chateau. The man with the concussion, apparently unaware of his circumstances, is propped up on a stake. A second prisoner goes before the firing squad weeping like a child. Only Corporal Paris is resigned to his fate.

The next day, General Broulard calls Colonel Dax and General Mireau to a meeting. Suddenly, without warning, he informs Mireau of Dax's charges. "There'll have to be an inquiry," Broulard says, matter of factly, casting Mireau to the winds.

"You're making me the goat," the shocked Mireau says as he storms out.

Turning to Dax, Broulard smiles and offers him the General's command. "Come, come," Broulard says, amused. "Don't overdo the surprise. You've been after the job from the start. We all knew that, my boy."

Dax, feeling that his motives have been totally misread, is infuriated. With controlled anger, he says, "I may be many things, sir. But I am not your boy."

Stung, the general offers him a warning: "It

would be a pity to lose your promotion before you get it—a promotion that you have so carefully planned for."

"Sir, would you like me to suggest what you can do with that promotion?"

"Colonel Dax, you will apologize at once or you will be placed under arrest."

"I apologize for not being entirely honest with you," Dax says, his voice rising with each phrase. "I apologize for not revealing my true feelings. I apologize for not telling you sooner that you're a degenerate, sadistic old man. And you can go to hell before I apologize to you now or ever again."

The general realizes that he has totally misjudged his junior officer. Dax is not playing by the rules. He is a maverick, a disappointment.

"You've spoiled the keenness of your mind by wallowing in sentimentality," Broulard says. "You really did want to save those men. And you were not angling for Mireau's command. You're an idealist. And I pity you as I would the village idiot."

Then Broulard tries to get Dax to understand the rationale for the execution from the general's point of view. "We're fighting a war, a war we've got to win. Those men didn't fight, so they were shot. You bring charges against General Mireau, so I insist that he answer them. Wherein have I done wrong?"

Dax says nothing for a moment. Then, measuring his words, he says quietly. "Because you don't

know the answer to that question, I pity you."

The final sequence shifts to a cafe not far from the battle scene. Dax is outside. Inside, his men are trying to forget the war for a few hours by getting drunk. The cafe owner (Roger Vagnoid) brings in a frightened German girl (Suzanne Christian),* evidently someone who has been captured, and orders her to sing for the soldiers. Slowly, haltingly, softly, she starts a simple ballad. At first it is lost in the laughter and din. Gradually, however, the soldiers become aware of her fragile presence, listen, become silent, and eventually join in the plaintive song of love in war. It translates, in part, roughly to:

Once there was a soldier who loved this girl
With a love that would never end. . . .
But then he got the word that his beloved
    lay dying,
And he hurried to her side. . . .

Outside, Dax listens until a soldier reports with orders for his unit to return to the front. "Well, give the men a few minutes, sergeant," Dax says. And again we hear the soldiers' strong voices singing the German ballad as the film ends.

*Miss Christian, a German actress, married Kubrick in 1958, a year after the film was made. They have three children. He was previously married to Toba Metz, a high school classmate, and Ruth Sobotica, a ballet dancer.

218

Peyton
Place

The book jacket of *Peyton Place*.

Peyton Place
(1957)

Directed by Mark Robson. Screenplay by John Michael Hayes, from the novel by Grace Metalious. Music, Franz Waxman. Orchestration, Edward B. Powell. Photography, William Mellor. Film editor, David Bretherton. Produced by Jerry Wald. CinemaScope, DeLuxe Color. 20th Century-Fox. 162 minutes.

Constance MacKenzie	*Lana Turner*
Selena Cross	*Hope Lange*
Michael Rossi	*Lee Philips*
Dr. Matthew Swain	*Lloyd Nolan*
Lucas Cross	*Arthur Kennedy*
Norman Page	*Russ Tamblyn*
Allison MacKenzie	*Diane Varsi*
Betty Anderson	*Terry Moore*
Rodney Harrington	*Barry Coe*
Nellie Cross	*Betty Field*
Ted Carter	*David Nelson*
Mrs. Thornton	*Mildred Dunnock*
Leslie Harrington	*Leon Ames*
Prosecutor	*Lorne Greene*
Seth Bushwell	*Robert H. Harris*
Margie	*Tami Conner*
Charles Partridge	*Staats Cotsworth*
Marion Partridge	*Peg Hillias*
Mrs. Page	*Erin O'Brien-Moore*
Joey Cross	*Scotty Morrow*
Paul Cross	*Bill Lundmark*
Matt	*Alan Reed, Jr.*
Pee Wee	*Kip King*
Kathy	*Steffi Sidney*
Judge	*Tom Greenway*
Bailiff	*Michael Lally*

Grace Metalious, *Peyton Place*'s author, at work in flannel shirt, blue jeans, and sneakers.

"When I was born, time was told not by the clock or the calendar but by the seasons. Summer was carefree contentment. Autumn was that bitter-sweet time of regret for moments that had ended and things that were yet undone. And then winter fell—with a cold mantle of caution and chill. It nipped our noses and our arrogance, and made us move closer to the warm stoves of memory and desire. Spring was promise. But there was a fifth season—of love. And only the wise or the lucky ones knew where to find it."

These are Allison MacKenzie's words as she reminisces about her New England girlhood at the opening of the movie *Peyton Place*. No mythical town is more closely identified with the 1950s than this one that came from the pages of Grace Metalious' best-selling novel.

The story of the scandalous sex life of this ostensibly prim and rock-ribbed American town shocked the nation in 1956. *Peyton Place* became synonymous with the hypocrisy of a small town in which sin ran rampant under the all but transparent cloak of respectability.

By today's standards, the goings-on seem mild, but in the decade of Harry Truman and Dwight D. Eisenhower, *Peyton Place* was the raciest thing in

print. It sold more than 300,000 hard-cover copies and eventually more than twelve million copies in paperback. That total made it the biggest selling novel in modern times until *Valley of the Dolls* broke its record in the early 1970s (with more than fifteen million copies sold).

But *Peyton Place* did more than set sales records. It created such a stir in Mrs. Metalious' real hometown of Gilmanton, New Hampshire (population: 700) that the school board declined to renew her husband's contract as principal of Gilmanton Corner School—even though the book was not yet in print.

The board denied that its contract decision had any connection with the book, but Mrs. Metalious felt otherwise. "Their attitude is that 'we know these things happen, but you're not supposed to write about them in a book so everyone else knows, too.' " "Actually," she added, "New York isn't a hell of a lot different from a small town. You can just hide things better here."

The book was a mixed blessing to this thirty-one-year-old housewife and mother of three who had married at twenty-one and lived in near poverty all her life. It catapulted her to instant success, and she sold the film rights for $125,000. Later, the book became the basis for a long-playing television series.* She appeared on television talk shows, went to Hollywood briefly, and wrote three other novels. None outdid *Peyton Place,* but their sales performances were impressive, nonetheless. *Return to Peyton Place* sold four million copies in paperback and drew $500,000 from Hollywood. *The Tight White Collar* sold more than two million copies, and *No Adam in Eden* earned $500,000 for movie rights. None of them got very favorable reviews, but this didn't faze Mrs. Metalious. "If I'm a lousy writer," she said, "a hell of a lot of people have lousy taste."

However, as her literary life thrived, her private life disintegrated. Her husband divorced her in 1958. Three days later, she maried a disc jockey named T. J. Martin. Within two years, she divorced Martin and remarried her original husband. But in 1964, when she died of a chronic liver ailment, they were again separating.** Before her untimely death at thirty-nine, she said in her candid style: "I'm really the last one in the world qualified to talk about love."

But talk she did. *Peyton Place* was not troubled by Negroes, Jews, or prejudice. Instead, it had more commercially palatable vices like rape, incest, adultery, premarital sex, illegitimacy, and suicide. It was also a tender tale of the beauty and innocence of young love as children growing into their teens tried to come to grips with the adult world. And it was this aspect of the book, as well as her cruder pictures of the seamier side of life, that intrigued the reading public.

When it was first announced that producer Jerry Wald would make a movie out of *Peyton Place,* people said that it couldn't be done. Wald went ahead anyway. His strategy to get the lurid story on the screen was a simple one. He turned *Peyton Place* into an expensively mounted soap opera. True, there was daring use of the word "miscarriage" (which replaces an abortion in the novel) and the phrase "sleeping with a man." There was also a nude swimming scene (although the swimmers were seen only in the distance). But, generally, the movie presented any sordidness through rose-colored glasses. Screenwriter John Michael Hayes

did this by carefully stripping the gutsy novel of its unpretty material while still retaining its storyline. "It is," commented *Variety,* "a shocker without shock."

The film was also carefully cast. Eighteen-year-old Diane Varsi, who had never before appeared in a movie, made an outstanding debut as Allison.† Hope Lange, who had begun her movie career in *Bus Stop* (1956) where she met and married Don Murray, got her first big part as the tragic Selena Cross. Lee Philips, another newcomer, left the Broadway stage to play school principal Michael Rossi. The veteran Lloyd Nolan all but stole the show as the compassionate Dr. Matthew Swain.

But most moviegoers were interested in Lana Turner's transition from glamour parts to motherhood. She played the frigid Constance MacKenzie who rediscovers the joys of love. "She probably turns in the best performance of her career," critic Ronald Johnston wrote half-cynically. "We'll leave it to the individual to decide whether that means anything."

Mrs. Metalious saw the movie at the now defunct Roxy Theatre in New York City. "I was pleasantly surprised," she said. "But I thought it was sugar-coated."

Here's the way she appraised the cast: "I thought Lee Philips was terrible. Lana Turner, good. Lloyd Nolan, great. Hope Lange did a good job but didn't look like Selena. I loved Hollywood for killing her father. Allison (Diane Varsi) came through fine."

The studio's decision to shoot the film on location added dimension to the movie. The original plan was to photograph it in Mrs. Metalious' New Hampshire hometown. But when the hierarchy in Gilmanton came out against the idea, the studio switched the locale to Woodstock, Vermont.††

---

*The TV "Peyton Place," which transplanted soap opera to nighttime video, was a proving ground for such young stars as Mia Farrow (Allison MacKenzie), Ryan O'Neal (Rodney Harrington), and Barbara Parkins (Betty Anderson). Dorothy Malone (Constance MacKenzie) also had a leading role.

**Her family contested a deathbed will in which she bequeathed her estate—reported at various figures between $250,000 and $1 million—to John Rees of Boston, an English journalist who had collaborated with her on her later books. Rees, however, relinquished all claims to the estate.

†Unfortunately, she quickly faded from the movie scene. After getting an Oscar nomination and appearing in a few more pictures, she quit Hollywood. She offered no explanation as she left with her two-year-old son. A couple of years later, she agreed to do an interview with movie writer Joel Hyams in her simple apartment in San Mateo, California. She told him that when she had decided to become an actress, she also decided that she would do it only for a while, only while it was still a learning process. "It was never meant to be permanent," she said. She was a rare Hollywood personality, Hyams said, an independent spirit who wanted to search out her own life. Nevertheless, she made a comeback in the 1970s and appeared in pictures like *Wild in the Streets* (1968), *Bloody Mama* (1971), and *I Never Promised You a Rose Garden* (1977).

††As late as 1976, twenty years after *Peyton Place's* publication, the Gilmanton Public Library contained no copy of the book. However, the situation was remedied in February of that year. Barbara Walters learned of the fact when she did a profile of the town on the "Today" show. During a televised interview, she presented a copy of the book to one of the town's leading residents and asked that it be donated to the library.

Allison MacKenzie (Diane Varsi) munches a hot dog as she and her date, Norman Page (Russ Tamblyn), enjoy a Labor Day picnic.

Again, town fathers rejected the plan. Finally, someone who had been in Maine during the filming there of *Carousel* (1956) remembered the picturesque town of Camden (population 3,300). This time the townspeople spread the welcome mat for the movie company. "This is a nice town," said Martha Clason, the gray-haired lady who runs the bookstore. "I don't see how anyone is going to identify us with *Peyton Place*. Anyway, we ourselves know better. And that's what really counts."

Local residents eagerly joined the production as extras. Almost six hundred of them appeared in the big picnic scene. They netted $10 each for their day's work. Many contributed their earnings to the local hospital building fund.

The townspeople still tell anecdotes about the exciting weeks of shooting. When director Mark Robson put out a call for 1938 vintage cars, some eighty old buggies turned up.

Weather, of course, is a key factor in outdoor shooting, and Robson grew to depend on an old bottle of emulsified oil shampoo. The bottle, which stood on the shelf of a local grocery, had served as a weather guide for a quarter of a century. It would cloud up inside if it was going to rain. Before the company left, it made believers out of the Hollywood crew.

Days of sunshine were busy ones. Actors had to be up at 5 A.M. to get made up so they could be on the set by 8 A.M. Shooting lasted until 6 P.M. In the evenings there were conferences and script study.

"I think what everyone was worried about was how this Hollywood crew would behave," said Hamilton Hall, editor of the *Camden Herald.* "Some people had notions about that. Actually, everyone's mighty pleased. We've found them very nice visitors. They've just gone ahead with their work, interfering as little as possible. I think they've made a lot of new friends for Hollywood."

Actually, only a small part of the picture reflected the scenes shot here. Miss Turner did not have to come to Maine. Her entire role was shot on the west coast. But director Robson felt the location shooting added much to the film. "You couldn't duplicate this scenery at the studio," Robson said. "It's the feeling of a small town that comes through. Every minute of our stay was worthwhile."

The movie opens in the days just before World War II. Michael Rossi (Lee Philips) is riding into the little town of Peyton Place where he is taking over the post of high school principal. He serves as a kind of touchstone to introduce us to the other characters.

On the outskirts of Peyton Place, Rossi passes the tarpaper shack where the Cross family lives. Paul (Bill Lundmark) is leaving home despite the efforts of his mother, Nellie Cross (Betty Field), and his seventeen-year-old sister, Selena (Hope Lange). He is going because his drunken stepfather, Lucas (Arthur Kennedy), stole his savings to spend on liquor.

At the high school, Rossi meets Mrs. Thornton (Mildred Dunnock), the senior teacher who had expected to get the principalship. To her surprise, she finds she is impressed by Rossi.

"I'm rather old-fashioned," he tells her as they chat in an empty classroom. "I have just two rules. I want this school to teach the truth, as far as we know it. I don't want any teacher making a fairy tale out of life. . . . And rule two—teaching a minimum of facts and a maximum of ideas. . . . If war comes, these kids shouldn't fight for historical dates but the ideas behind them."

That night, after strolling through the town, Rossi and Dr. Matthew Swain (Lloyd Nolan) go into the diner. A few minutes later, Constance MacKenzie (Lana Turner) comes in for coffee. She's been to the movies while her daughter, Allison (Diane Varsi), is having a birthday party at home. Swain tells Rossi that Constance is a widow who came back to Peyton Place after the death of her husband, a New York advertising executive. Struck by her beauty, Rossi asks to meet her. "Won't do you any good," Swain says. He tells Rossi that she is known as the Peyton Place "icicle," but he takes him over anyway and introduces him.

From the outset, he and Constance hit a discordant note. Rossi mentions that he intends to start a sex education course.

"Isn't that a function of the home?" Constance asks.

"You'd think it would be," Rossi says. "And yet, not one parent in ten does it. Sex is taboo in the home."

"And it should be in the schools," she snaps.

"Where will they learn it? In the alleys? In parked cars?"

"They'll learn it when they marry," Constance growls. With that, she bids him good night and struts out.

It's only a few blocks to her home, and when she gets there, Constance is shocked to find all the lights out. Allison and her friends are kissing in the dark. Furious, Constance sends all the kids packing. Allison tries to calm her mother, saying that they were only having innocent fun, but that far from satisfies Constance.

"Do you like being pawed over in the dark by some young animal with one thing on his mind?" Constance asks. "Oh, Allison, I want you to fall in love and, at the proper time, marry a man who respects you. I want you to have a good name. I want—"

"You want!" Allison cries. "You want! If any man would seriously ask me, I'd run away and be his mistress." At that, Constance slaps her daughter.

The next day, Sunday, an even more violent scene is played out at Selena's home. Lucas, alone with Selena, watches his stepdaughter dress for church. Suddenly he accuses her of showing herself off and they start a bitter quarrel. Just as Allison comes in, Lucas grabs Selena and slaps her angrily.

The camera cuts to a lofty mountain perch where Allison has taken an afternoon hike with shy Norman Page (Russ Tamblyn). Alone and away from their domineering parents, they begin to discuss their ambitions and emotions. Norman confesses that his shyness stems from his relationship with his mother. They both admit that their knowledge of sex comes from books sent in plain wrappers.

"You shouldn't be afraid of girls," Allison says.

"I know," Norman says. "But I don't know what I can do about it."

"I know what you can do," Allison says. "You can start with me. I'll prove anything your mother ever said was wrong. Would you kiss me, Norman?"

He kisses her tentatively, then tenderly.

A few weeks later when the school graduation dance comes, Allison goes with Rodney Harrington (Barry Coe), son of wealthy mill owner Leslie Harrington (Leon Ames). But at the dance, Rodney steals off with Betty Anderson (Terry Moore), a "fast" girl he has dropped under pressure from his father.

At the ball, Rossi succeeds in getting Constance MacKenzie to dance with him. As they part that night, Rossi kisses her. She doesn't resist, but she tells him she isn't interested in romance. "It's too late," Constance says.

The scene changes to the Cross shack, where Ted Carter (David Nelson), Selena's boyfriend, is saying good night to her. He tells her he wants to become a lawyer. She says she'll wait for him, then enters the shack. Inside, she finds her stepfather

Selina Cross (Hope Lange) saying goodbye to Ted Carter (David Nelson) as he leaves for the army in World War II.

Millionaire Leslie Harrington (Leon Ames) seated next to Betty Anderson (Terry Moore).

alone and drunk. "I thought you were something out of a dream," he says, bleary-eyed, attracted by her appearance in her white ball gown. "Let's have a drink and celebrate your growing up." She ignores him and goes to her room. Lucas follows her, storms in, and rapes her.

Two months later, Selena goes to see Dr. Swain who tells her she is pregnant. At first she refuses to say who the father is, but under pressure, she breaks down and names Lucas. Outraged, Swain rushes to Lucas and threatens to expose him and send him to jail unless he signs a confession. When Lucas weakens and consents, Swain orders him to get out of town for good. "If you do," Swain says, "I'll keep this paper in my safe. If you don't, I'll use it against you." Neither of them realize it, but Nellie Cross has overheard everything.

That night Selena returns home, and Lucas, furious at her for exposing him, tries to beat her. She eludes him and runs into the woods. As she escapes, she slips down a steep, rocky hillside. The next day, Dr. Swain discovers that she has had a miscarriage and performs an abortion. To keep Selena's secret, he lists it in his records as an appendectomy.

The summer passes quickly and then it is Labor Day, the occasion for the annual town picnic. Politicians make speeches, children stuff themselves with hot dogs and watermelon, and couples sneak off for a quiet swim. Among them are Norman and Allison. Unbeknownst to them, so are Betty and Rodney—who decide to do their swimming in the nude. They are seen and mistaken for Norman and Allison. By evening, word has gotten back to Constance that her daughter has been swimming with Norman.

When the two youngsters return, they hear the charges and are dumbfounded. Norman's mother takes him home, scolding him all the way, while Constance and Allison rage at each other in a bitter scene. In her fury, Constance tells her daughter that, though outwardly living a normal life, she has been concealing a dark, secret past: she has never married. Allison's father was wed to another woman when Constance had an affair with him. So Allison is an illegitimate child. In tears, Allison runs upstairs to her room. Suddenly, her scream is heard. In the bedroom closet, she finds Nellie Cross, the MacKenzie's maid, who has hanged herself.

Lee Philips and Diane Varsi, both of whom made their film debuts in *Peyton Place*. Each showed promise but neither lasted long on the Hollywood scene.

When World War II comes, most of the young men enter the army. Allison, disillusioned, goes to live in New York. Then, one Christmas, Constance, lonely with Allison away, goes to see Rossi. She tells him why her daughter left, but the news fails to shake him. "I told you I'm committing myself to you all the way," he says, embracing Constance. "I mean it."

Meanwhile, at the Cross shack, Selena and her little brother Joey (Scotty Morrow) are preparing to celebrate Christmas. There is a knock at the door and Lucas, now a sailor, enters. As if the years had never passed, he again attacks his step-daughter—even in the presence of his tiny son. Selena fights back desperately until Lucas stumbles by the fireplace. Then she grabs a piece of firewood and strikes him over the head.

Moments later, she realizes that she has killed him. She wants to give herself up, but Joey begs her not to. If they take her away, he'll be alone. Therefore, they bury Lucas behind the shack. However, as the days pass, Selena finds that she isn't strong enough to carry the burden of her crime. Eventually she turns herself in.

Selena's trial quickly becomes a major event in Peyton Place. Allison, hearing that her friend is in trouble, returns from New York. So does Norman, now a paratrooper. They both testify in Selena's behalf. But the prosecutor (Lorne Greene) makes a strong case against her because Selena is ashamed to disclose that Lucas once raped her. She has sworn Dr. Swain to secrecy, and by so doing, she has weakened her plea of self-defense. The prosecutor points out that Lucas owned the house and so was entitled to use it. And, he says, instead of acting like an innocent person and going to the police, Selena buried his body—like a criminal.

Allison testifies that she once saw Lucas beat Selena, but under cross-examination, she concedes she saw only a single slap. Constance further dilutes her daughter's testimony when she admits that Allison never mentioned it.

As the trial reaches its conclusion, it becomes clear that Dr. Swain is Selena's last hope. He accepts that challenge as soon as he takes the stand. The doctor stuns the packed courtroom by disclosing that he had assisted Selena in a miscarriage of Lucas' baby—then falsified his records to cover up the abortion. Next, he produces Lucas' signed confession. By doing this, Swain is jeopardizing his license to practice as a physician. But he says it's time someone spoke up to say that Selena killed Lucas out of fear she would have to submit to him a second time.

"I'm violating her secrecy," Swain says, "for a bigger purpose. We're all prisoners of each other's gossip, killed by each other's whispers. And it's time it stopped. Our best young people leave as soon as they are old enough to earn the price of a bus ticket. They contribute the best part of their character to other communities because they're stifled in Peyton Place. It's time you people woke up. There's something much bigger than the tragedy of Selena Cross on trial here—our indifference, our failure as a community to watch over one another, to know who needs help and to give it.

Selena has been living in a prison of her own long enough, one that we helped build."

Swain's plea is the turning point. The jury returns a not guilty verdict.

That evening, Constance returns home with Rossi with a bittersweet feeling—elated that Selena is free but saddened because Allison is leaving and still estranged from her. However, as they reach the porch, Allison is there waiting for Constance.

And so as night falls, the people of Peyton Place settle into their homes and begin again the normal everyday pace of life in a small town. Some are a little wiser from their experience. "We finally discovered that season of love," says Allison, musing to herself on the train to New York. "It's only found in someone else's heart. Right now, someone you know is looking everywhere for it. And it's in you."

Picnic

Verna Felton implores drifter William Holden to come in for breakfast, his reward for backyard chores.

Picnic
(1956)

Directed by Joshua Logan. Screenplay by Daniel Taradash, based on the William Inge play. Camera, James Wong Howe. Art director, William Flannery.* Editors, Charles Nelson* and William A. Lyons.* Music, George Duning. Orchestration, Arthur Morton. Conducted by Morris Stoloff. Produced by Fred Kohlmar. A Columbia Picture in CinemaScope and Technicolor. 115 minutes.

Hal Carter	*William Holden*
Rosemary Sydney	*Rosalind Russell*
Madge Owens	*Kim Novak*
Flo Owens	*Betty Field*
Millie Owens	*Susan Strasberg*
Alan Benson	*Cliff Robertson*
Howard Bevans	*Arthur O'Connell*
Mrs. Helen Potts	*Verna Felton*
Linda Sue Breckenridge	*Reta Shaw*
Bomber	*Raymond Bailey*
Christine Schoenwalder	*Elizabeth W. Wilson*
Juanita Badger	*Phyllis Newman*
First Policeman	*Don C. Harvey*
Second Policeman	*Steve Benton*
Trainman	*Abraham Weinlood*

*Academy Award Winner.

Holden's colorful yarns hold the attention of seventeen-year-old Susan Strasberg at the Labor Day picnic. Looking on are Rosalind Russell and Arthur O'Connell.

A freight train rumbles into a small Kansas town on a hot Labor Day morning and a young drifter alights. In the next twenty-four hours he will come in contact with the local belle who is tired of being thought of as just pretty, her tomboy sister who is crossing over into womanhood, and a spinster school teacher yearning for a husband. His presence will have a catalytic effect on all their lives.

This is the theme of *Picnic*, the movie based on William Inge's 1953 play that won the Pulitzer Prize and established him as a major playwright of the 1950s. Unlike many playwrights before him, Inge did not choose to focus on social problems. "I think we have to accept the world as it is," he said. "We can't make overnight changes."

Instead, he wrote about the humdrum lives of everyday people, most of them from small towns, and the frustrating boredom of their provincial existences. Ingel was particularly adept at delineating women whom he portrayed realistically, even harshly. He saw them as hypocrites in the

subtle game of sex. They were, he thought, caught up in a curious love-hate relationship. They longed for love, yet they were fearful of being taken advantage of. Therefore, some hid their emotions behind icy exteriors.

Inge once put his observations about courtship like this: "I was born in Independence, Kansas. As a child, I was struck by the fact that the women there were always protesting while men pursued. I got the idea that women hated men. I later came to the conclusion that this was an act—that there was a certain artificiality in their attitude. Some women love so passionately that they're embarrassed about it because it makes them dependent on men.

"In *Picnic*," Inge continued, "the school teacher protests at first, then humbly begs the man to marry her. You feel her deep loneliness. I've tried in it to catch a variety of female reactions to men...."

Although he had written one successful play previously *(Come Back, Little Sheba)* and two right afterward *(Bus Stop* and *The Dark at the Top of the Stairs), Picnic* was unquestionably the peak of his career. It was a simple work, but one in which his craftsmanship clearly showed through because he wove together the emotional traumas of half a dozen people.

Yet, as successful as the play was, the movie emerged as the more memorable version, and justifiably so. It deepened the relationship of the characters and turned the key scene, the picnic, into a kaleidoscopic highlight.

In the play the picnic was only mentioned in dialogue, but in the movie it became a major event. Like a play within a play, it had a beginning, a middle, and an end. Moviegoers saw the picnic's changing mood from the breathless, boisterous hilarity of afternoon fun and games to the quiet, subtle beauty of autumn dusk.

Joshua Logan, in his first full-fledged directing assignment, took his cast to the wheat and corn belt of Kansas. Logan, who had directed the stage play, filmed the picnic scene in the town of Halstead, and it would be an understatement to say that he was pleased with the outcome.

"There was no picnic in the play. It was only talked about," Logan said. "But we were able to stage the picnic in Halstead's public park, and it turned out to be one of the most important scenes in the picture.

"We employed nearly all of the townspeople as extras in this big scene and they were wonderful to work with. For natural effects, we had the little Arkansas River, which flows through the park, and a gorgeous sunset that [James Wong] Howe was able to capture on film. We had to work fast, as we were afraid of being interrupted by a cyclonic storm. But fortunately, the spiral cloud we saw coming toward us veered off in time to save the stage and sunsets."

Curiously, Logan took only three actors from the play—Reta Shaw, Elizabeth Wilson, and Arthur O'Connell—leaving behind such talented people as Janice Rule (the girl), Ralph Meeker (the boy), and Eileen Heckart (the school teacher). Two newcomers, Paul Newman and Kim Stanley, also appeared in the stage version.

In each case, in my judgment, their film counterparts failed to match the stage performances. For example, Kim Novak was pretty enough but too wooden and one-dimensional to show the loneliness and despair in Madge Owens' soul. And Rosalind Russell was much too loud and frenetic to bring out the softer, more pathetic nuances of the spinster. Some of this can be attributed to bad directing on Logan's part.

If it is true that many of Inge's characters have a quality of searching and unfulfillment, it is also true that he seems to share this tentativeness in his own life. A lifelong bachelor and the son of a traveling salesman, he went to the University of Kansas and grew up steeped in the tradition of the Middle West.

In his early years he was an amateur actor, a college instructor, and a drama critic for the *St. Louis Star-Times*. Then an event occurred that transformed his life. He interviewed Tennessee Williams and saw his play *The Glass Menagerie*. Said Inge: "I found it so beautiful and so deeply moving that I felt a little ashamed for having led what I felt was an unproductive life."

After a first work called *Farther Off from Heaven*, which was produced in Dallas in 1947, Inge wrote *Come Back, Little Sheba*. The play was his first hit and launched his career.

At the height of his success, he lived in New York City's famous Dakota apartment house, an old, musty, fortress-like structure on Central Park West. But he said he never liked New York "because I lost my identity there."

After three more successful plays, two stage disasters followed. Critics noted an emptiness in his later work. He went to Hollywood and got an Oscar for the screenplay for *Splendor in the Grass* (1961), but it was mostly downhill after that. Movie work became hard to find. He tried his hand at novels. Only one, *Good Luck, Miss Wyckoff*, published in 1960, had moderate success. In 1970, an off-Broadway play, *The Last Pad*, got brutal reviews. Critics found it embarrassingly bad, saying that Inge tried to bring in contemporary trends like nudity and vulgar language in a play whose storyline and structure were not right for them.

As the years passed, Inge felt that he was not fulfilling his potential. His sister, with whom he led a secluded life in Hollywood Hills, California, said that he became morose and depressed. He survived an overdose of barbiturates, but then, a few weeks later, in June 1973, his sister discovered him dead in his garage, slumped in the seat of his Mercedes-Benz. Police found the engine running and the windows rolled down. His autopsy listed carbon monoxide poisoning as the cause of death.

Inge left behind no great body of work. Some say that he never achieved the stature of such other playwrights of the 1950s as Williams and Arthur Miller. But he was a craftsman who knew how to strip away the subsurface of small-town life and portray the lonely striving of some of its people, a task he did best in *Picnic*.

Rosalind Russell is all aglow as she goes off to her long-awaited wedding. The same can't be said for Arthur O'Connell. Tossing rice and waving are Betty Field, Reta Shaw, Elizabeth Wilson, Susan Strasberg, and a glum-looking Kim Novak.

The movie opens as Hal Carter (William Holden), a broad-shouldered drifter, arrives in Salinson, Kansas. Hal is a former college football player who flunked out of school and ever since has been bouncing from one small job and minor scuffle to another. He has come to Salinson to see if his old college chum, Alan Benson (Cliff Robertson), son of the owner of a large grain elevator, will help him get a job.

Broke and hungry, Hal stops at a small house and asks to do some yard chores in return for breakfast.* Friendly, outgoing Mrs. Potts (Verna Felton) agrees. She is a tough little woman, still caring for her mother who, years ago, had her marriage annulled after one day.

Unbeknownst to Hal, his odd jobs are about to bring him into the vulnerable backyard world of Mrs. Potts' next-door neighbor, Flo Owens (Betty Field), and Mrs. Owens' two daughters—Madge (Kim Novak), who wants men to be attracted to her for qualities other than her face and figure, and Millie (seventeen-year-old Susan Strasberg, making her debut), an uninhibited adolescent.

In addition, there is Flo's school-teacher boarder, Rosemary Sydney (Rosalind Russell), a spinster who seems outwardly like a good sport but who is inwardly yearning for male attention. Finally there is Flo herself who hates Hal on sight. She is wary about the immediate attraction that her daughter and Hal have for each other. Hal reminds Flo of her happy-go-lucky husband who deserted her. She wants Madge to marry dependable Alan Benson and live the safe, rich life she never knew.

"A pretty girl doesn't have long—just a few years," Flo tells Madge. "Then she's the equal of kings. She can walk out of a shanty like this and live in a palace. [But] if she loses her chance when she's young, she might as well throw all her prettiness away."

"I'm only nineteen," Madge protests.

*Holden had to strip to the waist for the yard scene and that led to one of the sillier things he had to do in movies. "I had to shave my chest every day," Holden said, "because the Motion Picture Code said hairy chests were dirty."

233

"And next summer you'll be twenty," her mother says. "And then twenty-one. And then—forty."

The reunion of Alan and Hal is a boisterous one as they recall old college days. But Alan's exuberance quickly turns to apprehension when he learns that Hal has already met Madge, for Alan hasn't forgotten his school chum's way with girls.

Nevertheless, Alan agrees to lend Hal a car to take Madge's sister, Millie, to the picnic. Alan is escorting Madge, and Rosemary's date is Howard Bevans (Arthur O'Connell), a somewhat dull school supplier. Loaded with lunch hampers, everyone drives to the picnic grounds next to the river.

The day is sunny and warm and there is a swirl of frenetic activity. Bands are blaring. Tots tug to free themselves from their mothers. Adults and teenagers sprint together in a three-legged race. A baby gives an off-key vocalist a raspberry cheer. There are the watermelon and pie eating contests, a balloon popping competition, amusement rides, and tests of strength.

When night falls, the picnic takes on a different aura. A full moon and Japanese lanterns light up the festivities, and Madge, who has been named the picnic queen, floats down the river in a swan boat. Spectators on the river bank sing "Ain't She Sweet?" She is resplendent in crown and robe, and Hal, who has been jitterbugging with her kid sister on the boat landing, is suddenly struck by her loveliness. Minutes later, when Madge passes by, she and Hal are attracted to each other. They begin dancing.

Music helped create the mood of this key sequence. Columbia Pictures had commissioned composer George Duning to do the music, and he wrote a love song for this scene. But in the play, Logan had used the recording of "Moonglow." Since that number had worked to create just the right mood in the play, Logan did not want to see it eliminated in the picture.

However, when he saw Novak and Holden dancing to "Moonglow," Logan felt that it wasn't enough. So he asked Duning to blend the composer's own *Picnic* love theme with "Moonglow." After some hesitation, Duning agreed. The result was what movie audiences heard in the picture—one melody superimposed on another.

A rhythm section plays "Moonglow" as Novak and Holden dance. But as they look into each

O'Connell and Russell on the back porch.

234

other's eyes and move closer, a big string orchestra comes in with the *Picnic* love theme which soars above "Moonglow." It worked beautifully. Logan shrugged off the fact that the cameras showed only a small group accompanying the dance.

The score received wide acclaim, and the song was on the Hit Parade for three months. The Composers' Guild of America gave the movie an award for "best original underscore for a non-musical picture," and Steve Allen later wrote lyrics to the melody.

The episode marks the end of the picture's pastoral scenes. After the dance, Rosemary drinks too much, and with her inhibitions down, she storms after Hal. Embarrassingly aggressive, she insists on dancing with him. When he tries to pull away, she grabs him so tightly that she rips his shirt. Enraged, she tells Hal: "The gutter is where you came from. And the gutter is where you belong."

Humiliated, Hal rushes away. Madge follows him and they drive off in the borrowed car. He confesses that he feels unwanted and at loose ends. Madge senses that although Hal seems brash and confident, he is inwardly weak. And this awareness brings out the woman in her. "You've got lots of qualities," she says, trying to reassure him. Soon they are in each other's arms.

Meanwhile, Rosemary, realizing how badly she has behaved, becomes despondent. When Howard drives her home, she pours out her troubles. "It's no good living in a rented room," she says. "Each year, I tell myself it's the last. Something will happen. It never does." She turns to Howard. "You gotta marry me, Howard." Falling to her knees, she pleads pathetically. "Please marry me, Howard. Please!"

The next morning, Howard calls on Rosemary to tell her that marriage is out of the question. But before he can say anything, she rushes into his arms and proudly announces to everyone that they are eloping. Howard, overwhelmed, meekly accepts the situation. He drives off with her for their marriage and what will be, for Rosemary at least, fulfillment.

While all this is going on, Alan, wild with jealousy, has called the police and accused Hal of stealing his car. When Hal returns to Alan's estate, they exchange bitter accusations. Hal battles first with Alan and then with the police before he breaks away and runs off to Madge. He tells her that he has a job in Tulsa and begs her to come with him. Unsure of herself and of Hal, she is hesitant. Then Hal tells her that he wants her to marry him.

But Madge is frozen to inactivity. She is torn between her desire to go and her knowledge of two lives of misery—her deserted mother and frustrated Mrs. Potts next door. The freight train chugs by. Without a decision from Madge, Hal hightails it down the road, clambers aboard, and waves from the top of one of the cars.

Madge's mother, seeing his departure as good riddance, tries to console her daughter. But Madge remains despondent. Even the thought that Alan still wants her is of no comfort. In spite of his wealth, she doesn't really love him.

It is Madge's sister who finally gives her the courage she needs. Millie tells her to follow her heart. "Go with him, Madge," she says. "For once in your life, do something bright."

Suddenly her doubts vanish and Madge knows exactly what she must do. Her mother tries to stop her as she leaves to catch the bus, warning her that only misery lies ahead. "He's no good," she says. "He'll never be able to support you. And when he does have a job, he'll spend it all on drink. And then, there'll be other women."

"You don't love someone because he's perfect," Madge says, freeing herself and running off.

The last sequences show a bird's-eye view of the crazy-quilt pattern of the Kansas plains. Hal's freight train rumbles toward the city. The bus, too, speeds on its way. For better or worse, Hal and Madge will soon be together.

Inge was never satisfied with this ending. He originally had Madge stay behind. But he dropped this resolution and substituted its melodramatic windup at Logan's suggestion and under pressure to meet a rehearsal deadline. Some felt that this was the logical ending because Madge had grown as a person through her relationship with Hal, and so she had to follow him.

But Inge never felt quite comfortable with this outcome, and after the movie's success, he wrote a second version for his own satisfaction. His major revision was changing the ending to conform to his first instinct. Madge does not run after Hal. Instead she stays home, as in real life a girl like Madge probably would have done.

The new ending was, of course, a sadder one, but one that gave the play more character insight. Inge called his revision *Summer Brave* after a passage in a poem by Shakespeare.* It was this second version that Inge preferred, but even so he was realistic enough to accept the fact that the changes would have had a disastrous effect on the acceptance of his work by audiences in the 1950s.

"*Summer Brave* might not have enjoyed any success on Broadway whatever," Inge said, "nor won any of the prizes that were bestowed upon *Picnic*. But I feel it is more humorously true than *Picnic*. And it does fulfill my original intentions."**

*"Youth like summer morn, age like winter weather.
   Youth like summer brave, age like winter bare."

**Alexis Smith starred as Rosemary in the Broadway version that played in 1975. Nan Martin was Madge's mother, Ernest Thompson played Hal, and Jill Eikenberry was Madge. Unfortunately, the reviews were disappointing. Clive Barnes, the *New York Times* drama critic, said it was a well-constructed play that transcended *Picnic*. But on the whole, Barnes found *Summer Brave* "cornball, trivial, and fundamentally superficial." Another critic, Allan Wallach of *Newsday*, the Long Island daily, found even less to praise. He said that the play did not age gracefully and that Inge "didn't manage to say anything of great interest about women and their narrow lives or the young transient who briefly disrupts them." Summing up, Wallach wrote: "Inge has written that he regards this version as 'more humorously true' than the original. What seems truer still after seeing on stage the result of this rewriting is that it requires an act of will to care whether Madge stays or goes."

Pillow
Talk

Doris Day does a slow burn while Rock Hudson carries her—bed covers, pajamas and all—across the street to his apartment.

Pillow Talk
(1959)

Directed by Michael Gordon. Screenplay by Stanley Shapiro* and Maurice Richlin,* based on a story by Russell Rouse* and Clarence Greene.* Photography director, Arthur E. Arling. Art direction, Alexander Golitzen and Richard H. Riedel. Film editor, Milton Carruth. Music, Frank DeVol. Songs: "Pillow Talk" by Buddy Pepper and Inez James; "I Need No Atmosphere," "You Lied," "Possess Me," and "Inspiration" by Joe Lubin and I. J. Roth; "Roly Poly" by Elsa Doran and Sol Lake. Produced by Ross Hunter and Martin Melcher. CinemaScope and Eastman Color. Universal-International. 110 minutes.

Brad Allen	*Rock Hudson*
Jan Morrow	*Doris Day*
Jonathan Forbes	*Tony Randall*
Alma	*Thelma Ritter*
Pierot	*Marcel Dalio*
Mrs. Walters	*Lee Patrick*
Tony Walters	*Nick Adams*
Harry	*Allen Jenkins*
Dr. Maxwell	*Alex Gerry*
Nurse Resnick	*Mary McCarty*
Marie	*Julia Meade*
Entertainer	*Perry Blackwell*
Mr. Conrad	*Hayden Rorke*
Eileen	*Valerie Allen*
Yvette	*Jacqueline Beer*
Tilda	*Arlen Stuart*

*Academy Award Winner.

Hudson, hauling another load, this time lends special assistance to Nick Adams who has hoisted one too many.

Doris von Kappelhoff and Roy Scherer, Jr. Remember them? She was the freckled-faced girl next door, the wholesome, bouncy blonde with the sunny smile and the Pollyanna disposition. She was also a fresh-scrubbed virgin and nothing short of marriage would change that.

He was a threat to her chastity—a tall, dark, handsome bachelor with a strong jaw and finely chiseled features. A consummate wolf, he was eternally, but unsuccessfully, trying to get Miss Golden Girl in bed with him.

These movie lovers were better known as Doris Day and Rock Hudson. They never won Oscars, but they were favorites of every director and producer. The reason was simple—they were a sure-fire bet to pack theatres all over the country, and they made lots and lots of money.

In the 1950s and 1960s, Miss Day and Hudson led the list of top box office moviemakers time and time again. In 1970, Hudson tied for third with Elizabeth Taylor and Cary Grant in a *Motion Picture Herald* poll to pick the ten leading money-makers of the 1960s.

Yet, despite their runaway dollar success, they were both less than ecstatic about certain aspects of their professional life. The bugaboo for Hudson was his name. For Miss Day, it was her public image. Much to her dismay, she became a grown-up symbol of the girl-next-door. She doggedly tried to put that characterization to rest—but without much luck.

By the 1970s, despite her protests, "Doris Day" became to feminists the same sort of thing that "Uncle Tom" became to blacks. Women libbers used her name to epitomize the American soap opera ideal of what a woman should be—untouched by human hands, always wearing white, smiling. "To be called 'Doris Day,' " one feminist said, "means you're still fettered, still fawning, still trying to act out the cheerfully subservient role those in power—in this case, men—have assigned to you."

Over the years, Hollywood writers produced reams of copy about her un-Hollywood ways. They said she neither smoked nor drank, abhorred swearing, and crusaded against cruelty to animals.

Oscar Levant was widely quoted for quipping: "I knew Doris Day before she was a virgin." Some say she really is a "quiet swinger." Others assert that a dinner invitation at her home means starting with carrot juice at 5:45 P.M. and ending at 9 P.M. after ice cream from her soda fountain and a movie on her living room screen.

Whichever is closer to reality, Miss Day got so sick of trying to convince reporters she wasn't Miss Goody Two-Shoes that she once stopped giving interviews. She blamed it on exhaustion and a nervous breakdown. Nevertheless, the Hollywood Women's Press Club gave her its annual Sour Apple Award.

Later, she set up ground rules restricting the questions—or, as her late husband and manager, Martin Melcher, put it—setting up "areas of sensitivity" that reporters were not allowed to probe. An alternative was to give Melcher complete "control" of the story. That meant subjecting the article to his censorship.*

"Look, I'm a person," Miss Day told one writer. "I don't go around saying 'sweet darling, precious' all the time. Sometimes, it's _____ ," she said, filling in the blank with a ferocious growl. "I'm not a slice of pie."

In the 1970s, she surprised her fans when she said she thought a woman ought to live with a potential mate before marriage. She added that she would give that advice to a daughter who came to her with plans to marry. "I would strongly urge her first to have an affair with him. . . . It's terribly important to get to know someone," said Doris, who has strolled down the connubial aisle four times. "And you don't get to know that person well until you live with him."

But it wasn't until her surprisingly frank autobiography, *Doris Day, Her Own Story,* was published in 1975 that she really broke with her Snow White image. Written in collaboration with A. E. Hotchner, the book revealed some hitherto unpublicized romances and personality problems.

Among these items were the following facts:

—At the age of ten she found out that her father was having an affair with the mother of her best friend.

—At seventeen she was married—the first of three bad marriages. She said that her first husband, musician Al Jorden, turned out to be a "psychopathic sadist."

—Later she had real and rumored affairs. The rumored affairs—affairs she said were dreamed up by tabloid writers—linked her to such notables as Maury Wills, Elgin Baylor, Jerry West, Pancho Gonzalez, Glen Campbell, and Frank Sinatra. According to Doris, they were men whom she

knew only casually. One real liaison she did admit having was with an actor whose name she has never disclosed. The fact that he was married did not dissuade her from the affair. "I have no qualms about the other person's marital life," she said. "He [the actor] was an adult, a forceful man, and if he had honest feelings for me, that's all I asked of him."

—At forty-four, when Martin Melcher, her third (of four) husbands died in their seventeenth year of marriage, she discovered that he had squandered the millions she had earned and left her with a monumental debt.

Needless to say, the book was a best-seller.

For his part, Hudson never lived down his silly name which made him the butt of countless Hollywood jokes. It was coined by Henry Willson, his first agent, who also changed Arthur Gelien to Tab Hunter, Francis Timothy Durgin to Rory Calhoun, and Merle Johnson, Jr. to Troy Donahue.

When Willson met Hudson, the aspiring actor had by then adopted the name of his stepfather—"Fitzgerald." Impressed by his 6'4" height and two hundred pound muscular build, Willson changed it to "Rock" for the Rock of Gibraltar. "The Hudson part just came along, I guess from the motor car—although it might have been the river," Willson said. "Rock Hudson just seemed right for him."

One writer, Jerry Parker of *Newsday,* agreed—but for a different reason. "He has all the dignity of a slab of granite," Parker said. "And he is only slightly more talkative."

Hudson, who in real life is reported to be a gentle and unassuming person, says the name still embarrasses him. "I've never gotten used to it—never," he said. "I think I could have made good as Fitzgerald. It didn't hurt F. Scott."

If Rock Hudson fails to suit Roy Scherer-Fitzgerald, it is questionable whether Doris Day really fits Doris von Kappelhoff. In her salad days she was far from the typical teeny-bopper. While other girls were wearing bobby sox and starting to double date, she was out barnstorming the country as a band singer. At seventeen she was a wife and mother. Before she was twenty-three she had been divorced twice.

Born in Cincinnati in 1924 into a German-Catholic family,** her childhood memories included watching her father tiptoe with his extra-marital sweetheart (whose daughter was a classmate of Doris') through her bedroom to a rendezvous in the next room. "I heard everything," Doris said. Her parents were divorced when she was twelve.

---

*Refusing to accede to Miss Day's terms, cartoonist Al Capp once wrote an entire article on her without interviewing her.

**She later became a convert to Christian Science.

240

Doris wanted to be a dancer, so her mother helped pay for her lessons from the money she got working in a bakery. But her aspirations got a setback at thirteen when a car in which she was a passenger collided with a train. She suffered a badly broken leg that required extensive surgery, and she had to wear a toe-to-hip cast for more than a year. The doctors doubted that she would ever dance again. Therefore, showing a resiliency that was to stand her in good stead in years to come, Doris turned to singing.

She never learned to read music, but she had a natural voice and could pick up a melody after hearing it only once or twice. Her first big job was with Barney Rapp's orchestra. It was he who changed her name (because of a song she sang called "Day After Day").* Her first paycheck was $25 a week. Only later did she learn that Rapp was really paying her $50 and that the band manager was ripping off $25 for himself.

By the age of sixteen she was touring with the big name bands of Bob Crosby and Les Brown. A nervous, somewhat chubby girl with long blonde curls, she soon found that a touring musician's life is a lonely one. In 1941 she quit to marry trombonist Al Jorden.

It didn't last long. Jorden, she soon found out, was insanely jealous. She said he would beat her if he saw her showing the slightest attention to another man. These black rages continued even during her pregnancy. They broke up a year after the birth of Doris' only child, Terry, in 1942. Jorden later committed suicide.

Doris left her baby in her mother's care and rejoined Brown. Before long she recorded her first hit record, "Sentimental Journey" (on the Okey label), and her salary jumped to $500 a week. "She was a changed kid," Brown said. "Whereas she used to be scared but fascinated with life with the band, now she was moody and depressed."

Miss Day stayed with Brown until 1946 when she fell in love with saxophone player Gerry Weidler, brother of movie actress Virginia Weidler. Her second marriage fared no better, breaking up in less than a year. Weidler, she said, was as gentle as Jorden had been brutal. However, he apparently foresaw her impending success and could not accept what he thought would be a diminishing role in their marriage. He said he did not want to become "Mr. Doris Day."

Her third marriage, in 1951, was to her agent, Marty Melcher, who continued to manage her

career until his death from a heart ailment in 1968. When he died, Doris got the shock of her life. She had given him power of attorney, and he and lawyer-investment counselor Jerome B. Rosenthal had spent her fortune and left her $500,000 in the red.

Their ill-advised business deals ranged from amateurishly conducted oil and gas ventures to poorly conceived cattle and hotel investments. Rosenthal claimed that he had an oral agreement giving him half of the Day-Melcher empire. She sued, and a long and complex legal battle ensued. Five years later, in 1974, a California judge awarded her the staggering sum of $22 million. In a stinging judgment against Rosenthal, Los Angeles Superior Court Judge Lester E. Olson accused the lawyer of the "grossest negligence" and of conduct that was "outrageous and malicious." In his lengthy opinion, Olson characterized Rosenthal as an "attorney bent on personal gain at the expense of his clients."

In 1976 Doris married her fourth husband, Barry D. Comden, a forty-one-year-old Beverly Hills businessman. She was then fifty-two, his senior by eleven years.

But back to Doris' professional life. In 1947 she went to Hollywood where her career took a dramatic turn. She began appearing in musicals—her first was *Romance on the High Seas* (1948) with Jack Carson and Janis Paige. Doris' pert features, sparkling disposition, and fluffy charm caught on.

Some say she rose to stardom because her wholesome looks never really threatened women in the audience. "She isn't something out of their world. She's ordinary, believable," said Al Capp. "It makes them feel that, with a little effort, what happens to Doris could happen to them."

On the other hand, some foreign movie queens felt the nice girl roles she played were an outrage. One of Doris' critics was Isabel Sarli, an Argentine actress who was then appearing nude at least once in every picture. "In *That Touch of Mink* [1962]," Miss Sarli said, "this woman, who must be at least thirty-five, accepts many expensive gifts and a luxurious trip to Bermuda from Cary Grant. Naturally, he thinks this entitles him to make love to her. But, no! When he comes to the point, she tells him she didn't understand. This is immoral."

Immoral or not, Doris' career flourished in the 1950s. With *Love Me or Leave Me* (1955) and the Hitchcock film *The Man Who Knew Too Much* (1956), she showed her versatility in more sophisticated pictures.

But it was in 1959 in *Pillow Talk* that she really

*She never liked the name because she thought that it sounded as though she was a burlesque star.

241

Hudson and Day in one of their noncombative scenes.

came into her own. Ironically, Miss Day at first questioned whether she was right for the picture. The part was that of a sexy, chicly dressed New York career lady. Producer Ross Hunter changed her mind, convincing her, she said, that she was "God's gift to this part." Hunter also persuaded Rock Hudson to change the direction of his career and try his hand at comedy.

Pillow Talk was fabulously successful, and she and Hudson made two more pictures, *Lover Come Back* (1962) and *Send Me No Flowers* (1964). Other Doris Day movies in the *Pillow Talk* vein were *That Touch of Mink* (1962) with Cary Grant, *The Thrill of It All* (1963), and *Move Over, Darling* (1963) with James Garner. For better or worse, the Doris Day image was fixed.

Like Miss Day, Hudson was the child of a broken home. Born in 1925 in Winnetka, Illinois, he lived with his mother after his parents separated when he was four. After working as a telephone operator for three years, his mother married Walter Fitzgerald, a Marine sergeant, who legally adopted Rock and gave him his name. It, too, was an unhappy marriage that ended in divorce after several separations.

As a youngster, Hudson decided to be a movie star. He traces his ambition to a picture—probably *The Hurricane* (1937)—in which he saw Jon Hall dive off a whaling ship to save Dorothy Lamour. But his first experience with acting was less than reassuring. He couldn't hold a part in his high school play because he couldn't remember his lines.

After high school, he became an airplane mechanic, a piano mover, a mail carrier, and a truck driver. He held the latter job in Los Angeles. Between deliveries he stood outside studio gates leaning on his truck fender—with Lana Turner's soda fountain discovery in mind. No one noticed him until he took the more conventional route of sending his photograph to agents. Willson, then a talent scout for Selznick Studios, was impressed and called him for an interview. Although he was less than awed by Hudson's talent, Willson signed him.

"Only twice in my life have I asked young people I was interested in to read for me," Willson said, "and both times, thank God, I didn't let what I heard influence me. I signed them in spite of their readings. They turned out to be Lana Turner and Rock Hudson."

242

Although Rock was big and handsome,* he was shy and reticent and it took years of hard work for him to learn his trade. His first screen test for 20th Century-Fox was so bad that it was later shown to young actors as an example of what not to do.

Hudson persisted. He took drama lessons, eventually getting small parts. In six years, he made twenty-eight pictures, appearing as a soda jerk, prize fighter, soldier, fur trader, and the son of an Indian chief.

But he became a bigger star in the pages of movie magazines than he did on the screen. Universal said he got 4,000 fan letters a month, and Hudson, eager to promote himself, contributed $10,000 a year to maintain the Rock Hudson Fan Club.

Then, in 1954, he got his first big break. He played opposite Jane Wyman in *Magnificent Obsession*, the role that made Robert Taylor a star in 1935. Two weeks before shooting was to start, he broke his collarbone while surfing. But realizing the importance of the picture to his career, he convinced the doctors that he could work.

*Hudson's makeup man, Bud Westmore, said the main trouble with his face was that it was almost too pretty. In the 1950s, Westmore had to put in character lines. With most other stars, he had to take them out.

Some critics took his studio to task for casting him in this role. They said he was a "constructed hero . . . hatched out of the gilded egg of publicity." One critic said he was so wooden that his only impressive acting was "when he took off his shirt to wash his hands." But the film made $5 million and established him as a box office attraction.

With each succeeding picture, Hudson's acting improved. He went on to win critical praise as a Texas rancher in George Stevens' *Giant* (1956), his favorite role and one that earned him an Oscar nomination. Since then he has made over fifty pictures—including *Written on the Wind* (1957) and *Seconds* (1966), a modern horror film that has evolved into a cult movie—and the successful television series "Macmillan and Wife" with Susan Saint James. His performances in straight dramatic roles have been, by and large, uneven. In 1958, the *Harvard Lampoon* named him worst actor of the year for his role in *A Farewell to Arms*. But he did develop a flair for comedy, and he was at his best in this genre, which began with *Pillow Talk*.

This film revolves around a party line shared by song writer Brad Allen (Hudson) and interior decorator Jan Morrow (Day). They have become enemies without ever meeting because Allen, a

Pollyanna and the Rock of Gibraltar in another brief encounter.

243

swinging bachelor, monopolizes the phone—singing ballads and cooing to his stable of sweethearts. When Jan cuts in to try to make a business call, Brad accuses her of eavesdropping.

"She's always listening in," Brad tells his girl of the moment, "to brighten up a drab, empty life."

"If I could get a call through once in a while, my life wouldn't be so drab," she snaps.

In real life, Hudson and Doris hit it off from the start. "The very first day on the set I discovered we had a performing rapport that was remarkable," Miss Day said. "We played our scenes together as if we had once lived them. Every day on the set was a picnic—sometimes too much of a picnic."

Hudson, too, felt that they clicked naturally as an acting team. Why? In Miss Day's book, he answered this way: "I'd say, first of all, that two people have to truly like each other, as Doris and I did, for that shines through, the sparkle, the twinkle in the eye as the two people look at each other. Then, too, both parties have to be strong personalities—very important to comedy so that there's a tug of war over who's going to put it over on the other, who's going to get the last word, a fencing match between two adroit opponents of the opposite sex who in the end are going to fall into bed together. . . . But the great thing that Doris does in a film is the way she plays hurt when she realizes that she's been had. She is genuinely hurt. And the audience's heart goes out to her. She's not a vengeful woman. And when she plays hurt over what the man has done to her, she wins hands down."

But back to *Pillow Talk*. Jan's complaint to the phone company gets nowhere. There's so much construction going on, a phone official says, that there aren't enough trunk lines to put in private phones fast enough. "Of course, if some emergency came up," the official says, "if you'd become pregnant, for example, you'd jump right to the top of our list."

"Being single," says Jan dryly, in a typical Doris Day line, "I'm not quite ready for that type of emergency."

Finally Jan calls Brad and gets him to agree that they will each have the use of the phone on alternate half hours. However, her maid, Alma (Thelma Ritter),* perceives that Jan has more on her mind than telephones.

"If there's anything worse than a woman living alone, it's a woman saying she likes it," says Alma.

"Well, I *do* like it. I have a good job, a lovely apartment. I go out with very nice men to the best places. What am I missing?"

*She and Miss Day got Oscar nominations.

"When you have to ask, believe me, you're missing it," says Alma.

Actually, Jan is being courted by thrice-married millionaire Jonathan Forbes (Tony Randall).** Unbeknownst to Jan, Forbes is a friend of Brad Allen. In fact, Forbes is backing a show for which Brad is writing the music.

One day, when Forbes tells Brad about his current heart throb, Brad discovers that she is his party line neighbor and decides she might be worth knowing after all.

He gets his chance that night. When Jan attends a housewarming party given by a wealthy client, his son Tony (Nick Adams) offers to drive her home.† After making a few advances which Jan promptly counters, Tony insists on stopping at a nightclub for a drink. Of course, they happen to take a booth right next to the one where Brad and his date are sitting.

Overhearing their conversation, Brad realizes that the girl behind him is Jan Morrow. But how can he meet her without giving away his own identity? That old demon rum gives him his chance. When Tony gets drunk and passes out on the dance floor, Brad rushes to Jan's assistance—posing as a Westerner, Rex Stetson. To Jan's relief, he carries Tony outside and sends him home in a taxi. Then Brad drives Jan home, carrying out his impersonation of a chivalrous country boy.

"Don't tell me this young fellow was trying to

**Randall, in a 1977 interview with the author, said that his outstanding memory of *Pillow Talk* was an argument he had with director Michael Gordon. "It happened on the first day on the set," Randall said. "I didn't like the lines I had, and when I told my agent, he assured me that they'd be changed. They weren't. When I saw Gordon the first day, I told him I wasn't going to do the lines. He told me no one had changed them and he didn't have the authority to do it." Randall said that he and Gordon went round and round on that point in front of the cast and crew. It ended in a standoff. By noon, not a foot of film had been shot. When Randall went to lunch, producer Ross Hunter joined him in the commissary. He told Randall that Gordon had been blacklisted and that this was the first film he had undertaken in ten years. "If you destroy him now," Hunter said, "he'll never work again." Randall said he walked right back to the set. "In front of everybody, I apologized," Randall said. "Gordon threw his arms around me and hugged me. . . . I've never been able to get those arms off me. We've been close friends since that day." P.S. The lines were not changed.

†Dwayne Hickman was originally signed for the role. But the morning his scene was to be filmed, he woke up with flu and a 104-degree fever. Since 100 extras had been called for the day, the studio decided to find a substitute. Adams, responding to a rush call, got to the set within an hour and learned the dialogue while being made up. The son of a Pennsylvania coal miner, he later rode to brief fame and fortune. He was the troubleshooting Confederate veteran in the television adventure series "The Rebel." Then, he was nominated for a best supporting Oscar for *Twilight of Honor* (1963). Adams died in 1968 after a drug overdose at the age of thirty-six.

244

Tony Randall, who plays Rock's rival in *Pillow Talk*.

force his attentions on you!" Brad, as Rex, says. "We make short work of his kind back in Texas."

The next night, Rex invites Jan to dinner. "I get a nice, warm feeling being near you, ma'am," he says. "It's like being around a pot-bellied stove in the morning."

Before long, Jan finds she has fallen for the big guy. "It's so nice to meet a man you can trust," Jan tells Jonathan. Infuriated, Jonathan hires a detective to probe Rex's background. A few days later, the private eye produces a photograph, showing that Rex is really Jonathan's old chum, Brad.

What to do? Get Brad far away, Jonathan figures. He goes to see Brad and orders him to Jonathan's Connecticut home to finish the music for his show. Brad reluctantly agrees, but without telling Jonathan he invites Jan to come along. "Just make sure you do plenty of scoring up there," Jonathan says in the picture's best bit of *double entendre*.

At Jonathan's house, Jan notices a music sheet that has fallen to the floor. When she plays it on the

piano, she recognizes it as the tune Brad has sung to all his girl friends on their party line. The masquerade is over. Mad as a hornet, Jan tells Brad what a cad he is just as Jonathan walks in to whisk her away.

However, Brad won't quit. He decides to try to get to Jan through her maid, Alma. He waits for Alma outside the apartment and finds that she knows him through listening in on many of his calls. At a nearby bar, she advises him to engage Jan to decorate his apartment, thus giving him a chance to talk to her again. The ploy works. Jan agrees to take the job—though on a strictly business basis. She then proceeds to have her revenge. She decorates the apartment in the worst possible taste. When she's finished, it looks like a cross between a harem and a nineteenth-century bordello.

The minute Brad gets his first look at it, he storms over to Jan's apartment. He kicks in the front door, hauls her from bed, carries her in her pajamas through the lobby into the street, past a

245

cop, and over to his apartment.* Dumping her un-

*Hudson later made a small confession about that long, climactic scene: he didn't really carry Doris. "I hate to admit this," he said, "but Doris is a tall, well-built girl. And I just couldn't tote her around for as long and as far as the film required. So they built a special shelf for me with two hooks on it. And she sat on the shelf and all I did was hold her legs and shoulders." Hudson said he could have managed it if only one take had been involved. But they did it over and over, in part because there was a bit actor who played a cop on the street. "As we passed him, Doris' line was, 'Officer, arrest this man.' The cop was supposed to say to me, 'How you doing, Brad?' But that stupid actor kept calling me 'Rock.' So back to our marks we went for another take and another and another. I'll bet we did that scene twenty times."

ceremoniously on the sofa, he tells her that since she decorated the place, she can keep it and charge admission.

However, before he can storm out the door, Jan, in a sudden change of heart, flips a trick switch that snaps the lock and pipes music into the room. As Brad turns to her and smiles, she puts out the light and says, "All apartments look alike in the dark." The line was later deleted from the script. But no matter. We know all is well again in Rock Hudson and Doris Day land and they will live happily ever after.

A Place in the Sun

George Eastman (Montgomery Clift) sits in the rowboat in which he took Alice Tripp for her last boat ride as prosecutor Marlowe (Raymond Burr) points to an oar. That's Walter Sande (with hand on knee) in the center and Fred Clark next to him (hand on nose).

A Place in the Sun
(1951)

Directed by George Stevens.* Screenplay by Michael Wilson* and Harry Brown,* based on the novel *An American Tragedy* by Theodore Dreiser and the Patrick Kearney play adapted from the novel. Photography, William C. Mellor.* Music, Franz Waxman.* Costumes, Edith Head.* Editor, William Hornbeck.* Filmed at Lake Tahoe. Produced by Stevens. A Paramount Picture. 122 minutes.

George Eastman	*Montgomery Clift*
Angela Vickers	*Elizabeth Taylor*
Alice Tripp	*Shelley Winters*
Hannah Eastman	*Anne Revere*
Earl Eastman	*Keefe Brasselle*
Bellows	*Fred Clark*
Marlowe	*Raymond Burr*
Charles Eastman	*Herbert Heyes*
Anthony Vickers	*Shepperd Strudwick*
Mrs. Vickers	*Frieda Inescort*
Mrs. Louise Eastman	*Kathryn Givney*
Jansen	*Walter Sande*
Judge	*Ted de Corsia*
Coroner	*John Ridgely*
Marsha	*Lois Chartrand*
Mr. Whiting	*William B. Murphy*
Boatkeeper	*Douglas Spencer*
Dr. Wyeland	*Ian Wolfe*

A Place in the Sun was a remake of Paramount's *An American Tragedy* (1931).

*Academy Award Winner.

Elizabeth Taylor and Montgomery Clift. Elizabeth's gown is one of the two Oscar-winning gowns designed by Edith Head for the film.

During World War II, Francis Taylor and Sam Marx were air raid wardens in Beverly Hills. Marx was a producer at Metro-Goldwyn-Mayer, working on a picture called *Lassie Come Home*. Taylor was an art dealer who had recently returned to his native land* from England with his wife and young daughter. His little girl, he told Marx, was an unusually attractive child with coal black hair and radiant, violet eyes. Marx listened politely but he wasn't paying much attention. He already had a child actress, Maria Flynn, for the little girl's part in *Lassie Come Home*.

As things turned out, Marx was always grateful that he had his talk with Taylor. When the first rushes came in, Marx found, to his utter surprise,

*Contrary to studio publicity, the Taylors were American, not British. Both came from the sleepy midwestern town of Arkansas City, Kansas. Elizabeth was born in England where Taylor had moved to buy paintings for the U.S. market. In 1939, when Elizabeth was seven, the Taylors came back to the U.S. to escape World War II.

that Maria was a head taller than the star, Roddy McDowall.** Director Fred Wilcox put out an emergency call to half a dozen British girls who had tried out for *Mrs. Miniver* (1942). At the same time, Marx remembered Taylor's glowing description of his daughter. He called Taylor and invited him to bring Elizabeth to his office.

Late that afternoon, all the British children were assembled in Marx's office when his secretary buzzed on the intercom to tell him that another child had just arrived. Marx told her to send the youngster in.

**What happened to Maria Flynn? In her book *Who's Afraid of Elizabeth Taylor?* Brenda Maddox quotes Marx as saying that it fell to him to tell Maria that she was out of the picture. He called her into his office and said, "'This has nothing to do with you, Maria, but you're too tall for Roddy and we can't use you in the picture.' 'Thank you, Mr. Marx,' was all she said. And I was totally destroyed." Maria had just appeared in *Intermezzo* (1939) with Ingrid Bergman. Said Marx: "I never saw or heard from her again."

249

Marx never forgot his first sight of Elizabeth Taylor. The little girl entered wearing a blue velvet cape which set off her eyes and hair. "It was truly like an eclipse of the sun," he said. "She blotted out everyone else in the room. We never tested her for the part."

And so began one of Hollywood's great careers. At least this has become the standard version of its genesis. However, many Hollywood tales have become embellished over the years, and on close examination one finds at least three aspects of the Elizabeth Taylor discovery story that might be debated.

—In his book *Elizabeth*, Dick Sheppard writes a less dramatic variation. According to Sheppard, the original child hired for the *Lassie Come Home* role had to drop out of the picture at the last minute when her parents found that her eyes were too weak for the bright lights of the set. Edgar Selwyn, a studio official, learned of the situation when he heard Marx and Wilcox discussing the problem, and it was Selwyn who contacted Taylor.

—It was Universal, not MGM, that really first hired Elizabeth, although Universal was not perceptive enough to realize the prize it had captured. Universal signed her even though its casting director, Dan Kelly, had serious misgivings. "The kid has nothing," Kelly said. "Her eyes are too old. She doesn't have the face of a kid." The studio eventually agreed with Kelly's appraisal. It dropped her after a year during which it paid her $200 a week. But it was during her short stint with Universal that Elizabeth, then a nine-year-old singer and dancer, made her debut in a B-picture called *There's One Born Every Minute* (1942). It featured comedians Hugh Herbert, Edgar Kennedy, and Guy Kibbee. She sang one awful number with Alfalfa Switzer of *Our Gang* fame.

—Finally, according to Sheppard, Elizabeth did do a screen test for MGM, though it was an impromptu one without makeup or preparation. She was asked to pretend to pet a collie while director Wilcox read Nigel Bruce's lines off-camera. "We took one look at those eyes," Wilcox said, "and she was in."

Regardless of who discovered her, where she started, or whether she was or was not tested, there is no disputing Miss Taylor's superstar status. Some feel that she is more a celebrity than an actress. They say her lurid private life has made more headlines than her movies. She has been lauded more for her beauty than for her talent. In too many pictures, she has given wooden, one-dimensional performances.

On the other hand, her admirers say she has achieved stardom working under too many second-rate directors and with generally inferior material. Nevertheless, of the more than fifty movies she made, she won two Oscars—for *Butterfield 8* (1960) and for *Who's Afraid of Virginia Woolf?* (1966)—plus three Academy Award nominations. In her best pictures, she has proven she can be an actress of sensitivity and fire. And she has emerged as one of the most durable of stars. Only a handful of actresses, like Bette Davis, Katharine Hepburn, and Joan Crawford, matched her in the extraordinary length of her screen career.

Pushed into movies by her mother, who gave up acting to get married, Elizabeth first demonstrated her latent ability in *National Velvet* (1944). Audiences adored her as a thirteen-year-old who played opposite Mickey Rooney and rode her own horse to victory in the Grand National steeplechase.

With *A Date with Judy* (1948), *Little Women* (1949), and *Father of the Bride* (1950), she made the transition to young adult roles. Even so, as she grew out of the childhood parts, the best adjectives her performances inspired were words like "appealing" and "sweetly feminine." A harsher appraisal came from the *Harvard Crimson*. In 1950, it gave her its annual award for "gallantly persisting in her career despite a total inability to act."

Then came *A Place in the Sun*, a role she played with great feeling. She won nearly unanimous accolades from critics—*Variety* called her performance a "minor miracle"—and her stardom advanced another notch.

Meanwhile, she embarked on a stormy private life. Married at seventeen, she had five husbands before she was thirty-five. They were: Nicky Hilton (1949-1951); Michael Wilding (1952-1957), children: Michael and Christopher; Mike Todd (1957-1958), child: Elizabeth; Eddie Fisher (1959-1964); Richard Burton (1964-1973), remarried, (1975-1976), adopted child: Maria; John Warner (1976-   ). The Fisher marriage was an unpopular one with the public because he had divorced Debbie Reynolds to marry Elizabeth.

Elizabeth's movie career was as uneven and unpredictable as her private life. She did a series of forgettable pictures—including *Rhapsody* (1954) with Vittorio Gassman—and then scored as an oil-rich Texan's wife in *Giant* (1956) and as a southern belle in *Raintree County* (1957).

Her ascending career, combined with her public notoriety, put her picture on the cover of every fan magazine, and her salary soared to $500,000 a movie. Under Joseph L. Mankiewicz's direction, she played the neurotic Catherine Holly in *Sud-*

denly, *Last Summer* (1959). Acerbic critic Dwight MacDonald said that Mankiewicz had scored a "directional triumph; he has somehow extracted from Elizabeth Taylor a mediocre performance, which is a definite step up in her dramatic career." Obviously moviegoers didn't agree for she rose to number two in box office ratings.

In 1960 she won her first Oscar for *Butterfield 8*, a picture in which she did not want to appear because she didn't like the idea of playing a call girl. She called it a "sympathy award" because it came after she recovered from a nearly fatal case of pneumonia. Others said she got it because she hadn't won for *Raintree County, Cat on a Hot Tin Roof*, and *Suddenly Last Summer* (1959), although she had been nominated for each of those pictures.

Then came her much publicized appearance in *Cleopatra* (1963), for which she got $1 million. Her lucrative fee included $3,000 a week for expenses during filming plus ten percent of the gross. Fisher reportedly was paid $1,500 a day just to see that she showed up on time. Unfortunately for Eddie, Burton replaced Stephen Boyd in the cast and eventually replaced Fisher, too, on Liz's matrimonial list. The picture, which took years to make after scores of production problems and hassles,

became the most costly movie ever made—$37 million.

Capitalizing on their personal publicity, however bad, Liz and Burton appeared in a series of movies together, capped by *Who's Afraid of Virginia Woolf?* Playing a plump, vulgar wife, she won her second Oscar. Since then, her pictures have been disappointing—among them, *Reflections in a Golden Eye* (1967) with Marlon Brando, *The Comedians* (1967) with Burton, and *The Only Game in Town* (1970) with Warren Beatty.

Her failures notwithstanding, if an actress should be judged by her best work, then Elizabeth Taylor should be assessed by *A Place in the Sun*, where she turned in perhaps her most memorable performance.

As the movie opens, George Eastman (Montgomery Clift) is hitchhiking to his uncle's factory to look for a job.* Eastman comes from a modest

*In his book *Monty*, Robert LaGuardia said that Liz, then seventeen, had an adolescent crush on Clift. They dated and she wrote schoolgirlish love letters to him, proposing marriage in some. LaGuardia said Clift, who, unbeknownst to Liz then, was a homosexual, cruelly turned them over to his male lover, with vivid descriptions of how mad Liz was for him. The failed love affair, LaGuardia said, was a deep disappointment of Elizabeth's young life and the possible reason she rushed into marriage with Nicky Hilton, whom she had just met.

George, the boy from the wrong side of the tracks, tells society girl Angela Vickers that he loves her. Taylor wears her second Head-created gown, jet black with a "vestigial shred of white broderie anglaise edging her breasts."

George takes Alice (Shelley Winters), the working-class girl he has gotten in the family way, to the courthouse to get a marriage license. It is Labor Day and the office is closed, setting the scene for their fateful holiday outing.

midwestern background. His parents were Salvation Army workers but George aspires to a more worldly life. His unexpected arrival, however, is a bit unsettling to the wealthy, status-conscious Eastmans.

"What are we going to do about him socially?" Mrs. Eastman (Kathryn Givney) asks.

Charles Eastman (Herbert Heyes) assures his wife that there won't be any problem. "You don't have to meet him socially," he said. "He just wants to work and get ahead—that's all."

It is at this first awkward visit to the Eastman mansion that George sees Angela Vickers (Taylor) at a party. Vibrant and radiant, she flounces in gaily with her beau of the moment—not even noticing the skinny, bashful visitor.

At the plant, George's menial job consists of packing swim suits at the end of an assembly line. The Vickers family ignores him, so he starts dating Alice Tripp (Shelley Winters), a friendly but frumpy co-worker. One night a cop chases them from their lovers' lane parking spot. George drives her to her tacky rented room and goes to bed with her. It will be a night he will always regret.

Then George's luck takes a turn when the Eastmans finally invite him to a party. Shy and awkward, he shows up in a dark blue suit—everyone else is in black tie—and wanders aimlessly about until he finds himself alone in the billiard room. He starts playing until Angela passes by and, attracted by his boyish good looks, comes in.

"Wow," she says, admiring a difficult bank shot. "I see you had a misspent youth." He smiles but doesn't reply, and she senses his diffidence. "Why all alone? Being exclusive? Being dramatic? Feeling blue?" It is the beginning of an ill-starred relationship. Angela will find herself intrigued by the quiet, darkly handsome young man, and George, intoxicated by Angela's beauty, wealth, and social position, will fall in love with her.

The movie, of course, is a film version of Theodore Dreiser's famous 1925 novel, *An American Tragedy*, which was based on a real crime. Dreiser's theme was that man is a victim of his environment. If he is born poor, Dreiser felt, society almost certainly condemns him to a hard, dreary life.

When Josef von Sternberg made a picture out of the novel in 1931,* Dreiser denounced it because it put the major blame for the hero's tragic ending on

*It starred Phillips Holmes as the social climber and Sylvia Sidney as the poor girl who stands in his way.

himself rather than on his circumstances. And had he lived, Dreiser would have been unhappy, too, with Stevens' movie. Stevens made some attempt to show how George's poverty pushed him toward his terrible deed. However, the movie blunted the point because Stevens placed the greatest emphasis on the Clift-Taylor love story. He could have underscored how George's upwardly mobile yearnings drove him to disaster by switching the casting—making Elizabeth Taylor the factory girl and Shelley Winters the debutante. As it is, Liz is so pretty and idealized that it seems that Clift wants her even more than the good life that goes with her. But Stevens was not really interested in social commentary. He cared chiefly about filming a romance.

The next night, Angela telephones George, and they have a date. Soon George becomes part of her smart, young social set.

However, his plans of entering into society get a setback when Alice tells him that she's pregnant. While Alice stridently insists that he marry her, George stalls for time and keeps seeing Angela. It is soon clear that they are in the grip of an all-consuming passion. At a dance at Angela's home, the camera shows their enraptured faces. On the balcony, George confesses his love. They em-brace passionately and their close-ups fill the screen.

"I'm the happiest person in the world," George says.

"The second happiest," Angela replies.

George's joy is short-lived. He takes Alice to a doctor, but the physician refuses to do an abortion. The scene was played without using the word "abortion" because the Hays office did not consider abortions proper subject matter for movies. However, there was enough suggested to make clear what is going on. "I can't help you," the doctor (Ian Wolfe) tells Alice.

Alice now becomes hysterical, nagging George to quit delaying and marry her. "You just gotta marry me," she says, "future or no future."

George promises that he will, even while he steals away to join Angela for weekends of partying and power-boating at her summer lakeside home. Angela's parents are gradually becoming more comfortable with George who has shown a genuine zeal at the plant and won promotions. Then, one day, his weekend is interrupted by a telephone call from Alice. She has seen a newspaper picture of George boating on the lake with Angela and has taken a bus to the town closest to the Vickers' home.

George and Alice in happier days.

"You've lied to me for the last time," Alice says.

George leaves Angela, confused and dejected. When he joins Alice in a bus station, he again promises to marry her and convinces her that he means it. "You'll be happy and content with what you've got," she says, trying to console him, "instead of working yourself up about things you can't have."

The next day is Labor Day and the marriage bureau is closed. George's course of action is now clear to him. He takes Alice to a deserted lakeside area, rents a rowboat, and takes her to the loneliest part of the lake, intending to push her overboard. But at the last minute, he cannot find it in himself to do it. Instead, to his surprise, she gets up and starts over to him. She walks unsteadily, rocking the boat. "Stay where you are," he shouts. It's too late. The boat rocks crazily and then tips over. The two plunge into the water, but only George reaches the shore.

However, he is far from free, for he has left clues all along the trail to the lake. Police quickly find him, arrest him, and charge him with Alice's murder. The Vickers, stunned, hire prominent attorneys to defend George with the understanding that Angela will be kept out of the trial.

George's lawyers try to make the jury understand that he is on trial for the act of murder, not the thought. "Between the act and the deed lies a world of difference," one of his attorneys says.

They are no match for the aggressive district attorney—brilliantly played by Raymond Burr—who shows that George was leading a double life. Standing in the rowboat brought into the courtroom, the D.A. slams an oar on the floor and charges that George struck Alice with it. George denies this. However, the D.A. shows that George made no effort to reach Alice after the boat capsized when he was only a few feet from her.

"I wanted to save her," George says.

"Whom were you thinking of at that moment—Alice or that other girl?"

There is no answer.

"Then, in your heart, it was murder."

The jury, as expected, finds George guilty and the judge sentences him to death.

The film reaches its climax in an unlikely final scene when Angela, loyal to the end, comes to visit him in prison. It is the night of his execution.

"I know something now I never knew before," George says. "I'm guilty of a lot of things, most of what they say of me."

"All the same," Angela says. "I'll go on loving you as long as I live."

"Love me for the time I have left," George says. "Then forget me."

Minutes later, the warden leads George past death row cells to the execution chamber. "Goodbye, George," one prisoner says. "Be seeing you." George makes no response. His thoughts are of the lovely raven-haired girl whose perfume he can still smell.

The Quiet Man

John Wayne stands arms akimbo after knocking down burly Victor McLaglen during their marathon donney-brook. Barry Fitzgerald is the interested observer.

The Quiet Man
(1952)

Directed by John Ford.* Screenplay by Frank S. Nugent, based on a story by Maurice Walsh. Editor, Jack Murray. Photography, Winton C. Hoch* and Archie Stout.* Music, Victor Young. Songs: "Galway Bay" by Dr. Edward Colahan, and three traditional Irish songs, "The Wild Colonial Boy," "The Humour Is on Me Now," and "Mush Mush (Tread on the Tail of Me Coat)." Produced by Merian C. Cooper. Color by Technicolor. A Republic Picture filmed in Ireland. 129 minutes.

Sean Thornton	*John Wayne*
Mary Kate Danaher	*Maureen O'Hara*
Red Will Danaher	*Victor McLaglen*
Michaeleen Flynn	*Barry Fitzgerald*
Father Peter Lonergan and Narrator	*Ward Bond*
Sarah Tillane	*Mildred Natwick*
Dan Tobin	*Francis Ford*
Rev. Cyril Playfair	*Arthur Shields*
Elizabeth Playfair	*Eileen Crowe*
The Woman	*May Craig*
Forbes	*Charles FitzSimons*
Father Paul	*James Lilburn*
Owen Glynn	*Sean McClory*
Feeney	*Jack McGowran*
Guard	*Joseph O'Dea*
Engine Driver	*Eric Gorman*
Fireman	*Kevin Lawless*
Porter	*Paddy O'Donnell*
Station Master	*Web Overlander*
Father Paul's Mother	*Mae Marsh*
Children at Race	*Melinda and Pat Wayne*
Teenagers at Race	*Mike and Toni Wayne*

*Academy Award Winner.

Michaeleen Flynn (Fitzgerald) takes Squire Danaher (McLaglen) and the widow Tillane (Mildred Natwick) for a surrey ride. The squire has been courting the wealthy widow for years—unsuccessfully.

John Wayne first came into the public arena as a football player. Known then by his real name, Marion Michael Morrison, he was a hard-blocking guard for the University of Southern California in the 1920s. But his gridiron career was short-lived.

One day, the coach gave Tom Mix season box seats to the school's games. In return, Mix gave Wayne and a couple of other players summer jobs at Fox Studios.

Wayne didn't know it then, but that swap began a movie career that would lead to more than one hundred pictures. Wayne's powerful, larger-than-life performances as a rough but chivalrous Western hero would become legendary. Some felt that he never learned to read lines with any conviction, that his voice was flat and nasal, and that he remained awkward and stiff even in his later films. But his pictures made more money than those of any other actor in history—reportedly earning more than $400 million.

His popularity held up for decades. Only twice during the years from 1949 to 1974 did he not make the list of the top ten box office stars. And, in 1969, he capped his long career with an Oscar.

It was John Ford, then a contract director for Fox, who first gave the 6'4" athlete his start. Ford took a liking to him and hired him to play a bit part in *Hangman's House* (1928). However, it was director Raoul Walsh who gave Wayne his first lead role—in *The Big Trail* (1930)—and a new name. Walsh first came up with "Anthony Wayne," but aides felt that was too Italian. Walsh then tried "Tony" Wayne. That, they said, seemed too girlish. "What's wrong with just plain 'John'?" asked Winfield Sheehan, one of Walsh's assistants, and John Wayne it was.*

Over the years, Wayne would become one of Hollywood's most controversial and distinctive personalities. The reasons were legion:

—There were his politics. He was a staunch con-

*Wayne's nickname "Duke" comes from an Airedale dog he owned as a boy. Little Duke was the dog's name, and firemen at a station near his home began using the name Big Duke for Wayne. The nickname stuck.

servative, a fervent anti-communist, and a supporter of Senator Joe McCarthy in the 1950s and of the Vietnam War in the 1960s. On civil rights, he was once quoted as saying: "I believe in white supremacy until the blacks are educated to a point of responsibility. I don't believe in giving authority and positions of leadership and judgment to irresponsible people." Director Peter Bogdanovich defended Wayne's right-wing views as he defended Chaplin's left-wing leanings. Said Bogdanovich: "Neither of them [their political views] matters a damn in terms of their work or what they will leave behind."

—There were his stormy marriages. Josephine Saenz, his first wife, charged him with cruelty and drunkenness. Wayne's biographer, Maurice Zolotow, said he averaged a quart of whiskey a day through most of his life. Wayne and his second wife, the Mexican actress Esperanza (Chata) Baur, quarreled incessantly. She said he dragged her around by the hair one night, and she once threatened him with a loaded automatic after he kicked open the glass panel of their locked front door. In 1975, Wayne separated from his third wife, Pilar Palette, a Peruvian beauty. But his broken marriages did not damage his public image as a gentleman. In all, he had seven children and twenty grandchildren.

—There was his unique screen presence.* To cultivate a virile look, Wayne affected his slow, rolling gait and distinctive squint by practicing for hours in front of a mirror. However, he credits Ford with teaching him how to act. "He [Ford] taught me not to act but to react," Wayne said. That, of course, is the first lesson in every thespian school. But when Wayne did it, he projected a new dimension on the screen. "It was perhaps the particular way he reacted that so affected fans," said Richard Griffith in The Movie Stars. "It is slow. He watches and listens impassively. . . . Then he waits a while before he responds, either in speech or in action. If you've seen him often enough, you're pretty sure what he's going to say or do. But the fact that he makes you wait for it produces a kind of involuntary suspense which affects the reflexes even as the mind rejects it."

—There was his condemnation of contemporary movies. He deplores the trend toward sex and violence, yet he built a career on fist fights, brawls, and gun duels. The difference, he says, is that his

*It was really Wayne, and not Coach Vince Lombardi, who originated the famous macho line, "Winning isn't everything. It's the only thing." Wayne said it—or a reasonable facsimile—while playing a football coach in the movie Trouble Along the Way (1953).

he-man screen performances usually had a tongue-in-cheek quality to them.

—There was his heroic comeback from cancer (and later open-heart surgery). Wayne, a cigarette chain smoker, came down with a nagging cough in 1964. X-rays showed that he had a cancerous tumor in his left lung. When surgeons removed the affected area, his managers advised him to keep the operation secret, fearing that it might hurt his career. However, he insisted on announcing his condition, believing that it would focus attention on the need for early cancer detection. "I've licked the Big C," Wayne told a press conference, triumphantly. And he had.

Yet Wayne's career, as checkered as it was, took a long time in getting started. His first featured picture, The Big Trail (1930), was a failure. After a couple of other lacklustre efforts, he was relegated to quickie, low-budget Westerns. Through the 1930s, he shared the screen on Saturday matinees with such leatherslingers as Johnny Mack Brown, Bob Steele, and Gene Autry. Wayne was one of the first singing cowboys—a dubbed effort in a series in which he played Singin' Sandy. But he dropped the vocalist role because there were too many embarrassing requests for him to sing at parties.

It was around this time that Wayne developed his credo. "I made up my mind that I was going to play a real man to the best of my ability," he said. "I felt many of the Western stars of the 1920s and 1930s were too goddamn perfect. They never drank nor smoked. They never wanted to go to bed with a beautiful girl. They never had a fight. . . . I was trying to play a man who gets dirty, who sweats sometimes, who enjoys really kissing a gal he likes, who gets angry, who fights clean whenever possible, but will fight dirty if he has to. You could say I made the Western hero a roughneck."

Though he was paid fairly well, Wayne soon began to hate doing cheap poverty row pictures, some of which were shot in five days or less. John Ford ended his lean days when he cast Wayne as the Ringo Kid in the memorable Stagecoach (1939). It set a new standard for Westerns and made Wayne one of the most sought-after actors. Ford picked him again for Eugene O'Neill's somber The Long Voyage Home (1940), Cecil B. DeMille cast him for Reap the Wild Wind (1942), and Universal got him to play opposite Marlene Dietrich in Seven Sinners (1940), The Spoilers (1942), and Pittsburgh (1942).

Soon he began making quality Westerns. They included Ford's Fort Apache (1948), a Civil War tale with Henry Fonda; Howard Hawks' Red River

(1948), his biggest money-maker until then; and Ford's *She Wore a Yellow Ribbon* (1949), Ford's favorite among his Westerns and Wayne's favorite part. Wayne said that Hawks taught him "to do three scenes (outstanding sequences) in a picture and not annoy audiences in the rest."

Then came such memorable films as *Hondo* (1953), an off-beat Western with Geraldine Page; *The High and the Mighty* (1954), about a stricken airliner; and Hawks' *Rio Bravo* (1959), which, like *High Noon*, was about a sheriff who single-handedly defended a town against outlaws. Unlike *High Noon*, though, there was no contempt shown for the establishment, a contempt which Hawks and Wayne felt had degraded the Western hero. Finally, in 1970, he won his only Academy Award—for *True Grit* (1969), in which he portrayed a sloppy, hot-tempered, one-eyed marshal.*

Unquestionably, Wayne will be best remembered for his Western roles. But one part that

*In 1949, Wayne got an Oscar nomination for *Sands of Iwo Jima*, in which he played a tough leatherneck sergeant.

showed he could also play in a comic movie and hold his own with a seasoned cast came in *The Quiet Man*, a picture that was one of the most entertaining, fun-filled films of the 1950s.

In the beginning, Sean Thornton (Wayne) is returning to his native town of Innisfree in Ireland after growing up in America. Sean has become a celebrated boxer but has quit the ring after he accidentally killed a fighter. He is the quiet man of the title, seeking solace and a life of repose. However, it is clear from the outset that Ireland is the wrong spot for the peace and quiet Sean seeks, despite its lush scenery, gentle streams, and quaint customs.**

The Irish folks' garrulous, argumentative, and lackadaisical nature is immediately evident. Sean's train chugs in three hours late, a fact that seems to

**Director Ford went to Ireland for six weeks of shooting, during which only four days of unbroken sunshine occurred. But the company was rained out only once. The rest of the time, they worked in what the Irish called "nice soft days"—a little sun, some clouds, a bit of drizzle.

Sean moves his bride's trousseau into their new home. That's Maureen O'Hara on the wagon.

give nobody any particular cause for concern. When Sean asks directions to Innisfree, he nearly precipitates a riot as the train crew and passengers begin a loud debate on the platform. A little wizened man, Michaeleen Flynn (Barry Fitzgerald), leads him away to his horse-cart taxi and drives off. On the way, they pass a cottage that Sean says he wants to purchase.

"Now, why would a Yankee from Pittsburgh want to buy that?" Flynn asks.

"Because I was born in that little cottage over there. And I've come home."

Sean also spies a lovely barefoot colleen driving home a flock of sheep. She is Mary Kate Danaher (Maureen O'Hara). Sean immediately falls for the wild Irish beauty.

Miss O'Hara was one of a large troup of Irish expatriates, or Irish descendants, in the film, as was Ford himself. He was born in Maine but christened Sean Aloysius O'Feeney. The director also used many actors from the Emerald Isle's famous Abbey Theatre—including Eileen Crowe, May Craig, and Eric Gorman. He recruited extras from the countryside of Clark, Galway, and Mayo and shot all the location scenes in natural surroundings—pubs, churches, railway stations, villages, farms, and private residences.

Sean's troubles arise as soon as he starts courting Mary Kate. According to local tradition, a girl cannot marry without the consent of her parents or guardian. In Mary Kate's case, consent must come from her loutish, pig-headed brother, Squire Will Danaher (Victor McLaglen)—and therein lies a problem.

Sean has unwittingly aroused the squire's ire by buying the thatched-roof cottage of his parents. The house lies on land that the squire, a well-to-do farmer, wanted for himself because it divides his own property from that of Mrs. Tillane (Mildred Natwick), a wealthy widow the squire has taken a shine to.

"I've got you down in my book," fumes the squire after Sean outbids him for the house.

A few days later, Sean and Flynn, who also serves as a local marriage matchmaker, pay a call on the squire. They have come to ask permission for Sean to begin courting Mary Kate. The visit is a short one. "Get out," the squire roars. "If he was the last man on the face of the earth, I'd still say, 'No.' "

It turns out that Sean has some allies. The local priest, Father Lonergan (Ward Bond), is sympathetic to his cause. He joins in a conspiracy with Flynn, and on the day of the Innisfree horse race they spring a trap. They put the word out that Sean is now courting the widow Tillane. When the squire hears this, he nearly explodes. Flynn tells him that the only reason the widow has stood off the squire is that she did not want to marry into a house that already has another woman in it. "If you get rid of Mary Kate," Flynn says cagily, "the widow would have you like a shot."

"Is this true, Father Lonergan?" Danaher asks, seeking confirmation from a man of the cloth.

"I can't say it's true," the priest says, trying to avoid telling an outright falsehood. "And I won't say it's not. But there's been talk."

The Innisfree race is a traditional village affair at which single ladies put their bonnets on the finish line and riders compete for them by racing across a seaside steeplechase course. Sure enough, Sean wins Mary Kate's bonnet, and the squire relents and announces that he is allowing him to court his sister.

In time, Sean and Mary Kate are married. Still, their troubles are far from over. When the squire learns that he has been the victim of a fraud and the widow has no interest in him, he refuses to turn over Mary Kate's dowry. It means nothing to Sean. However, it's a severe blow to his new bride. Until she gets her dowry, she vows that her wedding will remain unofficial—meaning that she refuses to honor their marriage bed. "I'll wear your ring," she says. "I'll cook and I'll wash and I'll keep the land. But that is all—until I've got my dowry."

The only way out for Sean is to fight the burly squire for the money. But fighting is just what Sean has come to Ireland to forget, so he takes no action. As the weeks go by, and nothing happens, Mary Kate begins to doubt the virility of her new husband.

Eventually, of course, the bout does take place. One day Sean drags his wife to her former home, with the whole village following, to challenge the squire. The brawl is a battle royal. The fighting rages in and out of haystacks and up and down the countryside—with time out for a pint or two at local pubs. Most of the townfolk have a bet down on the slugfest and eventually join in the donnybrook themselves.

The scene is one of the film's memorable sequences—something Wayne was well prepared for by his many cowboy pictures. In fact, he helped develop the technique for movie fights. In the beginning, actors hit each other's shoulders and jerked their heads back to make it look real. That led to a lot of bruised shoulders. One day, Wayne said, director Robert N. Bradbury suggested a new approach. "Bradbury said that he thought if he placed the camera at a certain angle, it would look as if my fist was making contact with (stuntman) Yak's (Yakima Canutt's) face," Wayne said. "Actually my fist was passing by his (Yak's) face, not even grazing it. We tried it out one day, and when we saw the rushes, we saw how good it looked."

Bradbury reportedly invented this trick, which he called the pass system. Other stuntmen and directors adopted it, and it became the established way of staging a fight.

"The really nice thing about it was I could hit as hard as I wanted, put all my power into a punch and not have to hold back, because there was no body contact," Wayne said. "Remember that fight Vic McLaglen and I had in *The Quiet Man*? He didn't lay a hand on me and I didn't lay a hand on him. . . . We did not touch each other once. And yet we were punching away as hard as we could."

In the end, Sean's stout fists convince the squire that he has misjudged the big American. Mary Kate gets her dowry, Sean gets his wife officially, the squire and the widow begin courting, and everybody agrees that all's well that ends well.

While the brawl was one of the high points of the picture, it also was one of the scenes that drew criticism. Some native sons felt that Ford had overdrawn the Irish character, portraying them more as caricatures. They protested the characterization of the Irish as hard-drinking and tempestuous people, and, in one instance, as dishonest folk. "In spite of director John Ford's warm feeling for Ireland," said T. J. Sheehy in the *Irish Catholic*, "the film is a piece of complete stage Irishism. . . . He has exaggerated characters and situations to suit American audiences."

Still, most people recognize that the film was made in a tongue-in-cheek vein. Ford was really only inviting the Irish to laugh at themselves. Most audiences left the movie with a positive feeling toward Ireland and old traditions.

Rashomon

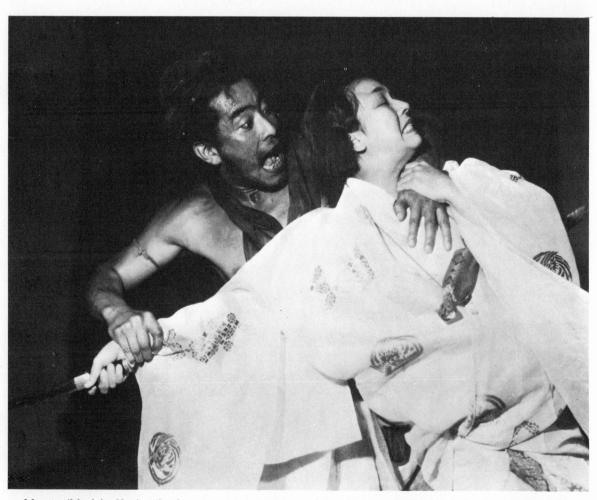

Masago (Machiko Kyo), wife of a samurai, is overcome and raped by a bandit (Toshiro Mifune) after he has killed her husband.

Rashomon*
(1950)

Directed by Akira Kurosawa. Based on the short story "In a Grove" by Ryunosuke Akutagawa. Screenplay by Shinobu Hashimoto and Kurosawa. Photography, Kazuo Miyagawa. Art direction, So Matsuyama. Music, Fumio Hayasaka. Producer, Jingo Minoru. A Daiei Production originally distributed in the U.S. by RKO, later by Janus Films, Inc. 88 minutes.

Tajomaru, the Bandit	*Toshiro Mifune*
Takehiro, the Samurai	*Masayuki Mori*
Masago, the Wife	*Machiko Kyo*
The Woodcutter	*Takashi Shimura*
The Priest	*Minoru Chiaki*
The Commoner	*Kichijiro Ueda*
The Police Agent	*Daisuke Kato*
The Medium	*Fumiko Homma*

(*The Outrage* [1964] was a Hollywood adaptation of *Rashomon*, with Paul Newman, Claire Bloom, Laurence Harvey, and Edward G. Robinson. Newman played a Mexican bandit who kidnaps a married couple [Bloom and Harvey] and allegedly rapes the wife. Conflicting stories follow. It got mixed reviews.)

*Special Academy Award as the most outstanding foreign language film released in the U.S.

The samurai (Masayuki Mori) and his wife (Machiko Kyo). In his version, he commits hara-kiri after hearing his wife urge the bandit to slay him.

In the summer stillness of a sun-dappled forest, a bandit rapes the wife of a samurai (a Japanese military officer) and then kills her husband in combat—or so it seems.

When the three tell about the double crime—the husband through the use of a medium—each tells a conflicting story. Then a fourth person, an eyewitness, gives his version, and a totally different account emerges.

Who is lying? Who is telling the truth? Is there any objective truth? Or is reality as things appear in the eye of the beholder?

These are some of the profound questions raised by *Rashomon*, a picture that many critics feel is the finest movie to come out of the Orient. Donald S. Richie, curator of film at the Museum of Modern Art in New York City and an authority on Japanese film, called it a "masterpiece." The *Saturday Review* hailed it as a "great film." Ten years after its premiere, Parker Tyler, in his anthology *Classics of the Foreign Film*, said *Rashomon* remains "a film in

which it is as hard to detect a flaw as to find anything dated."

Rashomon won its share of accolades. It captured the Grand Prize of the Venice Film Festival and got a special Academy Award for best foreign film—the first Asian movie to achieve the latter distinction—before going on to a long run in the United States and other Western nations.

Yet, ironically, it was not a big box-office attraction in Japan, nor was it well received by reviewers there. And it was only with the greatest hesitation that it was entered in film festivals abroad.

Many moviegoers were totally confused by its simple but intricate plot, and several critics were equally nonplussed. Its producer candidly said that he had no idea what to make of it. Masaichi Nagata, the Japanese studio head who has been compared to Darryl Zanuck in this country, did not even sit through the first screening. In fact, when it was released, a lecturer appeared before the filming in some theaters to discuss the movie's implications.

In a word, *Rashomon* was a puzzle, a problem, a mystery.

To find out why, let's take a look at its storyline. The picture takes place in twelfth-century Japan in a time of despair not unlike the defeated country's post-World War II era when the movie was made.

Under the ruined Rashomon gate leading to the ancient capital of Kyoto, three characters—a priest (Minoru Chiaki), a woodcutter (Takashi Shimura), and a stranger (Kichijiro Ueda)—huddle around a fire during a drenching rainstorm. Two of them are muttering to themselves.

"So strange, unbelievable," the woodcutter says. "I just can't understand it. It's beyond me."

"I hope I will be able to keep my faith in man despite what I have heard and seen this day," the priest says.

The stranger asks what is bothering them.

"Maybe you can figure it out," the woodcutter says. And so while the rain drives down, the woodcutter begins the story.

One day, when he went into the forest to gather firewood, he stumbled across the veil and hat of a lady, and then the body of a samurai. He went to the police who soon captured a bandit (Toshiro Mifune) and found the lady.

Before a magistrate, the bandit, the first to tell his story, freely admitted slaying the man. He said he was asleep in the woods when a samurai and his wife passed by. A sudden gust blew away the wife's veil, revealing a beautiful woman. In that moment, the bandit decided he had to possess her. "I meant to have that woman even if I had to commit murder," he said. "But if I could get her without murdering, then so much the better."

He waylaid the couple, overpowered the husband, and tied him to a tree. Then before the husband's eyes, the bandit raped his wife. At first, the woman resisted furiously with a dagger.

But through an ingeniously edited series of shots, we see that in the end she willingly succumbed. As the bandit kissed her, she closed her eyes, and loosened her grip on the dagger until it fell, quivering, into the ground. Her arm moved up his back, caressingly, then tightened.

As the bandit was about to leave, the woman stopped him. Her honor demanded that one of the two men must die. "To feel disgraced before two men is monstrous," she said. "I want to belong to whichever one of you survives."

The bandit then cut the husband free, and the two went at each other in a fierce battle in which each acquitted himself valiantly. Only after an exhausting struggle did the bandit prevail and slay the husband. But when he looked around, the woman was gone. He fled, leaving behind the dead man and the woman's dagger.

The woman's version agreed with the bandit's up to the account of the rape. After being assaulted, she said, the bandit ran away, laughing, while her husband's scornful eyes revealed that he had only contempt for her. "You have no right to blame me for this," she pleaded sobbingly. He said nothing.

Distraught and miserable, she got her dagger, approached him, and then fainted. When she came to, she found her husband dead, the dagger thrust into his chest.

The dead man, speaking through a medium, told a third version. He said that after the rape the bandit told the wife that her husband would not want her anymore, and he asked her to go off with him. To the husband's dismay, she not only agreed, but urged the bandit to kill him. "As long as that man lives," she told the bandit, "I will never be really yours."

But the bandit, repelled by her disloyalty, cut the man's bonds, and he and the woman fled in different directions. Alone and dishonored, the husband picked up his wife's dagger and plunged it into his heart. As he lay dying, sinking into oblivion, he faintly perceived someone pulling the dagger from his body.

Rashomon was not an old tale. It was based on the short story "In a Grove," written in the 1920s by Ryunosuke Akutagawa, who was considered to be Japan's Ernest Hemingway. Director Akira Kurosawa, in addition to adding the Rashomon gate prologue and epilogue, tacked on a fourth tale—that of the woodcutter.

The woodcutter, after hearing the three versions, asserts that they are all wrong because he witnessed the tragedy. He says that he did not disclose this before because he did not want to become involved with the police. But now, troubled over the conflicting accounts, he feels impelled to speak up.

When he came upon the woman's hat, he said that he heard sobbing and saw the trio in a grove. After the rape, he watched the woman cut her husband's bonds. However, the husband refused to risk his life to redeem her honor. "I give her to you freely, bandit," the husband said. "Take her. I mourn more the loss of my horse."

The woman, beside herself with rage, then denounced both men and goaded them to fight. "If you are my husband, why don't you kill this man?" she asked. To the bandit she said: "You are only half a man. A woman adores a man she can love

The bandit and the samurai in their death battle.

passionately. . . . Only the power of your naked sword can win her."

The two then begin a reluctant duel. Instead of fighting in the heroic manner that the bandit depicted, they go at each other timidly and awkwardly, like two terrified children. The husband finally trips in the undergrowth and the bandit runs him through. The wife, who has watched, fascinated, runs off.

Which one of these stories is the truth?

It would seem that the woodcutter, the observer, would most likely be the objective one, since he has had no personal part in the crime. And yet, as we return to the Rashomon gate in the final scene, we see that he himself is puzzled about what really happened.

"Now about all these stories," asks the stranger, "which one is the truth? You ought to think about it."

"I've been thinking about it," the woodcutter says. "And I'm not sure."

As they argue about the various versions, they suddenly hear the cry of a baby. The stranger finds an abandoned infant and immediately strips it of its blankets. When the woodcutter denounces him, the stranger says that someone else would only take them.

Then the stranger turns on the woodcutter and accuses him of lying three times about the crime. He has lied to the police by suppressing his eyewitness testimony. He has lied again in narrating the tale at Rashomon and still omitting his involvement. And he has lied a third time, says the stranger, because it was the woodcutter who stole the woman's dagger after he came on the scene. With this, the stranger hurries away in the rain with the baby's blankets.

The priest and the woodcutter stand in silence, the priest holding the baby. Suddenly the woodcutter reaches for the infant. However, the priest turns away. "What are you trying to do—strip it completely?"

"No," the woodcutter says. "I've six kids of my own. It wouldn't be much worse to have one more."

With the infant in his arms, the woodcutter

267

leaves with the baby as the sky clears and the rain stops. Standing on the steps of the gate, the priest watches him move off. "From the way you act," the priest says, "I'm able to keep my faith in men."

What do we make of *Rashomon*?

The movie seems to be questioning reality itself. Each participant in the drama tells a story that puts himself in the best light.

The bandit said he ravished a willing victim, then killed her husband in a noble duel only after his wife insisted that they fight to salvage her honor. The wife says she was the innocent victim of a brutal rape, and that she killed her husband after losing her senses when he scorned her. Not so, says the husband. He committed honorable hari-kiri after hearing his wife urge the bandit to slay the husband. Finally, the woodcutter says that it was the wife's hysterical goading that forced the sword fight, an awkward, cowardly battle. However, even his credibility is suspect because it turns out that he has lied about other aspects of the tragedy.

Through these conflicting versions of the same event, director Kurosawa seems to be demonstrating the many-sided nature of truth. The sum total of these diverse stories does not add up to a definite conclusion. Instead, it reflects the psychological states of the participants in the drama. As they struggle to justify their actions, they are revealing their own images of themselves. They have all recounted how they *should* have acted.

Kurosawa seems to be saying that there is no absolute truth, that it is all relative—a strange notion to Western minds. In our system of justice, we take it for granted that if enough people testify, the truth will come out. No such idea pervades this movie from the Orient. Says film curator Richie: "*Rashomon* is like a collection of prisms that reflect and refract reality and reverberate with Kurosawa's central theme—the world is illusion. You, yourself, make reality."

What confounded filmgoers most was the picture's ending. The compassionate scene at the Rashomon gate that restores the priest's faith seems to have no relation to what has gone before. Many critics found it jarring, sentimental, and redundant.

But Kurosawa was not content to make a cynical movie questioning moral values. Despite the fact that nothing prepared us for the final scene, he insisted on adding it—perhaps as a way of affirming his belief that not all men are evil, that there is hope ahead for mankind.

If one considers that Japan in 1950 was an occupied nation rising from its ashes, it is not difficult to understand why a director would seek an optimistic ending.

"The spirit of our time is suspicious," said Kurosawa. "And I am glad I have no part of it. I only want people to be happy—though perhaps you might find a kind of escapism in my attitude."

Rebel Without a Cause

Jim (James Dean), the new boy in school, is hazed by Buzz (Corey Allen) while Judy (Natalie Wood) looks on.

Rebel Without a Cause
(1955)

Directed by Nicholas Ray. From a story by Ray and a novel by Robert M. Lindner. Adapted by Irving Shulman. Screenplay, Stewart Stern. Music, Leonard Rosenman. Cinematography, Ernest Haller. Editor, William Ziegler. Art director, Malcolm Bert. Produced by David Weisbart. A Warner Bros. Picture in CinemaScope and Warner Color. 111 minutes.

Jim	*James Dean*
Judy	*Natalie Wood*
Plato	*Sal Mineo*
Jim's Father	*Jim Backus*
Jim's Mother	*Ann Doran*
Buzz	*Corey Allen*
Judy's Father	*William Hopper*
Judy's Mother	*Rochelle Hudson*
Jim's Grandma	*Virginia Brissac*
Moose	*Nick Adams*
Cookie	*Jack Simmons*
Goon	*Dennis Hopper*
Plato's Maid	*Marietta Canty*
Chick	*Jack Grinnage*
Helen	*Beverly Long*
Mil	*Steffi Sidney*
Crunch	*Frank Mazzola*
Harry	*Tom Bernard*
Cliff	*Clifford Morris*
Lecturer	*Ian Wolfe*
Ray	*Edward Platt*
Gene	*Robert Foulk*
Beau	*Jimmy Baird*
Guide	*Dick Wessel*
Sergeant	*Nelson Leigh*
Nurse	*Dorothy Abbott*

Furious when his father (Jim Backus) fails to understand his problems, Jim throws him across the livingroom. His mother's (Ann Doran) screams bring him to his senses.

The end came for James Dean in a silver blur on a darkening September afternoon in 1955.

Dean, who had just finished shooting *Giant*, was driving from Hollywood to a road race in northern California. He was in his $7,000 low-slung, light aluminum Porsche Spyder. With him was Rolf Weutherich, a mechanic from a Hollywood sports car garage. Nobody knows how fast they were going, but at a coroner's inquest, police officials estimated that Dean had been averaging more than eighty miles an hour.

Up ahead, still out of sight beyond a hill, Donald Gene Turnupseed was going home to Tulare that Friday night in his Ford sedan. Turnupseed, a twenty-three-year-old student, came around a bend where the two-lane blacktop Route 466 splits off into a "Y" intersection—left to Tulare, straight ahead to Bakersfield.

Turnupseed slowed down, glanced up the road, and then turned. Even if he had seen the silver gray sports car streaking over the rise in the lowering twilight, it would have been almost impossible to have gauged its speed from its head-on perspective.

But Dean, hurtling over the rolling horizon, saw the turning Ford, and he knew immediately that only one thing could save him. "That guy's gotta stop," he shouted. Turnupseed kept coming.

There was a shattering crash, the discordant sound of steel on steel. The little Porsche was crumpled like a pack of cigarettes, and it skidded one hundred feet into a ditch. Weutherich, thrown clear, suffered a broken leg and fractured jaw. Turnupseed escaped with a bruised nose. Dean was fatally injured, pinned behind the wheel, his head thrown back too far. His neck was broken

271

and he had many fractured bones. It has never been determined whether Dean, who was near-sighted, was wearing glasses.

The tragic death of the tousled-haired twenty-four-year actor came at the height of a meteoric career. He had just completed starring roles in three pictures and was the idol of millions of youths who saw in him their own image. A seemingly long and brilliant future loomed. "It is difficult to think of a contemporary figure who accomplished so much in so brief a time and with such fantastic results as Dean," said movie writer Gene Ringgold.

Dean's demise touched off a mass response unlike anything Hollywood had seen since the death of Valentino. Moviegoers refused to accept the fatality and formed fan clubs that flooded Warner Brothers with 7,000 letters a month. Even in the 1970s, screen magazines and national tabloids were running articles with headlines like: "James Dean Survives; He's Hidden, Paralyzed and Mutilated in a Sanitorium."

Despite the adulation, some feel that Dean's legendary stature has falsely inflated his true talent. These critics say that he derived his fame more from the fact that he was a symbol of his times than from his acting ability. He was a mirror of restless youth of the 1950s as well as a forerunner of the rebellion that flared into violence in the 1960s.

He was labeled Brando's successor, but some say that Dean showed none of his power and virtuosity. He was erratic, moody, and temperamental, and often difficult to direct. "He was never more than a limited actor," said Elia Kazan, who directed his performance in *East of Eden* (1955). "But he had a lot of talent. And he worked like hell."

Yet others called him a born actor, a natural talent. "He was very brilliant," said Julie Harris, who played opposite him in *East of Eden*. "There was nothing he couldn't do as far as acting went."

In David Dalton's biography *James Dean: The Mutant King*, Dennis Hopper vividly recalls Dean's improvisation in the prologue to *Rebel Without a Cause* (1955). The script merely called for Dean to lie drunk in the gutter and then to be taken to the police station.

"Well, first of all, the guy [Dean] is in the street playing with a toy monkey. And doing baby things—trying to curl up, to keep warm. . . .Then, he's searched, and this angry, drunk guy is suddenly ticklish. Where did that come from? It came from genius, that's where it came from. And that was all him. Nobody directed him to do that. James Dean directed James Dean."

It was only after *Giant* (1956) was shot that direc-

tor George Stevens realized his mistake in vetoing a suggestion by Dean. It was in a scene where Jett Rink, the ranch-hand who struck oil, goes to a big party at his former employer's ranch. Instead of drinking their liquor, Dean suggested that he pour himself something from his own flask.

"What Jimmy wanted to do would have been the cutest bit in the movie," Stevens said years later. It would have shown that Rink was still proud, still his own man. But Stevens turned Dean down and told him to enjoy the family booze. "His [Dean's] idea was too damn smart. And he didn't explain it to me. So I didn't get it then. But he really knew that character. And that's the best tribute I can pay to his talent as an actor."

Born in 1931 in Marion, Indiana, Dean was the only child of Winston and Mildred Dean. He acquired an early interest in the arts from his mother who had a fondness for poetry and music. In 1936 the Deans moved to California where James grew up as an introverted, self-absorbed boy who was often teased by his schoolmates. Three years later, cancer took his mother's life. It was a loss that made him strangely bitter. "My mother died on me when I was nine years old," he said years later. "What does she expect me to do? Do it all myself?"

Dean's father sent his son back to Indiana, where he lived with his grandmother, uncle, and aunt on their farm. In this easy-going rural environment, he became more outgoing and his circle of friends grew. In school he was a straight "A" student, a basketball star, and the winner of the state dramatic contest for a theatrical recitation of Dickens' "The Madman."

After graduation he went to UCLA and then joined a theatre group run by actor James Whitmore. It was here that Dean found his true calling. More than anything, he wanted to be a good actor. In the years to come he would impress many with the sensitivity of his performances. Hedda Hopper said that she sat "spellbound" through *East of Eden*.

But his talent and handsome features masked a stormy personality that offended many who befriended him. Some found him rude and conceited. "When he got success, he was victimized by it," said Kazan. "He was a hero only to the people who saw him just as a little waif, when actually he was a pudding of hatred."

Dean got roles in TV and radio productions, and bit parts in three movies—*Sailor Beware* (1951), *Fixed Bayonets* (1951), and *Has Anybody Seen My Gal?* (1951).

272

New York had more opportunities, so he went east. His first job was on "Beat the Clock" where he worked as a stand-by comic and helped with audience warm-ups. After he played in *See the Jaguar* on Broadway and won excellent notices, his stock began to soar. He got starring roles in such television shows as "Philco Playhouse" and "Kraft TV Theatre" and then a key part in a stage dramatization of Andre Gide's novel *The Immoralist*.

It was while he was in an out-of-town performance that Kazan saw him and offered him the part of the young, tormented Cal in *East of Eden*. On the screen, Dean projected a tense, emotional quality, and the role launched his film career.

Warner Bros. planned to put Dean in *Giant* next, but Elizabeth Taylor became pregnant and delayed its shooting. Studio executives, aware of Dean's box office potential, did not want him to stay idle, so they cast about for another movie in the interim. Juvenile delinquency themes like *The Wild One* (1954) and *The Blackboard Jungle* (1955) were just beginning to emerge. Warner Bros. had bought Robert M. Lindner's novel *Rebel Without a Cause* in 1946 but never filmed it. Dean seemed ideal for the lead, and Nicholas Ray, a young director who by chance had come to the studio with his own outline for a juvenile movie, got the directing assignment.

It was Ray's decision to do the picture from the vantage point of teenagers with adults far off in the background. He worked first with established writers Leon Uris and Irving Shulman before getting the screen treatment he wanted from a relative unknown, Stewart Stern. Shulman decided that the youths would be from a middle-class background and created the famous "chickie" run and the principal characters. But Stern—later to write the screenplays for *The Ugly American* (1963), *Rachel, Rachel* (1968), and *Summer Wishes, Winter Dreams* (1973)—molded all the elements into a lean, fast-moving scenario.

As the credits go up on the screen, Jim (Dean) is lying drunk on the sidewalk next to a toy monkey, trying to cover it with a paper blanket. Police haul him off to juvenile hall where he meets two other wayward youths—Judy (Natalie Wood) and Plato (Sal Mineo).* They are there for different reasons.

Plato has shot a puppy, while Judy has been picked up wandering about late at night. But the root cause of their troubles stems from the same source—their inability to relate to their parents.

It was in the police station scene that Dean began keeping the cast and crew waiting as he psyched himself in his dressing room—hitting a bongo and drinking wine. In this sequence, while Jim is being questioned by a detective, he is supposed to take a swing at him and miss. The cop then suggests that he take out his frustrations on the desk, and Dean was to bang away furiously. After an hour he finally came out and played the scene so convincingly that the film crew applauded. Yet it happened so suddenly in the movie that the first preview audience didn't know what to make of it. Some giggled.

"It wasn't, of course, what we intended," said Leonard Rosenman, who wrote the movie score. Discussing the scene in David Dalton's book *James Dean: The Mutant King*, Rosenman said: "We couldn't cut the scene because it was crucial. So I added about five seconds of music. And when the scene came on, the audience again started to laugh. But as soon as they heard the music, they shut up. It was as if the music was a second voice saying, 'Wait a minute. Take another look at this scene. It isn't funny.' and that's the only function of music in that scene—to keep the audience from laughing."

After the police release Jim in the custody of his embarrassed and disapproving parents, he goes to school where he inadvertently makes some remarks that get him in trouble with a gang led by Buzz (Corey Allen). The class is on a field trip to see a star show at the D. W. Griffith Planetarium. As soon as the lecture is over, the tension between Jim and the gang mounts until a knife fight breaks out outside.

Dean insisted on realism, so he and Allen used real switchblades (although they wore chest pads under their clothes). During the filming, Allen nicked Dean behind the ear, and director Nicholas Ray cut the shooting when he saw blood. Dennis Hopper, who had a small part as a gang member, remembers the enraged Dean yelling: "What the hell are you doing? Can't you see I'm having a real moment? Don't you *ever* cut a scene while I'm having a real moment. What the . . . . do you think I'm here for?"

---

*Mineo, who went on to play swaggering street punks with leather jackets and switchblade knives, was stabbed to death in 1976. He was attacked in an alley near the parking lot of his West Hollywood apartment. The Bronx-born actor, son of a Sicilian casket maker, was only seventeen when he got an Oscar nomination for his role as the mixed-up kid in *Rebel Without a Cause*. (He was nominated again in 1960 as a youthful Israeli terrorist in *Exodus*.) A loner who never married, Mineo found his career waning as he grew older, but he was always a hero to the kids on the street in his hometown. One day in 1959, hundreds of Bronx teenagers stayed home after Bob Hope told a TV audience that there would be no school in the Bronx the next day because it was Mineo's birthday. Hope, of course, was only joking. The kids weren't.

Jim, Plato, and Judy light candles and explore an old deserted mansion where they spend the night.

Jim wins the knife fight by disarming Buzz. But this only opens the way for a more dangerous confrontation. Buzz challenges him to a chickie run—a test of nerves where they will each drive a car toward a cliff and leap out seconds before their auto goes over.

That night Jim goes to his room, mulling over the whole affair and wondering what he ought to do. When his father (Jim Backus) comes in, Jim asks him for advice. His father, a kindly but weak and indecisive man, tells him not to show up: "In ten years you'll look back on this . . .and laugh at yourself, to think this was so important." But Jim sees the chickie run as a point of honor, so he slips out later that night, meeting Buzz and his cronies at a desolate bluff overlooking the ocean. The kids have lighted up a runway with the headlights of a dozen autos. Plato is there, and so is Judy, who turns out to be Buzz's girl.

Buzz and Jim walk alone to the edge of the cliff and Buzz explains that the one who bails out first is

"chicken." They share a cigarette and a certain camaraderie begins to surface.

"Why do we do this?" Jim asks.

"You got to do something, don't you?" Buzz answers cryptically.

Moments later, an exuberant Judy gives the signal, and Buzz's and Jim's cars roar toward the cliff. Wheel to wheel, they race through the night at breakneck speed. At the last moment Jim bails out, but Buzz's coat jacket catches in the door handle. While his gang looks on horrified, he plunges to his death on the rocks far below.

The sequence came from Ray's original conception of the film, which he called "Blind Run." It was a story of kids in trouble, and its key scene had two cars racing at each other with lights out from opposite ends of a tunnel. Ray realized that the outline needed changing. Still, he wanted to retain the dramatic car duel and the central idea of the story—putting youths in the forefront and showing adults, for the most part, only as kids see them.

274

The tunnel scene was eventually changed when Shulman, who did the movie adaptation, read a newspaper story of a fatal night "chickie run" on the Pacific Palisades. He felt that the oceanside car race would be more dramatic, and Ray agreed.

After the accident, Jim tells his parents. His mother's only concern is that he avoid being involved in any publicity about the tragedy. This enrages Jim. Confused, he reminds them that a boy was killed and that he played a part in the youth's death.

"You know you did wrong," his father says, trying to minimize the fatality. "That's the main thing, isn't it?"

"You better give me something, Dad," Jim says, pleadingly. "You better give me something fast. Dad, stand up for me."

When his father says nothing, Jim loses control, and he lunges at the older man. The two topple over an armchair, and Jim, his fingers on his father's throat, starts choking him. His mother's screams bring him back to his senses and he runs out into the night.

The next scene shows Jim at police headquarters. He has gone there to find the juvenile officer who had questioned him after he was drunk. The officer isn't there, but Buzz's gang is, and they think that Jim has gone to confess to the police.

Unaware that Buzz's crew is out to get him, Jim goes home, where he finds Judy waiting in the driveway. She, too, has had a falling out with her parents. As they talk under a clear moonlit sky, they find that they are kindred souls, and Dean gives Natalie Wood her first screen kiss.

Twenty years later, Natalie Wood recalled the touching, tentative nature of the scene. "We both felt embarrassed," Miss Wood said. "I was only a teenager. And it was the first time I played a love scene. . . . Jimmy was quite embarrassed, too. Some of the dialogue didn't quite come out because he mumbled a bit."

The part, which transformed her from a child actress into a star, was one she desperately wanted.

"It was a very important film for me personally," Miss Wood said. "Until then I had worked as a child and had always done as I was told. . . . When my parents read the script of *Rebel*, they said, 'Oh, no. Not this one.'

"You know, it shows parents in an unsympathetic light. And yet, I read it and for the first time in my life, I said, 'Oh, wait a minute. I have to do this.' I loved Judy. I felt an identification with the part. I guess I was going through my first rebellion.'"

Since Jim and Judy can't go home, they decide to spend the night at a deserted mansion that Plato has told them about. (It actually belonged to oil billionaire Paul Getty and was the same one used for the 1950 film *Sunset Boulevard*.) When Plato learns that the gang is looking for Jim, he joins them at the mansion after taking his father's gun.

Suddenly the mood of the movie shifts to a lighthearted vein as Jim and Judy pretend to be a rich married couple and Plato assumes the role of a real estate agent showing them a home.

> *Judy*: There's just one thing. What about—
> *Plato*: Children? Well, we don't really encourage them. They're so noisy and troublesome, don't you agree?
> *Judy*: Yes, and so terribly annoying when they cry. I just don't know what to do when they cry, do you, dear?
> *Jim*: Of course. Drown them like puppies.

Dean decided to do the "puppy" line in a Mr. Magoo voice to add more humor to the dialogue. Backus, of course, was well known to audiences as the voice of that cartoon figure. When one studio executive heard this, he buttonholed Dean on the set and tried to persuade him to do the line with a Bugs Bunny imitation instead. "That's a Warner's property," the executive explained. Dean was flabbergasted. He did the Magoo line as planned.

Later, Judy sings a lullaby to Plato and he falls asleep. When the gang members show up, they find Plato alone and wake him up. Startled, he runs away, then shoots one of the pursuing youths as they chase him through the gloomy mansion.

The cars outside and the gunshot attract the police, and Plato flees to the nearby planetarium. The police quickly surround it, throw up searchlights, and, using a bullhorn, call to Plato to surrender.

Alone and frightened, Plato stays put. Jim and Judy dash inside and persuade him to come out. As they all step outside, the searchlights terrify Plato and he bolts for freedom. A policeman sees that he has a gun, opens fire, and brings Plato down.

"But I've got the bullets," Jim shouts, shocked, and angered, as he runs to Plato's already dead body. Plato is wearing Jim's jacket and Jim zips it up as ambulance attendants carry him off. "He was always cold," Jim says.

Dawn is approaching and Jim's parents take him and Judy away. As police cars leave the scene, one of the planetarium astronomers arrives to start the new day. He looks at the departing cars quizzically, and then climbs the steps to go to work as the movie ends. The character is none other than director Ray, putting his signature on the movie à la Hitchcock.

After *Rebel Without a Cause*, Dean went into production with *Giant* almost immediately. He wanted the part of the surly Jett Rink and eagerly accepted it after Alan Ladd turned it down. The picture, a 197-minute color spectacle filmed on location in Marfa, Texas, drew mixed reviews, and so did Dean's performance. Bosley Crowther, the *New York Times* critic, called it a "haunting capstone to [his] brief career." (By the time it was released Dean had been dead almost a year.) But many other reviewers regarded it as his least effective role. They felt that he failed to create a convincing portrayal of the oil-rich Texan. In fact, director George Stevens was so dissatisfied with Rink's last speech that he dubbed in Nick Adams' voice in the final cut.

Nevertheless, Dean's performance was strong enough to get an Oscar nomination,* and the movie itself was an enormous box office success. It has since become one of the biggest money-makers of all time.

However Dean's *Giant* role was to be received, there is no doubt that when the shooting finished on that film, Dean was then the most publicized star in Hollywood. He was besieged with offers. MGM wanted him to play Rocky Graziano in *Somebody Up There Likes Me* (1956), a part that eventually went to Paul Newman. Paramount was dickering for Dean for the Jim Piersall role in *Fear Strikes Out* (1957), which was to go to Anthony Perkins. And Warner Bros., which was negotiating a new seven-year contract for Dean that would pay him $100,000 a picture and also allow him to make outside films, was thinking about starring him in a *Billy the Kid* Western. There was also talk that Dean would play the young ballplayer in the movie version of *Damn Yankees* (1958), the part that Tab Hunter was to get.

It was with these offers in the background that Dean decided to get away from it all on that fateful Friday in 1955. He was driving to a Sunday road race in Salinas, California—a race in which he was not destined to ride. A coroner's jury returned a verdict of accidental death. No charges were lodged.

Some feel that the cult that sprung up after his death began for the wrong reasons. Director

Stevens feels the Dean phenomenon might not have gathered steam had he lived a little longer. "He'd hardly broken water, flashing in the air like a trout," Stevens said. "A few more films and the fans wouldn't have been so bereft."

Others think his fans idolized him for traits he himself disliked. Leonard Rosenman, who wrote the score for *East of Eden* and *Rebel Without a Cause*, said: "Many of the things people adored about Jimmy were things he hated himself and tried to escape from—like his seeming to be a rebel and an eccentric. He actually had a conservative fantasy about what he wanted to do. He wanted tranquility, to create in some way, to be an intellectual, although I don't know how deep that was. . . . And I think the runaway, this leather-jacket man running from society—a middle-class version of *The Wild One*—was a thing Jimmy was compelled to do. But, at the same time, there was a side of him that didn't want to do it. And that's why he went into analysis at the end of his life. . . ."

Nevertheless, the infatuation for Dean was widespread. Fan clubs grew up all over the country. Indiana alone had twenty-six of them. The largest was one in New York City, founded by Mrs. Teresa Brandes and called the James Dean Memory Ring. Some people claimed to have contacted him after his death through automated writing or other supernatural ways. Sal Mineo said he had felt Dean's presence during a ouija board experiment.

On the anniversary of his death, pilgrimages are still made to his hometown of Fairmont, Indiana. Mourners put fresh flowers on his grave, and people chip away his tombstone as if they could take away a piece of him.

As the years passed, most of the fan clubs faded. Yet he still touches a responsive chord whenever youngsters see his movies for the first time.

Why has he had such a charismatic effect on youth?

Because, says author David Dalton, he was a "mutant," a sport of nature, an offshoot from the herd who served as a catalyst for his generation in their transition from the conformity of the 1950s to the freedom of the 1960s. "He became a psychological center around which adolescence organized itself into a community," Dalton said, "a sort of group soul."

Dean is an eternal symbol of the confusions and yearnings of young people everywhere and in every age. He has left behind three films. On their tiny celluloid frames his lonely, soulful features will stay forever young.

---

*The Oscar was won that year by Yul Brynner for his performance in *The King and I*. It was Dean's second Academy Award nomination. His first was for *East of Eden* in 1955. He lost out that year to Ernest Borgnine for *Marty*.

Room at the Top

Laurence Harvey as Joe Lampton, an ambitious social climber, in *Room at the Top,* a picture that took pot shots at Britain's rigid class system.

Room at the Top
(1959)

Directed by Jack Clayton. Screenplay by Neil Paterson,* from the John Braine novel. Photography, Freddie Francis. Art director, Ralph Brinton. Music, Mario Nascimbene. Editor, Ralph Kemplen. Producers, John and James Woolf. Associate producer, Raymond Anzarut. A Romulus Production released by Continental Distributing, Inc. 115 minutes.

Joe Lampton	*Laurence Harvey*
Alice Aisgill	*Simone Signoret**
Susan Brown	*Heather Sears*
Mr. Brown	*Donald Wolfit*
Mrs. Brown	*Ambrosine Philpotts*
Charles Soames	*Donald Houston*
Mr. Hoylake	*Raymond Huntley*
Jack Wales	*John Westbrook*
George Aisgill	*Allan Cuthbertson*
June Sampson	*Mary Peach*
Elspeth	*Hermione Baddeley*
Miss Gilchrist	*Avril Elgar*
Aunt	*Beatrice Varley*
Darnley	*Stephen Jack*
Mayor	*John Welsh*
Mayoress	*Everley Gregg*

*Academy Award Winner.

Thoughts of the emptiness and shallowness of his future life, now that he has made it to the top rung of society, register on Joe Lampton's face at his wedding with wealthy Susan Brown (Heather Sears). Donald Houston is on the left and Donald Wolfit, right.

We've seen his type before—the handsome opportunist, the dashing heel, the social climber consumed by ambition. He is a self-serving cad, an amoral schemer, a flatterer, a ruthless young man on the make. And yet there is a certain engaging quality—a softness in the eyes, a sincerity in the voice, a charm in the personality—that fools us because it masks the insidious nature of his character.

This was Joe Lampton in *Room at the Top*, a role that takes its place alongside Stanley Kowalski in *A Streetcar Named Desire* (1951) as one of those truly unforgettable movie creations. We had seen Joe's counterpart in Theodore Dreiser's *An American Tragedy*, a classic brought to the screen as *A Place in the Sun* in 1951. But *Room at the Top*, the film version of John Braine's first novel, had even more impact because it was set in Britain where the classes have been rigidly stratified for centuries.

Braine was one of England's "angry young men," railing at his country's staid and hoary conventions that make social mobility all but impossible for the working class. There was a bitter irony, too, in Braine's story. Unlike Dreiser's hero who is dragged to the gallows by his lofty goal, Braine's protagonist gets everything he sets out to achieve. In the end he finds that his room at the top has an empty and bleak view. His struggles have taken him to a spiritually sterile society where he can look forward to a dull and barren life—in a sense, a life worse than the slums and poverty from whence he came.

Despite its serious intent, the film proved to be a difficult one for censors of the 1950s to cope with. They did not object to its slap at the establishment. What troubled them was its earthy language (the words "bitch," "bastard," and "whore" were used) and its frank approach to extramarital love. One sequence had Laurence Harvey and Simone Signoret carrying on an intimate conversation in bed while partially clothed. The picture failed to get a Production Code Seal of Approval. Other officials banned the film in such far-flung places as Saskatchewan, Canada, and Australia.

Yet there was no denying its stinging social

commentary and adult realism—both brilliantly underscored by the cast's sensitive performances. They were so well done, in fact, that the story came through as if there were flesh-and-blood characters playing out real-life situations. "One feels that a whole new chapter is about to be written in motion picture history." said *Saturday Review* magazine.

The picture was successful both commercially and artistically. It got Academy Award nominations for best movie, best actor (Harvey), best actress (Signoret), best director (Jack Clayton),* best supporting actress (Hermione Baddeley), and best screenplay based on material from another medium (Neil Paterson). Paterson and Miss Signoret went on to win Oscars.

Hers was the first major acting award to go to a performer who had never made a Hollywood movie and the second to a performer in a foreign film.** (Laurence Olivier in *Hamlet* [1948] was the first to achieve this distinction.) In capturing the Oscar, Miss Signoret broke the Production Code barrier. It was the first time that a non-Code seal movie won one of the top Academy Awards.

Miss Signoret's one regret was her decision to turn down a contract offering a percentage of the profits. Instead, she opted for a salary. "In this way, I missed what was probably the most lucrative financial operation of my career," she said. "I was very well paid. But if I had accepted a percentage, I'd be very, very rich today."

Miss Signoret was then thirty-eight, the wife of actor Yves Montand, and an established foreign star who had scored an international hit in the French shocker *Les Diaboliques* (1954). But the *Room at the Top* part for Miss Signoret, who usually played prostitutes and kept women, was her most sympathetic role. Critics praised the warmth and unaffected naturalism of her performance, which turned out to be the pinnacle of her career. She became chubby and frumpy in her forties, and only character roles were offered. Never again would she make another box office hit, although occasionally she would win glowing reviews.

It was Harvey whose career profited most from *Room at the Top*. A veteran English actor who was virtually unknown to American audiences, he was perfectly cast and quickly became one of the highest paid movie stars. His trademarks were his

confident demeanor, his clipped speech, and his haughty look that could chill ice cubes. With his light gray eyes, high cheek bones, and shock of brown hair, he became the idol of scores of young actresses. Mothers who prized their daughters' virtue dreaded his appearance at parties. Some think that he brought so much to the Joe Lampton role because his own life wasn't far removed from that of the character he played.

Although his aristocratic manner gave the impression that he was of upper-class English heritage, Harvey was actually Lithuanian. His real name was Laruscka Mischa Skikne, and he was the son of a Jewish building contractor who moved his family from Joniskis, Lithuania, to South Africa when Laurence was six. A restless youth, he joined the Royal South African Navy at the age of fourteen. Though he was discharged as soon as his parents informed the authorities, he joined the army in 1943 a year later. This time they did not intervene, and he served in the North African and Italian campaigns of World War II. After the war he moved to England to study in a London drama school. He acted in a Shakespearean company and then broke into movies. Although he was then a low salaried actor, he attracted producers' attention by driving a borrowed Rolls-Royce and wearing expensive Saville Row suits. Over the course of a dozen years, he made thirty films—mostly British "B" programmers—before rocketing to the top in *Room at the Top*. The proceeds of the film and others that followed enabled him to buy plush Hollywood and London homes plus a $30,000 Rolls-Royce convertible and a $16,000 Maserati Mistral sports car.

Despite his early struggles, Harvey denied any kinship to Joe Lampton. "There's nothing of Lampton in me. True, my parents emigrated to South Africa, but they were well-to-do. I had an excellent schooling. True, I ran away to the sea at fourteen. But in my career in England, I've never had to scheme or flatter or cajole—though I've had to fight, mind you."

Like Lampton, Harvey loved older women. His first wife was actress Margaret Leighton. His second was Mrs. Joan Cohn, widow of Columbia Studios founder Harry Cohn. His third and last wife, however, was younger—London fashion model Paulene Stone, the mother of his only child, Domino.

Again, like Lampton, Harvey developed a reputation for arrogance with his colleagues. After working with him on *Walk on the Wild Side* (1962), Jane Fonda said: "There are actors and actors—

---

*It was the first feature-length film directed by Clayton, who later directed *The Innocents* (1961) and *The Pumpkin Eater* (1964).

**She also won the British Film Academy award, her third, and a prize at Cannes.

and then there is Laurence Harvey. With him, it's like acting by yourself."

Some said that Harvey had a phobia about women, and that he really loathed them. To this he replied dryly: "There are women who announce that they hate me. I am not conscious of hating them. They are not worth so strong an impulse."

Whatever his feelings about the opposite sex, his career flourished after *Room at the Top*. His reviews were seldom good, but he became so busy that he moved from one picture to another with hardly a day off in between. Though most of them were forgettable, he did have his share of hits. They included: *Butterfield 8* (1960), *The Manchurian Candidate* (1962), and *Darling* (1965). He also produced and directed, as well as acted in, one of his films—*The Ceremony* (1964), a movie about capital punishment—but it attracted little attention.

In 1972, Harvey's career abruptly slowed down when he underwent abdominal surgery for cancer. Despite cobalt treatments, he continued working for the next eighteen months—making the picture *Night Watch* (1973) with Elizabeth Taylor—until he died in his London home in November 1973. Harvey, who was forty-five at his death, left behind

a lengthy, if spotty, career. Of all his films, he will be remembered most for his convincing portrayal of the upwardly mobile Joe Lampton.

As the picture opens, Lampton arrives at the north country town of Warnley after spending three years as a prisoner of war. He is starting as a municipal clerk, one notch up from the factory work his father did. Handsome and full of life, Lampton tells his roommate Charles Soames (Donald Houston) of his plans to make a big splash in the social swim. Soames warns him of the locality's snobbishness, but Joe dreams of town houses and Riviera vacations. "I'm going to have the lot," he says.

On his first day Joe sets his cap for a beautiful brunette in a sports car—Susan Brown (Heather Sears), daughter of the local industrialist (Donald Wolfit), the town's wealthiest citizen. The Browns are among the close-knit group of wealthy and educated families who live at the "top" of Warnley's social hierarchy. Again, Soames tries to rein in Joe's ambition. "You're wasting your time," Soames says. "Susan's not for you, lad."

One of the town's few community activities that cuts across class lines is the amateur dramatic

Simone Signoret, playing an older woman who has a smoldering but tragic love affair with Joe Lampton (Laurence Harvey). Her performance won an Oscar.

group. It is there that Joe meets Susan, her fiancé Jack Wales (John Westbrook), and Alice Aisgill (Signoret), an unhappily married middle-aged French woman. In the Braine novel, Mrs. Aisgill was a Yorkshire housewife. However, the producers felt that a British actress would not seem sensual enough.

When Joe joins the group and makes advances toward Susan, Wales, an ex-RAF officer, reminds him of his "place" and tells him to stay put. Nevertheless, the curious Susan finally accepts one of Joe's many date proposals and goes to the movies with him. They are not unnoticed. A few days later, Joe's boss, Mr. Hoylake (Raymond Huntley), warns Joe that Susan's father will use his influence to cut short Joe's career unless he stops seeing her. "Find a girl of your own background," Hoylake advises.

One day after rehearsal, Joe accepts Alice Aisgill's invitation to take a drive. The older woman, who is sometimes publicly humiliated by her drunken husband (Allan Cuthbertson), is aware of Joe's interest in Susan and encourages him. Then, sharing a mutual unhappiness, they find themselves thrown together. One night, they make love on a hillside overlooking the city.

A few weeks later, Joe visits his hometown to look for a better job offer. It isn't hard to see what fired his social ambitions. The town is a dreary, soot-scarred factory slum. He comes away repelled by its poverty and by the revelation that his prospective employer depends on Mr. Brown for his business.

Back at Warnley, Joe learns that Susan has been sent abroad to forget him. Nevertheless, he tells Soames that this has made him more determined than ever to win her. In the meantime, he carries on a torrid affair with Alice. They meet at the home of her blowsy friend Elspeth (Hermione Baddeley),* who is skeptical about the consequences despite Joe's contention that he genuinely cares for Alice. "Don't hurt her," Elspeth says.

At the Civic Ball, which Joe attends in an ill-fitting rented tuxedo, Joe once again meets Susan. Her parents and their friends avoid him, but their rudeness only deepens her interest and sympathy for her. Soon they are meeting clandestinely. Eventually Susan lets him make love to her. "Isn't it super, Joe?" she says later. "Now we really belong to each other, really and truly, till death do us part."

Now it is Susan who has fallen for Joe, who in turn now realizes that the superficial pleasures he

has with Susan cannot compare with his deeply mature relationship with Alice. He spends an idyllic vacation with Alice in a seaside cottage, renouncing Susan and urging Alice to get a divorce. "I can't live without you," Joe tells her. "I've tried and I can't."

When they get back, Alice's husband storms into Joe's office, accusing him of trying to steal his wife, and tells him that he won't give Alice a divorce. Joe knows that any hope of a career would be ruined if they run off.

Before he can muster the courage to discuss the matter with Alice, Joe gets a luncheon invitation from Mr. Brown. The industrialist offers to set him up in business if he agrees never to see Susan again. When Joe refuses, Brown surprisingly announces that he will not only permit but demand that Joe marry his daughter, who is pregnant. After the marriage, of course, Joe would be taken into the firm, but first he must promise to end his affair with Alice.

Harshly, Joe breaks the news to Alice and they quarrel. The next day, while receiving congratulations on his engagement, Joe learns that Alice has been killed in a car crash on the hillside where they first made love. Her tragic death fills him with guilt, but his remorse does not deter him from going through with his wedding, the year's major social occasion in Warnley.

And yet his moment of triumph rings hollow. There is a long pause after the minister asks the traditional question, "Wilt thou have this woman as thy wedded wife?" Joe cannot but recognize his own shabby character and wonder if he has, after all, married the wrong woman. The years ahead will irrevocably bind him to a family that will inwardly always hold him in contempt and to a social circle that will forever bore him. "I will," he says flatly.

Later, as they are driving away from the church, Susan notices a tear rolling down Joe's cheek. "Darling, you're crying," she says. "I believe you're really sentimental after all."

Critics lauded the entire cast's performance, but many singled out the fiery brilliance of Harvey's acting. "It sounds," said Archer Winsten of the *New York Post*, "as if it had come right out of his bloodstream. . . . He throws himself into the bitterness of this role with an intensity that strikes out from the screen at you."**

*Mrs. Baddeley, an English actress, later played the housekeeper for "Maude" on television.

**Six years later, in 1965, Harvey played in a sequel called *Life at the Top*, with Jean Simmons as his wife. The picture, which proved out most of Joe Lampton's fears, followed the usual pattern of sequels—it flopped.

Shane

Wilson (Jack Palance), the hired gunman, draws on Torrey (Elisha Cook, Jr.), a fiesty little farmer who tries to defend his property against cattlemen. John Dierkes is seated behind Palance.

Shane
(1953)

Screenplay by A. B. Guthrie, Jr., based on the novel by Jack Schaefer. Additional dialogue, Jack Sher. Art directors, Hal Pereira, Walter Tyler. Cinematographer, Loyal Griggs.* Editor, William Hornbeck. Produced and directed by George Stevens. Associate producer, Ivan Moffat. Associate director, Fred Guiol. A Paramount Picture. 118 minutes.

Shane	*Alan Ladd*
Marion Starrett	*Jean Arthur*
Joe Starrett	*Van Heflin*
Joey Starrett	*Brandon de Wilde*
Wilson	*Jack Palance*
Chris Calloway	*Ben Johnson*
Lewis	*Edgar Buchanan*
Rufe Ryker	*Emile Meyer*
Torrey	*Elisha Cook, Jr.*
Shipstead	*Douglas Spencer*
Morgan	*John Dierkes*
Grafton	*Paul McVey*
Atkey	*John Miller*
Mrs. Shipstead	*Edith Evanson*
Wright	*Leonard Strong*
Johnson	*Ray Spiker*
Susan Lewis	*Janice Carroll*
Howells	*Martin Mason*
Mrs. Lewis	*Helen Brown*
Mrs. Howells	*Nancy Kulp*
Pete	*Howard J. Negley*
Ruth Lewis	*Beverly Washburn*
Ryker Man	*George Lewis*
Clerk	*Charles Quirk*
Ryker Men	*Jack Sterling*
	Henry Wills
	Rex Moore
	Ewing Brown

*Academy Award Winner.

With Ladd is Jean Arthur, who was playing in her last movie.

"Shane!" Brandon de Wilde is calling to the far-away ramrod-straight figure on horseback. But even as his voice echoes through the valley's wilderness, Shane, the gunfighter with a past, rides off into the hills. This memorable final sequence from the 1953 movie *Shane* is one of the scenes that sets it apart from other Westerns.

The idea of making a small boy both an observer and a participant in a struggle over a Wyoming range gives *Shane* an original stamp. Moreover, the bond that develops between the young farm boy and the strong, silent gunman touches a familiar nerve. De Wilde's total admiration of Shane epitomizes the boundless devotion all kids show toward an adult hero at some time in their childhood.

But *Shane* won its spurs as a classic Western for more than its qualities of uniqueness and nostalgia. It was a skillfully directed film, a truly meticulous job by George Stevens. Its color photography was lush and breathtaking, and its acting was first-rate. All this can be seen in the universal acclaim it won from critics:

—Said Paul Dehn in the London *Sunday Chronicle:* "It is a great film because its director has taken great and equal pains over every single component that goes to make a film. . . . Nothing in *Shane* is glamourized. But what is ordinary has been seen through the extraordinary eye of a director who, I believe, has genius."

—Said Bosley Crowther of the *New York Times:* "[*Shane* is] beautifully filmed in Technicolor. . . . It may truly be said to be a rich and dynamic mobile painting of the American frontier scene." In fact, cameraman Loyal Griggs won an Academy Award. One critic, Dehn, went so far as to call its color scenes "the most beautiful ever filmed." (Yet, ironically, as magnificent as they were, much of their effect was left on the cutting room floor. The film was cut at the bottom and top of each frame so that it could fit the new-size, wide screen, which had just come into vogue. In some scenes it had the mutilating effect of slicing off the tops of heads and bottoms of entire landscapes. Griggs' Oscar, said Pauline Kael, seemed like a "ghastly joke.")

—Said C. A. LeJeune in the London *Observer:* "The performances by Alan Ladd as Shane, Van Heflin and Jean Arthur as the parents, and Brandon de Wilde as the boy who idolizes the stranger, give the unusual sense of a ripening association. No character, however small, fails to leave a true mark on the picture."

There are some who maintain that *Shane* is the greatest Western ever made. In contrast to the inner psychological study made famous by *High Noon* (1952), this picture is in the old tradition of a man vs. man struggle in the great outdoors. Its plotlines are so simple that some have compared it to a morality play or a myth. Shane, a knight in buckskin, canters into the story alone on his trusty steed. At the end, he chivalrously leaves the same way after coming within an eyelash of breaking up a family by winning the affection of a homesteader's wife and son. He also leaves behind three dead hoodlums and, for the moment, blunts a cattleman's hard-nosed campaign to kick farmers off the range. "The story," said *Life* magazine, "comes straight from King Arthur's Round Table and the hero's real name is Galahad."

So pleased was Paramount with the film's initial reception that it re-released it only four years later in 1957. "There never was a picture like *Shane*," the studio's ads said.

But something unexpected happened during this second showing. Many moviegoers were bored. They felt that the film didn't hold up. As brilliant and evocative as it seemed on first viewing, it turned into a slow, mawkishly sentimental drama thereafter. Shane's final speech to Joey—in which he tells the boy to "grow up to be straight and strong"—is cliché-ridden. And so, disappointingly, is the gunfighter's final scene with Marion. All the trappings of a tender farewell are in the making as Shane goes off to a last shootout. But, again, the dialogue fails to rise to the occasion. Instead, it is hackneyed and trite.

> *Marion:* Shane, wait. You were through with gunfighting.
> *Shane:* I changed my mind.
> *Marion:* Are you doing this just for me?
> *Shane:* For you, Marion, Joe, and little Joe.
> *Marion:* And we'll never see you again?
> *Shane:* Never is a long time.
> *Marion:* Please, Shane, please take care of yourself.

"It is a film of diminishing returns," says movie historian William K. Everson. "Each viewing tends to leave one liking it a little less." Says Pauline Kael: "It is over-planned and uninspired. The Western was better before it became so self-importantly self-conscious."

Even so, most movies have their greatest impact on first viewing, and a first viewing of *Shane* is a totally absorbing experience. Part of the reason must inevitably stem from Stevens' craftsmanship and painstaking planning.

It was Stevens' idea to make the movie amid the sweeping, snow-capped peaks of Wyoming. Stevens, who directed the Oscar-winning *A Place in the Sun* (1951) and later *The Diary of Anne Frank* (1959), spent three weeks searching for a location near Jackson Hole, Wyoming. Then he took two months to shoot the film there. (The only scenes made in Hollywood were the ones at the Shipstead Ranch. Even here, to add realism, Stevens imported Wyoming willows to the set.)

In Wyoming, Stevens built an 1890 prairie town street as well as the Starrett ranch. He filled its kitchen with authentic antique western kitchenware. To decide which scenes to shoot each day, he called the weather bureau at 4:30 A.M. It was this policy that enabled Stevens to get the dark, brooding storm clouds that made the forbidding background in Torrey's famous death scene.

Stevens' attention to detail went beyond the weather. Because he thought it essential to emphasize the importance of water—both to the farmer and the herder—he diverted a stream and ran it past the Starrett ranch. At key points in the film, there is the sound of rushing water.

Background sound has always been an important part of Stevens' movies, and *Shane* is filled with bird melodies, horses' neighs, cattle lowing, and the clink of spurs. Like an orchestra director, Stevens brings up these noises, swelling them and magnifying them, so that at moments they seem to dominate the scene. The sound creates an offbeat emphasis. This is especially so during the saloon fight where wheezing gasps punctuate the tension of the struggle.

By the same token, the sounds can get in the way and throw a sequence out of focus. Bird songs, for example, get so distracting the fifth or sixth time around that you begin to think about what species they might be rather than what is going on.

But the deliberately paced story, building to its explosive climax, overcomes this excess, as do the cleanly etched performances of its cast.

Jean Arthur, in her last movie, convincingly portrays a woman loyal to her husband but strangely attracted by the mysterious Shane. Brandon de Wilde turns in a touching performance as the frontier farm boy. Van Heflin is outstanding as the hardy, stubborn homesteader. And so is Jack Palance as the icy-nerved hired killer. In minor roles, there are solid jobs done by Emile Meyer and Ben Johnson.

Shane (Alan Ladd), the drifter with a past, tries some target practice as little Joey (Brandon de Wilde), the frontier farmboy who idolizes him, flinches from the gun's report.

Ironically, it is Ladd who turns in the weakest performance.* Wooden, frail-looking, and small of stature—he was only 5'6"—he fell far short of creating the dramatic presence that won the love and devotion of Starrett's wife and son. Yet the disparity in the height of Shane and that of the

*Curiously, three of Shane's four leading players had violent or sudden deaths. Ladd, whose twenty-six movies for Paramount earned $60,000,000 for the studio, died in 1964 from the effects of alcohol and sedatives. He was fifty. In 1971, Heflin, a versatile supporting actor, was found clinging to a ladder at his Hollywood apartment house swimming pool—weeks after suffering a heart attack. He was sixty. De Wilde, who debuted at the age of seven in the Broadway play A Member of the Wedding, was killed in a 1972 highway crash. He was thirty.

lanky gunman Wilson adds emphasis to Shane's act of raw courage in taking on the giant killer. With the possible exception of his first film, This Gun for Hire (1942), Shane has become Ladd's most famous part.

The movie revolves around the age-old struggle between fence-building, Johnny-come-lately homesteaders and open-range, long-established ranchers. At the outset, Shane, a drifter, wanders onto the farm of Joe Starrett (Van Heflin), searching for water for his horse.

The family erroneously takes Shane to be a hostile cattleman because a bunch of cowhands ride up right behind him. They have come to tell Starrett that they have just signed a new beef contract. "I'm going to need all my range," says Rufe Ryker (Emile Meyer), the ranch boss. "You're going to have to get out before the snow flies. You and the other squatters. . . ."

"Homesteaders, you mean," Starrett says.

"I could blast you out of here right now," Ryker says, as tempers get edgy.

Just then, Shane steps in from behind the house, his hand near his gunbelt. He moves in next to Starrett.

"Who're you?" one of the cowhands asks.

"I'm a friend of Starrett," Shane answers.

His presence cuts down the odds quickly and gives the riders some second thoughts about any violence. They ride off without another word, trampling some garden vegetables as they go. Starrett, embarrassed for taking Shane to be an enemy, apologizes and invites him to join his wife Marion and son Joey for supper.

"These old-timers can't see it yet," says Starrett, expounding his philosophy during the meal. "But running cattle on open range can't go on forever. Takes too much space for too little results. Cattle that's bred for meat and are fenced in and fed right—that's the thing. A homesteader can't run but a few beef. But he can sure grow grain and cut hay. And what with his garden and hogs and milk, he'll make out all right. We make out all right, don't we, Marion?"

There is just a slight pause. Marion looks at the handsome blond stranger, then back at her sweat-stained, hard-working husband. "Of course," she says.

To repay Starrett for his meal, Shane helps the farmer pull up a huge tree stump. Then he accepts Starrett's offer to stay on and help with the farm work. But Shane's past remains a secret. When Starrett asks him where he was headed when he came, Shane says only, "One place or another. Someplace I've never been."

Shane's confident demeanor when trouble was brewing leaves us with the impression that he is a man who is no stranger to gunplay. But we feel this was all part of a past he wants to forget.

It doesn't take Shane long to run into trouble with Ryker's cowhands. On a trip into town to get supplies, Shane goes into the saloon to get some soda pop for Joey. Ryker's cowboys are playing poker, and one of them, Chris Calloway (Ben Johnson), starts hazing Shane.

"Oh, a new sodbuster," says Calloway. "Thought I smelled pigs."

When Shane orders a soda pop, the cowboy laughs and walks up to the bar. "What'll it be— lemon, strawberry, or lilac, sodbuster?"

Shane ignores him, but Chris splashes him with whiskey and warns him not to come back.

At a meeting that night, the homesteaders learn that Ryker's "war parties" have been around to threaten all of them. They resolve to hold on to their stakes. One of the toughest talking is a cocky, little Confederate veteran named Torrey (Elisha Cook, Jr.). "There ain't nobody pushing me off my claim," Torrey says. "And that's for certain."

The fur starts flying when the homesteaders go to town one Saturday. Shane goes into the saloon to cash in the deposit on his pop bottle. "That's one of the new ones," says Calloway, looking up from his poker hand. "They call him 'sody-pop.'" He walks up to Shane and tells him to get out. Shane orders two whiskies, tosses one in Calloway's face, and belts him so hard that he sails out the door. Calloway picks himself up and goes right after Shane. All the men get up from their card game to watch the battle royal, while Joey peeks in under the door.

Now Stevens' microphones add another dimension to the scene, picking up all the slight sounds surrounding the fight. "Tear him apart, Chris," whispers one of Ryker's men as they measure up the upstart. The soundtrack carries the heavy breathing of the men as they circle each other.

Shane ducks a roundhouse right, then bloodies Calloway's face with sharp punches, finally dropping him with a powerful overhand right.

Ryker, impressed by Shane's aggressiveness, offers him a job and says that he'll double what Starrett pays him. When Shane turns him down coldly, Ryker hints that it must be more than money that interests Shane.

"Pretty wife Starrett's got," Ryker says.

"Why, you dirty old man," Shane roars.

Before he can get at Ryker, the cattleman signals his men and they tear into Shane, then hold him while Ryker starts pummeling him.

Fortunately, Starrett is nearby and sees the beating Shane is taking. He grabs a two-by-four, clobbers Ryker, and then wades into the gang holding Shane. Between the two of them, Shane and Starrett whip the whole bunch.

So the homesteaders have won a battle. But the range war goes on. The next day Ryker sends one of his men to Cheyenne to hire a gunfighter. "I'm through fooling," Ryker says. "From now on, when we fight them, the air is gonna be filled with gunsmoke."

Meanwhile, out at the Starrett farm, Shane has won a firm place in the family circle, and he has turned out to be a willing and tireless worker. One day, Joey asks him how to shoot and Shane obliges. This is one of the key scenes of the movie. To demonstrate his prowess, Shane makes a fast draw and picks off some rocks about one hundred feet away. In an explosive instant, Shane, the gunfighter, has suddenly been exposed, and Marion, standing in the background, has seen him unmasked. But when she gently chides him for introducing Joey to firearms, Shane defends his action.

"A gun's a tool, Marion. No better and no worse than the man who uses it."

Shane is saying that the choice of right or wrong is up to the individual. Yet he has been put on the defensive, and this is the movie's point of departure. "Unlike most Westerns," says Otis L. Guernsey, Jr. in the *New York Herald-Tribune*, "Shane depicts the man who uses a gun as a thing apart, an outcast with an unpleasant smell of death lingering about him."

Later, at a July 4 celebration, Shane dances with Marion, and it's obvious that they make a fine couple. Then, one night as his mother tucks him into bed, Joey tells her that he loves Shane about as much as his father. His admiration is so deep-seated that it can readily be seen in his wide-eyed expression and in his voice. Some critics have even found a quality of hero-worship in the way Joey says Shane's name, pronouncing it in a kind of sing-song style as though it were a cheer.

"Do you like Shane, too," Joey asks his mother. "Yes, I like him, too, Joey," his mother says, her eyes with a faraway look. When she joins her husband, the faraway look is still there, and Starrett appears to notice it. "Don't say anything," Marion tells him. "Just hold me—tight."

Peace and quiet don't last long. Ryker's men cut their herd loose and the steers trample the plowed ground of a half-dozen farmers. Then the gunman shows up—Jack Wilson (Palance), a tall, lean man with steel-cold eyes and a sardonic grin. Wearing two guns, and a black hat and vest, he walks panther-like and his spurs jangle ominously. Before he does his shooting, he puts a black glove on his right hand.

However, Ryker is not quite ready to set Wilson

Shane buys farm supplies from Grafton (Paul McVey). Lewis (Edgar Buchanan) sits on counter.

loose. He wants to make one last attempt at conciliation, and so he offers to buy Starrett's homestead, promising him a job at top wages. Starrett turns him down, saying that the homesteaders are doing the right thing by holding onto their claims. This only enrages Ryker. But instead of painting him as an all-black villain, director Stevens does an interesting thing at this point. He gives Ryker a chance to state his case. Sitting atop his horse, looking like some bearded Old Testament patriarch etched against the night sky, Ryker makes a simple but eloquent argument.

He points out that it was the ranchers who opened the West and at great sacrifice. "I got a bad shoulder yet from a Cheyenne arrow," he says. "Then people move in. They fence off my range, fence me off from water . . . plow ditches, take out irrigation water. So the creek runs dry sometimes. I've got to move my stock. And you say the men that did the work and ran the risks have no right to the range?"

"I'm not belittlin' what you and others did," Starrett says. "At the same time, you didn't find this country. There were trappers here and Indian traders long before you showed up. . . . You talk about rights. You think you have the right to say nobody else has got any. Well, that ain't the way the government looks at it."

The next day, Ryker sends Wilson after his first victim. On a dark and dreary Saturday, Torrey comes to town, and Wilson calls him over. Storm clouds fill the sky and thunder rattles overhead. The gunfighter stands on the saloon porch baiting Torrey as the little farmer sloshes through ankle-deep mud.

"Stonewall Jackson was trash himself," Wilson says. "Him and Lee and all the rest of them rebels. You, too."

"You low-down lying Yankee," the hot-tempered Torrey says.

"Prove it," the gunfighter replies.

Torrey goes for his gun, but he's no match for Wilson. The gunman outdraws him easily, and the impact of Wilson's blast sends Torrey flying backward into the muck. Stevens staged the sequence, probably the most realistic gun battle seen until that time, by rigging wires to Cook. He fell back so far that he looked as if he had been hit head-on by a charging steer.

There is a simple funeral for Torrey—the camera shows the homesteaders framed against an azure sky while one of them plays "Dixie" slowly on a mouth organ. But even death won't stop Ryker. While the funeral takes place, his men burn a farm.

Then Ryker sends an invitation to Starrett to meet with him in town to work out their differences. It is, of course, a trap. Still, Starrett is determined to go, and nothing Marion can say will stop him—not even the thought of death. Starrett tells her that he knows she won't have to worry about things if he doesn't come back.

"I know I'm kind of slow sometimes, Marion. But I see things," Starrett says, alluding to the relationship that has developed between Marion and Shane. "I know if anything happened to me that you'd be taken care of better than I could do it myself."

Shane knows that Starrett is no match for Ryker and Wilson, but Starrett won't let Shane go in his place. As a result, a fight breaks out between Shane and the proud and determined farmer. With the camera shooting from low angles between the legs of frightened horses, the two stage a knockdown, drag-out slugfest that ends when Shane uses his gun butt to knock Starrett out.

Shane, at this point, has decided that, regardless of the outcome, he cannot come back. Although a genuine bond of affection has grown up between him and Marion, Shane respects Starrett too much to destroy his marriage. The cleanest, most honest way to extricate himself from this tangled situation is to leave. So Shane and Marion part with a handshake. "Please, take care of youself," says Marion.

The confrontation between Wilson and Shane is swift. When Shane walks quietly into the saloon, Ryker is at the bar.

"Your kind of days are over," Shane says. Then he turns to Wilson at a table. "I've heard you're a low-down Yankee liar."

"Prove it," Wilson says, now on his feet.

The two face each other and draw, but Shane is a shade faster. His bullet whizzes to the mark, thudding into Wilson's chest and toppling the gunman backward. As Wilson goes down, splintering tables and chairs, Shane turns like a flash toward Ryker, who is drawing his sidearm. Before Ryker can clear his holster, Shane sends two rounds into him.

Then, unaware that Ryker's brother (John Dierkes) is on a second story landing aiming a rifle at his back, Shane turns to leave. But Joey, who has trailed Shane to town, has watched the shootout beneath the saloon's swinging doors.

"Shane, look out," the boy yells. Even as Shane wheels, a bullet rips into his shoulder. However, his gun barrel is flashing, too, sending a spray of bullets into his assailant who goes crashing to the floor below.

The killings have sealed Shane's fate. He knows

Torrey is no match for the big gunfighter and Wilson blasts him into the mud.

now that he cannot stay on in the valley even if he were to live apart from the Starretts and stake out his own homestead. By his act of lawlessness, he has forfeited his right to live peacefully in the non-violent world of the homesteader. And so when Joey asks if he can ride home behind Shane, the gunfighter says that he has to move on. "A man has to be what he is, Joey. You can't break the mold. I tried it. It didn't work."

"We want you, Shane," Joey says, unwilling to give up his idol.

"Joey, there's no living with a killing. There's no going back. You run home to your mother. Tell her there are no more guns in the valley."

"Shane," Joey says, suddenly noticing his wound. "It's bloody. You're hit."

"I'm all right, Joey. You go home to your mother and father. And grow up to be straight and strong.

And, Joey, take care of both of them."

Shane starts off toward the mountains. The little boy looks after him, tears running down his face. "He'd never have been able to shoot you—if you'd have seen him."

"Bye, little Joe," Shane says quietly.

Shane's figure gradually gets smaller, fading in the distance. The boy never takes his eyes from him. "Pa's got things for you to do," he calls, pleadingly. "And Mother does. I know she does, Shane."

Shane keeps going, shrinking slowly as he rises into the jagged peaks that ring the valley. And as he rides away, never turning around, never replying, the mountains echo Joey's plaintive voice.

"Shane," Joey calls at the top of his lungs. "Come back, Shane."

And there is in his lonely cry all the poignancy and grief of a boy who has lost his hero forever.

Singin' in
the Rain

Gene Kelly and Debbie Reynolds keeping dry.

Singin' in the Rain
(1952)

Directed by Gene Kelly and Stanley Donen. Written by Betty Comden and Adolph Green. Musical director, Lennie Hayton. Orchestrations by Conrad Salinger, Wally Heglin, and Skip Martin. Songs by Arthur Freed (lyrics) and Nacio Herb Brown (music): "Would You?," "Singin' in the Rain," "All I Do Is Dream of You," "I've Got a Feeling You're Fooling," "Wedding of the Painted Doll," "Should I?," "Make 'Em Laugh," "You Were Meant for Me," "You Are My Lucky Star," "Fit as a Fiddle and Ready for Love," "Good Mornin'." By Comden, Green, and Roger Edens: "Moses." Camera, Harold Rosson. Art directors, Cedric Gibbons and Randall Duell. Special effects, Warren Newcombe and Irving G. Ries. Editor, Adrienne Fazan. Produced by Freed. A Metro-Goldwyn-Mayer Production. 103 minutes.

Don Lockwood	*Gene Kelly*	Olga Mara	*Judy Landon*
Cosmo Brown	*Donald O'Connor*	Baron de la Bouvet	
Kathy Selden	*Debbie Reynolds*	de la Toulon	*John Dodsworth*
Lina Lamont	*Jean Hagen*	J. C. Spendrill, III	*Stuart Holmes*
R. F. Simpson	*Millard Mitchell*	Don, as a Boy	*Dennis Ross*
Zelda Zanders	*Rita Moreno*	Villain in Western	*Bill Lewin*
Roscoe Dexter	*Douglas Fowley*	Phil, Cowboy Hero	*Richard Emory*
Dancer	*Cyd Charisse*	Man on Screen	*Julius Tannen*
Dora Bailey	*Madge Blake*	Ladies in Waiting	*Dawn Addams*
Rod	*King Donovan*		*Elaine Stewart*
Phoebe Dinsmore,			
Diction Coach	*Kathleen Freeman*	Villain, "Dueling	
Diction Coach	*Bobby Watson*	Cavalier" and	
Sid Phillips,		"Broadway	
Assistant Director	*Tommy Farrell*	Rhythm"	*Carl Milletaire*
Male Lead in		Orchestra Leader	*Jack George*
"Beautiful		Vallee Impersonator	*Wilson Wood*
Girl" Number	*Jimmie Thompson*	Audience	*Dorothy Patrick*
Assistant Director	*Don Foster*		*William Lester*
Wardrobe Woman	*Margaret Bert*		*Charles Evans*
Hairdresser	*Mae Clarke*		*Joi Lansing*
		Russ Saunders doubles for Gene Kelly	

Gene Kelly in the famous title song number from *Singin' in the Rain.*

It got good reviews in its day, but neither it nor any of its stars won an Academy Award.* Like most movies, it died out and disappeared, but it wouldn't fade away. A generation later it came back and began dazzling audiences in revival

*Jean Hagen was, however, nominated for best supporting actress, losing to Gloria Grahame for *The Bad and the Beautiful.*

houses and on television's late shows. Soon it was winning bouquets from nostalgic critics. And then there was no stopping its climb to celluloid immortality. Today, it has earned a niche in almost everybody's all-time favorite list.

In 1977 members of the American Film Institute voted it one of America's top ten movies. *Time* magazine has called the film one of the great "watershed" pictures. One reviewer, Pauline Kael, has even said it is "just about the best Hollywood musical of all-time." Vincent Canby, the *New York Times* critic, rates it "a Hollywood masterpiece."

The movie with the time-delay knockout punch was, of course, *Singin' in the Rain*. Like most of the best movie musicals, it was written directly for the screen, and yet it nearly didn't get as far as a script. Its authors, Betty Comden and Adolph Green, came that close to walking out even before they set a word on paper. According to Comden and Green, it happened like this:

In 1950, producer Arthur Freed summoned the two to Hollywood after they had done the movie version of their own first Broadway show, *On the Town*. They thought Freed had called them to write the lyrics as well as the original screenplay for a new musical.

Somehow, there had been a breakdown of communications. When they got to the coast, Freed told them that yes, they were to do a new screenplay, but no, they were not to do any lyrics. The words and music would come from songs turned out in the late 1920s and early 1930s by Freed himself (he was a former lyricist) and composer Nacio Herb Brown. Freed had just sold his catalogue of tunes to MGM. "We gulped a gulp that could be heard around the world," said Comden and Green.

For two solid weeks, the two scrapped with Freed and refused to work. But, in the end, they found that the small print in their contract upheld Freed's position, not theirs.

And so, beaten and disheartened, they wearily resigned themselves to go to the studio to hear a medley of Freed-Brown songs. At first they were bored stiff, but after a while the catchy tunes began to start their toes tapping. Many had become standards—"Broadway Melody," "Broadway Rhythm," "You Are My Lucky Star," "Fit as a Fiddle," "You Were Meant for Me," and the title song. Before the day was over, they were hooked.

But what would the plot be? "We knew one thing about the story," said Comden and Green. "There would have to be some scene where there would be rain and the leading man—Howard Keel? Van Johnson? Gene Kelly?—would be singin' in it."

The Comden-Green team took a closer look at the songs they were working with. Freed and Brown had written many of them from 1929-1931, those traumatic years in which Hollywood was teetering on the brink of the sound revolution. Eureka!

Instead of trying to shoehorn the songs into a contemporary musical, they decided to use them in their own period. *Singin' in the Rain* would be a story of Hollywood's greatest changeover, the mad upheaval of the film industry, the era when careers ended abruptly because a voice failed to match a classic profile.*

The classic case, of course, was John Gilbert. He was one of the leading male stars of the silent screen in 1928, but his career collapsed after his first talking picture in which he improvised his own love scene. Over and over he said, "I love you, I love you," exactly as he had done in silent films. However, for the first time the audience heard his rather odd soprano voice getting shriller each time, and they howled with laughter.

"Ah," said Comden and Green, "this was perfect." They decided that they wanted just such a star, only the trick was to put this tragedy into a musical and keep it light and funny. As for the hero, they felt that he should be a gent who could survive the transition. To give that story point an air of credibility, they thought that they should have a hero who had a song-and-dance vaudeville background before he got into the movies. "Such a character," they said, "felt more to us like Gene Kelly than Howard Keel."**

And so Kelly it was, and a happier casting choice may never have been made. Comden and Green knew there would be a scene where Kelly would be singing and dancing in the rain. "What the script didn't say was, 'Here Gene Kelly does perhaps the outstanding solo number of his career.'"

It was a career that began in Pittsburgh where he was born Eugene Curran Kelly in 1912. Even as a boy, Kelly, who had two brothers and two sisters, had a sunny disposition and an Irish temper. He found dancing easy because he was always athletically inclined. Before he was five, his father had him on ice skates whirling around a makeshift rink in their backyard.

His ego prompted him to pick dancing over

*An original concept, according to co-director (with Kelly) Stanley Donen, was to remake an early talking picture. One they considered was the Jean Harlow film *Bombshell* (1933). Somehow that idea got scrapped, but nobody remembers why because people are too fondly wrapped up in their memories of the original story that was done. "The nice thing about *Singin' in the Rain* [is] . . . that we didn't look back on the early talkies or silents and say we were superior to them," Donen said. "We looked back on them with great affection and appreciation. We weren't saying, 'We're doing it better.' We were just saying that they did it and we liked it. And I think that still comes through."

**Oddly, co-director Donen had a totally different recollection of Kelly's casting. "It [Green and Comden's story] isn't true. . . . Adolph is saying that they went off and wrote that script and then sent it to Gene and that Gene then said he would do it. The total opposite is true. We all met for weeks in California and talked about it. Gene was going to be in it. They were writing a part for him."

296

sports at Peabody High School. Kelly noticed that girls went for guys in school plays rather than football players—or, anyway, players who warmed the bench, which was where Kelly figured he'd end up.

"I was a little short then"—he is 5′9″ now—"and looking back, I can see it was pure self-aggrandizement. I wanted everyone to say, 'Gee, he's clever.' And they did, too. I'd do a nice buck-and-wing, and they all thought it was nifty. But I hated it at the time. No, there was no inner impulse. It was just a way to meet girls."

Kelly speaks in a soft, rasping voice, which somebody said sounds like fine sandpaper. His singing voice, not noted for its wide range, was not much different.

At sixteen Kelly went to Penn State University, later transferring to the University of Pittsburgh where, for some now unknown reason, he majored in economics. The Depression hit while he was in college, putting his father, a gramophone sales executive, out of work. Kelly quit school for a year to work for his tuition. He taught gymnastics at a YMCA camp, crated boxes, pumped gas, and dug ditches. After a while he began to count shovels and cars in his sleep.

"My kid brother, Fred, was dancing, going to amateur nights and making more dough in a couple of hours than I did in eight hours," Kelly said. "I thought maybe he had something."

With his brother, he started on the Pennsylvania amateur night circuit as a duo called "The Kellys." Then, he got a job teaching dancing in Pittsburgh's Temple Beth Shalom ("Why not? I was a nice Catholic boy") and opened a dance studio in the basement of his family's home. He did so well that he opened another in Johnstown, Pennsylvania.

At twenty-seven, an age when many other dancers are about ready to hang up their shoes, Kelly felt ready for the big time. He went to New York City to get a job as a choreographer, but things didn't quite work out the way he planned.

"I'd go around to the producers and say, 'I'm a choreographer.' And they'd say, 'Okay, what have you done?' And I'd say, 'Well, in Pittsburgh....' But

Kelly and Cyd Charisse
dancing a love duet.

I could always get a job as a dancer. I was better than any of the other guys around."

His first performance was as a chorus boy, but before the year was over, he landed the part of Harry the hoofer in William Saroyan's *The Time of Your Life*. He also acquired a wife, a dancer he met at Billy Rose's Diamond Horseshoe who became actress Betsy Blair.*

Kelly won raves in the 1939 Saroyan play, and by 1940 he got his name in lights with the title role in the Broadway musical *Pal Joey*. They gave him a Hollywood contract, and Kelly made his movie debut in *For Me and My Gal* (1942) with Judy Garland and George Murphy, later the Republican senator from California.

The rest is history. He appeared in thirty-four movies in a film career that ran from 1942-1967, often doing the choreography and sometimes the directing as well. His pictures include such well-known musicals as *DuBarry Was a Lady* (1943), *Cover Girl* (1944), *Anchors Aweigh* (1945), *On the Town* (1949), *An American in Paris*** (1951), and *Les Girls* (1957).

Inevitably he is compared with Fred Astaire, whose top hat, white tie, and tails set the style of movie dancing in the 1930s and 1940s. Kelly took off his jacket and rolled up his sleeves. He has made the best comparison of their very different approaches. "My own style was strong, wide open, bravura," he said. "Fred's was intimate, cool, easy."

"I searched for a form of my own," he said years after his dancing career was ended. "I tried to base it on male movements, athletic movements. I wanted to get rid of the suit. In dancing you speak with your anatomy. And you can't see it in a suit. A sailor suit was the best dance costume."

Wearing costumes as far-ranging as navy whites to the T-shirt of a truck driver, he pranced alongside Hollywood's most glamorous leading ladies. And he recalls the silver screen's dancing damsels candidly, if at times irreverently:

Cyd Charisse: She outweighed me ten to one. Astaire used to walk in every time I lifted her and say, "You're gonna get a hernia."

Ginger Rogers: When she danced with Astaire, it was the only time in the movies when you looked at the man, not the woman.

Rita Hayworth: She came from a Spanish family. I used to study with her uncle. He told me about all of her heel-clicking and castanets. It was amazing how well she could adapt to graceful movements. I thought she was wonderful in *Cover Girl*.

Judy Garland: No dancer. But she could pick up a step faster than I could. She had a computer mind. She could hear a tune once and walk away knowing every step. We called her "Old Tin Ear."

Not all his movie memories are happy ones. He lost the role of Sky Masterson in *Guys and Dolls* (1955). ("For a couple of months, I felt lousy. . . . Boy, that knocked me out. I was miserable, really sick.") And he had reservations about *Marjorie Morningstar* (1958). ("She [Natalie Wood] wasn't Jewish enough. It wasn't what [Herman] Wouk wrote.") And then there was the demise of the musical pictures that made him famous.† ("I certainly wasn't happy about the decline of musicals. But it gave me a chance to do things I always wanted to do.")

After a fling at a television series (he played Father O'Malley in "Going My Way" in 1962,†† he did less and less acting in favor of choreography, directing, and producing. His directing credits include *Gigot* (1962) with Jackie Gleason, *A Guide for the Married Man* (1967) with Walter Matthau, and *Hello, Dolly* (1969) with Barbra Streisand.

Unquestionably, though, Kelly will always be best remembered for his dancing days. And, in a 1966 interview when he was fifty-four (and wearing a toupee), he gave the feeling that this is the way he wants it to be.

"Dancing is a game for children," he said, explaining why he had not been seen on the screen in years. "You mature, but as a dancer matures he goes downhill physically. You reach a point of diminishing returns. By the time you learn your craft, your muscles won't respond. In a way, it's cruel. . . .

---

†The most common explanation for their disappearance is their extravagant budget. But many film experts trace the fall of the musical to the overseas market. American filmmakers depended on foreign audiences for more than half their revenue. However, musicals were not popular abroad because songs could not be dubbed well. In addition, many of them were about topical American subjects. Therefore, they usually ended up in the red—despite the occasional exception.

††Kelly was asked during the series' run if his life had been changed by playing a priest. His answer was a frank and refreshing one: "Do people really believe that nonsense about actors being affected by the roles they play? I told the guy if he believed that, he should go to Vince Edwards to have his tonsils taken out. What am I going to do, hear confessions now? Or if I play a rabbi, will I go around stomping on glasses?"

---

*They had a daughter, Kerry, then were divorced in 1957. In 1960, Kelly married his former dancing assistant, Jeanne Coyne. They had two children, Timothy and Bridget.

**The movie won an Academy Award and Kelly got the first special Oscar for screen choreography.

As Donald O'Connor looks on disinterestedly, Kelly and Debbie Reynolds share a romantic moment.

The thing is, people expect the same thing from you they saw twenty years ago. I guess I'll always be a song-and-dance man, even though the song-and-dance era is over."

In fact, seeing Kelly at a party is often a nostalgic occasion for ladies over forty who crowd up to dance with him. But Kelly is always aware that it's much different than it was in the old days.

"Their husbands don't want to dance with them. And they figure I'd love to. Then they always expect I'm going to drape them over a chair or toss them over the piano. I do this simple little fox-trot dance with them just like their husbands would with perhaps a little more style. And they just keep smiling like they think something wonderful is going to happen."

Even as Kelly has yielded to the changes of time, many of his films will never grow old—especially *Singin' in the Rain*, which seems to attract larger and younger audiences as the years roll on.*

The picture begins with a gala Hollywood opening night. The time is 1927, the year when the silent

*In 1975 it returned to Radio City Music Hall for a special one-week engagement. "It works just as well today as it did twenty-three years ago," said Canby of the *New York Times*.

film era was at its peak. The scene is Grauman's Chinese Theatre. Searchlights light up the sky. Crowds surge behind police barricades, oohing and aahing as the actors and actresses troop in.

Suddenly, two motorcycle policemen screech to a stop in front of a shiny limousine. Out step the stars of the picture, those two romantic screen lovers—Don Lockwood (Gene Kelly) and Lina Lamont (Jean Hagen). Fans push closer to get a look at Don in his belted white camel hair coat and Lina in her fur collared stole and glittering gown.

"You've come a long way together," says a radio interviewer (Madge Blake), sounding suspiciously like Louella Parsons. "Won't you tell us how it all happened?"

From this moment, Don does all the talking for the duo. While the bird-brained Lina smiles frustratedly, he begins talking of his early days—going to the finest schools, performing for Mom and Dad's society friends with his lifelong pal Cosmo Brown (Donald O'Connor), and studying at the conservatory of fine arts.

(While his voice carries over the sound track, the screen shows what really took place—tap-dancing for pennies in a poolroom, then playing the fiddle and piano in amateur nights and burlesque houses with Cosmo. They're seen doing a frantic song-and-dance number "Fit as a Fiddle.")

O'Connor was then under contract to Universal, and he proved to be a shrewd bargainer. Louis B. Mayer, MGM studio chief, offered Universal $50,000 for a loan-out on O'Connor. But O'Connor refused the part. "I said 'No,'" O'Connor said, "because in those days, under the terms of the contract, I wouldn't have seen a penny of the $50,000. Finally, Universal agreed to give me the $50,000. So I said okay."

"We played the finest symphony halls in the country," Don continues. (Montage of whistle stops: Dead Man's Fang, Arizona; Oat Meal, Nebraska; Coyoteville, New Mexico.)

"Audiences everywhere adored us." (The crowd is booing. Several people hold their nose.)

We go on to learn that Don and Cosmo started in Hollywood playing background music for B-Westerns starring Lina Lamont. One day, Don got his chance when the stuntman got knocked out in a barroom brawl. With nobody else left to substitute, Don volunteered, took an uppercut on the chin, somersaulted backward over a bar, and crashed in spectacular fashion into a shelf of glasses. So impressive was his three-point landing that he was then and there elevated to the role of stuntman.

"My roles were urbane, sophisticated, suave," says Don. (In quick sequences, we see him flying an airplane into a house, riding a motorcycle over a cliff, running into a burning shack which explodes.)

Next we see Don greeting Lina on the set and getting a chilly look in return. Stuntmen don't mix in her circles. Just then, producer R. F. Simpson (Millard Mitchell) walks over to Don. He says he's seen Don's stunts and thought he was a whole team of stuntmen. "I think you've got something," Simpson says. "Come over to my office after lunch. We'll discuss a contract." Lina is now smiling at Don.

"Well, Miss Lamont," says Don brightly. "Doing anything tonight?"

She puts her arm through his.

"That's funny," Don says. "I'm busy."

Now the camera returns us to the present. We are in front of the Chinese Theatre again and Don is telling his interviewer: "Well, Lina and I have had the same wonderful relationship ever since." As they disappear into the theatre, the crowd roars.

It is only after the successful premiere that we hear Lina's voice for the first time. Backstage, she

Kelly and O'Connor get the hook doing a slapstick vaudeville routine in their pre-Hollywood days.

The Kelly-O'Connor duo in the famous "Fit as a Fiddle" song and dance number.

turns to Don with a fury. "F' heaven's sake, what's the idea? Can't a girl get a word in edgewise?" Her voice is tinny, shrill, common. Filmdom's number one glamour girl is a blond dumbbell, a silent era Judy Holliday.

(Jean Hagen actually had a soft, modulated voice. The Lina Lamont intonation was her own creation. In fact, she did it so well, she actually dubbed her own voice in the later scenes when Kathy Selden is shown dubbing hers onto Lina's.)

Part of Don's job is to keep Lina's mouth firmly sealed in public. The other part is to make personal appearances with her. Fan magazines keep turning out pieces pairing the two off-screen. ("Lockwood and Lamont—Reel Life or Real Life Romance?") And so Don has to be seen with Lina for publicity purposes. The trouble is that Lina doesn't realize it's all part of the image game.

Anyway, with the deadly Lina as his constant companion, it's little wonder that Don takes a shine to the first girl he bumps into after freeing himself from Lina's clutches. She is none other than pert Kathy Selden (Debbie Reynolds), a girl in an open jalopy.

It happens this way: Don and Cosmo have a flat as they are riding away from the theatre and fans mob them. The crowd starts tearing off Don's clothes. Struggling to get away, he climbs on top of his car, leaps onto a passing trolley, and jumps into the first convertible he spies—Kathy's.

Kathy is startled at first, but when she finds out who Don is, she agrees to give him a lift. As they drive, she also innocently puts down Don's acting talents. She says she doesn't go to movies much.

"If you've seen one, you've seen them all," Kathy says. "The personalities on the screen just don't impress me. I mean, they don't talk. They don't act." She, on the other hand, is a real actress and one day she'll be on the stage.

As they pull up, Don gets out, laughs, and slams the door. "Farewell, Ethel Barrymore. I must tear myself away from your side." But Don has left the tail of his coat in the door, and as he walks away, it rips to shreds. Kathy drives off with the last laugh.

The two are fated to meet again. That same night, Don is at a party celebrating his new picture, and chefs wheel in a hugh cake. Out pops a leggy showgirl in a dancing outfit. Who is it? Who else but Kathy Selden.

"Well," says Don, relishing the moment. "If it isn't Ethel Barrymore!"

Kathy squelches her embarrassment long

Kelly tries to calm down Jean Hagen playing movie star Lina Lamont. O'Connor, Reynolds, King Donovan (rear), and Millard Mitchell (right) look on.

enough to prance through a lively song and dance rendition of "All I Do Is Dream of You" with a team of chorus girls. Then she beats a hasty retreat after hitting Lina with a pie intended for Don.

MGM considered a plethora of contract players as Kathy—Jane Powell, Gloria De Haven, and Leslie Caron, to name a few. But MGM chief Mayer decided to groom Miss Reynolds for stardom because he was convinced she was perfect for the role. It was a strange decision in view of the fact that she could then barely sing or dance. "I was totally untrained," Debbie said. ". . . All I knew was time step and soft shoe . . . and my voice was very weak. So they had to dub in the high notes." Nevertheless, she worked hard with choreographers Carol Haney, Ernie Flatt, and Jeanne Coyne, practiced long hours—sometimes working so late she slept in her studio dressing room—and came through with a yeomanlike performance.

Three weeks pass. *The Jazz Singer*, the first all-talking picture, opens and is a smash hit. The public is screaming for more, and every studio begins putting in sound equipment. The race is on to join the sound movie bandstand.

Meanwhile, Kathy has gotten a small role in a film at Don's studio. Of course, Don runs into her, helps her get a part in his new movie, and the two make up. On an empty studio lot, they do an old-fashioned dance together and Don sings, "You Were Meant for Me."*

Now diction lessons are going full swing around the studio, but they are too late to do much good for Lina. She can't even learn to say her lines into a hidden microphone. In a take for her first talking movie, she turns her head and the sound track picks up only half of what she says.

As a stopgap measure, the wardrobe woman sews a mike into the bosom of her dress, but it only punctuates her lines with a drumlike noise—her heartbeat. Next, a mike is sewn into the shoulder of her dress. As the cameras start cranking, producer Simpson walks on the set. He nearly trips over a second wire, which he is unaccustomed to seeing. Grumbling, he yanks it away. The wire is connected to Lina's mike and she flips backward, sailing head over heels into a bush. Despite the snafus,

*The song was the big hit of *The Broadway Melody* (1929), the first talking picture to win an Oscar.

the studio manages to finish the picture.

The scene shifts to a theatre where a preview of Don and Lina's movie, *The Dueling Cavalier*, is running. All the problems that cropped up in the studio are magnified on the screen. Though Lina is playing a French noblewoman, she sounds like a lady truck driver. Moreover, because she has moved her head from side to side, her voice is either too soft or so loud that it sounds like a foghorn. On one occasion, the sound slips out of synchronization. Whenever Lina speaks, the bass voice of the villain rumbles from her throat.

Outside the theatre, a man turns to the ticket-taker and says: "Sounds like a comedy inside."

It looks like Don's career is over, for the movie has to be released in six weeks. But later that night, he, Cosmo, and Kathy hit on a idea. Don was a singer and dancer in vaudeville. Why not turn *The Dueling Cavalier* into a musical? Okay, Don says. But how about Lina?

"Wait a minute," Cosmo exclaims. "I'm just about to be brilliant. Use Kathy's voice. Lina just moves her mouth and Kathy's voice comes over singing and talking for her."

With their problem resolved, Don takes Kathy home and kisses her in her doorway. Just then, a shower starts outside. As she says goodnight, Kathy tells Don to take care of his throat because it has just started raining.

"Really?" says Don. "From where I stand, the sun is shining all over the place."

In the picture's most famous scene, he closes his umbrella and starts strolling home in a downpour. As an invisible orchestra plays the title song,* he clicks his heels, sloshes through puddles, and balances on the street curb like a tightrope walker. Water from a drainpipe hits him in the face. He laughs it off and kicks up a storm in the flooded gutter until a policeman walks by and eyes him suspiciously. Don politely nods, collects himself, and walks off, sopping, but so in love that he can't tell wet from dry.

The original plan was for Kelly, O'Connor, and Miss Reynolds to do the sequence together. But Kelly decided to dance it as a solo. "We didn't know it was going to be such a great number," said co-

*"Singin' in the Rain" was first heard in *Hollywood Revue of 1929*. Ironically, four decades later, the gay, carefree melody was used as a background to a scene of unabandoned violence in *A Clockwork Orange* (1971).

O'Connor and Kelly do the "Moses Supposes" dance number around a bewildered studio diction coach (Bobby Watson).

director Donen. "It works because of its utter simplicity. There is no better idea for a movie than to dance for joy."

Don's studio buys his production ideas, and they rush through a new musical—including a big modern number (in which Kelly and Cyd Charisse dance a love duet to the tunes of "Broadway Melody" and "Broadway Rhythm").*

But Lina is not to be underrated. She heads off any attempt to credit Kathy as her voice by releasing a story to the papers about how her studio is excited about Lina's new-found musical talent. "You wouldn't want to call the papers and say Lina Lamont is a big fat liar," she tells producer Simpson. When she insists that Kathy continue dubbing her voice without credit, Simpson, unwilling to lose his investment in Lina, shrugs his shoulders resignedly.

The camera now takes us to the Chinese Theatre. The audience is applauding wildly after seeing the all-singing, all-talking, all-dancing premiere of Don and Lina in *The Dancing Cavalier.*

Don and Lina are taking one curtain call after another. The crowd starts calling for a speech, and suddenly Lina, overcome by the excitement of the moment, is out at center stage.

"Ladies and g'men," she says. "I cahn't tell you. . . ." There is a puzzled silence as her flat nasal tones echo through the theatre. As Lina screeches on, a man in the audience says, "Hey, she didn't sound that way in the picture." Someone in the balcony yells, "Sing."

Lina hesitates, and then runs to the wings. But

*Movie censors thought Miss Charisse's costume was cut too high. So, after the film was made, ruffles were painted over her thighs frame by frame in one shot where Kelly hoists her high in the air.

Don gets another idea. He tells Lina to just mouth the words to "Singin' in the Rain." Kathy will stand behind the curtain and dub the lyrics just as she did in the studio.

Confident and exuberant, Lina walks back onstage. The applause dies down, the orchestra starts up, and Lina begins mouthing her lines, making flapping gestures with her elbows. At the end of the first chorus, Don, Cosmo, and Simpson start flapping their elbows, too, and pulling the rope that draws back the curtain.

There, to the audience's amazement, is Kathy at a second mike, singing the lyrics. The crowd bursts out laughing, but Lina, still oblivious to what is happening, goes right on. Then Cosmo struts out on stage behind her, takes the mike away from Kathy, and picks up the lyrics in his baritone.

Lina goes on for a while with this strange masculine voice barreling out as if from her throat. Then, seeing the game is up, she dashes offstage. But Kathy, too, is running, fleeing into the audience, tearing down the aisle.

Don bolts out on stage. "That girl running up the aisle—stop her," he shouts. "That's the girl whose voice you heard and loved tonight. She's the real star of the picture. Kathy Selden."

The audience applauds, and some people get up and stop Kathy. Don starts to sing "You Are My Lucky Star" and Kathy, tears in her eyes, turns toward Don. He comes down the aisle, reaches out to her and leads her onstage as they sing together and finally embrace. The last scene shows them on a hill in front of a billboard announcing their first starring picture.

No, sir. They don't make musicals like that anymore.

Some Like It Hot

Marilyn Monroe as Sugar Kane, a ukulele player in an all-girl dance band. MM had some of her best comedy scenes in *Some Like It Hot*.

Some Like It Hot
(1959)

Produced and directed by Billy Wilder. Screenplay by Wilder and I. A. L. Diamond. Suggested by a story by R. Thoeren and M. Logan. Camera, Charles Lang, Jr. Art director, Ted Haworth. Editor, Arthur Schmidt. Costume design, Orry-Kelly.* Score by Adolph Deutsch. Songs supervised by Matty Malneck. Ashton Productions and Mirisch Company Picture released through United Artists. 120 minutes.

Sugar Kane (Kumulchek)	*Marilyn Monroe*
Joe (Josephine)	*Tony Curtis*
Jerry (Daphne)	*Jack Lemmon*
Spats Columbo	*George Raft*
Mulligan	*Pat O'Brien*
Osgood Fielding III	*Joe E. Brown*
Little Bonaparte	*Nehemiah Persoff*
Sweet Sue	*Joan Shawlee*
Sig Poliakoff	*Billy Gray*
Toothpick Charlie	*George E. Stone*
Beinstock	*Dave Barry*
Spats' Henchmen	*Mike Mazurki*
	Harry Wilson
Dolores	*Beverly Wills*
Nellie	*Barbara Drew*
Paradise	*Edward G. Robinson, Jr.*

*Academy Award Winner.

Tony Curtis in drag as Josephine and Jack Lemmon as Daphne, guises they have assumed as they flee Chicago mobsters.

Ironically, her future wasn't foreseen even by the most seasoned eyes in Hollywood. Twentieth Century-Fox dropped her contract when she was first starting. Darryl Zanuck later put her in lacklustre roles in lacklustre films, almost ignoring her, until her box office appeal could no longer be denied. At Columbia, Harry Cohn let her go after her twenty-week option expired. "I bet you a buck she never goes anywhere," he told a producer.

What they failed to see was that Marilyn Monroe's physical assets were only part of the reason for her screen success. As a sexpot, she had plenty of competition—Mamie Van Doren, Jayne Mansfield, Sheree North, and Diana Dors, among others. Those gals never made it. Marilyn did because her talent extended beyond cleavage, a toothpaste smile, and a cheesecake torso. She also projected a comedic quality that gave her a unique screen charisma. "She had," said Laurence Olivier, "a cunning way of suggesting naughtiness and innocence at the same time."

With her wide-open eyes, baby-like gurgle, and breathless voice, she was a comic-strip blonde come alive. She served up sex with a sense of humor—and it was a natural talent.

Had she lived longer, there might have been a third dimension to her screen personality. In *Bus Stop* (1956), perhaps her best picture, and in some scenes from *The Misfits* (1961), her last film, she showed promise of dramatic competence. Certainly, she lacked depth and seasoned professional skill. Still, her performance in *Bus Stop* drew surprisingly favorable reviews—even from her toughest critics.

Yet, this phase of her career was a subject of controversy. Some laughed off her aspirations of becoming a serious actress. Her two years in New York studying under Lee Strasberg, her detractors said, were a waste of time.

And this was not the only hostility directed her way. Much of it came from actors who worked with her. They accused her of being selfish, unprofessional, and psychotic, and it must be admitted that they had ample provocation. It wasn't only her widely resented habit of showing up late that set teeth gnashing; it was also her unpreparedness and lack of confidence after the camera started grinding. Some sequences had to be shot thirty, forty, even fifty times.

The result was that by the time the director was satisfied with Marilyn, the other actors' performances were often so stale and wooden that they looked bad by comparison. "Jack Lemmon and I had to get it perfect *every* take," said Tony Curtis, talking about *Some Like It Hot.* "Wilder told us privately that whenever she was right in a take, he was going to go with that one—even if one of us was scratching himself."

Little wonder that, in a fit of pique, Curtis compared making movie love to Marilyn to "kissing Hitler." Fourteen years later, in 1973, Curtis said that the oft-repeated remark was correctly quoted and that he really did make that crack. "Absolutely," he said. "She was a pain in the ---- in that film to everyone. I think Billy Wilder said it best when he said that Marilyn was the meanest seven-year-old he ever met."

Unwittingly, Wilder may have suggested the key to Marilyn's enigmatic character. Many who knew her said she never grew up emotionally. "I looked on her as an adolescent girl," said Maurice Zolotow, one of her many biographers.

Sadly, her lack of maturity made her an outsider even in her own profession. Joseph L. Mankiewicz, writer-director of *All About Eve,* remembers seeing her eating alone in restaurants during the cast's two weeks of location shooting in San Francisco. "We'd always ask her to join us, and she would seem pleased," Mankiewicz said. "But somehow she never understood or accepted our unspoken assumption that she was one of us. She remained alone. She was not a loner. She was just plain *alone.*"

If it was true that she was a figure of isolation even in the ascending years of her career, her solitariness remains a puzzle. The most widely held theories mention her abbreviated education, or her meteoric rise to fame, or her tragic childhood. It could have been all three.

As the daughter of Gladys Baker, a studio filmcutter, Marilyn had two strikes against her. She was an illegitimate child, and then an orphan. Her mother, who gave birth to Marilyn years after her husband had deserted her, came from a family with a history of mental illness. Before Marilyn was ten, her mother had been in and out of psychiatric institutions. As a result, Marilyn spent her childhood as a ward of Los Angeles County, living in a succession of orphanages and foster homes. In one of them, a lodger reportedly raped her when she was eight. At nine, she developed a stammer, a condition that is rare in a female.

At the age of sixteen she quit Van Nuys High School and married a nondescript aircraft worker named James Dougherty, probably because it meant independence and a break from her foster home environment. But the drudgery of housework bored her, so she soon got divorced and started a career as a model. Within a few years, her voluptuous form (37-24-36) was on view on the cover of several national magazines.

Twentieth Century-Fox signed her to a short-term contract, changed her name to Marilyn Monroe—Marilyn for Marilyn Miller, Monroe because it was her mother's maiden name—and then dropped her after giving her a few bit parts.*

Columbia picked up her contract, giving her the second lead in a B-musical called *Ladies of the Chorus* (1949). Then, despite a favorable review in the *Motion Picture Herald,* Columbia, too, let her go.

Undaunted, Marilyn stayed on the Hollywood scene, wangling more bit parts through the tenacious efforts of her agent, Johnny Hyde. The turning point came after she won recognition as Louis Calhern's mistress in John Huston's thriller *The Asphalt Jungle* (1950).

Fox invited her back and she scored again playing an aspiring actress—"a graduate of the Copacabana School of Dramatic Arts," as George Sanders phrased it—in *All About Eve* (1950).

She suddenly became a national figure in 1952 while she was making a now forgotten picture called *Clash by Night.* Stories broke about a nude calendar picture which she had posed for. However, she warded off adverse public reaction—and

*Her first movie is usually listed as *Scudda-Hoo! Scudda-Hay!* (1948), starring June Haver and Lon McCallister. But some Monroe buffs claim that this wasn't really her debut. They say she appeared in *Dangerous Years* (1947), which was made after *Scudda-Hoo! Scudda-Hay!* but released first. Others say she may have made an uncredited appearance in *The Shocking Miss Pilgrim* (1947) before either of those.

even won sympathy—by ignoring studio publicists' advice to deny that it was she who modeled in the buff. Instead, she candidly admitted she did it during her lean and hungry days as a starlet. The photograph, which reportedly made $500,000 for calendar manufacturer John Baumgarth, netted Marilyn only a $50 modeling fee.

Within a year, she rose to become Fox's top money-maker, turning in sparkling performances as mock dumb blondes in the musicals *Gentlemen Prefer Blondes* (1953) and *How to Marry a Millionaire* (1953).* She got the big glamour build-up and went on to score again as the girl upstairs in *The Seven Year Itch* (1955).

The memorable cheesecake shots of her dress flying came from that movie and put her in all the magazines. She was becoming the Hollywood sensation of the 1950s, and her marriages to Joe DiMaggio and Arthur Miller became front-page stories. So did her break with Fox, the first of many, after she demanded more and better parts. Less publicized then—but somehow perceived by the public—was her increasing instability under the pressure of divorce, miscarriage, and her stormy career. "In spite of all that was written and said about her," wrote film critic Richard Griffith, "people sensed that there was little in her life to envy."

As much as Marilyn may have needed to make movies to fulfill herself, she took a year off to study method acting in the famous Actors' Studio in New York. Outraged, Fox suspended her, and then sued her. However, the studio's stockholders began screaming when *The Seven Year Itch* blossomed into a box office bonanza. Therefore Buddy Adler, who succeeded Zanuck as production chief, lured Marilyn back with a lucrative contract at several times her previous salary. Then she made *Bus Stop* for Fox. It was a hit, but it was an ordeal, too. She was often late or absent from work, she feuded with the cast, and she complicated life for her director by bringing her own acting coach to the set.

For the rest of her career, she alternated between independent productions that were wide-ranging in their success. The worst was *Let's Make Love* (1960), a dull musical with Yves Montand with whom she had a short but well-publicized romance.

Some say that Marilyn's career had begun a downhill slide by the 1960s. Even if her name on a marquee still guaranteed a full house, her emotional state was deteriorating. Her reputation for being uncooperative, willful, even unmanageable, lost her film offers. Her last picture, *Something's Got to Give* (1962), could not be finished because of her frequent absences from the set. She showed up during only twelve of the thirty-two days of production. In that time, cameramen were able to make less than eight minutes of usable film of her.

As the months passed, she became more and more secluded in her suburban Los Angeles home as her hold on reality began slipping. She became more dependent on alcohol, sleeping pills, and psychiatric support. Finally, during the early morning hours of August 5, 1962, they found her dead from an overdose of barbiturates. She had gone to her bedroom with twenty-four Nembutol sleeping pills and taken them all. She was thirty-six.

No one can say for sure what it was that made her take her life. Perhaps what ultimately troubled her was the thought that she could not maintain her image as a sex symbol much longer. "Can you imagine Marilyn Monroe today, alive?" Joseph L. Mankiewicz asked ten years after her death when she would have been forty-six. "Existing as what? Where? How?"

Perhaps that wouldn't have been as crucial if she had had children or if she had developed a lasting and meaningful relationship with someone. Then again, perhaps this is too simple, and the real reason is deeper and more complex. Whatever the answer, we can only know for certain that the memories she left on the screen are indelible. And to the moviegoing public, she will always be the vivacious, dizzy blonde, bouncing her bountiful form on spike heels while tossing off zany innuendos with naive wonder.

Of all her movies, the one that best shows her off in this light—and the one that includes some of her most professional scenes as a comedienne—is *Some Like It Hot.*

The movie opens in Chicago in the pre-Depression, crime-rampant Prohibition era. Two seedy, jobless jazz musicians—a saxophonist

---

*Marilyn, who was not a real singer, surprised many of her fans by her spirited singing in these films. Some thought her voice was dubbed. It wasn't, but it took all the expertise of the studio's audio technicians to make the most of it. Edwin P. Hoyt, in his book *Marilyn: The Tragic Venus,* said that they worked it this way: "Marilyn put on head phones the first day and made twenty-five recordings of the song. One of her singing coaches, Ken Darby, then took the twenty-five pieces of tape home and cut them up and put them together so she had the proper phrasing in each part of the song. The next day, Marilyn listened to the paste-up and tried to recreate it—tried until she succeeded." It was a lot tougher for sound technicians to record her songs this way, for it involved the difficult process of keeping the orchestration and vocal records on separate tracks. But this is precisely the kind of technology that Hollywood has always excelled in, and the results were dazzling.

(Tony Curtis) and a bass player (Jack Lemmon)—inadvertently witness the St. Valentine's Day gangland massacre. Unfortunately, that spells their doom. Mob boss Spats Columbo (George Raft) orders his hoods to rub them out. But when police sirens momentarily divert his triggermen's attention, the musicians flee.

Running frantically for their lives, they masquerade as "Josephine" and "Daphne" and join an all-girl dance band bound for a Florida hotel job. At the train station, the two, bewigged and tottering on high-heeled shoes, ogle their shapely fellow musicians. The troup includes Sugar Kane (Monroe), a ukulele-playing, whiskey-swigging vocalist. She makes a hip-swinging entrance, sashaying down the platform as a cloud of steam startles her, swishing by her rear end.

"Look how she moves," says Lemmon, eye-

Director Billy Wilder going through a routine with Lemmon. Jack got an Oscar nomination.

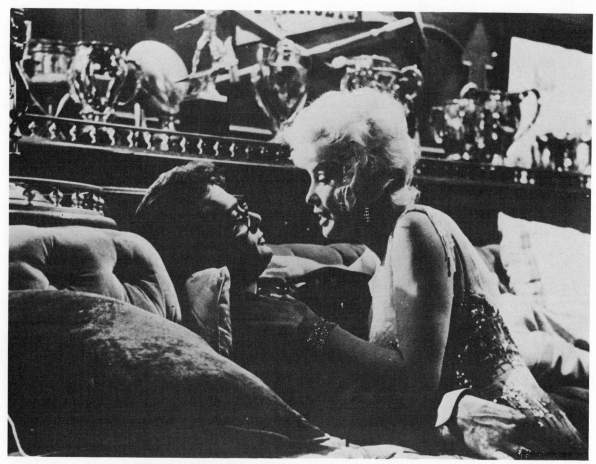

MM tries to help Curtis overcome his alleged insensitivity to sex.

brows raised. "That's just like Jello with springs."*

That inspired bit of business stemmed from a suggestion by Marilyn and Arthur Miller. They had seen that Marilyn's part called for her to be essentially an offbeat foil to Lemmon and Curtis. As the script stood, the first scene showed Marilyn as just one of the girls crowding onto the train. Marilyn and Miller felt it was important to have her character established at the outset—the first time she is seen. When they told Wilder this, he and his screen writer, I. A. L. Diamond, agreed, and they rewrote the sequence to include the squirt of steam.

Once on the train, the fun begins as Lemmon and Curtis share a Pullman with the shapely females. However, they know that the underworld's tentacles reach from coast to coast, so they are restrained by the fact that, for safety's sake, they can't let their disguises down. Even so, they are sorely tempted by this harem, particularly after Marilyn drops a whiskey flask and Lemmon covers up for her before the irate band manager. To ex-

press her gratitude, Marilyn climbs into Lemmon's upper berth in her nightie and innocently snuggles up, believing him to be another girl.

"If there is ever anything I can do for you," Marilyn says.

"I can think of a million things," Lemmon says, perspiring.

Curtis, too, has designs on Marilyn. In the ladies' room, she confides to Curtis her weakness for male saxophonists—which he is—and her ambition to marry a millionaire—which he will seem to be before too much longer.

Years later, Curtis confided that he could never figure out why Monroe had become a legendary figure. "They're making a big *megillah* out of a very ordinary person," Curtis said. "If you spent four months making a picture with her, you didn't want to see her again. . . . Jack Lemmon and I had to be ready at 9 A.M. We dressed as girls and we'd have to get into these steel jocks and go through hours on our hair and makeup. And she'd show up at noon . . . or even later."

In Florida, the plot thickens. An aging million-aire, Osgood Fielding III (Joe E. Brown), falls for

*The line is topped only by Constance Bennett's famous quip about the real-life Marilyn: "Now there's a broad with her future behind her."

311

Joe E. Brown and Lemmon in a zany windup to a zany film.

Lemmon and tries to woo him out to his yacht. Meanwhile Curtis impersonates the playboy yachtsman and bowls over Marilyn when he meets her on the beach.

"You own a yacht," she says breathlessly, looking out to the ocean. "Which one—the big one?"

"Certainly not," Curtis says in a clipped accent, parodying Cary Grant. "With all the unrest in the world, I don't think you should have a yacht that sleeps more than twelve."

Marilyn tells him that she sings with Sweet Sue and Her Society Syncopaters.

"Syncopaters? Does that mean you play that very fast music—jazz?" Curtis asks.

"Yeah—real hot."

"Oh, well, I guess some like it hot. I personally prefer classical music."

Later, Curtis prevails on Lemmon to keep Joe E. Brown, the real millionaire, occupied on shore, while he lures Marilyn to the yacht on the crew's night off.

Marilyn is wearing a gown that makes you look twice to see if there is anything there, but Curtis pretends that he couldn't care less. He tells her he's got a mental block. "When I'm with a girl, it does absolutely nothing to me. No feelings. Like my heart is shot full of novocaine."

Nobody has ever been able to help him, Curtis says, not even doctors, French upstairs maids, or Balinese dancers.

The ploy works. Marilyn asks if she can try to help, and then kisses him.

"Was that anything?"

"No. Just the same," Curtis says, his face expressionless.

"Could I take another crack at it?" Marilyn asks.

"If you insist," he says, looking bored, as he lies on a couch.

She kisses him again, long and hard.

"Anything this time?"

"I'm afraid not. Terribly sorry."

She pours champagne, turns the lights low, and puts on soft music.

"Don't fight it—relax," she says, climbing all over him as she kisses him torridly. There is no flicker of response.

"Like smoking without inhaling," Curtis says.

"So inhale," says Marilyn. Another long kiss.

About the twentieth go-round, Marilyn notices that Curtis' glasses are steaming. "I got a funny sensation in my toes," he admits. "I think we're on the right track."

On shore, Joe E. Brown has fallen so hard for Lemmon that he has proposed and given him an engagement bracelet. But before the romantic knots can be untangled, a convention of Mafia leaders, including Spats Columbo and his mob, invade the hotel. Spats and his men quickly see through the disguises of Curtis and Lemmon. "Those dames ain't dames," says Spats, and a wild chase starts in the hotel. Curtis and Lemmon temporarily take refuge under a banquet table in an empty hall.

The hall doesn't stay empty for long. It is filled in a few minutes by the gangsters' convention, whose cover name is "Friends of Italian Opera." Little Bonaparte (Nehemiah Persoff), the nationwide crime syndicate boss, opens the dinner by telling Spats that his "big noise" during St. Valentine's Day wasn't good for "public relations." Little Bonaparte is also displeased by Spats' carelessness in letting two witnesses get away. Suddenly, waiters wheel in a giant cake, but instead of a chorus girl jumping out, a hit man (Edward G. Robinson, Jr.) leaps up with a tommy gun and riddles Spats and his men.

Things start rushing to a quick conclusion. Police Sergeant Mulligan (Pat O'Brien), who has been tailing Spats, storms in, and his cops make a mass arrest. Meanwhile, Lemmon and Curtis beat a fast exit, but a few hoods manage to slip away and go after them.

Curtis and Lemmon outrun the plug-uglies and make it safely to a motorboat with Marilyn and Joe E. Brown. On the ride to Brown's yacht, Curtis clears the air. He confesses his hoax to Marilyn, and she says that she adores him anyhow.

At the same time, Lemmon tries to end his affair with Joe E. Brown. In what to me is the all-time funniest movie wind-up, Lemmon, still in drag, tells Brown there is something he ought to know.

"In the first place," Lemmon says, "I'm not a natural blonde."

"Doesn't matter," Brown says.

"I smoke. I smoke all the time."

"I don't care."

"I can never have children."

"We can adopt some."

"You don't understand," Lemmon says, exasperated, whipping off his wig. "I'm a man!"

"Well," replies Brown, "nobody's perfect."

A Star
Is Born

Judy Garland as young actress Vicki Lester, clutching her Oscar in *A Star Is Born*. The film was the second of three Hollywood versions of the story.

A Star Is Born
(1954)

Directed by George Cukor. Screenplay by Moss Hart, based on the Dorothy Parker, Alan Campbell, Robert Carson screenplay. From a story by William A. Wellman and Carson. Photography, Sam Leavitt. Art director, Malcolm Bert. Editor, Folmar Blangsted. New songs, music by Harold Arlen, lyrics by Ira Gershwin: "The Man That Got Away," "Gotta Have Me Go with You," "It's a New World," "Here's What I'm Here For," "Someone at Last," "Lose That Long Face." Song, "Born in a Trunk," music and lyrics by Leonard Gershe. Musical direction, Ray Heinsdorf. Assistant directors, Earl Bellamy, Edward Graham, Russell Llewellyn. Associate producer, Vern Alves. Dances, Richard Barstow. Produced by Sidney Luft. CinemaScope and Technicolor. A Warner Bros. Picture. 182 minutes.

Esther Blodgett (Vicki Lester)	*Judy Garland*
Norman Maine	*James Mason*
Libby	*Jack Carson*
Oliver Niles	*Charles Bickford*
Danny McGuire	*Tom Noonan*
Lola Lavery	*Lucy Marlow*
Susan	*Amanda Blake*
Graves	*Irving Bacon*
Libby's Secretary	*Hazel Shermet*
Glenn Williams	*James Brown*
Miss Markham	*Lotus Robb*
Justice of the Peace	*Emerson Treacy*
M.C.	*Rex Evans*
Judge	*Frank Ferguson*
Reporter	*Dale Van Sickel*
Gregory	*Percy Helton*
Esther at Six	*Nadene Ashdown*
Esther at Three	*Heidi Meadows*

Norman Maine reels drunk and rubber-legged into the Oscar awards ceremony and tells the audience he needs a job. As he rambles on, he accidentally slaps Vicki, his wife.

She was pushed into show business too early and stayed too late. While other girls were going to high school and double-dating, she was doped like a race horse to work twelve hours a day on the studio lot. She was married at nineteen to the first of five husbands. By the age of twenty-three, she had already had three nervous breakdowns. Before she was thirty she had attempted suicide and was seeing a psychiatrist. In her thirties she was hooked on pills—pills to sleep, pills to wake up, pills to lose weight, pills to relieve tension.

When Judy Garland died at age forty-seven from an overdose of sleeping pills, Vincent Canby, movie critic of the *New York Times*, wrote: "The greatest shock about her death was that there was no shock. One simply wondered how she survived as long as she did."

Yet she was an extraordinary talent. She had a strong, vibrant voice and a bubbling, enchanting personality that carried over into adulthood. She had legions of admirers who cheered her at concerts and flocked to see her films. On the screen she projected an aura of freshness and innocence. She was beguiling and beloved. She had exuber-ance and charm. These gossamer qualities never left her.

"Even after all these years of public peccadilloes and suffering," film historian Richard Griffin said, "the name of Judy Garland still evokes a sort of distilled essence of sweetness, of innate goodness of heart, of nostalgia for a time when everybody was young and life was not only better, but, in particular, somehow nicer."

Certainly, no one in Grand Rapids, Michigan, where it all started in the halcyon year of 1922, would have dreamed how it all would end in 1969.

She was born Frances Gumm, the youngest of three daughters of Ethel and Fred Gumm, who worked professionally as "Jack and Virginia Lee, Sweet Southern Singers." Years later she sang, "I was born in a trunk. . . ." It was literally true. She began her career at the age of thirty months at a theater her father was managing in Grand Rapids. During a Christmas show amateur night, her two sisters were singing while Judy sat on her grand-mother's lap.

"Grandmother got annoyed that I wasn't up there too," Judy said, recalling the incident. "So

317

she walked me down the aisle and put me on the stage. The only song I knew was 'Jingle Bells.' And I sang it over and over again. I liked the applause so much I wouldn't stop.

"My mother was playing the piano in the pit and kept saying, 'Get off. Get off.' My two big sisters had enough class to head for the wings. But my father finally embarrassed himself by coming onto the stage, picking me up, and carrying me off. The audience loved it. So did I."

Judy joined the act of her sisters, Jimmie and Susie. Soon Judy's domineering and ambitious mother, bent on a show business career for her daughters, began touring with them. Judy clearly stood out in the trio. In 1934, at the age of thirteen, she was singled out in her first notice in *Variety*. Reporting on the act at the famous Grauman's Chinese Theatre, a reporter wrote: "The girl is a combination of Helen Morgan and Fuzzy Knight. Possessing a voice that, without the public address system, is audible throughout a house as large as the Chinese, she handles ballads like a veteran, and gets every note and word over with a personality that hits audiences."

According to *Variety*, it was at a Chicago appearance that she got her stage name—a spontaneous bit of business by George Jessel. The comedian, who was emceeing the show at the Majestic Theatre, had sent a flowery telegram to Judith Anderson. Newspapers had reported that the actress had just scored a stage hit, and Jessel wired, ". . . these critical paeans become you like garlands of roses."

With that turn of phrase still in his mind, he stepped out to introduce the next act. "I now give you Miss Judith Garland," said Jessel. ("I just couldn't announce 'Frances Gumm,'" he said later.) Frances made it Judy, instead of Judith, and kept the new name.*

After the family moved to Hollywood, her mother wasted no time grooming her for a movie career. Metro-Goldwyn-Mayer signed her, but it was Fox that released her first picture, borrowing her for *Pigskin Parade* (1936), starring Stuart Erwin.

*Another version of the stage-name christening has it that their names were misspelled on the marquee as "The Glum Sisters." When Judy's mother was appealing to the management to change it, Jessel suggested that they switch their real name. Gumm rhymed with dumb, he said, a setup for a smart-alecky reviewer. Critic Robert Garland happened to be backstage and Jessel suggested that they use his name. Judy was then still called "Baby" by her mother and was tired of the nickname. She liked a popular song of the day called "Judy" by Hoagy Carmichael. So when Jessel stepped out on stage, he introduced the act as "The Garland Sisters—featuring little Miss Judy Garland with the big voice."

That same year she made *Every Sunday* at MGM, a short subject with teenaged Deanna Durbin. Louis B. Mayer saw it and liked her. When Miss Durbin's contract lapsed and another studio got her, Mayer decided to give Judy a chance to be the studio's major adolescent female star.

Now began the life of a studio child—going to the MGM school, taking singing and dancing lessons, and getting coaching in acting. She appeared in *Broadway Melody of 1938*, attracting attention with her song "Dear Mr. Gable." Then she was featured in *Everybody Sing* (1938) with Allan Jones, and *Love Finds Andy Hardy* (1938) with Mickey Rooney. But her big break came in 1939 when MGM decided to produce *The Wizard of Oz*.

Shirley Temple was the studio's first choice for the part of Dorothy. However, Fox and MGM couldn't get together on price, so Fox refused to lend out its star and Judy got the part. At seventeen she played the pigtailed Kansas schoolgirl who travels to the magic land of Oz. She sang "Over the Rainbow," the ballad that became her trademark. The song about the wistful pursuit of happiness just out of reach paralleled her own sad life in some ways. She, too, sought happiness at the other end of the rainbow, but never found it. "It [the song] is so symbolic of all my dreams and wishes," she once said, "that I'm sure that's why people sometimes get tears in their eyes when they hear it."

Ironically, the inclusion of the song in the movie was an afterthought. Studio executives had mixed feelings about it. Some felt it was too sentimental, and it was cut out of the final version. However, after a preview audience saw the picture, the producers felt that a change of pace was needed in one part, so they decided to splice it back—but only because it was too late to film a new musical sequence.

Judy got a special Oscar for her performance. Recognition, however, came at a high price. It was during this period that the studio first introduced her to drugs. "They'd give us pep pills," she said later. "Then they'd take us to the studio hospital and knock us cold with sleeping pills. After four hours, they'd wake us up and give us the pep pills again. That's the way we worked. And that's the way we got thin. That's the way we got mixed up. And that's the way we lost contact."

Judy asked for a year's layoff to rest, but MGM rejected the request. "I've got $14 million tied up in her," one studio executive said. At the time, she and Bette Davis were Hollywood's leading box-office attractions.

In 1941 she married composer-pianist David ("Holiday for Strings") Rose, but married life and financial security changed nothing. The studio pressures were still there. "If a star was box office one year, that didn't mean she would be box office the next," said E. Y. (Yip) Harburg, who wrote the lyrics for "Over the Rainbow." "The studio used her to the hilt—unwisely and inhumanely—with no concept of the psychological treatment of a human being."

Judy's marriage to Rose lasted only three years. One year later, in 1945, she married director Vincente Minnelli. Under his guidance, she became Hollywood's leading musical star, making such first-rate pictures as *Meet Me in St. Louis* (1944), the highest grossing musical up to that time, *The Pirate* (1948), and *Easter Parade* (1948).

But life for Judy was a roller coaster, and now the ride started down. She failed to report for work on three successive films, claiming that she was suffering from a nervous breakdown. In fact, the pills were beginning to take their toll. She was seeing a psychiatrist seven days a week and was in and out of sanitariums. In the one movie she did finish in this period, *Summer Stock* (1950), she appeared puffy and overweight.

In 1950, MGM quietly dropped her contract. That same year, she slashed her wrists. Later, she and Minnelli were divorced. She was twenty-eight.

Still, her resiliency was remarkable. She made a successful appearance at the London Paladium and then had a record-breaking run at the New York Palace. She began to regain her old authority and Hollywood asked her back. Producer Sid Luft, her third husband, arranged a deal with Warner Bros. for her to remake *A Star Is Born*. The picture, first made in 1937 with Fredric March and Janet Gaynor, tells the familiar story of the fading movie star who helps a young singer get into films.* He marries her and then watches her career rise while his declines.

*Produced by David O. Selznick, the first version of *A Star Is Born* was based on the 1932 RKO picture *What Price Hollywood?* In the *What Price Hollywood?* version, the storyline revolves around a waitress (Constance Bennett) whose movie career is boosted by an alcoholic director (Lowell Sherman). Cukor, who directed the 1954 version of *A Star Is Born,* also directed this early talkie. Some say that the death of John Bowers in 1936 revived interest in the film and led to the 1937 version. A silent screen actor whose career was cut short by sound, Bowers sailed out to sea in his boat one day and was drowned.

Garland and Mason on the set.

Now thirty-two and out of movies for four years, Judy began her film comeback with unbridled energy. But the picture, budgeted as a $2.5 million production, was stretched out over ten months by her insistence on retakes and demands for new songs. It ended up costing a whopping $6 million. Even so, the result was a brilliantly staged movie, a showcase for Judy. Not only was she in every musical number, but she did them single-handedly without the usual chorus and glossy sets. Her virtuoso performance has become one of the classics of the 1950s. One film writer, Douglas McVay, author of *The Musical Film*, considers the movie "not only clearly the greatest musical picture I have ever seen, but the greatest picture of any kind I have ever seen."

Judy was nominated for an Academy Award, but Grace Kelly got the Oscar for *The Country Girl* (1954). That was, said Groucho Marx, "the biggest robbery since Brinks." *A Star Is Born* was, in fact, one of the top grossers of the 1950s. Yet, it won no Oscars.

A Star Is Born begins and ends at the same place—Hollywood's Shrine Theatre. As the movie opens, Norman Maine (James Mason), a brilliant but alcoholic star, staggers onstage during a charity gala in the middle of a song and dance act. On impulse, Esther Blodgett (Garland), one of the performers, links her arm through his and gets him to dance off with her, while the unsuspecting crowd applauds.

Afterward, Maine thanks her for saving him from further embarrassment. Still feeling no pain, he takes her lipstick and draws on a backstage wall a heart with an arrow in it and their initials. Danny McGuire (Tom Noonan), Esther's pianist, rescues her and they drive off. But Maine can't get Esther out of his mind and goes looking for her. He finally locates her in a Sunset Strip musicians' hangout where, in an empty house filled with stacked chairs, she is singing the blues ballad "The Man That Got Away." The song by Harold Arlen and Ira Gershwin was to become another one of her great standards.*

Maine, impressed by her voice, tells her that she has "star quality" and persuades her to quit the band for a movie career. However the next day Maine is whisked off to a distant locale for a new movie. When he gets back, he can't recall Esther's address. Meanwhile, she has left the band. Broke and out of work, she has to do television commercials and hustle hamburgers in a drive-in. Then, one day, Maine sees her on TV and rushes off to find her.

Most people who see the movie miss this brief but touching separation which served to emphasize Maine's deep feeling for Esther in spite of his erratic ways. Warner Bros., after releasing the film, cut twenty-seven minutes from its marathon three hours and two minutes running time. The studio said it was responding to complaints from theater owners who felt that the film length was affecting audience turnover and therefore box office profits. The cuts have created a controversy that lingers on.

In addition to splicing the major portion of two musical numbers—"Lose That Long Face" and "Here's What I'm Here For"—the studio left out a sound-stage sequence in which Judy played a love scene beneath a "live" microphone. She had just recorded a song with Maine listening in the studio, and when he proposes to her, everyone around hears him.

Some critics felt that was a key romantic scene because it helped explain and justify the personal nature of their marriage. In a column called "A Star Is Shorn," *New York Times* movie writer Bosley Crowther said: "It is not the same picture we reviewed. . . .Virtually every cut in the picture leaves a gaping and baffling hole so that not only the emotional pattern but the very sense of the thing is shorn." Because of the cuts, Crowther refused to list it as one of his year's top ten.

George Cukor, the veteran director, never understood nor forgave the studio for those cuts, which were done without consulting him. "If they thought it was too long, there were other ways of shortening it besides chopping and hacking out vital bits," he said. "Had we been allowed, Moss Hart [author of the screenplay] and I could have sweated out twenty minutes which would have been imperceptible to the audience." Cukor said that the studio not only cut the film, but "they took the negative away and melted it down for silver."

For those who see the cut version—the one that plays on TV—the story picks up with Esther getting the brush-off at the studio. She gets a new name—Vicki Lester—but everybody treats her as Maine's girl-of-the-moment who will fade from the

*Gershwin said the use of the word "that" instead of "who"—which is grammatically correct—was deliberate. "It had to be 'The Man *That* Got Away,'" Gershwin said, "because, actually, the title hit me as a paraphrase of the angler's, 'You should have seen the one that got away.'" A problem with the lyrics came when Frank Sinatra wanted to record the song. The ballad is written for a female, but by substituting "girl" for "man" and making a few other changes in the last stanza, Gershwin was able to make it work for Sinatra. Despite the fact that it quickly became a jazz classic, the ballad lost out to "Three Coins in the Fountain" in the Oscar competition for best movie song.

Bailed out of jail on a drunk charge, Maine clings to his wife while press photographers take his picture. Producer Oliver Niles (Charles Bickford) does his best to clear the way.

scene as soon as he tires of her. In her first bit part, a director yells at her because she hasn't followed directions. She is waving a handkerchief in a farewell scene from a train. "We saw your *face*," he screams.

Then, one day, a singer in a big role cancels out, and studio head Oliver Niles (Charles Bickford) is under pressure to replace her immediately. Maine gets Niles to hear Vicki sing. Surprised and elated at her exciting voice, he puts her in the role and she rises to the occasion like a born trouper. In that movie within a movie, she sings the famous "Born in a Trunk" number which, in essence, tells the story of her own show business career.

Many feel that this is one of the film's highlights, but others believe it is too long and extraneous to the plot and thus slows down the film. Cukor, who had nothing to do with the sequence (which was added later), agrees with the latter opinion, and so does Mason, who commented: "I thought it was a liability to the film."

In fact, Mason, whom Pauline Kael thought stole the picture, was disappointed by the entire movie.

He, too, felt it was overlong and that the cuts were made injudiciously. "Also," he said, "we never really had a producer. Sid Luft was an amateur. There was nobody to check on or discipline Judy or George Cukor. As for Moss Hart, he just turned in the script, dealt very seriously with anyone who criticized it, and packed up and went to New York."

(Mason was actually a second choice for the role of Norman Maine. Jack Warner wanted Humphrey Bogart, who was under contract to Warner Bros. According to another version, Cary Grant was also sought for the part. However, Luft persuaded Warner to give the role to Mason. In his book, *My First Hundred Years in Hollywood*, Warner left little doubt that he had no great love for Judy's husband number three. Complaining about Luft's frequent absences from the studio, Warner said: "He's the only producer I know who has his office at Santa Anita." But Warner said he had to deal gingerly with Luft, because Luft could "make Judy go home [from the set] by snapping his fingers." Said Warner: "In order to get her [Judy] for the lead, I had to take her husband, Sid Luft, too, and bill him as producer. A charming fellow, Sid. He's one of the original guys who persuaded his parents he'd never work a day in his life—and made good.")

Vicki's film debut is a rousing success, and Maine and Vicki are married. But after their honeymoon, his drinking gets heavier, and his screen performances suffer until one day Niles reluctantly drops his contract. The days pass with Vicki at the studio and Maine sulking at home waiting for a part that never comes.

One night, Vicki, still in rehearsal costume of white shirt and black tights, comes home and tries to jolly him out of his black mood. She runs through the big production number she has been working on—taking all the parts. Maine, breaking out of his depression, joins in by playing the drums on her backside and tossing pillows at her. At the end of the sequence, he pulls her down with him behind the sofa. But then the doorbell rings. A package arrives and the delivery boy asks Maine if he is "Mr. Vicki Lester." He steps back inside grim-faced and says he's going to have a drink.

A few weeks later, the Academy Awards are held, and Vicki, the surprise winner, is on stage making her acceptance speech. Maine stumbles rubber-legged into the ceremony, interrupts her, and tells the shocked audience that he needs a job. As he rambles on, he swings his arms out and accidentally slaps Vicki. She only laughs, brushing tears aside, and shepherds him off.

The episode is the beginning of the end. Maine enters a sanitarium. He spends months there and is eventually discharged, but he is too far gone to win back his confidence. At the clubhouse of the Santa Anita Race Track, as he is drinking ginger ale, Libby (Jack Carson), the studio publicist who has always despised Maine, taunts him, making a crack about Maine living off Vicki's earnings. When Maine tries to hit him, Libby knocks him down. "Drunk again," says one onlooker. Stung and frightened, Maine picks himself up and orders a double scotch.

Days later, he turns up in night court on a drunk charge. After Vicki pleads with the judge (Frank Ferguson), he discharges Maine in Vicki's custody and she takes him to their Malibu house. There, while he is sleeping, she tells Niles that she is quitting Hollywood to go away with Maine. By so doing, she hopes to restore his health. But Maine overhears their conversation. We see him gasping, and then rolling over and burying his face in the pillow.

When Niles leaves, Maine enters in a gay, teasing mood. He is wearing bathing trunks and says that he is going to start reforming with a swim. He asks Vicki to sing for him, and we hear "It's a New World" as Maine wades into the surf for the last time.

For weeks, Vicki sits at home grief-stricken. One night, Danny McGuire, now her studio accompanist, comes to persuade her to keep an appointment to sing at the Shrine Theatre. When she refuses, railing bitterly at him, he berates her for wasting the career that Maine died to keep from destroying. It is only Vicki who can keep Maine's memory alive. "You're the only thing that remains of him now," he says. "And if you just kick it away, it's like he never existed."

Vicki, her back turned to him, is silent for a few moments. When she turns around, there are tears in her eyes. Cukor, who got the sequence in two takes, was impressed with the sincerity of Garland's performance. She shrugged off his compliment. "Come to my house any day. I do it every afternoon," she said, adding: "but I only do it once at home."

At the theatre, the M.C. (Rex Evans) has just told the capacity audience that Vicki Lester will not be able to appear when suddenly he gets a message saying she is backstage. There is a low hush as he corrects himself. Then, in one of the memorable endings of the movies of the 1950s, Vicki steps into the spotlight. In a strong and confident voice, she says, "Hello everybody—this is—Mrs. Norman Maine." There is a slight pause. And the audience bursts into prolonged applause, saluting her because she chose to honor her late husband's name.

This was the same line that ended the 1937 movie. The remake was a superior picture because it showed what made Vicki a star. In the Gaynor-March version, the heroine's talents were only alluded to in the dialogue, although in that version she was an actress, not a musical comedy star.*

Nevertheless, despite Judy's virtuoso performance, her work habits remained erratic. There

*The third version, a 1976 film with Barbra Streisand and Kris Kristofferson, shifts the plot from Hollywood to the contemporary rock music scene and ends with a seven-minute love song. Besides starring in the picture, Streisand was executive producer, songwriter, and designer of the movie's "musical concepts." The picture got mixed reviews. With notable exceptions, the majority of remakes of classics have been flops—financially and artistically. Failures include the 1966 remake of John Ford's *Stagecoach* (1939), the 1960 adaptation of Hitchcock's *The Thirty-Nine Steps* (1935), and the 1966 version of *Beau Geste* (1926 and 1939). *Variety's* list of all-time box office hits shows only two remakes among the top twenty films—DeMille's 1956 *The Ten Commandments* and William Wyler's 1959 *Ben-Hur*. But both those movies were remakes of silent films. Said Vincent Canby of the *New York Times:* "In addition to having a kind of suffocating effect on the imagination of the people who make them . . . remakes don't even make business sense."

322

Vicki is pensive because, try as she may, she cannot shake the depression clouding her husband's life. Eventually, it leads to his death.

were no offers for new films, so she began giving concerts again, and her shows met with spectacular success in England, Australia, and New York.* Her tour led to some one-woman TV shows, although a series for CBS flopped.

During the 1960s, she made only three pictures. They included a moving nine-minute role in *Judgment at Nuremberg* (1961) as a German hausfrau defending her marriage to a Jew (for which she got her second Oscar nomination) and a poignant performance as a teacher of the mentally retarded in *A Child Is Waiting* (1963).

All this time, her personal life remained disrupted. Her thirteen-year marriage to Luft ended in 1965. Her fourth husband was actor Mark Herron, eighteen years her junior. Her fifth spouse was Mickey Deans, a discotheque manager.**

*A recording of her 1961 Carnegie Hall concert, considered by some to be the highlight of her vocal career, sold two million copies.

**She had three children, Liza Minnelli, Lorna Luft, and Joseph Luft.

As the years passed, her voice began to fail. She tended to be overweight and she was late for performances. Some crowds booed her because of her poor showings, but she became a particular favorite of homosexuals who perhaps saw in her a reflection of their own loneliness and estrangement.

The end came suddenly in 1969 in London where she and husband number five, Deans, had a home in an exclusive section. One June night, Deans found her lying on the bathroom floor, silent and unmoving. A coroner said she had died from barbiturate poisoning and that she may have taken the fatal dosage—about ten of the 1½ gram tablets—while under the influence of a previous dose.

A few days later, an estimated 22,000 mourners stood in line—some for over four hours—to see her body in New York City. It was a tribute unequaled since the death of Rudolph Valentino. Of the many obituaries, a sentence by Peter Coutros of the *New York Daily News* perhaps tells the story best. He wrote: "Somewhere over the rainbow, the happy colors turned to rust, the champagne soured into vinegar, and for Judy Garland, who drank copiously of life, only the dregs were left."

She was doomed because her private life carried over into her career and her career into her private life, and she could never separate the two or put them in perspective. "I've heard how difficult it is to be *with* Judy Garland," she once said. "Do you know how difficult it is to *be* Judy Garland?"

Judy Garland made $8 million during her career. She left debts of $1 million at the end of the yellow-brick road to Oz.

A Streetcar Named Desire

Marlon Brando as the animal-like Stanley Kowalski, one of the screen's great characterizations.

A Streetcar Named Desire (1951)

Directed by Elia Kazan. Screenplay by Tennessee Williams. Adaptation by Oscar Saul based on the original play by Williams. Camera, Harry Stradling. Art director, Richard Day.* Set decorator, George James Hopkins.* Original music, Alex North. Musical direction, Ray Heindorf. Editor, David Weisbart. Produced by Charles K. Feldman. Released by Warner Bros. 125 minutes.

Blanche DuBois	*Vivien Leigh**
Stanley Kowalski	*Marlon Brando*
Stella Kowalski	*Kim Hunter**
Mitch	*Karl Malden**
Steve	*Rudy Bond*
Pablo	*Nick Dennis*
Eunice	*Peg Hillias*
A Collector	*Wright King*
A Doctor	*Richard Garrick*
The Matron	*Ann Dere*
The Mexican Woman	*Edna Thomas*
Sailor	*Mickey Kuhn*
Street Vendor	*Chester Jones*
Negro Woman	*Marietta Canty*
Policeman	*Lyle Latell*
Foreman	*Mel Archer*

*Academy Award Winner.

Kim Hunter, as Stella, puts her arms around Brando in the screen version of Tennessee Williams' Pulitzer Prize-winning play. Williams thought the movie improved on the play.

In 1947, Tennessee Williams electrified Broadway audiences with a brooding, haunting drama of the disintegration of a tarnished southern belle. The play, *A Streetcar Named Desire,* was not his first success. His 1945 work, *The Glass Menagerie,* won critical acclaim, too. But while *The Glass Menagerie* showed promise, *A Streetcar Named Desire* brought his writing talents to full fruition, stamping him as one of America's truly creative playwrights in the tradition of O'Neill, Saroyan, and Odets.

Williams' long and talky but powerful and poetic drama was puzzling. It posed no great social issue, it solved no penetrating moral problem, and when it ended, it came to no conclusion. However, Williams' play was more concerned with mood and character, and there was no doubt that he succeeded brilliantly in these areas.

No one who saw his play will forget the sultry, earthy ambience that Williams created in a squalid apartment in New Orleans' old French Quarter and the volatile characters who played out their star-crossed lives there. The names "Blanche

DuBois" and "Stanley Kowalski" became as familiar to the generation of the 1950s as "Jay Gatsby" and "Daisy Buchanan" were in the 1920s.

A Streetcar Named Desire won the Pulitzer Prize as a play and went on to take five Oscars as a movie. Yet it almost got derailed before it reached Hollywood.

Studio heads were not attracted by its strong, sordid plot, and they felt that the public would not like its unhappy ending. However, a talent agent, Charles K. Feldman, thought otherwise. He bought the screen rights for $350,000 and decided to produce it himself. "Everybody thought it was downbeat," Feldman said. "But I had faith in it."

His faith paid off when Warner Bros. agreed to release it. However, there still remained some large hurdles to clear.

For one thing, the studio faced the tricky problem of transferring the rough, violent drama to the screen without blurring its sensitive qualities. Some of the play's themes—homosexuality, prostitution, nymphomania, and rape—were taboo in movies. Compromises had to be made. The rape scene between Stanley and Blanche was cut. The homosexuality of Blanche's dead husband was only alluded to obliquely—she speaks of his "unmanliness"—rather than mentioned in stark detail. The sexual relationship between Stanley and Stella was toned down. And the ending was changed so that Stella walked out on Stanley.

But Williams was able to write the screenplay, and even with these modifications the story came across as a searing drama. Moreover, it seemed to gain dimension on the screen. The restless camera, with its shifting focus, made the action seem more fluid, alive, and dynamic.

The studio's next problem centered around casting. Elia Kazan, who directed the play and was hired to direct the movie, insisted on having the same actors he directed on the stage. This was almost unheard of in Hollywood, then. The standard formula called for stars with proven box office appeal to fill the key roles of a stage hit. However, Kazan had put together a magnificent production by melding the talents of gifted stage actors, and he insisted that they be signed for the film version as well. In the end, with the exception of Jessica Tandy, he prevailed. Vivien Leigh, who had played the role of Blanche DuBois in the London production, replaced Miss Tandy.

That immediately raised a question: Would Miss Leigh, a distinguished British actress, be able to work with the rest of the cast? They were all Americans, a tightly-knit group who had been together from the start.

"The gang from the play were all friends from New York, and Vivien was the only outsider," said Karl Malden. "We got together beforehand and decided to go all out to make her feel at home. We needn't have bothered. As soon as she walked on the set, we all got along beautifully."

Miss Leigh, who had played Scarlett O'Hara in *Gone with the Wind* (1939), was to win her second Academy Award for playing another southern belle.

Equally outstanding was the performance of Marlon Brando. He had acted magnificently in the Broadway play, but he had at that time appeared in only one other movie—*The Men* (1950). Nevertheless, Brando was able to enlarge on his stage performance to the extent that movie audiences were even more shocked by his conception of the vital, animal-like Stanley Kowalski who brought down the doomed Blanche.

Overnight, the film turned Brando into an entertainment celebrity. He became that strange phenomenon of the cinema world—an instant star. Moviegoers wondered who he was, where he came from, and how he had been able to immerse himself so completely in the role. And well they might, for Hollywood was a long way from Brando's small town, middle American roots.

Born in 1924 in Omaha, Nebraska, Brando was the only boy in a family of three children. He was the son of a businessman, a manufacturer of chemical feeds and insecticides, whose name traces back to the French "Brandeau." Young Marlon's interest in acting came from his mother who was an amateur sculptress, a painter, and a community actress.

However, it took him a while to find where his abilities lay. In school in Evanston and then Libertyville, Illinois, where his family later moved, Brando developed a reputation as a hell-raiser. Once, when a teacher shouted, "Order, order," Brando snapped back, "Make mine a beer." His family then sent him to a military school in Minnesota where he was soon expelled for planting firecrackers under a teacher's door.

He finally dropped out of school, went to New York City, and began a Bohemian existence. He bought a motorcycle and bongo drums and set up household with his old school friend, Wally Cox. New York also introduced Brando to Stella Adler, the noted drama coach. Acting gave him a chance to discover his rare natural talent.

Under Miss Adler, he learned the so-called Stanislavski method—named after the legendary Russian director who founded the famous Moscow Art Theatre. Stanislavski believed that acting was more than saying lines clearly and moving gracefully. It was a creative process in which the actor tried to penetrate to the very core of the character and project the inner truths of his soul. The actor had to feel what he was expressing. He had to understand the thought and problems behind the dialogue.

Brando, Miss Adler said, was able to understand the Method better than anyone she had ever seen. In 1944 Brando made his Broadway debut in John Van Druten's *I Remember Mama*. Two years later, critics named him the theatre's most promising actor.

Then, in 1947, Tennessee Williams wrote a new play called *A Streetcar Named Desire*. Brando read the script and decided to try for the part of Stanley Kowalski. The role was open because John Garfield had turned it down—partly over a contract dispute and partly because he underestimated the part. He reportedly didn't like it because he felt Kowalski was overshadowed by Blanche. The producers thought next of Burt Lancaster, but he was tied up with movie commitments so audi-

Vivien Leigh, playing Blanche DuBois, the seedy, neurotic southern belle who disintegrates after her clash with the coarse Stanley Kowalski (Marlon Brando).

tions were held. Brando was the choice of director Kazan, but by a prior agreement, Williams also had to approve.

Brando, who was then broke, hitchhiked to Williams' summer home on Cape Cod. By chance, he arrived in time to help Williams fix his faulty plumbing. He stayed most of the night, captivating the playwright with his intense, offbeat personality. When he left, the part was his.

On opening night, the audience gave the production a standing ovation. The twenty-three-year-old Brando drew rave notices. Most important, he laid the groundwork for a new introspective acting school later to be popularized by James Dean, Paul Newman, and Montgomery Clift, and later still by Dustin Hoffman, Jack Nicholson, and Al Pacino.

Brando was now the hottest young star on Broadway. Every studio sent him offers. The one he took was the part of a paraplegic veteran in Stanley Kramer's *The Men* (1950). It was a box office failure although Brando won impressive reviews. He went on to get Oscar nominations for his next three movies—*A Streetcar Named Desire* (1951), *Viva Zapata!* (1952), and *Julius Caesar* (1953). After he did *The Wild One* (1953), a sleeper anticipating the beat generation, he appeared in

On the Waterfront (1954), a performance that won him his first Oscar.

Still, Hollywood considered him a misfit, and his unorthodox acting style puzzled veteran movie stars. "The first thing I heard about Brando," said Joan Bennett, "was that he 'threw' other performers by rehearsing a scene one way and then playing it in an entirely different manner." He was rude and uncooperative with reporters,* wore T-shirts and blue jeans to parties, and made no bones about despising the whole movie scene. "The only reason I'm here," he said, "is because I don't have the moral strength to turn down the money." He earned enormous salaries. The $1,000,000 he got for *The Fugitive Kind* (1960) was the first time that amount of money was ever paid to a movie star for a single movie. Much more relevant to him were minority and racial causes that were beginning to gather strength in the 1960s. He took part in civil rights marches in the South, picketed San Quentin prison protesting capital punishment on the night

*Hollywood gossip columnist Sheilah Graham never forgot her introduction to Brando. "My first encounter with Marlon was during his New York stage appearance in *A Streetcar Named Desire*," she said. "When I asked Jessica Tandy, his co-star, to introduce us, he depressed me by asking her if I was her mother."

of Caryl Chessman's execution, and campaigned for fishing rights for the Puyallup Indians of the Northeast. He later became an outspoken critic of the Vietnam War.

Inevitably, his non-conformist ways carried over into his private life. His tempestuous affairs of the heart produced two children out of wedlock* and led to actress Rita Moreno's attempted suicide at his home. There was a stormy romance with actress France Nuyen, as well as two marriages and two divorces followed by extended court battles over the custody of his three legitimate children. Always attracted by dark women, he was married to Anna Kashfi (1957-1959), a minor actress whose origin—Indian or Welsh—was a mystery, and Movita Castenada, a Mexican actress older than Brando, who had played in the original *Mutiny on the Bounty* (1935).

Perhaps the most puzzling thing about Brando has been his acting career itself. Some feel that he squandered his talent on movies which, by and large, were mediocre. After *On the Waterfront,* he appeared in a long string of flops—including *Desiree* (1954), *The Fugitive Kind* (1960), the $26 million fiasco *Mutiny on the Bounty* (1962), and *A Countess from Hong Kong* (1967). However, he also turned in some memorable performances in *Guys and Dolls* (1955), *Sayonara* (1957), and *The Ugly American* (1963).

The 1960s were a doldrum decade for Brando, and his career was clearly waning in 1971 when he heard about the role of Don Corleone in *The Godfather.* For that film he made his first screen test in over twenty years. To transform himself into the elderly Mafia don, Brando slicked back his hair, dabbed shoe polish under his eyes, and stuffed cotton in his nostrils and cheeks. His performance in the title role brought him his second Oscar (which he refused) and marked a comeback that continued with his moving portrayal of an American widower in love with a young French girl in *Last Tango in Paris* (1971).

These recent triumphs notwithstanding, many moviegoers contend that Brando's masterpiece was *A Streetcar Named Desire.* His portrayal of the brute who shatters the sanity of his ladylike, half-demented sister-in-law ranks as one of the great performances of the stage and the screen. No one, says Tennessee Williams, has equaled Brando's portrayal of Stanley Kowalski.

* By Tarita, a Tahitian beauty he met while making *Mutiny on the Bounty* (1962).

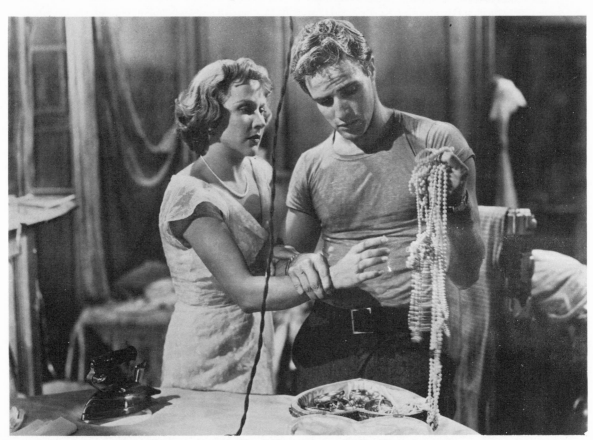

Kowalski goes through Blanche's jewelry as Stella tries to stop him.

Blanche berates her sister Stella for marrying "something sub-human . . . a stone-age cave man."

The movie takes its title from the New Orleans streetcar* that ran through the city's French Quarter to Desire Street and so bore its name. Blanche DuBois (Miss Leigh) has arrived at her sister's apartment by taking a symbolic journey. "They told me to take a streetcar named Desire," says Blanche, "and then transfer to one called Cemetery and ride six blocks and get off at Elysian Fields."

There, Blanche is dismayed to find her sister Stella (Kim Hunter) in a shabby, cramped flat in a rundown neighborhood. On her part, Stella is shocked by Blanche's frail, neurotic appearance and meandering disjointed tale of leaving her teaching job in Mississippi because of frayed nerves. Blanche, who has started drinking almost as soon as she arrives, says that their old homestead, Belle Reve (Beautiful Dream), has been lost to creditors, and that family deaths have left her alone and penniless.

The biggest surprise of all comes when Blanche meets Stella's husband, Stanley Kowalski (Brando), a loud, coarse-tongued roughneck. The two immediately clash.** Stanley can't stand Blanche's pretentious airs or her fanciful tales of rich and handsome suitors. He is also suspicious of her story of the family home. Blanche feels Stanley is obscene and common. She berates her sister for lowering herself to marry "something sub-human, thousands of years old, a stone-age cave man."

Stella defends her husband. She says that she has adjusted to this life, is happily pregnant, and feels fulfilled by her physical relationship with Stanley. "There are things that happen between a man and woman in the dark that sort of make everything else seem unimportant," Stella says.

One night, at one of Stanley's poker games, Blanche meets Mitch (Malden), and a common loneliness draws them together. An awkward hulk of a man, Mitch is a mother's boy with an Oedipus complex who desperately wants to escape his loyalty to her. Blanche sees Mitch as a gallant gentleman, a refuge she can escape to, a chance for

*There really was a Desire streetcar in New Orleans, but in the 1950s it became a victim of modern times and was replaced by a bus.

**The clash between Blanche and Stanley, some critics feel, represents the conflict between introspective idealism and open sexuality, between overrefined gentility and brutal coarseness. Blanche places great emphasis on many of the time-honored mores of civilization. Through her cruel downfall, writes critic Dorant du Ponte, the play is attacking "those disruptive forces in modern life that have shattered traditional values and rendered obsolete the older civilized refinements."

happiness. Only to him does she reveal the details of her tragic early marriage to a handsome youth who turned out to be homosexual and who later shot himself.

Stanley, bristling from Blanche's remarks about him, is intent on destroying this alliance. Through a friend who regularly travels to Mississippi, Stanley learns the truth about Blanche's past. When creditors took over the family home, she went to nearby Laurel where memories of her failure to cope with her first love twisted her life. She stayed at the Flamingo Hotel and gradually took up with many men. One day she had an affair with an adolescent. Finally, she had to resign her teaching job and leave town because of her behavior.

Stanley sees that Blanche's tales of a gaudy past filled with rich admirers have been made up to cloud a life she cannot face. He tears down that gossamer facade, not with moral indignation but with a cruel pleasure that makes his actions even more painful.

First, he tells Mitch about Blanche's past, destroying his illusion of her. Drunk and vindictive, Mitch comes to rape her. He rips off a colored lampshade and holds a naked light bulb to her haggard, hysterical features. He tells Blanche she "isn't clean enough to bring into the house with Mother." Her screams send him running into the street.

Then Stella is rushed to the hospital to have her baby, and Stanley comes home to confront Blanche alone. Half-drunk and highly confused, Blanche is walking around in a white satin gown and rhinestone tiara. She rambles on about getting a telegram from an old beau inviting her on a Caribbean cruise.

Stanley will not let her seek salvation in a dream world. He accuses her of inventing the telegram. He taunts her about her pretensions to gentility, her lies, and her conceits.

Face facts, he says. He tells her to look at herself and her ragtag outfit. She may think of herself as a queen, but she has only been swilling his liquor.

Frightened and desperate, Blanche makes pointless calls to Western Union. Stanley watches, grinning, then moves toward her until he corners her. Blanche smashes a bottle and holds up the jagged ends to twist in Stanley's face. He snatches her wrist and says: "Tiger, tiger. Drop that bottletop. Drop it." The scene ends with Stanley overcoming Blanche, leaving her rape to the audience's imagination. (In the play, he picks up her limp form and carries her to the bed. Recognizing the inevitability of their encounter, he says: "We've had this date with each other from the beginning.")

The end has now come for Blanche. It is a few days later and Stella has returned with her baby. While a poker game is going on, a doctor and a matron come to take Blanche to an asylum. Now totally unable to distinguish between illusion and reality, she gives herself over to their care with a childlike expression of trust that has become a memorable farewell line: "Whoever you are—I have always depended on the kindness of strangers."

The play actually ended here, but the studio felt that it had to make Stanley suffer for his cruel treatment of Blanche. So as Blanche is led away, Stella, guilt-ridden and miserable, tells Stanley she is through with him. Then, with her baby in her arms, she goes upstairs to a neighbor's apartment, refusing to heed her husband's pleading calls.

A Streetcar Named Desire won three of the four acting Oscars—for best actress (Leigh), best supporting actor (Malden), and best supporting actress (Hunter)—as well as Academy Awards for art direction (Richard Day) and set decoration (George James Hopkins).*

Despite the accolades, director Kazan was miffed by cuts made without his approval. The studio made twelve cuts that removed about three minutes from the film to avoid getting a "C" (condemned) rating from the Catholic Church's Legion of Decency.

The cuts ranged from a minor deletion of three words—"on the mouth" (following the words "I would like to kiss you softly and sweetly")—to a forty-second splice of a wordless scene in which Stella comes down a stairway to Stanley after a quarrel. The scene was worked out in an alternation of closeups and medium shots to show Stella's conflicting revulsion and attraction to her husband. Kazan said he was told that the close shots combined with the music made the girl's relation to her husband "too carnal." Many of the cuts, Kazan also was told, stemmed from the thought that "if one character [Stella was the candidate] could be shown as 'good' the film would be redeemed."

Nevertheless, Kazan felt that the cuts were minor, by and large, and did not hurt the total impact of the picture. Williams, who hasn't always felt too kindly about Hollywood, agreed. Said Williams: "I shall know now, regardless of what happens to me or my work afterward, that at least one thing I have done has survived with whatever honesty and beauty it had in the beginning, and even more. This is the first time I have seen a stage play actually increase in stature when transferred to the screen."

*Many feel that the picture deserved a sixth Oscar—for Brando's performance. He lost out to Humphrey Bogart who got it for his portrayal of Charlie Allnut in *The African Queen*.

Summertime

Rossano Brazzi and Katharine Hepburn teaming as a middle-aged Venetian proprietor and a love-starved American tourist in *Summertime*.

Summertime
(1955)

Directed by David Lean. Screenplay by Lean and H. E. Bates, based on the play *The Time of the Cuckoo* by Arthur Laurents. Music, Sandro Cicognini. Camera, Jack Hildyard. Editor, Peter Taylor. Filmed in Venice in Eastman Color. Produced by Ilya Lopert. United Artists. 99 minutes.

Jane Hudson	*Katharine Hepburn*
Renato Di Rossi	*Rossano Brazzi*
Signora Fiorina	*Isa Miranda*
Eddie Jaeger	*Darren McGavin*
Phyl Jaeger	*Mari Aldon*
Mrs. McIlhenny	*Jane Rose*
Lloyd McIlhenny	*MacDonald Parke*
Mauro	*Gaitano Audiero*
Englishman	*Andre Morell*
Vito	*Jeremy Spenser*
Giovanna	*Virginia Simeon*

Jane Hudson, the old maid from Ohio, admires the patio of her Pensione hostess Signora Fiorina (Isa Miranda).

She had more than her share of liabilities. She had freckles, frizzy hair, a flat, strident voice set off by a clipped Bryn Mawr accent, and an ironing board figure.* Few of her films were box office smashes. Some were just plain flops.

On screen, critics sometimes described her as cold and intellectual, haughty and aloof. At RKO, her studio nickname was "Katharine of Arrogance." Her stage performances brought sharp reactions, too. Dorothy Parker once said, "She ran the gamut of emotions from A to B."

But Katharine Hepburn confounded her critics and endured to enjoy one of the longest Hollywood careers. Many consider her the movies' greatest actress. Adept at both comedy and drama, she won three Oscars—a feat equalled among actresses only by Ingrid Bergman. Hepburn's career even transcended pictures. She invariably showed up on lists of the world's most admired women.

In short, she was a celebrity larger than life. "I'm a personality as well as an actress," she once said. "Show me an actress who isn't a personality, and you'll show me a woman who isn't a star."

*Commenting on it in the movie *Pat and Mike* (1952), Spencer Tracy quipped: "There ain't much meat on her. But what there is, is cherce."

There was no question that Hepburn knew she was to be a star long before her career was in high gear. Even in her thirties, Hepburn was a shrewd negotiator—she was one of the few performers who got the best of Louis B. Mayer in a deal—and frequently bought her way out of contracts to avoid doing pictures she didn't like. She did the play *The Philadelphia Story* without salary, insisting, instead, on ten percent of the gross and movie rights. It made $1.5 million. MGM later bought it for $250,000. For *The African Queen* (1951), she passed up a salary for a percentage deal. The picture grossed $4 million.

George Stevens got these words of advice when he began directing her in *Alice Adams* (1935): "Yell 'No!' at her seven times. If you try to be tactful, she thinks she must be right."

Her failure to listen to directions once brought a physical rebuke from the usually placid George Cukor. During the filming of *Little Women* (1933), he told her to be careful with a dish of ice cream. She had to hold it while running up a flight of stairs, and Cukor was concerned because there was no replacement for the dress she was wearing. But she became so caught up in the spontaneity of the scene that she spilled the ice cream. "She ruined the dress and then she laughed—and I hit her and called her an amateur," Cukor said. Hepburn shrugged the slap off and played the scene again in a different version of the costume.

Her burning ambition was to play Scarlett O'Hara, and she made a personal appeal for the role to David O. Selznick. She felt that her spirit and outspoken demeanor mirrored Scarlett's character.

"The part was practically written for me," she told the producer. "I *am* Scarlett O'Hara."

However, Selznick felt that she wasn't alluring enough. "I just can't imagine Rhett Butler chasing you for ten years," he replied.

The Hepburn encounters were not limited to studio heads, producers, and directors. She sometimes rubbed other performers the wrong way. However, Spencer Tracy instinctively knew how to handle her quixotic personality. According to legend, when she met Tracy, she noticed that he stood only an inch taller than she. Hepburn, who was wearing three-inch platform heels, said, "I think I'm a little too tall for you, Mr. Tracy," to which he replied, "Don't worry, I'll cut you down to size."*

So began a friendship that lasted until Tracy's death in 1967. They made nine pictures together, beginning with *Woman of the Year* (1942) and ending with *Guess Who's Coming to Dinner* (1967). Their screen partnership was captivating. It revolved around a clash of wills. She came on strong at the outset—acerbic, flinty, willful, headstrong, aristocratic. He was down-to-earth, tolerant, rough-hewn, a man of strength and character who tamed her and freed her spirit from the inhibitions of hidebound class strictures.

Their relationship continued off-screen, although Tracy was not the only man in her colorful life. She had a short marriage to stockbroker Ludlow Ogden Smith (her career made this an incompatible situation) and romantic interludes with Leland Hayward, her agent and later a producer, and with Howard Hughes. But the twenty years she spent with Tracy marked the real love of her life. She was devoted to him, taking on the chores of a wife, nursing him back to health after he went on periodic drinking benders, and cheering him up when he became despondent over his career. Tracy, separated from his wife, would not divorce her because he was a Catholic.

The life styles of Tracy and Hepburn comple-

mented each other beautifully. She brought him into her circle of literary and society friends and introduced him to intellectual pursuits. He showed her how to relax, let down her hair, and enjoy life. Theirs was a very private affair. They rarely were seen together in public, and they gave no interviews. When they traveled, they stayed in separate hotels. The relationship was no secret to the Hollywood press corps. However, they treated it with discretion. Sheilah Graham called it "the greatest story never told."

That was all right with Hepburn. Like Garbo, Hepburn never liked the press and always tried to keep her personal life separate from her career. Born in 1909 to a well-to-do, liberally inclined Connecticut family—her mother was a suffragette and her father was a physician—she launched a stage career after acting in college at Bryn Mawr. She overcame early failures to become a Broadway star and then moved on to Hollywood. When she arrived, her eyes were red from a cinder she had picked up on the dusty train ride. John Barrymore, who met her at the station, looked deeply into her bloodshot orbs and said sympathetically, "I have that trouble, too." Hepburn explained that she hadn't been drinking. Barrymore only smiled knowingly: "That's what they all say, my dear."

At first the film capital did not know what to make of her angular looks and tempestuous spirit. However, her first movie, *A Bill of Divorcement* (1932) with Barrymore, immediately established her as a unique talent. In her third picture, *Morning Glory* (1933), she won an Oscar. There followed a long string of movies whose results were wide-ranging. Some were so bad that, by 1937, she headed a list of stars labeled "box office poison." Part of this was due to poor scripts. But part of the problem was that her personality limited her range as an actress, and not all her movies were intelligently cast.

Still, the best of her work ranks among the best by any actress. Her most memorable pictures include *Little Women, The Philadelphia Story, The African Queen* (1951), *Guess Who's Coming to Dinner, Long Day's Journey into Night* (1962), and *The Lion in Winter* (1968). And, of course, there was her *tour de force* performance in the bittersweet *Summertime*, a movie that in many ways was the culmination of all the stiff-upper-lip heroines she played in the 1930s.

Kate as plain Jane Hudson, a love-starved, middle-aged secretary from Akron, Ohio, on her first trip to Europe, arrives as a tourist in Venice. Almost immediately we can see the conflict boiling inside. She is yearning for romance, hoping that

*However, Gary Carey, in his biography of Hepburn, said that it was actually Joseph L. Mankiewicz who produced the topper. "Don't worry," Carey quoted Mankiewicz as saying, "he'll cut you down to size."

All dressed up but no place to go. Poor Jane has lost a date because she proudly turned up a chair at her table. She did it to make some other American tourists she spotted think she had an escort. But it also made a handsome Italian (Brazzi) who approached her table move on.

someone will come along to fulfill her dreams. Inwardly, we know she is too straitlaced to relax and enjoy herself when, and if, any opportunity should crop up.

Jane stays at the modest Pensione Fiorina where fellow Americans Mr. and Mrs. Lloyd McIlhenny (MacDonald Parke and Jane Rose) and Eddie Jaeger (Darren McGavin), an unproductive artist, and Phyl (Mari Aldon), his wife, are also guests. The two couples have dinner out. And so Jane, gowned in picturebook fashions, spends her first night alone in the ancient city. Actually, she has always been alone. But wandering through Venice's beautiful piazzas and narrow winding streets, she meets Mauro (Gaitano Audiero), an enterprising street urchin who becomes her guide. Then, while sitting at a cafe in the San Marco Piazza, she is stared at admiringly by a handsome middle-aged Italian. Nothing comes of it—at least not right away. The movie's lovely theme music weaves in and out of the background, underscoring her estrangement.

Sightseeing the next day with Mauro, Jane is attracted to a red goblet in the window of an antique shop. When she goes in, she discovers that the proprietor is Renato Di Rossi (Rossano Brazzi), the same man she had seen in the cafe.

Flustered, she buys the goblet, which Renato says is authentic eighteenth-century Venetian. He promises to find another to make a pair. The next afternoon, when Jane returns to his shop, he is not in, so she goes out to take some 16mm movies of the store. However, as she tries to frame the picture, she keeps backing up until she falls into a canal.

The sequence appeared as a spread in *Life* and turned out to be the most famous scene in the picture. Hepburn did it reluctantly, for the Venetian canals are filthy and filled with all sorts of refuse. However, there was no way to fake the scene. And so she went ahead, covered with all sorts of oils and lotions. Only her eyes were unprotected, and they became inflamed and watery. In fact, she never quite overcame the condition. The weepy look she has in later films is a carryover from her plunge into the canal.

337

After the accident, Renato comes to the Pensione. Jane assumes that he has found another goblet, but he says he's there for social reasons. "I came to see you," he says. Before he can explain, the McIlhennys come in and proudly show off six red goblets that were made for them that afternoon. They resemble the one Jane bought at Renato's shop.

Renato, embarrassed, implores Jane to believe that her goblet is a genuine antique. Eventually she does, and she agrees to have dinner with him.

After an enchanted evening of good food and music, a flower lady comes by and Renato asks Jane to pick one. She chooses a white gardenia. Why that flower? he asks. "I once went to a ball . . . the first one I'd ever been to," she tells him. "Somehow, I got it in my mind that I had to wear a gardenia. I don't know why. . . . [But] gardenias cost two dollars apiece. And the boy I was going with was still in college. But it was a nice dream."

"Well," Renato says, "now you have your gardenia. Everything happens sooner or later."

As they stroll through Venice, she accidentally drops it in a canal. Try though he may, Renato cannot retrieve it. It floats away—a symbol of the elusiveness of love—just beyond his outstretched fingers.

Nevertheless, she breathlessly confesses that Venice has become "more than I ever dreamed of back in Akron." At the end of their first evening together, he kisses her and she rushes off to her Pensione room.

Jane spends most of the next day preparing for her next date with Renato. As she waits for him in the piazza, a young man named Vito (Jeremy Spenser) comes to tell her that Renato will be a little late. Jane invites him to sit down and then discovers Vito is Renato's son. Hurt by what she takes to be Renato's deception, she leaves.

Actually, Renato is separated from his wife, but

Shopping in Venice, Jane is attracted to an antique store. It turns out to be Brazzi's shop.

Hepburn uses her hands to drink water from an outdoor fountain with Gaitano Audiero, who played a street urchin who acted as her unofficial guide.

Jane doesn't know this. Later, when Renato finds her at the Pensione, she tells him that she despises dishonesty. He, too, has some harsh words.

"You Americans get so disturbed about sex."

"We don't take it lightly," Jane replies.

"Take it. Don't talk it. . . . You are like a hungry child who is given ravioli to eat. My dear girl, you are hungry. Eat the ravioli."

Renato insists that they dine together, and Jane, ashamed of her behavior, agrees. They go dancing and nightclub hopping and wind up in his bedroom while fireworks flash in the Venetian sky.

They spend the next week together on the colorful island of Burano, across the Adriatic Lagoon from Venice. The days are carefree and idyllic until, finally, Jane is reminded of the futility of their relationship.

When they return to Venice, she tells him that she has to leave. "I come from such a different world," she says. He tells her that he loves her and begs her to stay. But she says she can't. "You and I would only end in nothing," Jane says. "All my life I've stayed at parties too long because I didn't know when to go. Now, with you, I've grown up. I think I do know when to."

So she does. And the movie ends with a poignant scene. At the railroad station, Jane is on the train as it is ready to leave, her eyes nervously sweeping the station. Renato is nowhere to be seen.

Then, suddenly, she sees him running down the crowded platform, holding a box. He bumps into someone and drops it. By the time he picks it up, the train is moving, picking up steam.

Renato sprints to the end of the platform but he cannot quite put the box into her outstretched hand. And so he tears it open and holds up a white gardenia.

Never looking away, Jane hangs out the window and waves to the tiny figure shrinking and then vanishing in the distance. And then, when the train turns round the bend, she brings her body back into the train and we see the despair etched into her face.*

*Summertime was based on the successful play The Time of the Cuckoo, in which Shirley Booth starred. Dramatically, the play was a more subtle, complex work, and Miss Booth played the role quite differently, emerging more as a mature but selfish woman than as an uptight spinster. But there was no denying Summertime's visual beauty and the consummate art of Hepburn. The combination made up for the movie's slender love story.

Sunset Boulevard

Gloria Swanson in her great comeback role as the eccentric silent film star Norma Desmond. William Holden played Joe Gillis, the broke, young Hollywood writer who comes to live with her.

Sunset Boulevard
(1950)

Directed by Billy Wilder. Screenplay by Wilder,* Charles Brackett* and D. M. Marshman, Jr.*
Camera, John F. Seitz. Sets, Sam Comer* and Ray Moyer.* Score, Franz Waxman.* Editors,
Doane Harrison and Arthur Schmidt. Art directors, Hans Dreier* and John Meehan.* Produced
by Brackett. Released by Paramount. 110 minutes.

Joe Gillis	*William Holden*
Norma Desmond	*Gloria Swanson*
Max von Mayerling	*Erich von Stroheim*
Betty Schaefer	*Nancy Olson*
Sheldrake	*Fred Clark*
Morino	*Lloyd Gough*
Artie Green	*Jack Webb*
Undertaker	*Franklyn Farnum*
First Finance Man	*Larry Blake*
Second Finance Man	*Charles Dayton*
Electrician (Hawkeye)	*John Skins Miller*
Jonesy (Old Security Man)	*Robert Emmett O'Connor*
Captain of Police	*Howard Negley*
Captain of Homicide	*Ken Christy*
Police Sergeant	*Len Hendry*
Themselves	*Cecil B. DeMille*
	Hedda Hopper
	Buster Keaton
	Anna Q. Nilsson
	H. B. Warner
	Ray Evans
	Jay Livingston

*Academy Award Winner.

Norma and Joe dancing alone at a New Year's Eve party in her Sunset Boulevard mansion.

She was one of Hollywood's legendary figures, and her career epitomizes a crazy, extravagant era that we will probably never see again.

Between 1923 and 1926 she made $20,000 a week and spent more than that. When she traveled, she rented country estates or whole floors of hotels for her huge entourage. When she gave dinners, she invited hundreds of guests. When she shopped, she often bought three fur coats at a time.

She was one of the first movie stars to make a picture abroad, the first to have a child while she was an actress, and the first to marry a titled nobleman. But she will be known for none of those things. She will be remembered for disproving the notion that a fallen star never rises again.

Gloria Swanson did that in 1950 when, at the age of fifty-two, she made a remarkable comeback in the brilliant, sardonic *Sunset Boulevard.*

The story, an original screenplay, was the result of an idea hatched by an already proven team of collaborators. Charles Brackett, the producer, and Billy Wilder, the director, had pooled their talents to do the Academy Award winning *The Lost Week-*

end (1945). A few years later, they turned their attention from alcoholism to another subject rarely screened with candor.

"We decided we wanted to do a story about Hollywood," Brackett recalled. "We closed the doors and said, 'What sort of story shall we do?' Someone suggested a relationship with a silent-day queen and a young man."

And so work began on a screenplay for a picture that was to become a classic of the 1950s. With another writer, D. M. Marshman, Jr., the Brackett-Wilder team proceeded to flesh out the story line. At first they ran into a blind alley, however, for they couldn't figure out how to develop the plot without running into clichés.

So, after many frustrating false starts, they abandoned their meetings. Three weeks later, they were discussing a French novel when suddenly, out of the blue, one of them remarked, "Suppose the old dame shoots the boy?"

That, said Brackett, put them right back on the track, and a cross-pollination of ideas began to blossom forth. "We decided the opening scene would show the body of the writer floating in the movie queen's swimming pool," Brackett said. "But why did she kill him? From this point, it became only a job of filling out the story."*

The next hurdle was casting. "Though we liked the story, we knew we could never hope to make it seem real to the public without Gloria," Brackett said. "She knew nothing about all this. Suppose now we didn't get her? Or, if we did, this being a pretty strong story, would she demand changes?"

It turned out that none of these fears materialized. "Gloria responded magnificently," Brackett said. "She worked slavishly without complaint, often to two or three o'clock in the morning. It's the kind of trouping we don't have too much of in Hollywood nowadays."**

So perfect was her casting, in fact, that many thought Miss Swanson was merely playing herself. Like Norma Desmond, she had worked for Cecil B. DeMille (who used to call her "young fellow" as he does in the picture). Like Norma, she had lived in a mansion off Sunset Boulevard during her heyday in the 1920s. And like Norma, she nurtured the belief that she would one day return to past glories. But unlike Norma, Miss Swanson was able to make a triumphal return to the screen after her film career ended. Her manic, mercurial portrayal of Norma Desmond remains one of the screen's enduring performances.

Sunset Boulevard opens with a shot of the body of Joe Gillis (William Holden),† a hack movie script writer, floating in the pool of a Beverly Hills mansion. Three bullets lie embedded in his body. "Let's go back about six months," the voice of the dead man says, "and find the day when it all started."

In the flashback, we see Gillis, pursued by creditors, swerving his car into a driveway of what he thinks is a deserted estate on Sunset Boulevard. The immense, gloomy house, a throwback to another era, stands dark and brooding in the midst

of unkept, overgrown grounds. Rats scuttle across the bottom of its empty pool. Inside, wind whispers eerily through the pipes of an organ.

To his surprise, Gillis finds that the mausoleum-like home is not empty. Two relics of the past live there—Norma Desmond (Swanson), a once regal silent movie queen, still wealthy but living in a dream world, and Max von Mayerling (Erich von Stroheim), her former director and ex-husband, now her servant.

Gillis is mistaken for a funeral director called for a macabre burial of Miss Desmond's pet chimpanzee. He is about to leave when he sees Miss Desmond remove her dark glasses.

"You're Norma Desmond," he says. "You used to be in silent pictures. You used to be big."

"I am big," she says. "It's the pictures that got small."

The strange, egocentric woman takes a fancy to the young man. His contemporariness is a counterpoint to her decadent life style. When she learns he is a script writer, she asks him to stay and patch up a dreadful scenario of *Salome* that she has written as a comeback vehicle. Broke, and seeing a chance for some easy money, he accepts her proposition. And so he is introduced to her huge mansion—a gaudy, baroque structure with too much furniture in every room.

For this key set, Paramount rented a twenty-five-room French-Italian mansion, unoccupied for years, owned by the Getty oil family.†† Producer Brackett carefully furnished it with bizarre mementos—an oversize nut bowl, a Louis XV commode, a gondola-shaped bed. Everywhere he placed photographs of Swanson in her salad days.

Gillis is vaguely fascinated by Norma's past glory. "She was the greatest of them all," von Mayerling, her butler, says. "In one week she received 17,000 fan letters. Men bribed her hairdresser to get a lock of her hair."

Now she lives like a hermit, fearful of the outside world that might remind her of times past. At night she occasionally has her cronies over for bridge. They are actor friends from her silent days (played by Buster Keaton, H. B. Warner, and Anna Q. Nilsson). "I used to think of them as her waxworks," says Gillis.

*According to Maurice Zolotow in his book *Billy Wilder in Hollywood,* the movie originally began and ended in a morgue with Joe Gillis' corpse talking to others who had recently joined him in the next world. But sneak preview audiences laughed at this scene and never got into the true mood of the picture thereafter. Wilder reluctantly cut the sequences.

**Zolotow said that Swanson was not Wilder's original choice. Wilder first approached Mae West (when the story line had not taken its sardonic turn), Mary Pickford, and Pola Negri. For one reason or another, nobody was interested. Miss Negri, for example, was enraged that Wilder thought her suitable for the part of a has-been. It was director George Cukor who suggested Swanson to Wilder.

†Montgomery Clift was first offered the part, but he turned it down reportedly because he thought that his fans would be repelled by his playing a male prostitute living off a woman twice his age. Fred MacMurray also rejected the role, which he found demeaning.

††The family didn't want a swimming pool, so Paramount assured them that it would restore the grounds when the picture was finished. Later, the Gettys were so pleased with the attractive pool the studio built that they withdrew their objection. When they found that it wasn't practical, Paramount installed a filter and other things and made them a gift of the pool. In 1957, the Getty family tore down the mansion and erected a twenty-two-story office building in its place. The building, headquarters of the Getty Oil Company, stands at 3810 Wilshire Boulevard in Los Angeles.

Other nights she watches movies in her living room. The bill of fare is always one of her silent pictures. Watching her image on the screen, she tells Gillis, "We didn't need dialogue. We had faces then."

For the closeup of Swanson in the oldtime film, Paramount used one of her monumental flops called *Queen Kelly* (1928). The picture is about an Irish girl who ends up in a brothel after a military officer seduces her. It was never released in this country because of the brothel scenes. Ironically, von Stroheim, who shows the film in *Sunset Boulevard,* was its director.

Eventually, the aging actress falls in love with Gillis, but her eccentric ways begin to turn him off. When Gillis discovers that he is the only guest at her New Year's party complete with orchestra, he leaves to attend a party of his own generation.

There he sees Betty Schaefer (Nancy Olson), a studio script reader who persuades him to start writing again. However, in the midst of the festivities, Gillis gets a phone call from Max telling him that Norma has attempted suicide.

Out of pity, Gillis decides not to leave Norma, but at the same time he wants to continue writing. So, in the evenings he slips away to work on a

Joe becomes bored with Norma as the weeks pass. But she becomes even more possessive and demanding of his time.

Erich von Stroheim persuades Norma to leave with the police who have come for her after she shoots Joe.

script with Betty, who has also begun to fall in love with him.

The weeks pass, with Gillis living a double life—staying with Norma by day, working with Betty by night. One day Norma gets a call from Paramount. Believing that it is DeMille, her old director, asking her back, she rides in her vintage, leopard-skin upholstered Isotta-Faschini to the lot. However, the studio has called only to ask to borrow Norma's car to use in a scene.

DeMille, embarrassed, tries to make her welcome. "Well, hello, young fellow," he says, greeting her as he did two generations earlier. "It's good to see you."

Some technicians from her silent days are on the set and they welcome her enthusiastically. Eventually, she feels she has been missed. She believes that it's just a matter of time before she will start playing Salome.

Meanwhile, Joe has been seeing more of Betty, and Norma has begun to notice his absences. Trying to head off a tragedy, Max tells Joe that he is worried about his mistress.

"Sure you are," Gillis says disgustedly. "And we're not helping her any, feeding her lies and more lies. Getting herself ready for a picture. What happens when she finds out?"

"She never will," Max says. And then Max discloses his whole weird relationship with Norma. Max says he discovered her when she was sixteen and made her into a star. He was a top director then.

"And she's turned you into a servant," Gillis tells him.

"It was I who asked to come back, humiliating as it may seem," Max says. "I could have continued my career—only I found everything unendurable after she had left me. You see, I was her first husband."

But Gillis cannot play the deceitful game. One day when Norma discovers that Joe is seeing Betty and tries to break up their romance, Gillis tells her the truth about her career. The movies don't need her, he tells her, and they never intended to star her again. The studio only wanted to rent her car.

"Wake up, Norma. The audience left twenty

346

In one of the memorable closing scenes of the 1950s, Swanson descends the stairs of her mansion, believing she is playing Salome. Police are waiting to take her in. Swanson remembered the scene as a difficult one. "I had to do it barefoot," she said. "It was hard because it had to be done in rhythm to music with little dance steps."

years ago," he says, trying to get her to face up to reality. "You're a woman of fifty. There's nothing tragic about being fifty—not unless you try to be twenty-five."

With that he starts to leave. "No one ever leaves a star," Norma says, going for a gun. As Gillis lugs his typewriter alongside the pool, she calls to him. He doesn't stop and she fires. A bullet tears into his back. He keeps walking. A second slug sends him staggering toward the pool. A third topples him into the water.

And so Gillis, who started as Norma's collaborator, and then became her lover, has now become her victim. Their alliance has ended in tragedy for them both, but it brings Norma one brief moment of glory in her twisted mind.

As police take her to be booked and charged with murder, a battery of press photographers have set up their cameras at the bottom of her stairs. In the picture's finale, she comes out dressed in her Salome costume. Max, in an effort to get her to go quietly, tells her that she is descend-

ing the staircase of the palace. With reporters and police looking on, she sees herself once again in the spotlight of a studio set.

"All right," Max says. "Camera. Action."

Before she goes on, she has a word for the crew. "I just want to tell you all how happy I am to be back in the studio making a picture again. You don't know how much I've missed all of you. And I promise you, I'll never desert you again. . . . You see, this is my life. It always will be. There's nothing else . . . just us . . . and the cameras . . . and those wonderful people out there in the dark. All right, Mr. DeMille, I'm ready for my closeup." Then she glides down the long winding stairs, smiling and dancing, as the camera moves in.

As brilliant a movie as *Sunset Boulevard* was, it failed to lead to any other major pictures for Miss Swanson. There were offers of roles like Norma Desmond, but she turned them all down. Paramount proposed to put her in *Darling, How Could You!* (1951). However, she refused to test—an idea she thought was impertinent—and Joan Fontaine got the part. Hedda Hopper suggested Frances Parkinson Keyes' best-selling novel *Dinner at Antoine's* as a follow-up movie. Swanson declined, saying that she "couldn't possibly play the mother of an eighteen-year-old daughter." She was then a grandmother.*

*She did end up doing *Three for Bedroom C* (1952) as the mother of a young child, and *Nero's Big Weekend* (1955), as Nero's mother, in Italy.

However, even though *Sunset Boulevard* did not restore Miss Swanson to any lasting favor with the studios, it was in every sense her ultimate triumph, her masterwork. Her scintillating portrayal of the bitter, neurotic Norma Desmond was a feat unmatched by any star returning to pictures after a prolonged absence. "The signature of the artist is all over her performance," said critic Richard Griffith.

Tea and
Symphaty

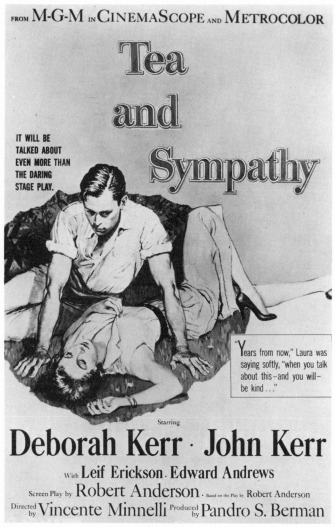

Newspaper ads for *Tea and Sympathy*, which dealt with the delicate
theme of homosexuality, showed the play's memorable final scene.

Tea and Sympathy
(1956)

Directed by Vincente Minnelli. Screenplay, Robert Anderson, based on his play. Camera, John Alton. Editor, Ferris Webster. Music, Adolph Deutsch. Art directors, William A. Horning and Edward Carfagno. Produced by Pandro S. Berman. MGM. 122 minutes.

Laura Reynolds	*Deborah Kerr*
Tom Robinson Lee	*John Kerr*
Bill Reynolds	*Leif Erickson*
Herb Lee	*Edward Andrews*
Al	*Darryl Hickman*
Ellie Martin	*Norma Crane*
Ollie	*Dean Jones*
Lilly Sears	*Jacqueline de Wit*
Ralph	*Tom Laughlin*
Steve	*Ralph Votrian*
Phil	*Stephen Terrell*
Ted	*Kip King*
Henry	*Jimmy Hayes*
Roger	*Richard Tyler*
Vic	*Don Burnett*

Laura (Deborah Kerr) does her best to instill confidence in troubled Tom (John Kerr).

One of Hollywood's memorable closing lines—or near-closing lines, as it turned out—came in MGM's adaptation of the Robert Anderson play *Tea and Sympathy.*

Deborah Kerr plays a prep school housemaster's wife who sympathizes with a sensitive student haunted by the thought that he may be homosexual. His classmates cruelly taunt him, and even Deborah's own husband gives him no solace until he is driven to the brink of emotional crisis.

However, she is determined to see that he isn't shaken by doubts that will leave him psychologically crippled. The only way she can accomplish this, she decides, is to give herself to him. At the end of the movie, as she takes his hand and looks deeply into his eyes, she tells the youth, "Years from now, when you talk about this—and you will—be kind."

Tea and Sympathy was Anderson's first Broadway play. Nevertheless, he was anything but an overnight success. A Harvard graduate, he taught playwriting at the American Theatre Wing in New York City, and then wrote more than seventy radio and television shows, mostly play adaptations. In

one year, he produced twenty-five such scripts. But his goal had always been the theatre. Therefore, in between teaching and doing radio and television work, he wrote original plays. He did fourteen of them without a single New York City production. "So I tried one more," Anderson said. "And it worked."

Tea and Sympathy ran for 720 performances during its ninety-one-week run on Broadway and continued on the road for an additional thirty-five weeks. Miss Kerr, in the starring role, became as acclaimed on stage as she was in pictures, John Kerr (no relation) blossomed forth as an outstanding new star, and Anderson was established as a ranking playwright. He was later to write, among other works, the plays *You Know I Can't Hear You When the Water's Running* and *I Never Sang for My Father* (later a movie), plus the screenplay for *The Nun's Story* (1959) and *The Sand Pebbles* (1966).

When MGM bought the movie rights to *Tea and Sympathy,* it kept the stage team intact. Anderson, then thirty-four, was signed to do the screenplay, and its original stars, Deborah Kerr, John Kerr, and Leif Erickson, were recruited to repeat their roles, and Vincente Minnelli was picked to direct.

Even before the cast came to Hollywood, they anticipated the problem of censorship. In a letter to Minnelli, Deborah Kerr, then touring in the play, said she had heard that the movie might have difficulties with the Breen Office because the story dealt with the delicate subject of homosexuality. If that were so, she said, she felt it quite ironic. "Adultery is O.K. Impotence is O.K. But perversion is their *béte noire.*"

Miss Kerr maintained that homosexuality was not the play's underlying point. "It really is a play about persecution of the individual, and compassion and pity and love of one human being for another in crisis."

Anderson, too, had always played down the homosexual aspect. "The accusation made against this boy, who did not quite fit in with the crowd, could have been applied to any number of other things," Anderson said. "The point is a guy has to be allowed to lead his own life, to part his hair on the right side or the left, whichever he wants to. There has to be room in the world for the off-horse."

Despite these disclaimers, homosexuality was, in fact, an intricate part of the play, and it was an issue that had to be dealt with in shaping the movie. The Production Code clearly stated: "Sex perversion, or any inference of it, is forbidden."

The Breen Office, Minnelli said, insisted that a prologue and epilogue be added to show that the wife is punished for her acts. "We gritted our teeth," Minnelli said. In the end, MGM acquiesced to the censors.

These were the major changes:

—The movie left out the schoolmaster's fear of his own latent homosexuality. This only weakened and confused the character. In the play, his fear of a "taint" of femininity within himself drives him to wear a belligerent macho mask. It is his own self-doubt that clearly motivates his persecution of the boy. Since all this is omitted from the picture, movie audiences could only link his hatred of the student with jealousy—the school master's envy of the close relationship between his wife and the boy.

—Less drastic but as mindless was a change in the climactic scene with the wife and the student— moving from the privacy of his bedroom to a moonlit woods. Also, the play ended as the wife leaned

Tom's father (Edward Andrews) cannot understand why his son isn't a "regular guy." He makes Tom call his dramatics coach and give up a girl's part in the school play.

Instead of muscular pursuits, Tom chooses the non-contact game of tennis and plays it with clever cuts and lobs instead of aggressive serves and volleys.

over the boy, unfastening her shirt-front blouse. In the picture, the unbuttoning business was excised.

—The major change was the addition of the prologue and epilogue, showing the student, now a man, returning to school ten years later. He learns that the wife's act of compassion has had a drastic effect on her life. It is a jarring final scene and casts a deadly pall of remorse over the film. Ironically, Minnelli said he later saw a French version of the play starring Ingrid Bergman. It was produced only after great debate, Minnelli said, for from the French view, the conflict was not easily seen. "So the boy thinks he's a homosexual," the French producer told Minnelli. "And the wife of the headmaster gives herself to him to prove that he's not. But what is the problem?"

Despite the changes, the theme of homosexuality is still implicit in the film—the youth is called "sister boy"—and the over-all impact is that of a moving, forceful picture. If the play's values are not abandoned, it is helped in no small way by the expert characterizations by the two Kerrs and Erickson.

Set in a New England boys' school, the movie opens at a class reunion as Tom Lee (John Kerr) visits his old quarters and reminisces. In a flashback to his student days, we see him dash from his room to help Laura Reynolds (Deborah Kerr) with her gardening. They are great friends, and she is constantly touched as well as amused by his puppy-like devotion.

This bright scene only hides painful undercurrents sweeping through Tom. Because his ways are different—he wears his hair long, walks with a light gait, and likes classical music and poetry instead of athletics—he suffers the ridicule of classmates. At a school battle royale, pitting new boys against old boys, his classmates haze him by form-

Leif Erickson played Laura's husband who was preoccupied with mountain climbing and macho pursuits. With Erickson are Kerr and Andrews.

ing a ring around him so that "sister boy" won't get roughed up. Bill Reynolds (Leif Erickson), Tom's housemaster, who makes an obsession of mountain climbing and muscular pursuits, thinks that Tom is getting his just deserts.

All of this distresses Laura, who tries her best to comfort and reassure Tom. That only draws a rebuke from her husband who asserts that the boys have to learn to overcome their difficulties themselves. A housemaster's wife, Bill tells her, has to be a disinterested bystander. "All you're supposed to do is . . . give the boys a little tea and sympathy." Laura tells him that she thinks their marriage is drifting, but Bill only glosses over her dissatisfaction.

Meanwhile, the ribbing of Tom never ceases. The kids scrawl nasty epithets on the door to his room. They gradually shun him and put pressure on his roommate Al (Darryl Hickman) to move out.

Tom's father (Edward Andrews), an active alumnus, comes to the school. A hail-fellow-well-met type, he is puzzled that his son is not a "regular

guy." Before his visit ends, he makes Tom give up a girl's part in the school play.

That only adds to Tom's torment, which comes to a head when he decides to prove his manhood with the town trollop (Norma Crane). Even though he risks being kicked out of school, he calls her for a date. The idea proves to be a disaster, for he is repelled by her, and his clumsy sexual efforts wind up in a fiasco.

The affair leads to Tom's expulsion and a bitter encounter between the housemaster and his wife. Laura wants Bill to defend Tom, but he won't. In fact, he says that he thinks expulsion is the right course.

It is at this point in the play that Laura discloses she is aware of Bill's own weakness. She tells him that he never really wanted a wife and that he is persecuting in Tom the very thing he fears in himself. Because this is cut out in the movie, when Laura goes to Tom in his moment of deep humiliation, we wonder if her act is motivated as much by altruism as by her own unhappiness. That is, there is some doubt that her act is totally sacrificial because it is not clear that she herself may not be craving emotional release or vengeance on her husband.

At any rate, she tells Tom that last night was no test of virility because he wasn't in love. "One day, you'll meet a girl and it will be all right."

And so follows the poignant scene that ended the play.

In the movie epilogue, we see Tom return to school at an alumni affair. He is ten years older, married, and a successful author. From his old housemaster, he gets a letter Laura left for him in which she tells him that her indiscretion brought about the end of her marriage. This tacked-on ending is all wrong. Bosley Crowther, the *New York Times* critic, advised moviegoers to leave after Miss Kerr delivered her famous line, "Years from now. . . ."

As a kind of postscript, it is interesting, I think, to note that in interviews in the 1950s, Anderson insisted that the movie was not autobiographical. However, a decade later, he told Rex Reed a somewhat different story.

"I guess it was autobiographical, in spirit if not in fact," Anderson said. "Some of my problems with my father were reflected in the role of the husband. I had also been very lonely at prep school (Exeter), the way all people are lonely when they are young, and I had been in love with an older woman."

Like Tom in the movie, Anderson returned to Exeter, his old prep school. "I was afraid they'd never let me back," he said. "I went there to give a talk and said, 'I hope this play hasn't caused you any embarrassment.' And the housemaster's wife where I lived said, 'Nobody has been so kind as to call me Laura.' What a wonderful thing to say."

That's My Boy

Jerry Lewis, playing myopic weakling Junior Jackson, is sandwiched between leading ladies Marion Marshall and Polly Bergen.

That's My Boy
(1951)

Directed by Hal Walker. Story and screenplay, Cy Howard. Camera, Lee Garmes. Editor, Warren Low. Music score, Leigh Harline. New song, Jay Livingston, Ray Evans. Songs include: "Ballin' the Jack," "I'm in the Mood for Love," "Ridgeville Fight Song." Produced by Hal B. Wallis. Paramount. 98 minutes.

Bill Baker	Dean Martin
"Junior" Jackson	Jerry Lewis
Ann Jackson	Ruth Hussey
"Jarrin' Jack" Jackson	Eddie Mayehoff
Terry Howard	Marion Marshall
Betty Hunter	Polly Bergen
Coach Wheeler	Hugh Sanders
Benjamin Green	John McIntire
Henry Baker	Francis Pierlot
May (Maid)	Lillian Randolph
Doc Hunter	Selmer Jackson
Sports Announcer	Tom Harmon

Jerry trips the light fantastic with Chester Conklin, a former Keystone Kop, while Marie Wilson looks on in *My Friend Irma Goes West* (1950). It was the Martin-Lewis team's second movie. They made eighteen pictures before splitting in 1956.

Ⓞne of them was a frenetic, rubber-faced clown. The other was a lazy, likeable crooner. Together, they clicked with a spontaneous quality that won them loyal audiences—first in nightclubs, then in the movies. The public enjoyed the way they played off each other with a free-wheeling, spoofing humor. By their fifth picture, their films had catapulted them into the gilt-edged circle of top-grossing movies.

Then, one day, they stunned their fans, when at the height of their career they split up. Movie columnists predicted that they would quickly become has-beens. But they confounded their critics. They both rose to loftier heights, rocketing to such fame that they became superstars of the 1960s and millionaires many times over in the 1970s.

The frenetic guy, Jerry Lewis, ended up as a versatile money-making talent. He became a comic lionized by European critics (who would compare him to Keaton and Chaplin), a producer and director, a college lecturer, a chain movie-theater owner, a restaurateur, and a tireless campaigner for charity.

The lazy guy, Dean Martin, established himself as a low-key comedian in his own right, a dramatic actor, and a TV success whose weekly network show stayed on the tube for a decade. He also became a successful recording star and owner of part of the famous Sands Hotel in Las Vegas, a Lake Tahoe lodge, and a restaurant, Dino's, on Hollywood's Sunset Strip.

How did they do it? There's no single answer.

Martin attracted audiences because he is a big, darkly handsome charmer with a lazy baritone voice. People liked him, too, because he didn't seem to take himself or life very seriously. He cultivated the image of a generous, fun-loving boozer, a woman chaser, and a swinger.* And late at night when his TV show flickered on, he touched a responsive chord among the nation's army of viewers seeking to relax and forget their workaday tensions.

To many, Lewis' rise to fame is the more baffling

*In point of fact, Martin insists he really is not a heavy drinker. Unless he is working at Las Vegas, he says he is usually in bed by 10 P.M.

enigma. Critics in France and England consistently praise his work as first-rate social satire, and an organization of French film writers voted one of his pictures, *The Nutty Professor* (1963), the best movie of the year. Twice, Lewis has been named director of the year in that country.*

Yet he has never won a receptive audience among discriminating adults in his own country, nor has he gotten a favorable press from critics. The most common complaint is that his humor is erratic, but the gripes are as long as a laundry list. He has been called self-conscious, shallow, vulgar, grotesque, and egotistical. His movies—which are devoted entirely to himself—are uneven, weakly plotted, and strained.

"The sad thing is that he has all the makings of a good clown," said critic Dwight Macdonald, "if only he didn't always give it 'the works.'" Said Mike McGrady, former columnist for *Newsday:* "When he is good, he is excruciatingly funny. When he is bad, he is excruciating." Lewis is the only American comedian doing slapstick. But, says Andrew Sarris, he still hasn't put together "one comically coherent work of art."

If critics are still pondering the secret of Martin and Lewis' success, there is no secret about where it all started. They first teamed up in a New Jersey cabaret in 1946.

Lewis, who had been doing an act mimicking celebrities by synchronizing his lip movements to their records, was the son of vaudevillians. Born Joseph Levitch in Newark, New Jersey, in 1926, he followed his parents to the borscht circuit in the summers. Before he was seventeen he dropped out of school to launch a showbiz career of his own. His stage name became a modification of his parents' names—Rea and Danny Lewis.

Martin, a barber's son, born Dino Crocetti in Steubenville, Ohio, in 1917, was, like Lewis, a high school dropout.** He had a checkered career before he became an entertainer. He was a gas station attendant, a gambling house croupier, and a boxer. As a welterweight, he won twenty-four out of thirty bouts, but a broken nose cut short his ring aspirations and he had plastic surgery.

Martin had always loved to sing. So he changed his name and worked in nightspots around his hometown. Later he toured with bands, and then moved on to nightclubs as a single.

Martin and Lewis' famous first meeting actually took place in New York City. They appeared as separate acts until they were booked at the 500 Club in Atlantic City. Their first routine reportedly was a flop. However, when they started doing an impromptu act—Lewis would clown around the stage and try to break Martin up as he sang—audiences howled. They began to trade insults and ad libs, squirting seltzer water and wandering onto the floor to trip passing waiters. In eight months, their salaries jumped from $350 to $3,500 a week.

Soon they appeared at the Copacabana in New York, on television, and in nightclubs throughout the country. Hal Wallis saw them at Slapsie Maxie's in Hollywood and signed them to a five-year contract.

Wallis billed them fifth and sixth in their first movie, *My Friend Irma* (1949), based on Marie Wilson's radio series, but they stole the picture. Bosley Crowther found "genuine comic quality" in Lewis' antics. From 1949 to 1956, they made sixteen movies. None won critical acclaim, but they drew enthusiastic audiences, mostly composed of youngsters. Eventually fan clubs sprang up and Martin and Lewis quickly supplanted Abbott and Costello as the nation's top comedy duo.

All this time, however, there was a dissonant undercurrent in their private relationship. Martin, nine years older, felt that he was playing second fiddle and that the partnership never gave him a chance to exploit his own talent. Some say he also thought that Lewis took himself too seriously.

For his part, Lewis disliked Martin's casual attitude, feeling that his partner didn't work hard enough. No reason was given when they split up in 1956.† However, insiders felt that Martin would have the harder time as a single.

In fact, Martin's first picture, *Ten Thousand Bedrooms* (1957), was a failure, and his movie offers soon dried up. However, he stayed on the Hollywood scene and wangled the part of the Broadway soldier in *The Young Lions* (1958). He

*One theory for Lewis' high regard overseas is that his pictures' often inane dialogue is not understood. He is, in effect, being seen as a pantomimist. "Lewis should be seen," said film critic Andrew Sarris, "not heard." Another theory, espoused by French writer Jean-Pierre Coursodon, holds that U.S. critics were not prepared to deal with Lewis because he was exploiting a slapstick style popularized by silent comedians, a genre that they thought had had its day. "The merit of the French critics," said Coursodon, "was their willingness to look at what Lewis was doing as a filmmaker, rather than with some preconception of what film comedy should be."

Unlike Lewis, who has married only once, Martin has had three wives: his childhood friend, Betty McDonald (1940-1949); former model Jeanne Bigger (1949-1972); and former model Catherine Mae (Kathy) Hawn (1973-). Martin, who has seven children by his first two wives, was fifty-five when he married the twenty-five-year-old Miss Hawn.

†The final parting of the ways reportedly came over *The Delicate Delinquent* (1957), a film whose script Lewis had written. When Martin refused to play the part of a policeman, Lewis said matter of factly, "We'll have to get somebody else." Martin coolly replied: "Start looking."

scored a surprise hit and followed it with two more first-rate dramatic performances in *Some Came Running* (1959) and *Rio Bravo* (1959).*

Thereafter, Martin had little trouble getting film parts. He made one after another—the *Matt Helm* series, *Texas Across the River* (1966), *Bandolero* (1968)—though few of them were particularly distinguished. Then came an outstanding coup, a fabulous deal he made for *Airport* (1970). He took no salary, working instead for ten percent of the gross. This weak film, for some reason, became a box office smash and earned $7 million for Martin—believed to be the biggest actor's take for a single movie. However, Martin's major outlet became television, not movies. In 1965 he started a variety show on NBC. He sang, danced, displayed an engaging sense of humor, and established himself as one of television's major stars.

Ironically, television was the one medium in which Lewis was not able to score any sustained success. He did guest appearances in which he showed himself to be a master of the impromptu one-liner. But an attempt at his own continuing program—a two-hour live network comedy show—failed dismally.

Whether Lewis fared better in his movies is also open to debate. After the 1956 Martin breakup through 1974, he appeared in thirty movies. Most of them did brisk box office business, but some feel that this is their only claim to fame.**

At first Lewis used Darren McGavin as his foil, replacing Martin in *The Delicate Delinquent* (1957). But gradually he struck out entirely on his own, taking over as producer, director, and eventually writer of his own movies.† On the plus side, his versatile talent gave him total control of his pictures. On the negative side, it meant that he was not subject to any discipline except his own. For example, decisions have to be made on where to cut a comedy sequence so that it does not lose its sparkle by running too long. When the director and

the star are the same person, the system of checks and balances can be upset. Many felt that Lewis the director at times was too indulgent with Lewis the actor.

Nevertheless, Lewis ground out two films a year, pegging them around a gawky simpleton known variously as The Idiot, The Nut Kid, and The Little Fellow. "At his best," said columnist Mike McGrady, "the Nut Kid reflects the integrity and innocence of a child suddenly tossed into an adult world of grown-ups; at his worst, shallow stupidity."

Some say that he has no equal in the extensive comic vocabulary expressed in his face. His features are so mobile and eccentric and his pantomime is sometimes so brightly conceived that he can bring belly laughs to any audience in the world. French critic Robert Benayoun calls him "the finest comic artist since Buster Keaton."

What sets Lewis apart from the truly great movie comedians like Keaton and Chaplin is his penchant to rush through a shooting. He often shows up on a set without knowing his lines, ad-libbing as he goes along. He will, as often as not, settle for a first take. Sometimes it works, adding spontaneity to the picture. Often, it just doesn't play. "His range from excellent to awful," said critic John Crosby, "is probably faster than anyone else's in the business."

Newsweek critic Charles Michener once expressed his own disenchantment with Lewis like this: "At the age of nine, I knew there was something exquisitely forbidden about laughing at Jerry Lewis. I first saw him as a parking lot attendant in *My Friend Irma*, scampering across the tops of parked cars and plunging feet first through the canvas of a convertible—and I cracked up. 'Dreadful,' my parents said of Jerry. . . . It was the best recommendation anyone could have made.

"Ten years later, I couldn't stand Jerry Lewis. Now on his own, he seemed mindless and mawkish in *Rock-a-Bye Baby* (1958) and tiresome in *Cinderfella* (1960). . . . I had joined my parents."

Yet, no one can deny Lewis' appeal to the young.†† And certainly when the movies of the 1950s are brought to mind, they have to include a Jerry Lewis picture. One of the best from the Dean Martin days was *That's My Boy*.

As the picture opens, the camera shows us a two-story home in a pleasant, small-town community. The camera zooms in on a mailbox with a metal football affixed over the name "Jarrin' Jack"

---

*Martin also kept making records. He made his first major breakthrough with "That's Amore," which sold more than three million copies. Thereafter, he earned a dozen gold discs. He was also a hit in Las Vegas. By the time he started his network TV series, he already had become a top solo headliner.

**The best Lewis-directed opuses, in my opinion, are: *The Bellboy* (1960), *The Errand Boy* (1961), *The Nutty Professor* (1963), *The Patsy* (1964), and *Three on a Couch* (1966).

†His commercial success also supports his lavish tastes. Lewis, who is married to the former Patti Palmer (who used to sing with Jimmy Dorsey's band), and has six sons, lives in a thirty-one-room mansion in Bel Air outside Los Angeles. The house, once owned by Louis B. Mayer, has seventeen bathrooms and reportedly cost $350,000. Lewis has equipped it with expensive film and recording equipment which he often uses to edit his own movies.

††Lewis once explained his popularity with kids this way: "I get paid for doing what children are punished for. . . . In doing this, I help the audience get rid of its hostility." Said one fourteen-year-old: "Kids love him [Lewis] because he's one of us."

Jerry and Dean get mixed up with ghosts and haunted castles in *Scared Stiff* (1953), a remake of *Ghost Breakers* (1940), a Bob Hope vehicle. In the background is Lizabeth Scott.

Jackson. Then it pans through a bedroom window where, under a blanket that says "All-American Jackson," a hefty, middle-aged man (Eddie Mayehoff) rises to greet the morning.

Jackson, an aging jock, is a caricature of a gridiron star twenty years later. He starts the day with a shower, the cold water going full blast, all the while singing his college football song, "Stand up and cheer for Ridgeville. Hail the red and blue. . . ."

As he starts his exercises, his wife (Ruth Hussey) calls him for breakfast. "Another thirty-five push-ups and I'll be right down," he answers. Even as Jackson's baritone echoes downstairs, we hear about the offspring of this Neanderthal.

"Is young Junior going to have breakfast with us, Miz Jackson?" asks the maid (Lillian Randolph).

"I think so," Mrs. Jackson says. "I hope he gets back from the doctor in time."

"Not sick again?"

"Nothing serious. Just his old trouble, his eyes. And what with this rainy weather, his sinuses have been none too good."

Dad whizzes downstairs via the banister. "Pretty

good shape for a man of forty-one," he roars. "Still could get out on the football field at Ridgeville U. and make those youngsters watch their step. . . . The kids today just don't play guts football."

Suddenly, inspired, he enlists the aid of his wife and maid to run off a play and slams into his son Junior (Lewis) coming in the front door. Junior, of course, is the antithesis of his father—skinny, awkward, and myopic. For good measure, he wears braces.

The disparity between father and son is underscored that night at the high school graduation dance. Bill Baker (Martin), the school's top athlete, is called up to the stage for a picture. "That's my son Bill," says someone. Jarrin' Jack looks around to see a tiny, bald man with a chronic cough and a wheeze.

"This heredity business is all cockeyed," Jackson mumbles.*

*In this Martin and Lewis picture—the fourth of eighteen they did together—the pair was not on-camera as much as in later efforts. The emphasis was more on plot and gave other actors a chance to share the spotlight. In this case, Mayehoff all but stole the show.

Also called to the stage is Betty Hunter (Polly Bergen), the most beautiful girl in the class. The principal then summons Junior, but when he steps alongside Betty and Bill, the principal pulls him back. "No, not for the picture," the principal says. "I want you to hold the flash."

When the dancing starts, poor Junior has no partner. He asks an old maid teacher to dance and then launches into a wild, herky-jerky solo when the band plays a hot number. The teacher's frowning looks cut short Junior's antics, but this sequence foreshadows some of Lewis' later routines.

Junior gets to borrow his dad's car to take Betty home. However, his romantic notions are squelched when she brings along Bill Baker. While Junior chauffeurs them through the park, they neck in the back seat, and Bill croons, "I'm in the Mood for Love."

The next day, Ridgeville University football coach Wheeler (Hugh Sanders) pays a call on Junior's dad at his plant. On his desk is his motto, "Guts is what counts." The coach says that Ridgeville has a chance for the championship if it can recruit Baker. The only trouble is that Baker doesn't have the money to go to college. Will Jarrin' Jack finance his education?

"On one condition," he says. "You've got to see that my son makes the team and gets a letter." The deal clinched, Jackson calls in Bill Baker and asks him to be Junior's roommate. "Maybe you could inspire him to be an athlete. You know, the strong looking out for the weak."

At Ridgeville, Baker and Junior have a little difficulty adjusting to each other. Baker is taken aback by Junior's one piece pajamas. "What are you trying to do, grow up to be a rabbit?"

But Junior soon warms up to Baker and proudly shows him his vast inventory of medications— nasal sprays, vitamins, tranquilizers, and pills. "If you ever have sinus trouble, this stuff will clear it up in a minute," Junior says. "Just two drops in each nostril and you'll breathe again." Junior demonstrates and suddenly starts a coughing fit. "Of course a little will trickle down your throat," he explains. "But I have a pill for that."

When they go to bed, Junior nearly drives Baker to distraction by insisting on switching beds three times because he feels a draft. Then they battle over whether the window stays up or down. Baker grins and bears it.

At football practice, Baker is a standout. Junior, as expected, is pitiful. When he reports, thick glasses and all, the coach looks at him and offers some advice: "The Ping-Pong team needs an anchor man." But when the coach learns who Jun-

ior is, he remembers his bargain.

"Must you wear glasses?" the coach asks.

"Oh, no sir," says Junior. "Only when I want to see."*

Terry Howard (Marion Marshall), Bill Baker's campus sweetheart, gives Junior a pep talk. She tells him that confidence is all a matter of building up one's ego. "You've got to believe in yourself. You've got to keep saying, 'I'm big, I'm big.'" When Junior says it, it comes out, "I'm big???"

Junior's dad shows up at the first game and gives him his old jersey. "Live up to number 66," he says. Late in the game after Baker's spectacular running has secured Ridgeville's victory, the coach finally puts Junior in.

To his Dad's everlasting embarrassment, Junior proceeds to do everything wrong. First, he takes too much time in the huddle and the team is penalized five yards. Then he is snowed under and fumbles. Finally he loses his glasses, runs the wrong way, and scores for the other side. "Believe me, ladies and gentlemen, Junior Jackson is nothing like his father," says the radio announcer (Tom Harmon, former Michigan All-American). "He'll win games—but for the other team."

At home after the game, Jarrin' Jack is berating himself. "How did my own son do this to me? The son of Jack Jackson disgraces himself. Is there anything worse?"

"Yes," his wife says. "He could have been a criminal."

At this point, the movie makes an abrupt switch. Its comedic line suddenly dissolves and it starts taking itself seriously.

Junior decides to quit school so that he won't shame his father anymore. But Terry, even though she is Baker's girl, asks him to keep plugging. Junior agrees to do so if she will wear his fraternity pin. "It'll give me a reason to stay," he says.

Day after day, Junior takes extra practice with Baker and Terry. A dummy knocks him flat. Sometimes, the hard knocks discourage him. "Is this good for me? Then how come I'm getting nauseous?" But he keeps plugging.

The climax comes at the homecoming game. Baker can't play. He's had a tiff with Terry over her attentions directed toward Junior, gotten drunk, and been kicked out of school. Without Baker, Ridgeville has no real offense. Wilton College is leading 7-0 with a couple of minutes left.

*Some other Lewis one-liners from later flicks were: (Lewis to Martin) "I knew you'd do the right thing. After all, we're cousins. Your mother and my mother were mothers." (Lewis to Martin after Martin asks him to sing): "With my voice, if I sing 'The Star-Spangled Banner,' they'd arrest me as an enemy agent."

Finally, the coach decides to give Junior a chance. Just before he goes in, Terry runs over to him and makes a confession. She tells him that she's been going with him only to help build his confidence. She's really Bill's girl, and Bill's been expelled all because of a misunderstanding. The only way Junior can make amends, she says, is to go out and show everybody that he can stand on his own two feet.

Junior pulls on Bill's jersey and dashes out on the field. On the first play, he starts back toward his own goal, then suddenly cuts back, reverses field, and with the cheers of a million kids ringing out at Saturday matinees all over the nation, he darts through the entire Wilton team.

That makes it 7-6. The extra point fails. But with seconds left, Junior is back in the game to try a field goal. Up goes the pigskin, end over end, through the uprights, and Ridgeville wins 9-7.

At the football dance, Junior proudly shows his varsity letter to his dad, but Jarrin' Jack doesn't seem particularly pleased. There is a kind of mind reversal as he says: "Son, you've taught me there are more important things in life than football."

Just then a group of students surrounds Junior, asking for his autograph. One of them says that he's going out for football next year. Could Junior give him some advice?

"Well, there are three things to remember when you play football," Junior says, his voice resonating like his Dad's. "You hit 'em low. You hit 'em fast. And you hit 'em hard. And if they get up, you hit 'em again. Yes, sir, you've got to play guts football."

Dad is all smiles. He puts his huge hand around Junior and off they walk, arm in arm. "That's my boy," says Jarrin' Jack.

The Third Man

Holly Martins (Joseph Cotten) waits at the Ferris wheel in Vienna's famous amusement park, the Prater.

The Third Man
(1950)

Directed by Carol Reed. Screenplay by Graham Greene. Director of photography, Robert Krasker.* Edited by Oswald Hafenrichter. Sound, John Cox. Zither music by Anton Karas. Art director, Vincent Korda. A British Lion release of the Alexander Korda-David O. Selznick-London Films production. 104 minutes.

Holly Martins	*Joseph Cotten*
Anna Schmidt	*Alida Valli*
Harry Lime	*Orson Welles*
Major Calloway	*Trevor Howard*
Sergeant Paine	*Bernard Lee*
Porter	*Paul Hoerbiger*
Porter's Wife	*Annie Rosar*
"Baron" Kurtz	*Ernst Deutsch*
Dr. Winkel	*Erich Ponto*
Mr. Popesco	*Siegfried Breuer*
Crabbin	*Wilfrid Hyde-White*
Anna's Landlady	*Hedwig Bleibtreu*
Hansl	*Herbert Halbik*
Brodsky	*Alexis Chesakov*
Hall Porter at Sacher's	*Paul Hardtmuth*

*Academy Award Winner.

Police take Anna (Alida Valli) into custody for having a forged passport as she turns with pleading eyes toward British Major Calloway (Trevor Howard). Sergeant Paine (Bernard Lee) holds briefcase.

He isn't seen until halfway through the movie. He appears in only one extended scene of dialogue. And he is killed off at the end.

Nevertheless, Orson Welles' portrayal of Harry Lime in *The Third Man** has become the most memorable character role of the 1950s. Yet it took all the persuasion that director Carol Reed could muster to get Welles accepted for the part. Then, when Reed finally pulled it off, he faced another sales task. He had to convince Welles himself to do the famous chase scene in the Vienna sewers.

As Reed remembered, he wanted Joseph Cotten, Alida Valli, and Welles for the picture. David O. Selznick, the co-producer, was agreeable to Cotten and Valli, who were under contract to him, but not to Welles. Also, Reed recalled, Welles had once paid a little too much attention to Mrs. Selznick (Jennifer Jones). Selznick wanted Noel Coward to play Harry Lime.

"Of course, that would have been disastrous," Reed said. "It [the argument] went on and on. . . .

*The movie won the Best British Film Award, and the Grand Prix for best feature film in the 1949 International Film Festival at Cannes. Although it was made and shown in Europe that year, it was not released in the United States until 1950.

When I started the film, Selznick was still going on about Noel. But Alexander Korda (the film's co-producer) didn't care. So in the end, I got Orson."

It was Welles who wrote the colorful and justly renowned speech about the Swiss cuckoo clock. He also turned in what some critics feel was his best performance after *Citizen Kane* (1941).

Moreover, Reed said, Welles, despite his reputation as a temperamental actor, was easy to work with—that is, except for the underground manhunt sequence. It was shot on location the day Welles arrived—several weeks after filming had started. Reed took him right down to the sewers, and Welles immediately balked.

In an interview with Charles Thomas Samuels for his book *Encountering Directors*, Reed recalled their conversation.

Welles: Carol, I can't play this part.
Reed: What's the matter?
Welles: I can't do it. I can't work in a sewer. I come from California. . . .
Reed: Look, Orson, in the time it's taking to talk about this, you can do a shot. All you do is stand there, look off, see some police after

367

you, turn and run away. . . ."

Welles: Carol, get someone else to play this. I cannot work under such conditions.

Reed: Orson, Orson. We're lit for you. Just stand there.

Welles: (Finally relenting) All right. But do it quickly.

With that, Reed said, Welles dashed into the sewers. The next moment, Welles was shouting, "Don't cut the cameras. I'm coming back." Then Welles began improvising, rushing through the waters, running beneath a cascade and emerging dripping wet.

"With Orson, everything has to be a drama," said Reed. "But there were no arguments of any sort at all."

The idea for *The Third Man* came from Korda. He was pleased with Reed's and author Graham Greene's collaborative effort for his film *The Fallen Idol* (1948), a superb drama of an adult's world as seen through the eyes of a child. He wanted them to stay together as a team, so he asked Greene to do a scenario for Reed about the four-power occupation of Vienna.

For years Greene had been intrigued by the opening sentence of an unfinished story he had written on the flap of an envelope. It read: "I had paid my last farewell to Harry a week ago, when his coffin was lowered into the frozen February ground, so that it was with incredulity that I saw him pass by, without a sign of recognition, among the host of strangers in the Strand."

Greene had always wanted to flesh out the idea of a dead man turning up alive. Korda gave him the chance to pursue the tracks of Harry Lime in Vienna.

Script preparation went smoothly. Greene wrote a story and then turned it into a movie script. At this point Reed joined him, and they went over and over every line together, acting out scenes while they revised and cut.

One of the few major disagreements came over the ending. "I held the view," Greene said, "that an entertainment of this kind, which in England we call a thriller, was too light an affair to carry the weight of an unhappy ending."

So in Greene's version, Anna, the mistress of Welles, took the arm of Joseph Cotten, the awkward hero, and they walked off together from the cemetery. In Reed's closing scene, Anna walked scornfully by Cotten, avoiding his confused, unbelieving eyes.

Selznick supported Greene's version. Reed argued that the whole point of Anna's character was

that she had experienced a "fatal love and then along comes this silly American." Reed later told an interviewer: "At one time it was thought that every picture must end with an embrace so that the audience could go home happy. But I don't think that's so. A picture should end as it has to. I don't think anything in life ends 'right.' "

Greene eventually deferred to Reed's judgment and now agrees that the years have proven Reed "triumphantly right." Said Greene: "I had not given enough consideration to the mastery of Reed's direction. And, at that state, of course, neither of us could have anticipated Reed's brilliant discovery of Mr. [Anton] Karas, the zither player."

Reed found Karas playing in a tiny Viennese beer and sausage restaurant. He had never heard a zither before, but he thought that its sounds were attractive, and he decided to use the forty-stringed box instrument for background music. In doing so, he abandoned a completed orchestral score which had already been written and recorded for the sound track. Reed felt the zither's sad-sweet melody was so unique that it offered him a chance to weave it into the film—almost as an additional character. In fact, its twanging, zinging sounds followed the plot closely. Its phrases and chords matched the dialogue and movement as if it were a commentator on the action.*

Reed was also able to tell Karas exactly where and how he wanted certain types of musical passages. "For example, in the cat scene," Reed said, "I asked him to play a few sort of walking notes while the cat crossed the street and then, as it looked at Harry's shoes, ascending chords, which break into 'The Third Man Theme' when it finally sees Harry, and we hold on the cat's little face.

"That's the advantage of working with a single instrument. Usually, I talk to my composer, saying, 'You know, we should have something romantic here.' Then, after three or four weeks, he comes to me, plays the piano, and says, 'Here's what the drums are going to do,' and then, 'The strings are doing this.' It doesn't mean a bloody thing to me. I just cross my fingers but don't know until we get to the first recording session, when it's too late to change."

Music was only one of the many elements that helped make *The Third Man* a masterpiece in its genre. It brought together all the elements of a classic thriller—a gripping, fast-moving plot, a first-rate

*After the movie opened to international acclaim, Karas became a local hero. Before Reed found him, he was playing for a small salary plus tips. When Karas' "The Third Man Theme" became a worldwide hit, his fee rocketed to $1,600 a week, and he was booked for months in advance.

cast and director, and realistic-style filming. Reed's imaginative use of Vienna's baroque architecture, its narrow, winding streets, and its gloomy bombed-out rubble made a perfect setting for the picture's twisting, Byzantine-like plot.*

Reed also made deft use of off-angles, filming some sequences with the camera slightly askew. "I intended it," said Reed, "to make the audience uncomfortable."**

The picture opens in the uncertain days after World War II when Austria was still under Allied army occupation. Holly Martins (Cotten), a pulp Western writer, comes to Vienna in response to a vague job offer from an old school friend, Harry Lime (Welles). He is shocked to find that he has arrived just in time for Lime's funeral after an accident.

Only a few people are at the graveside—two men in heavy overcoats, a young lady, and a British major named Calloway (Trevor Howard). Calloway offers Martins a ride back to the city and gives him his second shock. He says that Martins' chum, Lime, was a racketeer wanted by the police. Martins, who has never even imagined anything about these alleged darker tendencies of his pal, refuses to believe Calloway's story. Instead, he decides to stay in Vienna to clear his friend's reputation.

His first stop is the Mozart Cafe, one of Harry's favorite haunts, where Martins meets "Baron" Kurtz (Ernst Deutsch), who says he was a friend of Lime.† Kurtz, a seedy aristocrat who has fallen on

hard times like many others in the war-torn city, denies knowing anything about any racket Lime was mixed up with. In response to Martins' request, he reluctantly takes him to the accident scene outside Harry's apartment. Kurtz says that Harry walked into a truck while he and a second man, a Romanian named Popesco (Siegfried Breuer), looked on in horror. A porter (Paul Hardtmuth), sweeping the apartment steps, watches the two men talk.

When Martins asks who the girl at the funeral was, Kurtz replies matter of factly that she works at the Josefstadt Theatre. However, he tries to discourage Martins from seeing her. "It would only cause her pain," he says.

Martins goes to the theater that night anyway and introduces himself to her backstage. She is an actress named Anna Schmidt (Valli), a melancholy girl with full lips and dark soulful eyes who was Lime's mistress.

Anna says that she wasn't at the accident scene. Nonetheless, she is able to add some details about the fatality. She says Harry's doctor passed by right after the accident. Witnesses testifying at the inquest, she adds, said it wasn't Harry's driver's fault.

"He was Harry's driver?" Martins says, puzzled. "I don't get this. Kurtz? His own driver knocking him down? His own doctor? Not a single stranger?"

"I've wondered about it a hundred times," says Anna, "if it really was an accident."

Martins returns to Harry's apartment with Anna and asks the porter (Paul Hoerbiger) what he knows of Harry's death. The old man says that he did not see it happen, but that he heard the brakes and saw three men carry Lime across the road.

"No," Martins says. "Only Kurtz and the Romanian."

"There was a third man," the porter says. "He didn't give evidence."

That evening, at a nightclub where "Baron" Kurtz plays violin ("A man has to live," he says, embarrassed), Martins meets Popesco. He asks the Romanian about the third man, but Popesco insists that the porter was mistaken. "He remembered wrong," the Romanian said.

The next day, Martins visits Anna in her apartment and they talk about Harry, their mutual friend. To Martins, Harry was a boyhood idol. He knew how to manipulate things, to get what he wanted in life. "He could fix anything," Martins says. "[He knew] how to put up your temperature before an exam, the best crib, how to avoid this and that."

---

*In Vienna, the media gave the picture a mixed reception. Under the front-page headline "Is Vienna a Robbers' Den?" the communist paper *Abend* launched an impassioned broadside. It said the film had indicted the Austrian capital as a center of espionage, kidnapping, black marketeering, and assorted skullduggery. However, since most of the population was fully aware of the lurid activities going on there after World War II, the story was not taken seriously. Other noncommunist dailies saw the picture as a triumph for Vienna. In fact, some criticized the Austrian film industry for continuing to grind out imitations of Hollywood productions when a genuine dramatic theme and setting was right under its nose.

**Although his most famous pictures were thrillers like *Odd Man Out* (1947) and *The Fallen Idol* (1948), Reed won his only Oscar for the musical *Oliver* (1968), based on Dickens' *Oliver Twist*. It was one of his last films. Reed died in 1976 of a heart attack in his London home. He was sixty-nine. He had been knighted in 1952.

†Deutsch was one of a number of European actors in character roles who added mood and dimension to the film. Born in Prague, the son of a German-Jewish businessman, he won favor as a leading man in Max Reinhardt's Deutches Theatre in Berlin. Nazi persecution forced him out of Germany in 1933 and he acted in Hollywood and on Broadway, but he returned to Germany after World War II. "I'm a German actor. I speak the German language," he explained. "I could not speak the English language well. There were not too many parts I could play in this country." In Europe, he appeared with distinction in both modern and classic works—he played Hamlet, Richard II, and Shylock—until he died in 1969 at the age of seventy-eight.

Eyes wide and gun leveled, Harry Lime (Orson Welles) looks for his pursuers behind an iron stairway in Vienna's sewers.

"He fixed papers for me," Anna says. "He heard the Russians were repatriating people like me who came from Czechoslovakia."

Earlier, when Anna had opened the door, she at first thought it was Harry, and it is in this conversation that Anna first inadvertently calls Martins "Harry." It is a dialogue clue indicating that Greene may have intended Lime to be Martins' alter ego. In fact, in an article called "The Theme of the Double in *The Third Man*," Joseph A. Gomez suggests that Lime represents something Martins has aspired to, but never been—a success. Where Martins has been a blunderer, awkward and naive, Lime has been a man of confidence, suavity, and sophistication.

Now things take a darker turn. The porter, who told of the third man, is slain. When Martins goes to

Calloway to tell the major what he has learned, Calloway discloses that Lime's racket was diluting scarce penicillin to make it go further, and selling it on the black market. This deed, Calloway says, has caused the death of scores of sick people, including children. "The lucky children died," Calloway says. "The unlucky ones went off their heads. You can see them now in the mental ward. That was the racket Harry Lime organized."

Disillusioned, Martins goes to Anna's apartment in the middle of the night. He tells her that he is leaving Vienna, and then tries to make love to her. But Anna, numbed by a loyal, grieving devotion, is cold and unresponsive.

At this point, director Reed introduces a bit of business that points up how a first-rate director can improve a script. There is a cat on Anna's bed, and

Martins tries to get it to play with a string. Much as Anna shows indifference, the cat is unresponsive and jumps away. It was Reed's idea to use this cat as a plot device.

"When Cotten had been trying to get the cat to play, I had him say, 'Bad tempered cat,'" Reed said. "Then I worked in the line for Valli, 'He only liked Harry.'"

The cat then slips out the window. When Martins leaves the apartment, we next see it running across the dark street to a figure standing in the shadows of a doorway. "It might be anything," Reed said. "But by going over to him and playing with his shoelace, the cat establishes that it's Harry."

Suddenly the lights go on in an apartment and shine on Harry's face. But before the startled Martins can reach Lime, a car hurtles down the street between them. By the time it has passed, the figure in the doorway is gone. All that is left is the sound of his fleeing footsteps.

Now comes the famous meeting between Lime and Martins. Holly goes to Kurtz and Popesco and tells them to have Lime meet him at the Ferris wheel in the Prater, Vienna's famous amusement park. The once gay pleasure ground, a ghost of its old self, has still not recovered from the war's devastation. Weeds push up around the foundations of the carousel. In the bleak autumn afternoon, only a few people are in the park. However, the great Ferris wheel is still running, so they meet in this ride that will take them high above the city.

Lime's first words are: "It's grand to see you, Holly."

He goes on affecting a warm air of friendship, but his true feelings surface when Martins tells him that Anna is in danger of being turned over to the Russians. "What can I do, old man?" Lime asks, smiling. "I'm dead, aren't I?"

Martins then discloses that he knows what Lime has been doing and asks if he has seen any of his victims.

"Victims? Don't be melodramatic," Lime says as the wheel continues its slow ascent. He points to the people far below. "Would you really feel any pity if one of those dots stopped moving forever? If I offered you twenty thousand pounds for every dot that stops, would you really, old man, tell me to keep my money—or would you calculate how many dots you could afford to spare? Free of income tax, old man."

The car swings to a standstill at the peak point of the ride. Martins looks out the window. They are sizing each other up.

"I carry a gun," Lime says. "You don't think

they'd look for a bullet wound after you hit the ground."

There is a silence. Then Martins says: "They dug up your coffin."

This is Martins' trump card. It means that Lime's ploy of substituting another person as his corpse to throw the police off his trail has failed.

"Found Harbin?" Lime says without emotion. "Pity."

Again the car begins to move, swinging slowly earthward, and Lime suddenly changes his mood. "Holly, what fools we are—talking like this, as if I'd do that to you." Ever the businessman, Lime makes a proposition to Holly, offering to cut him in on his black market scheme for old time's sake. As they get off the wheel, Lime adds his famous parting speech:

"Don't be so gloomy. After all, it's not that awful. You know what the fellow said. In Italy for thirty years under the Borgias, they had warfare, terror, murder, and bloodshed. But they produced Michelangelo, Leonardo da Vinci, and the Renaissance. In Switzerland, they had brotherly love. They had five hundred years of democracy and peace. And what did that produce? The cuckoo clock. So long, Holly."*

Meanwhile, British police have taken Anna into custody with the intention of handing her over to the Russians, but Martins makes a deal. In exchange for Anna's freedom, he agrees to meet Lime with the police staked out so that they can arrest him.

When Anna learns what Martins plans to do, she is furious. She tries to warn Lime as he meets Martins at a cafe, but it is too late. The police close in.

Lime bolts for the sewers and in a chase sequence brilliantly filmed by Robert Krasker (who won an Oscar for his camera work), police of four nations pursue him through the subterranean network, throwing searchlights about the stone walls and dark, rushing waters.**

Lime kills one policeman before a bullet brings him down. Struggling to escape, he crawls up an iron stairway to reach a manhole cover. The camera shows his straining fingers—actually the

*Ironically, it was not Martins, the hero, but Lime, the villain, who became the protagonist of a television series based on the movie. Also called "The Third Man," it made Lime a spy for the British and, thus, a good guy. Michael Rennie, the British actor, played the role.

**The heroes of this scene—actually shot in the labyrinth of low tunnels running beneath Vienna—were the city's sewer brigade. Their job is to patrol the sewers daily, looking for would-be suicides and burglars thinking of new ways of housebreaking.

The famous closing sequence shows Anna, Harry Lime's girl, walking down the cemetery road while Martins waits for her. Instead of stopping, as the audience expects, she walks by Martins without a word.

fingers of director Reed because the scene was shot before Welles' arrival—emerging through a grill, too weak to budge it. Then Martins reaches him. They look at each other for a moment, and Martins, standing in the sewer waters with a gun, fires a shot that finishes Lime.

So Lime is buried for a second time, and for a second time Martins is driven from the cemetery by Calloway. As they ride down the dreary strip of road, Martins sees Anna walking back from the graveyard. "One can't just leave," he says and gets out.

Off in the distance, like a faraway train seen down the ties of a railroad, she is, at first, a dot, then a shadow, then a woman. The audience is set for the conventional embrace, but there is one more surprise left.

Martins has been Lime's friend for what he has imagined him to be, but Anna has loved him for what he really was and she cannot forgive Martins for betraying his friend like a Judas—even if her own freedom has been bought by the thirty pieces of silver. And so she walks past Martins—without a word, without a look, without a gesture.

It is a bitter and ironic ending. Martins stands amidst the leafless trees of winter, a totally bankrupt person—devoid of friends, money, a job, even a hoped-for lover.

Twelve Angry Men

Henry Fonda as the determined juror who turns around a murder panel. Jack Warden is in the background.

Twelve Angry Men
(1957)

Directed by Sidney Lumet. Screenplay by Reginald Rose, based on his television play. Produced by Henry Fonda and Reginald Rose. Associate producer, George Justin. An Orion-Nova Production. Released by United Artists. 95 minutes.

Juror Eight	*Henry Fonda*
Juror One	*Martin Balsam*
Juror Two	*John Fiedler*
Juror Three	*Lee J. Cobb*
Juror Four	*E. G. Marshall*
Juror Five	*Jack Klugman*
Juror Six	*Edward Binns*
Juror Seven	*Jack Warden*
Juror Nine	*Joseph Sweeney*
Juror Ten	*Ed Begley*
Juror Eleven	*George Voskovec*
Juror Twelve	*Robert Webber*
Judge	*Rudy Bond*
Guard	*James A. Kelly*
Court Clerk	*Bill Nelson*
Defendant	*John Savoca*

A tense moment in the jury room. E. G. Marshall, Fonda, and Robert Webber listen intently but don't seem to be swayed by what they hear.

Twelve Angry Men broke the cardinal rule of filmmaking.

It was a movie that did not move. All but three or four minutes of its ninety-five-minute running time was shot on a single set—a cramped, stuffy jury room. The characters were all men, and the only plot development came through dialogue.

On paper, the picture seemed to have all the ingredients of a highly forgettable, static, talky melodrama. On film, just the opposite happened. It was a swift-moving, absorbing, suspenseful movie. With deftness and precision belying his years, Sidney Lumet, the movie's thirty-two-year-old director, created a picture that showed how the delicate balance of opinion shifts among a dozen jurors to decide the fate of a slum youth. Over the years, the film has become a classic portrayal of the little-known atmosphere in which justice takes place.

But *Twelve Angry Men* was a far from perfect movie, and it produced more than its share of headaches for its director. For openers, the fact that the picture primarily focused on the faces of a dozen men arguing and debating created a multitude of problems.

"You go elaborately nuts," said Lumet, "trying to be consistent about who is looking where and at whom."

The reason: the camera did not follow the action as it shows up in the final film version. Instead, to save film (and thus money), the camera went around the jury room's conference table shooting character by character in order.

"Once lights and camera were pointed at a chair, then every speech, no matter its order in the movie, was shot," Lumet said. "That meant that often you had only two or three actors in or near chairs, talking and arguing across the table with actors who were not there. You had to figure out where the non-existent actor's eyes would be, so that the existent actor could stare him down."

In a *Life* magazine article, Lumet said that he spent nights studying the script—adapted by Reginald Rose from his television play*—and making so many notes that it became a maze of diagrams. People thought he was doing things the wrong way a dozen times. But, he said, the diagrams came out

*It was a grabber, too, and included such first-rate performers as Franchot Tone and Robert Cummings.

right all but once. "One [time] we had to reshoot because I had the stockbroker looking the wrong way as he spoke to another actor."

Perspiration was another concern. The movie starts on a sweltering summer day. The actors sweat—but not at the same rate. Then a storm comes up and they all cool off—except for one, the juror played by Lee J. Cobb. "So with every scene, we stood before the actor with an atomizer," Lumet said, "trying to figure out whether or not to squirt on sweat. And, if so, just how much to squirt."

Lumet also tried to use the camera to heighten the drama by emphasizing the confinement of the tiny room. "We created a claustrophobic tension by gradually changing camera lenses to narrow the room and crowd up the table," he said. "Little by little, we lowered the camera level to shoot up at the furious jurymen. And the rate of changes in the camera angles is stepped up as the talk grows louder and more furious."

Superb performances also heightened the drama. One reason they were consistently good, said Henry Fonda, was because ample time was provided for rehearsal. "Rehearsals [for movies] are usually on the run," Fonda said in a 1976 interview with the author. "But we rehearsed around a table in a rehearsal room for two weeks. And then we did [filmed] it in twenty to twenty-one days.

"The only scene that took all day to shoot was the first day. That was the introductory scene as we all walk into that [jury] room. If you remember the scene, the camera was so mobile that it seemed to be anyplace you wanted it to be without stopping.

"You met every one of those twelve men and in enough of a scene to know something about them. That was all in one take. It took all day to get that, but it was worth it. Once we got it, then we just sailed."

All these effects add to the film. But unquestionably what makes it a memorable drama is its original story:

The movie opens in a New York City courtroom in the middle of summer. A murder trial has ended and the judge (Rudy Bond) is charging the jury. In even, unemotional tones, he tells the twelve-man panel that its verdict must be unanimous, and that a reasonable doubt must result in a verdict of not guilty. He adds that if a guilty verdict is reached, the death sentence is mandatory. Watching intently as the jurors file out are the dark eyes of the defendant (John Savoca), a frightened-looking Hispanic youth.

In the small, stifling conference room, the jurors take their places around a long table and begin their task. They are a divergent group. They include a stockbroker, a house painter, a small businessman, a watchmaker, an advertising executive, and a salesman.

The foreman (Martin Balsam) starts by calling for a preliminary vote with a show of hands. "Yeah, who knows?" one juror says. "Maybe we'll all get out of here." The vote is eleven for a guilty verdict, one for acquittal.

"Boy, oh boy," says juror number ten (Ed Begley), shaking his head. "There's always one." The lone holdout is juror number eight (Henry Fonda).

"You really think he's innocent?" asks juror number three (Lee J. Cobb), puzzled at how Fonda could vote for acquittal in the face of the overwhelming evidence to the contrary.

"I don't know," Fonda says.

"I mean you sat in court with the rest of us," Cobb says. "You heard what we did. The kid's a dangerous killer."

But Fonda says he wants to talk about the case for a while before sending the youth off to the chair. He's a slum kid, says Fonda. He's been kicked around all of his life. His mother died when he was nine. His father served a jail term for forgery. "I just think we owe him a few words," Fonda says.

Some jurors are perturbed. They are looking for a quick verdict. "Listen," says Begley, making clear his feeling. "I've lived among them all my life. You can't believe a word they say. They're born liars."

However, the other jurors grudgingly agree that they at least owe the boy the decency of a discussion of his case.

The key points are these:

—The youth is accused of fatally stabbing his father in the chest. The killing took place in his father's apartment around midnight during the summer. Neighbors said they heard the two argue around 8 P.M. and the father strike his son. Then the boy ran out.

—An old man, who lived under the room where the stabbing occurred, said he heard loud noises around midnight that sounded like another fight. He testified he heard the kid yell, "I'm gonna kill you." A second later, he said he heard a body hit the floor. The old man said he went to the door and saw the defendant running down the stairs. Police later found the father with a four-inch knife buried in his chest.

—Another neighbor, a woman who was in bed in her apartment across the street, said she looked out the window just when the boy stabbed his father. The street has an elevated subway track and a train was passing. But she said there were no passengers and she could see through the windows to the other side.

—The boy, who had a police record that included arrests for mugging and knife fighting, said he was at the movies during the killing. Yet, an hour later, when police questioned him, he couldn't remember what pictures he had seen.

"It's these kids, the way they are nowadays," says Cobb. "When I was a kid, I used to call my father 'sir.' Do you ever hear a kid call his father that anymore?" Cobb trails off into a personal monologue. He says he has a grown son who ran away from a fight when he was nine. Cobb says he was so embarrassed he told the boy he'd make a man out of him if he'd have to break him in two trying. "Well, I made a man out of him," Cobb says. "When he was sixteen, we had a fight. Hit me on the jaw. He was a big kid. Haven't seen him for two years. Kids—work your heart out. . . ."

The discussion finally gets back to Fonda. Why, his fellow jurors ask, is he holding out? Fonda says he thinks the youth got a poor defense. "Everybody [all the witnesses] sounded so positive. . . . His lawyer let too many things go by."

What about the switchblade knife, one juror says. The boy admitted buying a knife after the fight in a neighborhood junk shop. It had a carved handle. The storekeeper said it was the only one of its kind he had in stock.

"He [the defendant] claims the knife fell through a hole in his pocket on the way to the movies and he never saw it again," says E. G. Marshall. "Now there's a tale. I think it's quite clear that the boy never went to the movies."

Fonda says it's possible the boy's story is true. "It's possible the boy lost his knife and somebody else stabbed his father with a similar knife."

The jurors ask the guard to bring in the knife and take another look at it. Cobb jabs its blade into the table. "I've never seen one like it," he says. "Neither had the storekeeper."

Fonda then reaches into his pocket, pulls out a duplicate of the murder weapon, and sends its blade quivering into the wood next to the first one.

Ed Begley has the floor. Listening are (clockwise) Fonda, Joseph Sweeney, Lee J. Cobb, E. G. Marshall (face obscured), Edward Binns, and Jack Klugman.

He says he bought the second knife the night before, just to show that the murder weapon could be duplicated.

The second knife touches off a loud discussion. "You're asking us to believe that someone did the stabbing with exactly the same kind of knife," one juror says. "The odds are a million to one."

Fonda suggests another vote, this one by secret ballot. He will abstain. If there is not a single vote of "not guilty," he will switch his vote to guilty.

The second ballot shows: Guilty: 10; Not Guilty: 1; Abstaining: 1.

Cobb suspects that juror number five (Jack Klugman) is the one who changed his mind, and their dialogue gets so emotional that they almost come to blows. But it turns out that it is actually juror number nine (Joseph Sweeney) who has switched—only because he admires Fonda's lone stand. He demands that the panel review all the facts.

Therefore, the jurors start by going over the testimony of the old man. He said he had heard the death threat and then the father's body hit the floor a split second later. Fonda wonders how clearly the old man could have heard these sounds over the noise of a passing train.

"Why should he [the old man] lie? What does he have to gain?" asks one juror.

"Attention—maybe," another says. "He's a very old man . . . an insignificant old man who has never had recognition . . . or his name in the newspaper."

A second vote is held. A third juror votes not guilty.

Now the jurors begin to find more holes in the prosecution's case. Fonda points out that even if the boy had threatened his father, it doesn't mean he was serious about it. "How many times have all of us used the phrase, 'I'm going to kill you'? Probably thousands."

Another juror says that he doubts that the boy would have returned to his father's apartment hours after he had killed him.

A third ballot shows four voting not guilty and eight voting guilty.

It has started raining, and darkness creeps over the jury room. Begley wants to call it a hung jury. Juror number seven (Jack Warden), who has tickets to a night baseball game, agrees. But Fonda will have none of that. He wants more discussion. For instance, there was the telling point of the old man seeing the boy run down the stairs fifteen seconds after the killing. One juror points out that the old man said he was sitting in the bedroom. By examining the apartment floor plan, they calculate that he was nearly fifty feet from the hallway. Tak-

ing into account the fact that he had had a stroke and dragged one foot when he walked, they simulate his trip through the apartment and estimate that it would take him over forty seconds to get to the door. The old man may have heard someone racing down the stairs and assumed it was the boy, Fonda says.

Cobb, enraged by the swing away from a guilty verdict, loses his temper. "You all know he's guilty," he rages. "He's got to burn. You're letting him slip through our fingers."

"Slip through our fingers?" says Fonda. "Are you his executioner?"

"I'm one of them," Cobb says.

"Perhaps you'd like to pull the switch?"

"For this kid, you bet I would."

"I feel sorry for you," Fonda tells him. "Ever since you walked into this room, you've been acting like a self-appointed public avenger. You want to see this boy die because you personally want it. Not because of the facts. You're a sadist."

"I'll kill you," Cobb shouts as he lunges at Fonda. Other jurors head him off and restrain him.

Recalling the same threat by the defendant, Fonda says: "You don't really mean . . . you'll kill me . . . do you?" Fonda has obviously made a point. On the fourth ballot, the vote is tied, six to six.

Now the jury turns to the boy's alibi—the movie he went to and couldn't remember. "Put yourself in the boy's place," Fonda says. "Do you think you could remember details . . . under great emotional stress?" As a test he asks the stockbroker, E. G. Marshall, about a recent double-feature Marshall saw. It turns out that he cannot remember the correct title of the second film or the names of the actors who played in it. "And," Fonda reminds him, "you weren't under emotional stress, were you?" Score another point for Fonda.

Juror number two (John Fiedler) wants to talk about the stab wound. The boy was 5'7". The father was 6'2". Since the knife went in at a downward angle, it doesn't seem to add up.

Cobb disagrees. It isn't awkward at all, he says, and asks for another juror to serve as a mock victim. Fonda volunteers. A hush falls over the room as Cobb raises the knife and plunges it to within an inch of Fonda's chest. Obviously the wound could have been made with an overhand motion.

But juror number five (Jack Klugman), who seemed to be a solid middle-class citizen, now steps forward. He comes from a slum background, he says, and has been a knife-fighter in his time. Switchblade knives are always used with an underhand thrust.

The vote swings to nine for acquittal, three for

guilty. The panel now turns to the testimony of the woman across the street. "That's the whole case," says Cobb. "You can throw out all the other evidence. The woman saw him do it. What else do you want?"

One juror notices E. G. Marshall rubbing his nose to relieve pressure marks from his eyeglasses. It reminds him that the woman who testified she saw the killing had not worn glasses in court, but she had those same marks on her nose. She had rubbed them, too. Fonda points out the woman, obviously weak-eyed, undoubtedly wore no glasses in bed. Nonetheless, she had to be able to identify a person sixty feet away at night through the windows of a passing train. She might have thought she saw the defendant, Fonda says. But she certainly would not have had time to put on her glasses to insure a positive identification.

Fonda has succeeded in raising the most crucial of "reasonable doubts." He admits that he still doesn't really know what the truth is. "But," he adds, "we have a reasonable doubt. . . . No jury can declare a man guilty unless it is sure."

The next vote shows eleven for acquittal, one for conviction. Now Cobb, the last holdout, is asked for his reasons for still feeling that the defendant is guilty. Doggedly he launches into a rambling tirade, flailing out at the gullibility, naiveté, and softness of the other jurors. "Everything that's gone on has been twisted and turned," Cobb says. "You're not going to intimidate me. I'm entitled to my opinion."

During his speech, he takes his wallet out and a picture of his son falls on the table. Suddenly he stops, looks at it, and a change comes over him. "Rotten kids," he says, his voice breaking as he stares at the picture. "You work your life out." Then he sinks to the table, covers his head, and sobs quietly. It is clear that the hatred he has displayed toward the young defendant was part of a general hatred he has toward all youth because of his own son's estrangement.

"Not guilty," he moans without looking up. In a few minutes, the jurors file out to the courtroom to return their verdict—for acquittal.

Like many Hollywood films based on a somber theme, the movie was not a box office success, although it did win general critical acclaim and a few prizes. One of them was the French Film Academy's best picture award. The movie got an Oscar nomination, too, but it lost to *The Bridge on the River Kwai*.

Vertigo

James Stewart as ex-detective John (Scottie) Ferguson. Here, his sometimes girlfriend (Barbara Bel Geddes) comforts him.

Vertigo
(1958)

Produced and directed by Alfred Hitchcock. Screenplay by Alec Coppel and Samuel Taylor, based on the novel *D'Entre Les Morts* by Pierre Boileau and Thomas Narcejac. Photography, Robert Burks. Editor, George Tomasini. Music, Bernard Herrmann. Music conducted by Muir Mathieson. Special photographic effects, Hal Pereira and Henry Bumstead. A Paramount release in Technicolor and VistaVision. 126 minutes.

John (Scottie) Ferguson	*James Stewart*
Madeleine Elster and Judy Barton	*Kim Novak*
Midge	*Barbara Bel Geddes*
Gavin Elster	*Tom Helmore*
Official	*Henry Jones*
Doctor	*Raymond Bailey*
Manageress	*Ellen Corby*
Pop Leibel	*Konstantin Shayne*
Older Mistaken Identity	*Lee Patrick*

Stewart tries to restrain Kim Novak, playing Madeleine, who believes she has been possessed by the soul of a despondent ancestor who took her life after an unhappy love affair.

A detective is chasing a robber over rooftops above San Francisco. Suddenly the detective loses his balance. Just as he topples over, he manages to grab a gutterpipe. A policeman goes to his rescue. But, in the end, it is the policeman who slips and plunges to his death while the detective dangles in space.

The spectacular sequence is the opening of *Vertigo*, one of Alfred Hitchcock's most controversial pictures. Reaction to it was wide-ranging when it came out, and it remains so today. Some insist that it is an overpraised, second-rate work. Others say that it ranks among Hitchcock's finest efforts, perhaps his masterpiece.

Based on the French novel *D'Entre Les Morts*, by Pierre Boileau and Thomas Narcejac, the team

that wrote *Les Diaboliques* (1955), *Vertigo* is a complex but engrossing story of false identity and murder with supernatural overtones. Its major weakness, some contend, is Hitchcock's daring decision to give away the mystery well before the movie ends.

If you have never seen *Vertigo*, read no more. There are few more fascinating moviegoing experiences than watching this film for the first time— unaware of what will happen next as the picture unfolds.

If, however, you have seen *Vertigo*, you will remember it tells how a detective (James Stewart) resigns from the force because of acrophobia (fear of heights that produces dizziness or vertigo). An old college friend hires him to trail his blonde wife,

Madeleine, whom he fears has become suicidal and neurotic. Little by little, the ex-detective falls in love with her, but his phobia stops him from saving her when she throws herself off a steeple.

The second part of the movie shows the former detective, shattered by guilt feelings, walking aimlessly in the streets searching for his lost love. For a while the picture seems to be going nowhere. Then, one day, he meets a dark-haired shop girl, Judy, who resembles Madeleine, and he persuades her to let him take her out. Eventually they, too, seem to fall in love. The truth is that Judy is Madeleine. She had pretended to be the friend's wife as part of a plan to get rid of his real wife.

This is where the movie's great point of departure comes. In the novel, the reader does not learn Judy's dual identity until the very end. That's the final twist. In the picture, however, Hitchcock makes a major change. He discloses Judy's link with Madeleine halfway through the film's second part—more than twenty minutes before the end.

It was not a change that Hitchcock made without careful thought. In an interview with filmmaker Francois Truffaut, Hitchcock disclosed that, during the shooting, even his assistants argued against the plot change. They thought that the disclosure should be saved for the last sequence, but he held out. He later explained why:

"I put myself in the place of a child whose mother is telling him a story. When there's a pause in her narration, the child always says, 'What comes next, Mommy?'

"Well, I felt that the second part of the novel was written as if nothing came next. Whereas, in my formula, the little boy, knowing that Madeleine and Judy are the same person, would then ask, 'And Stewart doesn't know it, does he? What will he do when he finds out about it?'

"In other words, we're back to our usual alternatives: Do we want surprise or suspense?* We followed the book up to a certain point. At first, Stewart thinks Judy may be Madeleine. Then he resigns himself to the fact that she isn't—on the condition that Judy will agree to resemble Madeleine in every respect. But now we give the public the truth about the hoax so that our suspense will hinge around the question of how Stewart is going to react when he discovers that Judy and Madeleine are actually the same person. . . ."

Hitchcock had planned to have Vera Miles play the dual role. A year earlier he had cast Miss Miles as Henry Fonda's wife in *The Wrong Man* (1957).

Hitchcock had a wardrobe created for her for *Vertigo* and made final tests with her. The part, he thought, was going to turn her into a star. But then she became pregnant. After that, he lost interest. "I couldn't get the rhythm going with her again," he said.**

Her replacement was Kim Novak, who two years earlier had been named Hollywood's most popular star—ahead of William Holden, Doris Day, and Marilyn Monroe—in a *Boxoffice* magazine poll. The daughter of a Chicago railroad worker, she came to Hollywood as a model after working as an elevator operator and a five-and-dime store clerk. She got a walk-on role in *The French Line* (1953), but her career was really launched after Columbia's Harry Cohn decided to make her his studio's replacement for Rita Hayworth.

She went on to score major successes in *Picnic* (1955) and *The Man with the Golden Arm* (1955). She combined a childlike beauty with sultry sex appeal. However, even at the height of her career, she projected little warmth. She was, for the most part, emotionless, frozen-faced, and somnambulistic.

When she attempted roles beyond her limited range, critics were quick to blast her for the inadequacy of her talent. "She has no personality beyond a publicity handout," said *Photoplay* magazine. She also began to develop a quarrelsome nature on the set. Hitchcock, who always favored blonde leading ladies, was struck by her ethereal qualities. However, his decision to cast her led to problems.

He found her difficult to direct, he said, because she came to work with preconceived notions that Hitchcock felt were ill-suited to the part. "You know, I don't like to argue with a performer on the set," he said. "There's no reason to bring the electricians in on our troubles. I went to Kim Novak's dressing room and told her about the dresses and hairdos that I had been planning for several months. I also explained that the story was of less importance to me than the over-all visual impact on the screen, once the picture is completed."

Some feel that Miss Novak brought little to the film. She played the dual identity role with "equal ineptitude," said *Saturday Review*. However, others disagreed. "I thought she was perfect for the role," said Truffaut. "Those who admire *Vertigo* like Kim Novak in it."

To me, her cold, porcelain demeanor seems right for Madeleine, and her change to the earthy,

---

*Hitchcock's thesis is that suspense is based on prior knowledge. To get real suspense, the audience must be aware of something happening before the characters are.

**Nevertheless, he chose her two years later to play the important role of Janet Leigh's sister in his thriller *Psycho* (1960).

common shop girl is carried off well, too. As Judy, her sensual quality is accentuated by the fact that she plays the role without a bra. That feat, unusual for the 1950s, was something she was particularly proud of, Hitchcock said.

If critics are divided on Miss Novak's performance, many were also at odds in their assessment of the film. Some were unhappy to see him abandon his taut, terrifying, suspense-filled thrillers for what seemed like an intricate chess problem in which the beauty of the San Francisco Bay area sometimes overshadowed the leisurely paced story.* Nevertheless, as the years pass, most Hitchcock buffs have come to rate *Vertigo* among his five best films—alongside *The Thirty-Nine Steps* (1935), *The Lady Vanishes* (1938), *North by Northwest* (1959), and *Psycho* (1960). Several writers, including Molly Haskell of *The Village Voice* and Donald Spoto, author of *The Art of Alfred Hitchcock*, feel it is his masterpiece.**

As the movie opens, John (Scottie) Ferguson is at loose ends after resigning from the police force. "I'm not going to do anything for a while," he tells Midge (Barbara Bel Geddes), his long-time girl-friend.

One day, Scottie gets a call from an old college chum, Gavin Elster (Tom Helmore), now a wealthy shipbuilder. Elster has a strange story to tell. His wife, Madeleine, has developed neurotic tendencies. She thinks she is a kind of Bridey Murphy, possessed by the spirit of a mad ancestor. She has periods of complete withdrawal from her own life. Sometimes she sits looking at her old family jewelry. Sometimes she drives alone for hours, not realizing how far she has wandered. Knowing that Scottie has resigned from police work, Elster asks him to shadow his wife to see that no harm comes to her.

At first Scottie turns Elster down, but he does agree to go to a restaurant where Elster and Madeleine are dining so that he can at least look at her. There, Scottie, sitting at the bar far from their table, sees a lovely blonde creature. When she gracefully sweeps out in her red evening dress, he sees her only remotely in profile, but intrigued and tantalized by this aura of mystery, he accepts the assignment.

*In 1976, Brian De Palma and writer Paul Schrader did a suspenseful but shallow reworking of the *Vertigo* theme in the film *Obsession*. The story told about a businessman, guilt-ridden after the death of his wife, who finds a look-alike replacement for her. It starred Cliff Robertson and Genevieve Bujold.

**Adding to *Vertigo*'s over-all impact is its exceptional score by Bernard Herrmann, particularly its lyrical and haunting love theme.

For the next ten minutes, there is practically no dialogue as Scottie trails Madeleine through scenic areas of San Francisco and its environs. He follows her to a florist shop, a Spanish mission, a cemetery, an old hotel, and a museum in which she sits for hours in front of a portrait of a woman named Carlotta Valdez. The woman in the painting turns out to be a beautiful but tragic dancer from a nearby mission settlement whose life was plunged into gloom by an unhappy love affair. After her child was taken from her, she lost her mind and then took her life. It turns out that Carlotta was Madeleine's great-grandmother.

Until now, Scottie has seen Madeleine only from a distance, and she has been like a dreamlike vision. But that illusion ends abruptly one day when, without warning, she jumps into San Francisco Bay. He rescues her and, since she is unconscious, takes her to his apartment and puts her to bed. When she opens her eyes, they talk for the first time.

Now that they have met, they seem to find a mutual fascination in each other, and he accompanies her on her trips. At a dark sequoia forest, she feels uncomfortable in the presence of the ancient trees, the oldest living things. "I don't like it," she says, "knowing I have to die." When she sees a felled tree, she runs her fingers over its cross-section. "Somewhere here I was born. And there I died."

The sunlight slants through the tall trees, giving the forest a dreamlike quality. She tells Scottie that she is haunted by weird images of death. "It's as though I'm walking down a long corridor that once was mirrored," she says. "And fragments of that mirror still hang there. And when I come to the end of the corridor, there's nothing but darkness. And they know, when I reach the darkness, that I'll die . . . ."

She tells of seeing in her dream a tower and a bell and a garden below. "It all seems to be in Spain," she says, frightened. "I'm not mad. I don't want to die. But someone within me says I must die." She clings to Scottie and he kisses her.

A few days later, she comes to Scottie's apartment breathless and tells him that her dream about the tower has returned. When she describes the scene, Scottie recognizes it as the old San Juan Baptista Spanish Mission, now preserved as a museum one hundred miles south of San Francisco. He takes her there, hoping that when she sees it is a real place, it will end her nightmares. "No one possesses you," he says, kissing her in the lonely mission. "You're safe with me."

However, she remains distraught, speaking

cryptically. "If you lose me, then you'll know I loved you. And I wanted to go on loving you." (It is only later, when we learn Madeleine's true identity, that these lines take on meaning.) Suddenly Madeleine breaks away, runs into the church, and disappears up a narrow stairway winding to the top of a bell tower. Scottie goes after her, but, halfway up, his acrophobia returns. He is frozen to the spot, helpless when he is most needed.

Then the shrill cry of a woman breaks the silence. We see a body flash by an aperture in the tower, and then see it lying inert and crushed far below.

It is a shocking scene not only to Scottie but to the audience. "No one, I think, seeing *Vertigo* for the first time unprepared, thinks that Madeleine is going to die halfway through," says Robin Wood in his book *Hitchcock's Films*. "She is the heroine of the romance. . . . We are prepared for a happy ending, or perhaps full-grown tragedy, but not for this brutal midway rupture."

The film now moves into a second stage, with the audience totally puzzled as to where the plot is headed. Bewildered and conscience-stricken, Scottie ends up in a mental institution, blaming himself for Madeleine's suicide. After he gets out, he wanders the streets, morosely revisiting places that Madeleine frequented and occasionally seeing women whom he imagines are Madeleine. One day he notices a shop girl who resembles Madeleine, although she is a brunette. He follows her to her hotel and knocks on her door. Her name is Judy Barton, and when he explains the situation, she responds angrily. Her voice is harsh and her manner brusque. But when she sees how vulnerable he seems, she gradually softens and finally agrees to have dinner with him.

Now the camera flashes to Madeleine's death and we see how it was engineered. Elster held his wife at the top of the tower until Madeleine broke away from Scottie. To be sure of her silence, he had already killed her. Then, while Madeleine hid in

Stewart with Judy Barton, a shop girl who resembles Madeleine and whom he tries to make over in Madeleine's image.

the belfry, he threw the body of his wife over.

This is one of the weakest parts of the crime. If Elster wanted to kill his wife, why would he trump up such a Rube Goldberg-like scheme? The question occurred to Hitchcock even years after he made the movie. "How could he [Elster] know that Stewart wouldn't make it up those stairs?" Hitchcock asked. "Because he became dizzy? How could he [Elster] be sure?" Also, how could Elster be certain that Stewart wouldn't examine the body on the ground and see that it wasn't Madeleine?"

If the movie's first part has these gaping loopholes, the rest of the story unfolds, for the most part, compactly. Judy writes a note admitting the hoax. "I made a mistake. I fell in love," she writes. "That wasn't part of the plan. I'm still in love with you. And I want you to love me . . . as I am, for myself, and forget the other and the past." But the note is only for her diary. Stewart never sees it.

For the next few weeks, Scottie begins taking Judy out, trying to recreate her in Madeleine's image. He buys her clothes and shoes like those Madeleine wore. Then he persuades her to bleach her hair.

When she walks in, Scottie seems to have a dazed look in his eyes. He thinks that he is seeing the reincarnation of his lost love. However, the spell is broken abruptly when Judy puts on a necklace that she forgets had once belonged to Madeleine.

Now there is a change in Scottie's voice. It has lost its warmth, its boyish charm. It has become brittle, businesslike.

There's one last thing he must do to get free of the past, he says, and he takes Judy to the mission where Madeleine died. "I have to tell you about Madeleine," he says. "We stood there and I kissed her for the last time. And she said, 'If you lose me, you'll know that I loved you and wanted to keep on loving you.' And I said, 'I won't lose you.' But I did. And then she turned and ran into the church."

He pulls Judy into the church and starts up the tower where his fear of heights had returned. "I want to stop being haunted," he says. "You're my second chance." She struggles vainly to free herself and warns him that his vertigo will come back. But he pushes her ahead and follows her up the terrifying stairway.

The famous shot of Scottie looking down the steep tower well was done by what is known as a "track-out and forward zoom" combination. The orthodox way to shoot this bird's-eye view would have been to put the camera at the top of the stairs, point it downward, and zoom in. But since it would

have cost $50,000 to build the gear to lift it, Hitchcock hit on the idea of having a miniature of the stairway built, putting the miniature on its side, and then photographing it, using a tracking shot and zoom-in from the ground. The shot could be made this way because no characters were involved. It saved $31,000.

Now Scottie and Judy are at the top of the stairway. "You played the young wife very well, didn't you?" Scottie says, shaking Judy violently. She admits everything but says that she wanted to back out at the end. She says she screamed at the moment of the crime because she wanted to stop it. However, she was so convincing before that Scottie can't be sure she isn't acting now. "He made you over, didn't he? Just like I made you over. Only better. Not only the clothes and the hair. But the looks and the manner and the words. . . . You were a very apt pupil, too, weren't you? Why did you pick on me? Why me?"

He takes her still higher, to the belfry, the scene of the crime. The horror and irony of the whole thing turns over in his mind. "Oh, I loved you so, Madeleine," he says, confusing Judy's dual identity even as he has forced her confession.

Judy can only plead for forgiveness. "I was safe when you found me," she says, sobbing. "There was nothing you could prove. When I saw you again, I couldn't run away. I loved you so. I walked into danger, let you change me because I loved you and I wanted you. . . . You love me now."

"It's too late. There's no bringing her back."

"Please. . . ."

Suddenly, a figure looms in the shadows. "Oh, no," Judy says, startled, believing she is seeing the ghost of the murdered wife.

"I hear voices," the figure says.

Terrified, Judy lurches backward, a kind of involuntary reflex. There is no place to go. She pitches back through an opening in the tower, shrieking, as she reels into space.

"God, have mercy," says the figure from the shadows. It turns out to be a nun from the mission.

The mission bells begin tolling. As the camera pulls away, Scottie is seen standing out on the belfry ledge, peering down from that great height on the tragic scene. His vertigo is gone, but at a terrible price. The woman he has loved and hated, who has been both vision and reality, lies dead on the pavement far below.*

*Author Donald Spoto feels the final sequence suggests Scottie's own suicide. Says Spoto: "Hitchcock has even reflected that Scottie might—as his only alternative for having three times caused death—hurl himself over for the final union with his beloved in death."

The Wild One

Johnny (Marlon Brando), leader of a motorcycle gang, manhandles sassy Kathie Bleeker (Mary Murphy).

The Wild One
(1953)

Directed by Laslo Benedek. Screenplay by John Paxton, based on a story by Frank Rooney. Musical director, Morris Stoloff. Scored by Leith Stevens. Camera, Hal Mohr. Editor, Al Clark. Produced by Stanley Kramer. Columbia. 79 minutes.

Johnny	*Marlon Brando*
Kathie Bleeker	*Mary Murphy*
Harry Bleeker	*Robert Keith*
Chino	*Lee Marvin*
Sheriff Singer	*Jay C. Flippen*
Mildred	*Peggy Maley*
Charlie Thomas	*Hugh Sanders*
Frank Bleeker	*Ray Teal*
Bill Hannegan	*John Brown*
Art Kleiner	*Will Wright*
Ben	*Robert Osterloh*
Wilson	*Robert Bice*
Jimmy	*William Vedder*
Britches	*Yvonne Doughty*
Gringo	*Keith Clarke*
Mouse	*Gil Stratton, Jr.*
Dinky	*Darren Dublin*
Red	*Johnny Tarangelo*
Dextro	*Jerry Paris*
Crazy	*Gene Peterson*
Go-Go	*Alvy Moore*
Boxer	*Jim Connell*
Stinger	*Don Anderson*
Betty	*Angela Stevens*
Simmonds	*Bruno Ve Sota*
Sawyer	*Pat O'Malley*

Johnny holds the trophy that his gang pilfered and he and his guys share a good laugh. The crew-cut cyclist is Jerry Paris, later a TV director. Second right (with cap on) is Gil Stratton, Jr., formerly of the Bowery Boys.

First they appear as a blur on the horizon. Then, accompanied by an ominous buzz, they race closer—darting at us from the screen, getting nearer every second. Now they are almost upon us—a squadron of motorcycle riders roaring down a ribbon of highway.

This is the opening of *The Wild One*, a movie that created little attention in its time but which became a landmark film of the 1950s. It paved the way for a host of motorcycle and youth culture pictures that culminated in *Easy Rider* (1969). "It also," said *Life* magazine, "helped create an image of motorcycling that non-violent bike riders have been trying to live down for a quarter of a century."

The Wild One was a clear case of a movie made before its time—a fact that, in retrospect, could have been discerned even before its release. Its ambiguous storyline confused and bewildered preview audiences. Columbia waffled over its title—calling it first *The Cyclist Raiders*, then *Hot Blood*.* Exhibitors, the theatre owners who show the

Hot Blood became the title of a 1956 Columbia movie with Cornel Wilde and Jane Russell about gypsies.

Hollywood films, predicted that it would be a financial flop. And, indeed, its New York premiere was no great triumph. It was relegated to the RKO Palace where it served chiefly as a break between eight acts of vaudeville.

Reviews were mixed. *Saturday Review* called it "first-rate movie making," but *Time* and most newspapers panned it. Overseas, the British, upset by its mayhem, banned the picture, and it remained unseen there until 1968.

In truth, the movie was a flawed and unsatisfying picture. Nevertheless, as the years passed, it became obvious that it was the first film to spell out the division between the two worlds of America—the straight and the hip—that were to clash in the 1960s. "It was one of the few pictures to pose a style of life, however inarticulate, directly in conflict with middle American values," said Andrew Dowdy in *Movies Are Better Than Ever*. And it did so "without copping out into a sociological explanation of misfits and what to do about them."

The idea for *The Wild One* stemmed from a real-life incident. On July 4, 1947, a band of marauding bikers terrorized the town of Hollister, California. They plowed their motorcycles into bars and restaurants, broke up furniture, and drank the town dry. The brutal invasion inspired Frank Rooney to write the short story "Cyclists' Raid" that *Harper's* published in 1951.

Stanley Kramer bought the screen rights and reworked the story with screenwriter John Paxton to shift the emphasis to the town's hostility toward the motorcyclists. The Breen Office recoiled, since the Kramer version made the cyclists seem like good guys. It suggested that there was a narrow-minded intolerance in middle America more worrisome than the aimless hijinks of the hipsters. Kramer, who was not in good standing then with Columbia studio boss Harry Cohn, was in no position to battle the censors. He made changes, playing up the rampage itself. Thus, the attempt to explore the growing restlessness of youth became just another mindless exercise in violence.

Marlon Brando had been attracted by the social commentary of the picture, and the revisions disappointed him. He fought against the changes, and he even tried to rewrite some of the scenes himself. But, in the end, time ran out. The picture had to start on schedule.

As the movie opens and the credits come on, we hear Brando's voice saying: "It began here for me on this road. How the whole mess happened, I don't know. But I know it couldn't happen again in a million years." Far away, a cloud of riders appear on the horizon. As they loom closer, Brando continues off-camera: "Maybe I could have spotted it early. But once the trouble was on its way, I was just going with it. Mostly, I remember a girl. I can't explain it—sad chick like that. But something changed in me. She got to me. But that's later, anyway. . . ."

The gang of cyclists—it calls itself the Black Rebels Motorcycle Club—storms into a motorcycle meet, spoiling for trouble. We don't know where they're from, or where they're going, or even why they're spending their weekends dressed in black leather jackets, T-shirts, skin-tight jeans, and boots. Seventy-nine minutes later when the movie is over, we still have no real inkling of what makes these self-made outcasts tick.

The cyclists' stay at the meet is short-lived. They disrupt the race, mock officials, and, in general, make a nuisance of themselves. Police quickly send them on their way. "Get goin'," says a tough cop. As they shamble to their bikes, one of them swipes a race trophy, a second-place statuette, and gives it to the riders' leader, Johnny (Brando).

They blast away, and a man asks the cop where

the gang is from. "I dunno—everywhere," the cop says. "I don't even think they know where they're going."

Then the man adds (in an obvious studio attempt to head off protests by cycle manufacturers and riders): "Guys like that give people the idea that everybody driving a motorcycle is crazy."

Their next stop is a quiet little town that doesn't stay quiet long. Minutes after they blow in, the gang is dragging for beers on the main street. The fun and games quickly get out of hand. During the scramble, they force old Art Kleiner's (Will Wright) car into a hole, partially wrecking it and breaking the leg of one of the bikers (Gene Peterson).

In Bleeker's Cafe, Johnny meets Kathie (Mary Murphy) and, attracted by her good looks, he makes a pass at the pert waitress. The scene was written to make two points: (1) that Kathie is not part of the hip scene and (2) that the cyclists go on their rampage weekends as a release from meaningless, dead-end jobs. However, the Breen Office rejected as socially dangerous the explanation for the bikers' outings, and so director Laslo Benedek inserted a bland, innocuous speech instead.

According to Bob Thomas in his book *Marlon: Portrait of the Rebel as an Artist*, Brando protested: "We've got to explain why these guys need to break out and be somebody." When Brando, a cyclist himself, went on to expand on this argument, Benedek thought that Brando was doing better than the revised script, so he asked him to ad-lib the scene. Benedek told Mary Murphy to draw him out with questions. When the cameras rolled the scene came out like this:

Kathie: Where are you going when you leave here? Don't you know?
Johnny: Oh man, we just gonna go.
Kathie: Just trying to make conversation. It means nothing to me.
Johnny: Look, on weekends we go out and have a ball.
Kathie: What do you do? Do you just ride around? Or do you go on some sort of picnic or something?
Johnny: A picnic? Man, you are too square. I'll have to straighten you out. Listen, you don't go to any one special place. That's cornball style. You just go (snaps his fingers). The idea is to have a ball. Now if you gonna stay cool, you got to wail. You got to put something down. You got to make some jive. Don't you know what I'm talking about?
Kathie: Yeah. Yeah, I know what you mean.
Johnny: Well, that's all I'm saying.

Middle America couldn't dig Johnny's jive talk in the mid-1950s. There was a ripple of unrest stirring in some counter-culture pioneers like Jack Kerouac. But it wasn't until the 1960s that the rebellion against the humdrum but respectable nine-to-five workaday world got up steam. Nevertheless, Kathie seems to share Johnny's yearnings. In her own vague, inarticulate way, she tries to convey a sense of suppressed restlessness, too.

Kathie: My father was gonna take me on a fishing trip to Canada once.
Johnny: Yeah?
Kathie: We didn't go.
Johnny: Crazy.

However, Johnny is quickly turned off when he learns that Kathie's father is Harry Bleeker (Robert Keith), a town cop. "I don't like cops," Johnny says. The word "cops" hisses through his teeth.

He grabs his trophy, ties it on his cycle, and starts to pull out with his gang. At this moment, Chino (Lee Marvin), a crazy-acting hooligan, rides in with his outlaw band, who have broken away from the Black Rebels. Chino and Johnny trade insults, then punches, after Chino tries to swipe Johnny's trophy.*

Townspeople gather around during the brawl. One of them, Charlie Thomas (Hugh Sanders), tries to drive through the bunch, and the kids respond by tipping over his car. The angry residents then demand that Harry do something. He complies by arresting Chino. So, for the time being, Johnny stays on.

Inside the cafe again, Johnny tells Kathie that her father ought to have arrested the motorist, too, because he precipitated the rough stuff. Kathie says that her father didn't do it because he was afraid of offending townspeople and losing his job. Then, in a sudden switch in tone, she finds a parallel between her father and Johnny.

*The two had a similar experience on the set, reportedly not getting along during the picture. One day, Marvin went over to Brando and told him that he was thinking of changing his name. When Brando asked what he was planning to change it to, Marvin replied, "Marlow Brandy." Brando didn't crack a smile. Instead, he told Marvin that he was thinking of changing his name, too. "What to?" Marvin asked. "Lee Moron."

Johnny and his Black Rebels Motorcycle Club. That's Yvonne Dougherty in the center and Keith Clarke on her right. Jerry Paris is on the extreme left and Gene Peterson is extreme right.

"He's the town joke and I'm stuck with him," Kathie says. "He doesn't have any business being a cop. No more than you have with that fake trophy. . . . You've impressed everybody now, big motorcycle racer. Why don't you take that back so they can give it to somebody who really won it?"

"Nobody tells me what to do," says Johnny, stung by these surprisingly cutting remarks. "You keep needling me, and, if I want to, I'm going to take this joint apart. And you're not going to know what hit you."

Night comes. The townspeople shiver, wondering what the cyclists will do next. They don't have to wonder long. First, a bunch sits outside the jail, blaring their horns. Then other riders invade the telephone office, cutting the lines so that Harry can't get through to the sheriff. Confident that they are safe from the law, they then drive into stores, breaking windows and wrecking furniture.

Even while this mayhem is going on, Johnny's thoughts are on Kathie, and it's lucky they are. A group of cyclists pursue her when she gets off from work. They catch her and terrorize her, circling her with their cycles until Johnny pulls up. He yanks her onto his jump seat behind him and roars off. Some see this scene as something akin to the horseback rescue in a Western.

At any rate, Brando takes her to a little park where he can get a few things off his chest. He doesn't like the fact that Kathie has labeled him as a phony.

"You think you're too good for me," Johnny says. "Nobody's too good for me. Somebody's too good for me, I make sure I can knock them over sometime. Right now, I can slap you around to show you how good you are. And tomorrow, I'm someplace else and I don't even know you or nothing. . . ."

That little lecture seems to thaw the ice maiden. "Johnny," she says, in a soft voice. "Crazy isn't it? You're afraid of me. I don't know why, but I'm not afraid of you. . . ."

Johnny is now more puzzled than ever. What's happened, of course, is that the two are from different backgrounds and they are not communicating.

"I'm afraid of you?" Johnny says. "Are you cracked?"

"I wanted to touch you," Kathie says. "I wanted to try anyway."

"Try what?"

"I dunno. I wanted to make it the way I always thought it would be sometime—with somebody. The way I always thought it might be. . . . You're still

fighting, aren't you? You're always fighting. Why do you hate everybody?"

There is no answer, so Kathie rambles on, saying that she has never ridden on a motorcycle before, but has dreamed about leaving the town with some motorist who'd come into the cafe for coffee. Finally, she asks Johnny for his trophy. "I just wondered if you still wanted to give it to me. It's crazy. . . . I wish I were going somewhere. I wish you were going somewhere. We could go together."

When Johnny doesn't respond to this disjointed pitch, Kathie, embarrassed, runs, slaps him when he catches her, then flees, crying. Some townspeople see Johnny chasing her and mistakenly think he is trying to rape her. They round up a group who yank Johnny behind a store and work him over.

"We'll pound a little respect for law and order into this guy's thick skull," one citizen says. Johnny defiantly answers, "My old man used to hit harder than that." Just as the citizens try to make him eat those words, Harry and Kathie show up and stop the beating at the point of a gun.

Johnny's troubles aren't over. As he tries to ride out of town, another citizen group cuts off his retreat. Someone tosses a tire iron at him. It catches in the spokes of his cycle and throws it out of control, causing it to run down and kill an old man (William Vedder).

The townspeople, now an angry mob, swarm around Johnny, ready to lynch him—just as Sheriff Singer (Jay C. Flippen) arrives. He takes Johnny to the jail. There, the sheriff tells Johnny that he has found himself some real trouble, maybe a manslaughter charge.

Things are looking black when Frank Bleeker (Roy Teal), Kathie's uncle, comes forward and says that Johnny is really innocent. Bleeker tells the sheriff that he saw someone throw a tire iron. That turns the case around in the sheriff's mind.

"A man's dead on account of something you let get started, even though you didn't start it," Singer says. "I don't know if there's any good in you. I don't know if there's anything in you. But I'm going to take a big fat chance and let you go."

If the sheriff thinks that his speech has made Johnny repentant, he's wrong. Johnny walks out without a word of thanks either to the sheriff or to the man who has spoken up in his behalf. "He doesn't know how," Kathie says.

Next the sheriff turns to Johnny's pals. "Every one of you monkeys is down in my book, and every stick of damage will be paid for. . . . Stick your nose back in this county, any of you, and you'll never see daylight again as long as you live."

On his way out of town with his gang, Johnny stops at the Bleeker Cafe. He wants to say something to Kathie, but he can't find the words. Instead, he pushes his pilfered trophy down the counter to her and smiles. She returns the smile. And then he's off, gunning down the highway the same way he came.

Columbia boss Harry Cohn hated the picture. So did Brando, who considered it a failure. "We started out to do something worthwhile, to explain the psychology of the hipster," Brando said. "But somewhere along the way, we went off the track. The result was that instead of finding why young people tend to bunch into groups that seek expression in violence, all that we did was show the violence."

Nevertheless, *The Wild One* has become a milestone of its decade, a picture that anticipated the nationwide youth protest that followed in the 1960s.

Wild Strawberries

Isak Borg dreams of Sara (Bibi Andersson), his childhood sweetheart, picking wild strawberries with Isak's rival, his younger brother Sigfrid (Per Sjostrand).

Wild Strawberries (1959)

Directed by Ingmar Bergman. Photography, Gunnar Fischer. Assistant cameraman, Bjorn Thermenius. Music, Erick Nordgren. Music directed by E. Eckert-Lundin. Sound, Aaby Wedin and Lennart Wallin. Editor, Oscar Rosander. Assistant director, Gosta Ekman. Screenplay by Bergman. Produced by Svensk Filmindustri. Distributed in the U.S. by Janus Films. 90 minutes.

Doctor Isak Borg	*Victor Sjostrom*
Sara	*Bibi Andersson*
Marianne	*Ingrid Thulin*
Evald	*Gunnar Bjornstrand*
Agda	*Julian Kindahl*
Anders	*Folke Sundquist*
Victor	*Bjorn Bjelvenstam*
Isak's mother	*Naima Wifstrand*
Mrs. Alman	*Gunnel Brostrom*
Isak's wife	*Gertrud Fridh*
Her lover	*Ake Fridell*
Aunt	*Sif Ruud*
Alman	*Gunnar Sjoberg*
Akerman	*Max von Sydow*
Uncle Aron	*Yngve Nordwall*
Sigfrid	*Per Sjostrand*
Sigbritt	*Gio Petre*
Eva Akerman	*Anne-Mari Wiman*
Charlotta	*Gunnel Lindblom*
Angelica	*Maud Hansson*
Anna	*Eva Noree*
The Twins	*Lena Bergman*
	Monica Ehrling
Hagbart	*Per Skogsberg*
Benjamin	*Gorgan Lundquist*
Promoter	*Professor Helge Wulff*

Borg gives a ride to three hitchhikers—Bjorn Bjelvenstam, Folke Sundquist, and Andersson.

He never allows outsiders on the set, and once the day's work has begun, no actor may leave. No improvisations are permitted, nor deviations from the script—no matter how minor. And no stand-ins are used even when the action is rough-and-tumble.

Dressed in a baggy sweater and old corduroys, he works swiftly and surely, rehearsing each scene four times, then shooting three sequences. Each day he winds up with about three minutes of finished film, using up only 20,000 feet for a 7,000-foot picture. Then, when everything is finally shot, he cuts ruthlessly. "Kill all your darlings," says Ingmar Bergman, Sweden's master director.

If an objective way is ever found to pick the century's greatest director, it might well turn out to be Bergman. He has created an original style—focusing on what he calls "the inner landscape." His movies are lyrical, mystical, and allegorical. Since 1945, audiences have been fascinated by their pictorial loveliness and beguiled by their technical brilliance. At the same time, they have also been perplexed by their baffling nature.

Said Bosley Crowther, the *New York Times* film reviewer, after seeing *Wild Strawberries* in 1959: "If any of you thought you had trouble understanding what Ingmar Bergman was trying to convey in his film *The Seventh Seal* (1958), wait until you see his *Wild Strawberries*. This one is so thoroughly mystifying that we wonder whether Mr. Bergman himself knew what he was trying to say."

Another critic, Stanley Kauffmann, found even the best of his pictures "pretentious . . . illogical . . . unsatisfying." Bergman's movies, however beautiful, said Kauffmann, raise expectations that are not fulfilled.

Yet Crowther, and to some extent Kauffmann, too, grew to recognize Bergman for the genius he is. "He is," said Crowther later, "a motion picture artist for whom we must have the highest regard." Most reviewers agree. *Time* has called him "one of the most forceful and fascinatingly original artists who now confronts the U.S. in any medium." Critic John Simon feels he has no peer. "Bergman," says Simon, "is the greatest filmmaker the world has seen so far."

If Bergman is obscure, it is partly because he is filming things that grow out of his own consciousness. Like a novelist, he uses his own private thoughts and experiences as the basis for his movies. Thus at times they may be too private for the average audience to share with him. But their difficulty also stems from the fact that he has taken a new approach to moviemaking. He is trying to change film from a purely derivative art form—one that borrows plots and ideas from short stories, books, and plays—to an original one. If the message of his movies is elusive, it is, then, because he is sometimes more interested in using the picture to convey emotions, impressions, and states of mind rather than merely to entertain or tell a straightforward story.

Harry Schein, chairman of the Swedish Film Institute and husband of actress Ingrid Thulin, credits Bergman with starting a whole new school of cinematography. "He was the first to use film as a writer does paper and typewriter, as a personal medium. . . . That idea of just expressing yourself in film was the beginning of the 'auteur' [author]* theory of filmmaking, long before this new wave (the group of *Cahiers du Cinema* critic-filmmakers like Godard, Chabrol, Truffaut, who became auteurists in the late 1950s)."

Yet, as dominant a figure as Bergman is, he remains as puzzling a personality as some of his movies. Married six times, he is described by his intimates as a character out of Strindberg—insomniac, hypochondriac, neurotic. For one thing, he rarely leaves Sweden. Liv Ullmann, who had an out-of-wedlock child by Bergman, tells of his strange reluctance to leave familiar surroundings.

"When I was 'married' to Ingmar, he would sometimes travel to Rome, which is practically the only foreign city he ever goes to. But he is so afraid to go away from everything he knows and is familiar with that I have to go a day in advance, take the luggage, and set things up in the hotel suite so he will not feel himself in an environment too alien to him."**

Some say beneath his Scandinavian *sangfroid* lies a volatile temper. Once, after a bad review, he socked Bengt Jahnsson, theatre critic for the

---

*This controversial theory, first espoused by Andrew Sarris, holds that it is the director—rather than the screen writer—who is really the "author" of the movie.

**All this, of course, changed drastically one day in 1976 when Stockholm police hauled Bergman out of a rehearsal and arrested him on a charge of tax fraud. Swedish tax collectors said Bergman owed $120,000 in 1970 taxes, and the statute of limitations for tax evasion was running out. The charges were later dropped, but not before Bergman went to a mental institution, reportedly suffering a nervous breakdown. The affair was widely publicized, and soon afterward Bergman exiled himself to Munich. His self-banishment lasted until 1978 when he returned to Sweden and resumed directing.

Stockholm newspaper *Dagens Nyheter*. He was fined $1,000. It was worth it, Bergman said, because Jahnsson was "dangerous" to Swedish dramatic art.

A tall, reedlike man who neither smokes nor drinks, Bergman lives an insulated, disciplined existence. Through the 1950s and 1960s, his most creative period, his yearly schedule seldom varied. A director at the Royal Dramatic Theatre in Stockholm in the winter, Bergman entered a hospital in May when the theater season closed. He stayed six weeks, writing his next movie. He filmed it during Sweden's long summer days, shooting it in an intense and hectic two months of concentration. Then, in the late fall, he was back in the theatre again, directing.

There were no gaps. Everything ran precisely, and his rigid regime left little time for socializing. Once it soured a friendship. That happened in 1971 after Elliott Gould had finished Bergman's first film in English, *The Touch*. Gould, whom Bergman had handpicked to be its star, was returning to Stockholm to be taped with Bergman on the Dick Cavett TV show. He had flown to London, expecting to spend some time with his idol Bergman before the taping. However, this was in May, and *The Touch* was past history to Bergman. He was now deeply involved in writing his fall film. When Gould telephoned, Bergman said that he couldn't see him. Gould never got over the slight.

However, most actors respect him highly. They say that he has the gift of inspiring an actor to give his finest performance.

Says Bibi Andersson: "He knows what he wants before he starts directing. He will know the script thoroughly and have an opinion on every line. He gives you total confidence, the feeling that right now you're the most important person in the world."

Says Ullmann: "Bergman gives very few script directions. And his instructions before each scene are brief. A bad director suppresses an actor's spontaneous creativity by giving you exhaustive directions. He puts into words that which should only exist in your fantasy. But Ingmar tells you only what he wants the end result to be and lets you arrive at it your own way."

Says Thulin: "He is not so much directing as imagining what your secret life is, and what of that secret life he can express in his film."

Just what is it that Bergman is trying to convey in his movies? He generally avoids the question. "My films," he once said, "are a part of me. I can't explain what they mean—each person must discover that for himself."

This much he has explained:

—"I try to tell the truth about the human condition, the truth as I *see* it."

—"My idea is that film and music are much the same. They are a means of expression and communication that bypass man's reason and touch his emotional centers. The film isn't just a picture. Music isn't just a sound. Both of them work with rhythmic sequences, harmonies, colors, relations, forms. . . . Film should communicate psychic states, not merely project pictures of external action."

—"Somebody studying sleep discovered that if they prevent you from dreaming, you go crazy. . . . Dreams are a sort of creative process. . . . My films come from the same factory. They are like dreams in my mind before I write. And they are made from the same materials. From everything I have ever seen or heard or felt, I use reality the same way dreams do. Dreams seem very realistic—and so are my films. . . . All my films are dreams."

The son of an Evangelical Lutheran minister who became chaplain to Sweden's royal family, Bergman recalls his childhood as a restrained, emotionally cold, rigidly moral period. Some say that his church background prompted Bergman, a shy, introverted child, to withdraw into a private world of fantasy. It also gave him his major themes—God and the devil, life and death, and the tragic isolation of existence.

Whether this is true or not, Bergman himself has traced his interest in the world of make-believe to a toy—a beat-up magic lantern that he got on his ninth birthday. Later he was given an old projector and a puppet theatre. With great joy, he quickly became an expert puppeteer. He improvised dramas, built scenery, created his own marionettes, and worked the strings. He even produced a full-length Strindberg play, speaking all the parts from memory.

All this activity foreshadowed his directorship of a youth club theatre group while he was a student at Stockholm University. After the German invasion of Norway in 1940, Bergman produced an anti-Nazi version of Macbeth—playing the role of Duncan himself—and created a minor sensation. It was also about this time that he discovered the movies. He soon was going two and three times a week, building his own private film library. In fact, so obsessed did he become with movies and plays that he quit the university to follow a Bohemian life and a career in the theatre.

He began as a playwright, and one of his earliest works had a strange twist. One day a clergyman goes to a striptease show and finds that he is the only customer. To return the favor, the stripper goes to his church, where she finds that she is the only worshiper. The two have a love affair, and the clergyman, conscience-stricken, castrates himself. Bergman saw it as a comedy, but when friends took issue with this interpretation, he produced it as a tragedy, *Murder in Batjaerna*.

Bergman finally got a steady job as an assistant stage manager and began to rise quickly. He became an assistant director with the Stockholm Royal Opera, getting important training in music, production, and lighting. Then he joined the script department of Svensk Filmindustri, Sweden's biggest movie company, and submitted his first screenplay, *Torment*. It became an international hit. The picture won eight "Charlies"—the Swedish equivalent of the Oscar—and a 1946 grand prix at Cannes. Thus began Bergman's career.

The next year, he did both the writing and directing for his film *Crisis*—a practice which he has generally continued and which has given him total control over his pictures. Unlike most directors, he even supervises the cutting and film editing. Yet, with all this authority, he has not abandoned the theatre. In 1959, at the age of forty-one, he became the youngest director of the Royal Dramatic Theatre in Stockholm. In this way he began his two-sided love affair—the theatre in the fall and winter, the movies in the spring and summer. Of the two, Bergman maintains that the theatre remains his first interest. He has said that he can live very well without movies, but not without the theatre. "The theatre is my faithful wife," he says. "The film is my mistress."

Nonetheless, he unquestionably owes his worldwide reputation to his movies. Disciplined and driving, he has surrounded himself with a tiny but efficient and loyal eighteen-man film crew. Many have worked for him for twenty years or more. His actors, too, were hand-picked—most of them veterans of the Swedish stage—and seemingly became projections of his own personality. Perhaps the most famous is Max von Sydow, the tall, gaunt thespian whose expressive features, some feel, seem to capture Bergman's theme of spiritual torment.

With this elite repertory unit of technicians and actors, a group unique in cinema history, Bergman has turned out pictures that have enthralled audiences for three decades. The impressive list includes: *Smiles of a Summer Night* (1955), *The Seventh Seal* (1956), *The Magician* (1958), *The Virgin Spring* (1959), *Wild Strawberries* (1959), *Through a Glass Darkly* (1961), *The Silence* (1962), *The Touch* (1970), and *Cries and Whispers*

At the university in Lund where Borg got his medical degree, he is honored after fifty years as a physician.

(1973). These pictures bear little resemblance to Hollywood productions, and, increasingly, their meanings have become more ambiguous and obscure. Even so, the first vision of any Bergman movie is an experience not to be forgotten.

Only time will tell which of his films will be called his masterpiece. However, *Wild Strawberries*, perhaps the simplest of his screenplays, has been his most commercially successful picture. It is also probably his best-known work.

The movie opens as Isak Borg (Victor Sjostrom),* a seventy-eight-year-old physician, starts on a day's journey from his retirement home in Stockholm. He is going to his old school, the University of Lund, where he is to receive an honorary degree in recognition of his fifty years as a doctor. It is to be the crowning glory of his career.

The impending award sets off the old man's thought processes. What has my life been like? he

*Sjostrom, one of Sweden's greatest actors and directors, came to the United States in the 1920s to direct such memorable silent films as *He Who Gets Slapped* (1924) with Lon Chaney, *The Scarlet Letter* (1926) with Lillian Gish, and *The Wind* (1928) also with Gish. Sjostrom (or Seastrom as it was listed in U.S. credits) died in 1960, one year after *Wild Strawberries* opened. He was eighty-one.

wonders. What have I done to earn such a signal honor? Before his trip is over, the highway that the old doctor travels will be transformed to the road of life. On it, the sweep of years will rush back and he will confront the past in memory and dreams and reality.

Even before he leaves, the ominous day begins with a Kafka-like nightmare. He finds himself alone, lost amidst forbidding facades of decayed buildings in an unfamiliar part of the city. He sees a clock without hands, and a man without a face who collapses into air when Borg approaches. Then, a horse-drawn funeral carriage rumbles through the streets. Suddenly it sways, a wheel comes loose, and a coffin falls out and breaks apart. A hand reaches out to pull Borg in. Then, inside the casket, he sees himself, smiling scornfully.

That morning as he is about to leave, Marianne (Ingrid Thulin), his daughter-in-law, who has been staying with him after a fight with her husband Evald, asks to go along. On the way, she tells Borg that she has been estranged by his son's coldness. In many ways, she tells the doctor, Evald is the image of him.

"What do you have against me?" the doctor asks, somewhat startled by her frank tone.

"Do you want an honest answer?" Marianne asks.

"Tell me the truth."

"You are a completely selfish person," Marianne says, quite calmly. "You are terribly inconsiderate. And you've never listened to anyone beside yourself. But you cunningly hide behind the mask of gentleman-like civility and cultural charm."

The old man tries to look into her eyes, but she stares straight ahead, talking quietly. She tells him that he is aloof and remote. When she came to Stockholm a month ago, she reminds him, the doctor took her in with the proviso that he not be dragged into her affairs. "I got the idiotic notion you were going to help Evald and me. This is what you said: 'Now, don't try to draw me into your and Evald's marital difficulties. I don't care a hoot about them. We must all handle our own problems.' "

Finally, Marianne points out that Evald still has to work nights to pay off a $5,000 student loan the old doctor gave him years ago. It means, Marianne says, that they rarely have a holiday together.

"A bargain is a bargain," the doctor says. "And I know that Evald understands me and has respect for me."

"Certainly," Marianne says. "And he hates you also."

Ironically, we feel no harshness toward the old man in spite of Marianne's accusations. This is because Sjostrom's lined face is as open as a child's and because he comes across as a warm and sympathetic character. That, in my opinion, is the picture's fundamental weakness. We see Borg only with his best foot forward, so to speak, but never in any of his weaker moments that have characterized his life. Thus it is hard to imagine that they ever existed.

Suddenly Borg turns down a side road and drives through a forest. He has decided to stop off at a lakeside house where his family spent its summers when he was a boy. While Marianne takes a swim, he looks at the abandoned home.

In his mind's eye, he sees his mother and father, his eight brothers and sisters, and his cousin Sara (Bibi Andersson), the lost love of his youth. She is picking wild strawberries in the woods. As she puts

A closeup of Victor Sjostrom, who capped his long and distinguished acting career with *Wild Strawberries*. He died in 1960, at eighty-one, one year after the film was made.

them in a basket, his younger brother, Sigfrid (Per Sjostrand), a bold and adventurous type, joins her. He flirts with Sara and steals a kiss. And so we see that the wild strawberries of the title is the place where Isak's first love forsook him.

Then Borg overhears Sara tearfully tell a girl-friend that she can't love young Isak because he's a stuffed shirt. "Isak is terribly refined and moral and true. He always talks about sin and life after death and plays duets on the piano . . . and only tries to kiss me when it's absolutely dark. I hate these extremely high-minded people. Sigfrid is so wild and passionate."

Borg remembers that he has gone on to have an unhappy marriage. "A feeling of emptiness and sadness invaded me," the old man says.

He is soon roused from his dream by a young girl in shorts and a boy's shirt (Miss Andersson again). Her name is Sara, too, and she asks for a lift for herself and two boys traveling with her on a vacation to Italy. As Sara, a light-hearted, ebullient blonde, seems a reincarnation of Borg's childhood sweetheart, the boys (Folke Sundquist and Bjorn Bjelvenstam) parallel the personalities of Sigfrid and Isak. The three hitchhikers remind him of his salad days, particularly Sara.

"The girl I loved when I was young was named Sara, too," Borg says wistfully.

"Really?" Sara replies. "She was like me, of course, huh?"

"Oh, to tell the truth, she was quite like you."

"What happened to her later?"

"She married my youngest brother, Sigfrid. They had three boys. Now she's seventy-five years old and quite a fine-looking woman."

Suddenly, on a blind curve, a little black car speeds straight toward them. Borg swerves off the road into a pasture. The other car rides into a ditch and rolls over. Two people crawl out, a couple named Alman (Gunnar Sjoberg and Gunnel Brostrom) who have been quarreling bitterly. This was the reason for their erratic driving.

They join the entourage, continuing their bickering, humiliating and berating each other. Their plight reminds Borg of his own marital difficulties. When the wife suddenly slaps her husband, Marianne stops the car and asks them to get out. They stand on the road and fade into the distance, two forlorn and miserable figures held together by a hellish bond.

Then there is a happier scene. Borg stops for gas near a little town where he started his practice and where his mother still lives. The man who runs the station, Akerman (Max von Sydow), and his wife, Eva (Anne-Mari Wiman), remember the kindness and dedication Borg showed them during the fifteen years he lived there. "You know," says the gas station man, "Mother and Father and all the people in the district are still talking about you. The greatest doctor in the world. Eva, I propose we name our next baby after the doctor." They refuse to let him pay for his gas. "Perhaps I should have stayed here," Borg mutters.

After lunch, Borg goes to see his aged mother, now ninety-six. In a large, solemnly appointed house, she is a lonely cantankerous figure. Feeling unloved and forgotten, she is cut off from the real world and attended only by memories.

"Nine children and all dead, except Isak," she says. "Twelve grandchildren and not one visits me except Evald, once a year. Now I'm not complaining. Only [I have] fifteen great-grandchildren I've never seen. I send telegrams and presents on fifty-three birthdays every year. Oh, I get letters and thanks. But nobody visits me except on those occasions they wish to borrow money. And I have another fault. I don't die. And unfortunately, the inheritance is behind the schedule figured out by the younger generation."

Back in the car with Marianne at the wheel, Borg falls asleep and dreams again. This dream is strange and humiliating. He finds himself back in the strawberry patch with Sara, only she can see him now. She is young and he is an old man. She puts a mirror up to his face to show him how he looks. "You are a frightened old man who will die soon," she says mockingly. "But I have my whole life before me." She tells him that she is about to marry Sigfrid.

Then she goes off to a house, lifting a child from a crib. Borg tries to follow, but instead of Sara, Alman, the quarreling motorist, greets him at the door. Inside, in a large lecture hall where Sara and students sit in an amphitheatre, Alman begins giving Borg an examination. He asks the doctor to identify specimens in a microscope, but Borg sees nothing. The doctor is asked to read words on a blackboard, but he cannot translate them.

Alman asks Borg if he knows what a doctor's first moral duty is. Borg says he has forgotten. It is, says Alman, to ask forgiveness. Borg is then asked to diagnose a woman on a stretcher. "But the patient is dead," he exclaims. The patient, who turns out to be Alman's wife, rises and laughs as if she had just heard a joke.

Finally, Alman tells Borg that he has been accused of the offenses of indifference, selfishness, and lack of consideration. The accusations have been made by Borg's dead wife. And now, says Alman, Borg shall see her. Opening a door, Alman

Isak reminisces as he revisits the strawberry patch at his childhood summer home.

leads the old doctor into a forest where, in a clearing, they come upon a man and a woman. The woman is Borg's wife, and she is making love with the man. While Borg looks on, pale and shaken, Alman reminds him this is not just an illusion. It is the same scene Borg saw on May 1, 1917, a scene he has never forgotten.

And what is the penalty for all this? Borg asks Alman. Loneliness, Alman replies.

After he wakes up, Marianne asks Borg if he slept well. Yes, the old man answers, but he had peculiar dreams. "It's as if I'm trying to tell something to myself I don't want to recall when I'm awake," he says. "That I'm dead although I live."

Evald has said exactly that about himself, Marianne says. In the picture's only flashback by a character other than Borg, Marianne recounts how two months ago she asked Evald to drive her to the seashore on a rainy day. There she told him that she was pregnant. He stiffened and recoiled. Then he got out of the car and walked off in the rain. When she reached him, he told her that he wanted no children. She will have to choose between him and the child. "Living in this world is absurd," he says. "But it's also absurd to keep adding new victims,

and even more absurd to think they'll have it any better than us. I myself was an unwelcome child in a marriage that was a nice imitation of hell."

Marianne has laid bare this common thread to Borg's family. As Borg and his mother have become insulated figures, so Evald is on the verge of becoming just as lonely and cold. His inability to relate to others, to commit himself to things outside himself, is cutting him off from the joy of life. "Somehow," Marianne says, "there must be an end to it all."

Then a small but important thing happens. Borg asks Marianne if he can help her. She turns him down. But her frankness and the events of the trip have made an impression.

At Lund, after the ceremony where Latin is intoned and the doctoral hat is placed on his head in the great university cathedral, Borg asks Evald about his marriage. Evald says that he has asked Marianne to stay with him and have the baby. Borg then brings up the matter of the loan—in an effort to wipe it out—but Evald misconstrues his remarks. Irritably, he cuts off his father, assuring him that he will get his money.

As he prepares to go to bed, Borg thanks Marianne for her company on the trip. "I do love you, Marianne," he says. She kisses him lightly on the cheek.

Outside his window, Borg hears singing. The hitchhikers are serenading him. They have come to say goodbye. "You're the one I really love," Sara says, waving and smiling as she shrinks in the summer night, "today, tomorrow, and forever."

"Let's hear from you once in a while," Borg says softly, more to himself than anyone else.

Critics debate whether Borg has really changed. There surely are signs that he has shucked off his formal demeanor of indifference and become aware of the problems of others. But Bergman, when asked this question, responded by denying that there has been any change of heart. "He doesn't change," says Bergman. "He can't. That's just it. I don't believe that people can change, not really, not fundamentally. They may have a moment of illumination. They may see themselves, have awarenesses of what they are. But that is the most they can hope for."

However, Jorn Donner in his book *The Personal Triumph of Ingmar Bergman,* says that it isn't important if Borg really changes. In the deeper, artistic sense of the film, says Donner, "the important thing is that he realizes the meaning, or meaninglessness, of his life, that he looks himself in the face."

And so, having done this, Borg lies down in bed. It is dark now, and his head is on the pillow. He closes his eyes, and once more he dreams. This time it is a dream of peace and harmony. He is back at his boyhood summer home. Far away, he sees his father, dressed in white with an old pipe in his mouth and a pince-nez, fishing by a still lake. Nearby, his mother sits on the shore in a bright summer dress and a big hat that shades her face. They see Borg as a boy and they wave. We see Borg as he is now, waving to them, an old man looking back on his life with all the poignancy of passing time.

Selected Bibliography

Baxter, John. *Science Fiction in the Cinema.* Barnes, 1970.

_____ *Sixty Years in Hollywood.* Barnes, 1973.

Brosnan, John. *The Horror People.* St. Martin's, 1976.

Butler, Ivan. *The Horror Film.* Barnes, 1967.

Chaplin, Charles. *My Autobiography.* Simon and Schuster, 1964.

Comden, Betty and Green, Adolph. *Singin' in the Rain,* Viking. 1972.

Cowie, Peter. *Seventy Years of Cinema.* Barnes, 1969.

Crowther, Bosley. *The Great Films: Fifty Golden Years of Motion Pictures.* Putnam, 1967.

Dalton, David. *James Dean: The Mutant King.* Straight Arrow, 1974.

Druxman, Michael B. *Make It Again, Sam: A Survey of Movies Remade.* Barnes, 1975.

Gow, Gordon. *Hollywood in the Fifties.* Barnes, 1971.

Herndon, Venable. *James Dean: A Short Life.* Doubleday, 1974.

Hotchner, A. E. *Doris Day: Her Own Story.* Morrow, 1975.

Hyams, Joel. *Mislaid in Hollywood.* Wyden, 1973.

Jordan, Rene. *Marlon Brando.* Pyramid, 1973.

Kaminsky, Stuart M. *Don Siegel: Director.* Curtis, 1974.

LaGuardia, Robert. *Monty: A Biography of Montgomery Clift.* Arbor House, 1977.

Maddox, Brenda. *Who's Afraid of Elizabeth Taylor?* Evans, 1977.

Madsen, Axel. *William Wyler.* Crowell, 1973.

Malton, Leonard. *Movie Comedy Teams.* Signet, 1970.

Mankiewicz, Joseph L. *More About All About Eve.* Random House, 1972.

Michael, Paul (Editor-in-Chief). *The American Movies Reference Book: The Sound Era.* Prentice-Hall, 1969.

Nolan, William F. *John Huston: King Rebel.* Sherbourne Press, 1965.

Quigley, Martin, Jr., and Gertner, Richard. *Films in America: 1929-1969.* Golden, 1970.

Richie, Donald S. *Focus on Rashomon.* Prentice-Hall, 1972.

Samuels, Charles Thomas. *Encountering Directors.* Putnam, 1972.

Sheppard, Dick. *Elizabeth: The Life and Career of Elizabeth Taylor.* Doubleday, 1974.

Shipman, David. *The Great Movie Stars: The Golden Years.* Crown, 1970.

_____ *The Great Movie Stars: The International Years.* St. Martin's, 1972.

Steinbrunner, Chris and Goldblatt, Burt. *Cinema of the Fantastic.* Saturday Review Press, 1972.

Stine, Whitney. *Mother Goddam: The Story of the Career of Bette Davis.* Hawthorne, 1974.

Thomas, Bob. *Marlon: Portrait of the Rebel as an Artist.* Random House, 1973.

Truffaut, François. *Hitchcock.* Secker and Warburg, 1968.

Tyler, Parker. *Classics of the Foreign Film.* Citadel, 1962.

Warner, Jack L. *My First Hundred Years in Hollywood.* Random House, 1965.

Wood, Robin. *Hitchcock's Films.* Barnes, 1965.

Zolotow, Maurice. *Billy Wilder in Hollywood.* Putnam, 1977.

Index